CHARTERS OF ST PAUL'S, LONDON

ANGLO-SAXON CHARTERS

SUPPLEMENTARY VOLUMES

ANGLO-SAXON CHARTERS · X

CHARTERS OF ST PAUL'S, LONDON

EDITED BY

S. E. KELLY

Published for THE BRITISH ACADEMY
by OXFORD UNIVERSITY PRESS

Oxford University Press, Great Clarendon Street, Oxford OX2 6DP

Oxford   New York
Auckland   Bangkok   Buenos Aires   Cape Town   Chennai
Dar es Salaam   Delhi   Hong Kong   Istanbul   Karachi   Kolkata
Kuala Lumpur   Madrid   Melbourne   Mexico City   Mumbai   Nairobi
São Paulo   Shanghai   Singapore   Taipei   Tokyo   Toronto

Published in the United States
by Oxford University Press Inc., New York

© The British Academy, 2004
Database right The British Academy (maker)

First published 2004

Data available

ISBN 0-19-726299-6

Typeset by Latimer Trend & Company Ltd
Printed in Great Britain
on acid-free paper by
Antony Rowe Limited
Chippenham, Wiltshire

FOREWORD

Dr Susan Kelly's edition of the charters of the cathedral church of St Paul's, London, forms the tenth fascicule in the series, Anglo-Saxon Charters, sponsored by the British Academy and the Royal Historical Society. It is also the sixth volume that has been edited by Dr Kelly herself, the project's consulting and co-ordinating editor, and is a work of highly expert scholarship. The superb expertise that Dr Kelly has gained through editing these difficult documents has been facilitated by the generous support of several funding bodies, most recently by the British Academy itself and by the Arts and Humanities Research Board. Their successive funding has sustained this project's momentum through difficult and rapidly changing times and has now given it a new lease of life. Several other volumes (some by other editors, some by Dr Kelly) are also now nearing completion. This is therefore a most encouraging time to serve as Chairman of the Anglo-Saxon Charter committee. In addition to Dr Kelly this committee currently comprises Professor Simon Keynes (the Honorary Secretary), together with Professor James Campbell, Dr Julia Crick, Dr Margaret Gelling, Professor Peter Sawyer (a founder member), Professor Richard Sharpe, Professor Eric Stanley and Mr Patrick Wormald. As with previous volumes, the editor has received detailed comments and assistance on her early drafts both from the committee members and from other scholars, as indicated by Dr Kelly. It is indeed only through such collaboration that we can provide an edition of the quality that has been so long sought.

None of the original single-sheet charters from St Paul's have been preserved. Though copies of the charters of St Paul's were entered during the medieval centuries into a number of cartularies and charter rolls, their survival thereafter has been very uncertain. Many of the crucial manuscripts have been lost since the Reformation and this edition has therefore had to have something of the character of a rescue mission. Several charters are now only known as fragments, from short extracts or summaries made by seventeenth-century antiquarians. The presentation of them here is the product of scholarly detection in which many earlier scholars have had an important part. By gathering all the evidence in a single volume concentrated upon St Paul's, it is possible to appreciate the fortunes of the archive and of its component charters and to make considered

judgements of their authenticity. Given London's importance as a political, economic and religious centre, it is an enormous boon to have these texts critically
edited as a group for the first time. This edition is therefore a major event in
making the sources for the early history of London accessible. For this reason
the opportunity has also been taken to include in this volume another London
charter, a writ of Edward the Confessor, which is the single pre-Conquest charter that was preserved at Holy Trinity, Aldgate. It takes its place in a London-
centred volume, rather than in a miscellany of charters from small archives.

NICHOLAS BROOKS

CONTENTS

LIST OF ILLUSTRATIONS

ACKNOWLEDGEMENTS

This volume has been many years in the writing. During this time I have been supported by the generosity of the British Academy and the Arts and Humanities Research Board, and I have been attached to various institutions, including the Universities of Cambridge and Birmingham. Especial thanks are due to Simon Keynes, for sharing his discovery of Selden's transcripts and for his comments on an early draft. I am also grateful to Nicholas Brooks for his comments, and for his hard labour on the funding applications. Pamela Taylor has been extremely helpful, and I should like to extend my warmest thanks for her kindness in discussing and commenting on the evidence for the endowment. As always, Margaret Gelling has provided invaluable assistance on place-names. Thanks also to Julia Crick, Nigel Ramsay and the members of the Anglo-Saxon Charters Committee for advice and ideas; also to London Guildhall Library, Lincoln's Inn Library and the Bodleian. Katie Lowe kindly supplied a text of Bishop Theodred's will from her forthcoming edition.

I wish to thank the Public Record Office and the Fellows of Corpus Christi College, Cambridge, for permission to reproduce photographs, and Mr Harry Buglass for the magnificent maps.

ABBREVIATIONS

BL	London, British Library
Bodleian	Oxford, Bodleian Library
CCCC	Cambridge, Corpus Christi College
D. & C.	Dean and Chapter
GDB	Great Domesday Book
GL	London, Guildhall Library
LDB	Little Domesday Book
PRO	London, Public Record Office
s.	*sæculo*
TRE	*Tempore Regis Eadwardi*
TRW	*Tempore Regis Willelmi*

BIBLIOGRAPHICAL ABBREVIATIONS

Abels, *Lordship*	R. Abels, *Lordship and Military Obligation in Anglo-Saxon England* (London, 1988)
Anton, *Studien*	H.H. Anton, *Studien zu den Klosterprivilegien der Päpste im frühen Mittelalter* (Berlin and New York, 1975)
ASC	*Anglo-Saxon Chronicle*
ASNL I	V. Horsman, C. Milne and G. Milne, *Aspects of Saxo-Norman London: I, Buildings and Street Development near Billingsgate and Cheapside*, LMAS Special Paper xi (London, 1988)
ASNL II	A. Vince (ed.), *Aspects of Saxo-Norman London: II, Finds and Environmental Evidence*, LMAS Special Paper xii (London, 1991)
ASNL III	K. Steedman, T. Dyson and J. Schofield, *Aspects of Saxo-Norman London: III, The Bridgehead and Billingsgate to 1200*, LMAS Special Paper xiv (London, 1992)
Attenborough, *Laws*	F.L. Attenborough, *The Laws of the Earliest English Kings* (Cambridge, 1922)
Bailey 1989	K. Bailey, 'The Middle Saxons', in Bassett, *Kingdoms*, pp. 108–22

BAFacs.	*Facsimiles of Anglo-Saxon Charters*, ed. S. Keynes, Anglo-Saxon Charters, Supplementary ser. i (London, 1991)
Ballard, *Borough Charters*	*British Borough Charters, 1042–1216*, ed. A. Ballard (Cambridge, 1913)
Barlow, *English Church*	F. Barlow, *The English Church 1000–1066: a History of the Later Anglo-Saxon Church*, 2nd edn (London, 1979)
Bassett, *Kingdoms*	*The Origins of Anglo-Saxon Kingdoms*, ed. S. Bassett (London and New York, 1989)
Bates, *RRAN: Acta of William I*	D. Bates, *Regesta Regum Anglo-Normannorum: the Acta of William I (1066–87)* (Oxford, 1998)
BCS	For 'Birch' in citations of charters
Bede, *HE*	Bede, *Historia Ecclesiastica*
Biddle, *Winchester*	M. Biddle, *Winchester in the Early Middle Ages: an Edition and Discussion of the Winton Domesday* (Oxford, 1976)
Biddle 1989	M. Biddle, 'A City in Transition: 400–800', in Lobel, *City of London*, pp. 20–9
Birch	W. de G. Birch, *Cartularium Saxonicum*, 3 vols (London, 1885–93)
Bishop and Chaplais	*Facsimiles of Royal Writs to A.D. 1100, presented to Vivian Hunter Galbraith*, ed. T.A.M. Bishop and P. Chaplais (Oxford, 1957)
Blackburn and Dumville, *Kings, Currency and Alliances*	*Kings, Currency and Alliances: the History and Coinage of Southern England*, ed. M.A.S. Blackburn and D.N. Dumville (Woodbridge, 1998)
Blackmore 1997	L. Blackmore, 'From Beach to Burh: New Clues to Entity and Identity in 7th- to 9th-Century London', *Urbanism in Medieval Europe*, i. 123–32
Blackwell	*The Blackwell Encyclopedia of Anglo-Saxon England*, ed. M. Lapidge, J. Blair, S. Keynes and D. Scragg (Oxford, 1999)
Blair, *Minsters and Parish Churches*	*Minsters and Parish Churches: the Local Church in Transition 950–1200*, ed. J. Blair, Oxford University Committee for Archaeology, Monograph no. 17 (Oxford, 1988)
Blair, *Surrey*	J. Blair, *Early Medieval Surrey: Landholding, Church and Settlement* (Stroud, 1991)
Blair 1985	J. Blair, 'Secular Minster Churches in Domesday Book', in *Domesday Book: A Reassessment*, ed. P. Sawyer (London, 1985), pp. 104–42
Blair 1989	J. Blair, 'Frithuwold's Kingdom and the Origins of Surrey', in Bassett, *Kingdoms*, pp. 97–107
Blake, *Liber Eliensis*	*Liber Eliensis*, ed. E.O. Blake, Camden Third Ser. xcii (London, 1962)
Brett, *English Church*	M. Brett, *The English Church under Henry I* (Oxford, 1975)

Brigham 2001 — T. Brigham, 'Roman London Bridge', in Watson *et al.*, *London Bridge*, pp. 28–51

Brooke 1951 — C.N.L. Brooke, 'The Composition of the Chapter of St Paul's, 1086–1163', *Cambridge Historical Journal* x (1951), pp. 111–32

Brooke 1956 — C.N.L. Brooke, 'The Deans of St Paul's *c.* 1090–1499', *Bulletin of the Institute of Historical Research* xxix (1956), pp. 231–44

Brooke 1957 — C.N.L. Brooke, 'The Earliest Times to 1485', in Matthews and Atkins, *St Paul's Cathedral*, pp. 1–99

Brooke 1970 — C.N.L. Brooke, 'The Church in the Towns, 1000–1250', *Studies in Church History* vi (1970), pp. 59–83

Brooke 1989 — C.N.L. Brooke, 'The Central Middle Ages 800–1270', in Lobel, *City of London*, pp. 30–41

Brooke and Keir, *London* — C.N.L. Brooke, with G. Keir, *London 800–1216: the Shaping of a City* (London, 1975)

Brooks, *Church of Canterbury* — N. Brooks, *The Early History of the Church of Canterbury: Christ Church from 597 to 1066* (Leicester, 1984)

Brooks 1971 — N. Brooks, 'The Development of Military Obligations in Eighth- and Ninth-Century England', *England Before the Conquest*, ed. P. Clemoes and K. Hughes (Cambridge, 1971), pp. 69–84

Brooks 1992*a* — N. Brooks, 'The Career of St Dunstan', *St Dunstan: his Life, Times and Cult*, ed. N. Ramsay, M. Sparks and T. Tatton-Brown (Woodbridge, 1992), pp. 1–23 (repr. in Brooks, *Anglo-Saxon Myths: State and Church 400–1066* (London and Rio Grande, 2000), pp. 155–80)

Brooks 1992*b* — N. Brooks, 'Church, Crown and Community: Public Work and Seigneurial Responsibilities at Rochester Bridge', *Warriors and Churchmen: Essays to Karl Leyser*, ed. T.A. Reuter (London and Ronceverte, 1992), pp. 1–20

Brooks and Kelly, *Christ Church* — *Charters of Christ Church, Canterbury*, ed. N.P. Brooks and S.E. Kelly, Anglo-Saxon Charters (forthcoming, 2004)

Brown and Farr, *Mercia* — *Mercia: an Anglo-Saxon Kingdom in Europe*, ed. M. Brown and C.A. Farr (London and New York, 2001),

Bullough 1974 — D.A. Bullough, 'Social and Economic Structure and Topography in the Early Medieval City', *Settimane di studio del Centro italiano di studi sull'alto medioevo* xxi (Spoleto, 1974), pp. 351–99

Campbell, *AS State* — J. Campbell, *The Anglo-Saxon State* (London and New York, 2000)

Campbell, *Essays* — J. Campbell, *Essays in Anglo-Saxon History* (London and Ronceverte, 1986)

Campbell, *Rochester* — *Charters of Rochester*, ed. A. Campbell, Anglo-Saxon Charters i (London, 1973)

Campbell 1987	J. Campbell, 'Some Agents and Agencies of the Late Anglo-Saxon State', *Domesday Studies*, ed. J.C. Holt (Woodbridge, 1987), pp. 201–18 (repr. in Campbell, *AS State*, pp. 201–25)
Campbell 1989	J. Campbell, 'The Sale of Land and the Economics of Power in Early England: Problems and Possibilities', *Haskins Society Journal* i (1989), pp. 23–37 (repr. in Campbell, *AS State*, pp. 227–45)
Campbell 1996	J. Campbell, 'The East Anglian Sees before the Conquest', *Norwich Cathedral: Church, City and Diocese, 1096–1996*, ed. I. Atherton *et al.* (London and Rio Grande, 1996), pp. 3–21 (repr. in Campbell, *AS State*, pp. 107–27)
Carlin, *Southwark*	M. Carlin, *Medieval Southwark* (London, 1996)
Chaplais, *Essays*	P. Chaplais, *Essays in Medieval Diplomacy and Administration* (London 1981)
Chaplais 1965	P. Chaplais, 'The Origins and Authenticity of the Royal Anglo-Saxon Diploma', *JSA* iii.2 (1965), pp. 48–61 (repr. in Ranger, *Prisca Munimenta*, pp. 28–42)
Chaplais 1966	P. Chaplais, 'The Anglo-Saxon Chancery: from the Diploma to the Writ', *JSA* iii.4 (1966), pp. 160–76 (repr. in Ranger, *Prisca Munimenta*, pp. 28–42)
Chaplais 1968	P. Chaplais, 'Some Early Anglo-Saxon Diplomas on Single Sheets: Originals or Copies?', *JSA* iii.7 (1968), pp. 315–36 (repr. in Ranger, *Prisca Munimenta*, pp. 63–87)
Chaplais 1978	P. Chaplais, 'The Letter from Bishop Wealdhere of London to Archbishop Brihtwold of Canterbury: the Earliest Original "Letter Close" Extant in the West', *Medieval Scribes, Manuscripts & Libraries: Essays presented to N.R. Ker*, ed. M.B. Parkes and A.G. Watson (London, 1978), pp. 3–23 (repr. Chaplais, *Essays*, XIV pp. 3–23 with Addendum)
Chaplais 1985	P. Chaplais, 'The Royal Anglo-Saxon "Chancery" of the Tenth Century Revisited', *Studies in Medieval History presented to R.H.C. Davis*, ed. H. Mayr-Harting and R.I. Moore (London, 1985), pp. 41–51
ChLA	*Chartae Latinae Antiquiores: Facsimile Edition of Latin Charters Prior to the Ninth Century*, ed. A. Bruckner and R. Marichal, part iii (Olten and Lausanne, 1963)
Chron. Abingdon	*Chronicon Monasterii de Abingdon*, ed. J. Stevenson, RS, 2 vols (London, 1858)
Clark 1999	J. Clark, 'King Alfred's London and London's King Alfred', *London Archaeologist* ix (1999), pp. 35–8
Clarke, *English Nobility*	P.A. Clarke, *The English Nobility under Edward the Confessor* (Oxford, 1994)
Colgrave and Mynors, *Bede's Ecclesiastical History*	*Bede's Ecclesiastical History of the English People*, ed. B. Colgrave and R.A.B. Mynors, Oxford Medieval Texts (Oxford, 1969; rev. edn 1991)

Colker 1965	M.L. Colker, 'Texts of Jocelyn of Canterbury which relate to the History of Barking Abbey', *Studia Monastica* vii (1965), pp. 383–460
Coote 1881	H.C. Coote, 'The English Gild of Knights and their *Socn*', *TLMAS* v (1881), pp. 477–93
Councils & Synods	*Councils and Synods with other Documents Relating to the English Church, I: A.D. 87–1204*, ed. D. Whitelock, M. Brett and C.N.L. Brooke, 2 pts (Oxford, 1981)
Cowie 2001	R. Cowie, 'Mercian London', in Brown and Farr, *Mercia*, pp. 194–208
Cowie and Harding 2000	R. Cowie and C. Harding, 'Saxon Settlement and Economy from the Dark Ages to Domesday', *The Archaeology of Greater London*, MLAS (London, 2000), pp. 171–206
Cox 1976	B. Cox, 'The Place-Names of the Earliest English Records', *Journal EPNS* viii (1975–6), pp. 12–66
Crawford Charters	*The Crawford Collection of Early Charters and Documents*, ed. A.S. Napier and W.H. Stevenson (Oxford, 1895)
Crick, *St Albans*	*Charters of St Albans Abbey*, ed. J. Crick, Anglo-Saxon Charters (forthcoming)
Crosby, *Bishop and Chapter*	E.U. Crosby, *Bishop and Chapter in Twelfth-Century England* (Cambridge, 1994)
Cubitt, *Councils*	C.R.E. Cubitt, *Anglo-Saxon Church Councils c. 650– c. 850* (London, 1995)
CUHB	*The Cambridge Urban History of Britain: I, 600–1540*, ed. D.M. Palliser (Cambridge, 2000),
Davis, *Cartularies*	G.R.C. Davis, *Medieval Cartularies of Great Britain: a Short Catalogue* (London, 1958)
Davis 1925	H.W.C. Davis, 'London Lands and Liberties of St Paul's: 1066–1135', *Essays in Medieval History presented to Thomas Frederick Tout* (Manchester, 1925), pp. 45–59
Davis 1972	R.H.C. Davis, 'The College of St Martin-le-Grand and the Anarchy 1135–54', *London Topographical Record* xxiii (1972), pp. 9–26
DB Beds.	*Domesday Book: Bedfordshire*, ed. J. Morris (Chichester, 1977)
DB Essex	*Domesday Book: Essex*, ed. A.R. Rumble (Chichester, 1983)
DB Herts.	*Domesday Book: Hertfordshire*, ed. J. Morris (Chichester, 1976)
DB Suffolk	*Domesday Book: Suffolk*, ed. A. Rumble (Chichester, 1986)
DB Middx	*Domesday Book: Middlesex*, ed. J. Morris (Chichester, 1975)
DB Surrey	*Domesday Book: Surrey*, ed. J. Morris (Chichester, 1975)
DEPN	E. Ekwall, *The Concise Oxford Dictionary of English Place-Names*, 4th edn (Oxford, 1960)

Diceto, *Abbreviationes*   Ralph Diceto, *Abbreviationes Chronicorum*, in *The Historical Works of Master Ralph de Diceto, Dean of London*, ed. W. Stubbs, RS, 2 vols (London, 1876), i.

DNB   *Dictionary of National Biography*

Dodwell, *AS Art*   C.R. Dodwell, *Anglo-Saxon Art: A New Perspective* (Manchester, 1982)

Douglas and Greenaway,   *English Historical Documents 1042–1189*, ed. D.C. Douglas
  EHD II   and G.W. Greenaway, English Historical Documents ii, 2nd edn (London, 1981)

Dugdale, *St Paul's*   W. Dugdale, *A History of St Paul's Cathedral in London* (London, 1658)

Dugdale, *St Paul's* (2nd edn)   W. Dugdale, *A History of St Paul's Cathedral in London*, 2nd edn with author's corrections and additions (London, 1716)

Dugdale, *St Paul's* (3rd edn)   W. Dugdale, *A History of St Paul's Cathedral in London*, reissue with further continuations by H. Ellis (London, 1818)

Dumville, *Wessex and*   D.N. Dumville, *Wessex and England from Alfred to
  England*   Edgar: Six Essays in Political, Cultural and Ecclesiastical Revival* (Woodbridge, 1992)

Dyson 1978   T. Dyson, 'Two Saxon Land-Grants for Queenhithe', *Collectanea Londoniensis: Studies ... presented to R. Merrifield*, ed. J. Bird, H. Chapman and J. Clark (London, 1978), pp. 200–15

Dyson 1980   T. Dyson, 'London and Southwark in the Seventh Century and Later: a Neglected Reference', *TLMAS* xxxi (1980), pp. 83–95

Dyson 1990   T. Dyson, 'King Alfred and the Restoration of London', *London Journal* xv (1990), pp. 99–110

Dyson and Schofield 1984   T. Dyson and J. Schofield, 'Saxon London', *Anglo-Saxon Towns in Southern England*, ed. J. Haslam (Chichester, 1984), pp. 285–313

Edwards, *Charters*   H. Edwards, *The Charters of the Early West Saxon Kingdom*, British Archaeological Reports (British ser.) 198 (Oxford, 1988)

Edwards, *Secular*   K. Edwards, *The English Secular Cathedrals in the
  Cathedrals*   Middle Ages*, 2nd edn (Manchester, 1967)

Ekwall, *London*   E. Ekwall, *Early London Personal Names* (Lund, 1947)
  Personal Names*

Ekwall, *London Street*   E. Ekwall, *The Street Names of the City of London*
  Names*   (Oxford, 1954)

EPNS   English Place-Name Society

Felix, *Life of Guthlac*   *Felix's Life of Saint Guthlac*, ed. B. Colgrave (Cambridge, 1956)

Faith 1994   R. Faith, 'Demesne Resources and Labour Rent in the Manors of St Paul's Cathedral, 1066–1222', *Economic History Review* xlvii (1994), pp. 657–78

Faith 1996   R. Faith, 'The Topography and Social Structure of a Small
                                        Soke in the Middle Ages: the Sokens, Essex', *Essex
                                        Archaeology and History* xxvii (1996), pp. 202–13

Fernie, *Architecture of*   E. Fernie, *The Architecture of Norman England* (Oxford,
  Norman England   2000)

Finberg, *ECW*   H.P.R. Finberg, *The Early Charters of Wessex* (Leicester,
                                        1964)

Finberg, *ECWM*   H.P.R. Finberg, *The Early Charters of the West Midlands*,
                                        2nd edn (Leicester, 1972)

Foot, *Veiled Women*   S. Foot, *Veiled Women: the Disappearance of Nuns from
                                        Anglo-Saxon England*, 2 vols (Aldershot, 2000)

Gelling, *ECTV*   M. Gelling, *The Early Charters of the Thames Valley*
                                        (Leicester, 1979)

Gelling, *Signposts*   M. Gelling, *Signposts to the Past: Place-Names and the
                                        History of England* (London, 1978)

Gelling and Cole,   M. Gelling and A. Cole, *The Landscape of Place-
  Landscape of Place-Names   Names* (Stamford, 2000)

Gibbs   *Early Charters of the Cathedral Church of St Paul,
                                        London*, ed. M. Gibbs, Camden Third Series LVIII
                                        (London, 1939)

Gransden, *Historical*   A. Gransden, *Historical Writing in England c. 550–1307*
  Writing   (London, 1974)

Haddan and Stubbs   *Councils and Ecclesiastical Documents Relating to Great
                                        Britain and Ireland*. ed. A.W. Haddan and W. Stubbs, 3
                                        vols (Oxford, 1869–78)

Hale, *St Paul's Domesday*   *The Domesday of St Paul's of the Year MCCXXII*, ed.
                                        W.H. Hale, Camden Society Old Series LXIX (London,
                                        1858)

Harmer, *Writs*   F.E. Harmer, *Anglo-Saxon Writs* (Manchester, 1952)

Hart, *Danelaw*   C.R. Hart, *The Danelaw* (London and Rio Grande, 1992)

Hart, *ECE*   C.R. Hart, *The Early Charters of Essex*, Department of
                                        English Local History, Occasional Papers x, 2nd edn
                                        (Leicester, 1971)

Hart, *ECEE*   C.R. Hart, *The Early Charters of Eastern England*
                                        (Leicester, 1966)

Hart, *ECNE*   C. Hart, *The Early Charters of Northern England and the
                                        North Midlands* (Leicester, 1975)

Hart 1973   C.R. Hart, 'Æthelstan "Half-King" and his Family',
                                        Anglo-Saxon England ii (1973), pp. 115–44

Haslam 1988   J. Haslam, 'Parishes, Churches, Wards and Gates in
                                        Eastern London', in Blair, *Minsters and Parish
                                        Churches*, pp. 35–43

Haynes *et al.*, *London*   *London Under Ground: the Archaeology of a City*, ed. I.
  Under Ground   Haynes, H. Sheldon and L. Hanning (Oxford, 2000)

Hill, *Atlas*   D. Hill, *An Atlas of Anglo-Saxon England* (Oxford, 1981)

Hill and Cowie, *Wics*   *Wics: the Early Medieval Trading Centres of Northern
                                        Europe*, ed. D. Hill and R. Cowie (Sheffield, 2001)

HMC 9th Report	Ninth Report of the Royal Commission on Historical *Manuscripts* (London, 1883), Appendix
Hodgett, *Holy Trinity Cartulary*	The Cartulary of Holy Trinity Aldgate, ed. G.A.J. Hodgett, London Record Society (London, 1971)
Hollister, *AS Military Institutions*	C. Warren Hollister, *Anglo-Saxon Military Institutions on the Eve of the Conquest* (Oxford, 1962)
Holtzmann, *Papsturkunden*	W. Holtzmann, *Papsturkunden in England*, 3 vols (Berlin, 1930–52)
HRH	D. Knowles, C.N.L. Brooke and V.C.M. London, *The Heads of Religious Houses England and Wales 940–1216* (Cambridge, 1972; new edn 2001)
Jaffé	P. Jaffé, *Regesta Pontificum Romanorum ad annum 1198*, ed. W, Wattenbach, S. Loewenthal, F. Kaltenbrunner and P. Ewald, 2 vols (Leipzig, 1885–8)
John of Worcester	The Chronicle of John of Worcester, ii: the Annals from 450 to 1066, ed. R.R. Darlington and P. McGurk (Oxford, 1995)
JSA	*Journal of the Society of Archivists*
KCD	For 'Kemble' in citations of charters
Keene 2000	D. Keene, 'London from the Post-Roman Period to 1300', *CUHB*, pp. 187–216
Keene *et al.*, *St Paul's Cathedral*	The History of St Paul's Cathedral, ed. D. Keene et al. (forthcoming, 2004)
Kelly, *Abingdon*	Charters of Abingdon Abbey, ed. S.E. Kelly, Anglo-Saxon Charters vii–viii (Oxford, 2000–1)
Kelly, *Chertsey*	Charters of Chertsey Abbey, ed. S.E. Kelly, Anglo-Saxon Charters (Oxford, forthcoming)
Kelly, *Malmesbury*	Charters of Malmesbury Abbey, ed. S.E. Kelly, Anglo-Saxon Charters (Oxford, forthcoming)
Kelly, *St Augustine's*	Charters of St Augustine's Abbey, Canterbury, and Minster-in-Thanet, ed. S.E. Kelly, Anglo-Saxon Charters iv (Oxford, 1995)
Kelly, *Selsey*	Charters of Selsey, ed. S.E. Kelly, Anglo-Saxon Charters vi (Oxford, 1998)
Kelly, *Shaftesbury*	Charters of Shaftesbury Abbey, ed. S.E. Kelly, Anglo-Saxon Charters v (Oxford, 1996)
Kelly 1990	S.E. Kelly, 'Anglo-Saxon Lay Society and the Written Word', in McKitterick, *Literacy*, pp. 36–62
Kelly 1992	S.E. Kelly, 'Trading Privileges from Eighth-Century England', *Early Medieval Europe* i (1992), pp. 3–28
Kemble	J.M. Kemble, *Codex Diplomaticus Aevi Saxonici*, 6 vols (London, 1839–48)
Ker, *Catalogue*	N.R. Ker, *Catalogue of Manuscripts Containing Anglo-Saxon* (Oxford, 1957; repr. with addenda, 1990)
Ker 1969	N.R. Ker, 'Books at St Paul's Cathedral before 1313', *Studies in London History presented to Philip Edmund Jones*, ed. A.E.J. Hollaender and W. Kellaway (London,

1969), pp. 43–72 (repr. N.R. Ker, *Books, Collectors and Libraries: Studies in the Medieval Heritage*, ed. A.G. Watson (London, 1985), pp. 209–42)

Keynes, *Diplomas* S. Keynes, *The Diplomas of King Æthelred 'the Unready' 978–1016: a Study in their Use as Historical Evidence* (Cambridge, 1980)

Keynes 1985 S. Keynes, 'King Athelstan's Books', *Learning and Literature in Anglo-Saxon England*, ed. M. Lapidge and H. Gneuss (Cambridge, 1985), pp. 143–201

Keynes 1988 S. Keynes, 'Regenbald the Chancellor (*sic*)', *Anglo-Norman Studies X* (1988), pp. 185–222

Keynes 1990 S. Keynes, 'Royal Government and the Written Word in Later Anglo-Saxon England', in McKitterick, *Literacy*, pp. 226–57

Keynes 1991 S. Keynes, 'The Æthelings in Normandy', *Anglo-Norman Studies XIII* (Woodbridge, 1991), pp. 173–205

Keynes 1993a S. Keynes, 'A Charter of King Edward the Elder for Islington', *Historical Research* lxvi (1993), pp. 303–16

Keynes 1993b S. Keynes, 'The Control of Kent in the Ninth Century', *Early Medieval Europe* ii (1993), pp. 111–31

Keynes 1994a S. Keynes, 'The West Saxon Charters of King Æthelwulf and his Sons', *English Historical Review* cix (1994), pp. 1109–49

Keynes 1994b S. Keynes, 'Cnut's Earls', in Rumble, *Cnut*, pp. 43–88

Keynes 1998 S. Keynes, 'King Alfred and the Mercians', in Blackburn and Dumville, *Kings, Currency and Alliances*, pp. 1–46

Keynes and Lapidge, *Alfred the Great* S. Keynes and M. Lapidge, *Alfred the Great: Asser's 'Life of King Alfred' and other Contemporary Sources* (Harmondsworth, 1983)

Kissan 1940a B.W. Kissan, 'An Early List of London Properties', *TLMAS* n.s. viii (1938–40), pp. 57–69

Kissan 1940b B.W. Kissan, 'The London Deanery of the Arches', *TLMAS* n.s. viii (1938–40), pp. 195–223

Knowles, *Monastic Order* D. Knowles, *The Monastic Order in England*, 2nd edn (Cambridge, 1963)

L. & P. Henry VIII *Calendar of Letters and Papers, Foreign and Domestic: Henry VIII*, xix.1, ed. J, Gardiner (London, 1903)

Lawson, *Cnut* M.K. Lawson, *Cnut: the Danes in England in the Early Eleventh Century* (London and New York, 1993)

Lawson 1984 M.K. Lawson, 'The Collection of Danegeld and Heregeld in the Reigns of Aethelred II and Cnut', *English Historical Review* xcix (1984), pp. 721–38

Le Neve, *Fasti 1066–1300* J. Le Neve, *Fasti Ecclesiae Anglicanae 1066–1300: i. St Paul's, London*, compiled D.E. Greenway (London, 1968)

Le Neve, *Fasti 1300–1541* J. Le Neve, *Fasti Ecclesiae Anglicanae 1300–1541: v. St Paul's, London*, compiled J.M. Horn (London, 1963)

Le Neve, *Fasti 1541–1857*	J. Le Neve, *Fasti Ecclesiae Anglicanae 1541–1857: i. St Paul's, London*, compiled J.M. Horn (London, 1969)
Levison, *England and the Continent*	W. Levison, *England and the Continent in the Eighth Century* (Oxford, 1946)
Liebermann, *Gesetze*	F. Liebermann, *Die Gesetze der Angelsachsen*, 3 vols (Halle, 1903–16)
Liebermann 1900	F. Liebermann, 'Matrosenstellung aus Landguetern der Kirche London um 1000', *Archiv für das Studium der Neueren Sprachen und Literaturen* civ (1900), pp. 17–24
Life of Wilfrid	*The Life of Bishop Wilfrid by Eddius Stephanus*, ed. and transl. B. Colgrave (Cambridge, 1927)
Lobel, *City of London*	*The City of London from Prehistoric Times to c. 1520*, ed. M.D. Lobel, British Atlas of Historic Towns iii (Oxford, 1989)
Martin 1991	G.H. Martin, 'Domesday London', *Middlesex Domesday*, pp. 22–32
Matthew Paris, *Gesta Abbatum*	Matthew Paris, *Gesta Abbatum S. Albani*, ed. H.T. Riley, RS (London, 1867)
Matthews and Atkins, *St Paul's Cathedral*	*A History of St Paul's Cathedral and the Men Associated with It*, ed. W.R. Matthews and W.M. Atkins (London, 1957)
McKitterick, *Literacy*	*The Uses of Literacy in Early Medieval Europe*, ed. R. McKitterick (Cambridge, 1990)
MGH	Monumenta Germaniae Historica
Middlesex Domesday	*The Middlesex and London Domesday*, Alecto Historical Editions (London, 1991)
Miller, *New Minster*	*Charters of New Minster, Winchester*, ed. S. Miller, Anglo-Saxon Charters ix (Oxford, 2001)
Milne and Goodburn 1990	G. Milne and D. Goodburn, 'The Early Medieval Port of London A.D. 700–1200', *Antiquity* lxiv (1990), pp. 629–36
MLAS	Museum of London Archaeology Service
Mon. Angl.	R. Dodsworth and W. Dugdale, *Monasticon Anglicanum*, 3 vols (London, 1655–73)
Morey and Brooke, *Gilbert Foliot*	A. Morey and C.N.L. Brooke, *Gilbert Foliot and his Letters* (Cambridge, 1965)
Nightingale, *Mercantile Community*	P. Nightingale, *A Medieval Mercantile Community: the Grocers' Company and the Politics and Trade of London 1000–1485* (New Haven and London, 1995)
Nightingale 1987	P. Nightingale, 'The Original of the Court of Husting and Danish Influence on London's Development into a Capital City', *English Historical Review* cii (1987), pp. 559–78
O'Donovan 1973	M.A. O'Donovan, 'An Interim Revision of Episcopal Dates for the Province of Canterbury, 850–950: Part II', *Anglo-Saxon England* ii (1973), pp. 91–113
Page, *London*	W. Page, *London: its Origins and Early Development* (London, 1929)

Page 1965	R.I. Page, 'Anglo-Saxon Episcopal Lists, Parts I and II', *Nottingham Mediaeval Studies* ix (1965), pp. 71–95
Pierquin, *Recueil*	H. Pierquin, *Recueil général des chartes anglo-saxonnes: les Saxons en Angleterre, 640–1061* (Paris, 1912)
Pinder 1991	T.G. Pinder, 'An Introduction to the Middlesex Domesday', *Middlesex Domesday*, pp. 1–21
PN Beds.	A. Mawer and F.M. Stenton, *The Place-Names of Bedfordshire and Huntingdonshire*, EPNS iii (Cambridge, 1926)
PN Essex	P.H. Reaney, *The Place-Names of Essex*, EPNS xii (Cambridge, 1935)
PN Herts.	J.E.B. Gover, A. Mawer and F.M. Stenton, *The Place-Names of Hertfordshire*, EPNS xv (Cambridge, 1938)
PN Middx	J.E.B. Gover, A. Mawer and F.M. Stenton, *The Place-Names of Middlesex Apart from the City of London*, EPNS xviii (Cambridge, 1942)
PN Surrey	J.E.B. Gover, A. Mawer and F.M. Stenton, *The Place-Names of Surrey*, EPNS xi (Cambridge, 1934)
Ranger, *Prisca Munimenta*	*Prisca Munimenta:Studies in Archival and Administrative History presented to Dr A.E.J. Hollaender*, ed. F. Ranger (London, 1973)
Redin, *Personal Names*	M. Redin, *Studies in Uncompounded Personal Names in Old English* (Uppsala, 1919)
Richter, *Professions*	*Canterbury Professions*, ed. M. Richter, Canterbury and York Society (Torquay, 1973)
Robertson, *Charters*	*Anglo-Saxon Charters*, ed. A.J. Robertson, 2nd edn (Cambridge, 1956)
Robertson, *Laws*	*The Laws of the Kings of England from Edmund to Henry I*, ed. and transl. by A.J. Robertson (Cambridge, 1925)
Round 1891	H. Round, 'An Early Reference to Domesday', *Domesday Studies* II (1891), pp. 539–59
RS	Rolls Series
Rumble, *Cnut*	*The Reign of Cnut: King of England, Denmark and Norway*, ed. A.R. Rumble (London, 1994)
Sawyer	P.H. Sawyer, *Anglo-Saxon Charters: an Annotated List and Bibliography*, Royal Historical Society Guides and Handbooks viii (London, 1968) (new edn with additions, ed. S.E. Kelly *et al.*, forthcoming; see meanwhile http://www.asnc.cam.ac.uk)
Sawyer, *Burton*	*Charters of Burton Abbey*, ed. P.H. Sawyer, Anglo-Saxon Charters iii (Oxford, 1979)
Sawyer 1983	P.H. Sawyer, 'The Royal *Tun* in Pre-Conquest England', in Wormald, *Ideal and Reality*, pp. 273–99
Sawyer 1986	P.H. Sawyer, 'Anglo-Scandinavian Trade in the Viking Age and After', *Anglo-Saxon Monetary History: Essays in Memory of Michael Dolley* (Leicester, 1986), pp. 185–99

Scharer, *Königsurkunde*   A. Scharer, *Die angelsächsische Königsurkunde im 7. und 8. Jahrhundert*, Veröffentlichungen des Instituts für Österreichische Geschichtsforschung xxvi (Cologne and Vienna, 1982)

Schofield, *Building of London*   J. Schofield, *The Building of London from the Conquest to the Great Fire*, 3rd edn (Stroud, 1999)

Sharpe, *Letter-Book C*   *Calendar of Letter-Books preserved among the Archives of the Corporation of the City of London at the Guildhall: Letter-Book C, circa A.D. 1291–1309*, ed. R.R. Sharpe (London, 1901)

Sharpe 2002   R. Sharpe, 'Martyrs and Local Saints in Late Antique Britain', in *Local Saints and Local Churches in the Early Medieval West*, ed. A. Thacker and R. Sharpe (Oxford, 2002), pp. 75–154

Simpson, *Registrum statutorum*   W. Sparrow Simpson, *Registrum statutorum et consuetudinum ecclesie cathedralis sancti Pauli Londiniensis* (London, 1873)

Simpson 1887   W. Sparrow Simpson, 'Two Inventories of the Cathedral Church of St Paul's, London, dated respectively 1245 and 1402', *Archaeologia* l (1887), pp. 439–524

Sims-Williams, *Religion and Literature*   P. Sims-Williams, *Religion and Literature in Western England 600–800* (Cambridge, 1990)

Smith, *Bede*   Bede, *Historia Ecclesiastica Gentis Anglorum*, ed. J. Smith (Cambridge, 1722)

Stenton, *ASE*   F.M. Stenton, *Anglo-Saxon England*, 3rd edn (Oxford, 1971)

Stenton, *Preparatory to ASE*   *Preparatory to Anglo-Saxon England, being the Collected Papers of Frank Merry Stenton*, ed. D.M. Stenton (Oxford, 1970)

Stevenson, *Asser*   *Asser's Life of King Alfred*, ed. W.H. Stevenson (Oxford, 1904)

Symeon of Durham   Symeon of Durham, *Historia Regum*, in *Symeonis Monachi Opera Omnium*, ed. T. Arnold, 2 vols (London, 1882–5), ii

Tangl   *Die Briefe des Heiligen Bonifatius und Lullus*, ed. M. Tangl, MGH Epistolae Selectae vol. 1 (Berlin, 1916)

Tatton-Brown 1986   T. Tatton-Brown, 'The Topography of Anglo-Saxon London', *Antiquity* lx (1986), pp. 21–8

Taylor 1980   P. Taylor, 'The Bishop of London's City Soke', *Bulletin of the Institute of Historical Research* liii (1980), pp. 174–82

Taylor 1990   P. Taylor, 'Clerkenwell and the Religious Foundations of Jordan de Bricett: a Re-Examination', *Historical Research* lxiii (1990), pp. 17–28

Taylor 1992   P. Taylor, 'The Endowment and Military Obligations of the See of London: a Reassessment of Three Sources', *Anglo-Norman Studies XIV* (Woodbridge, 1992), pp. 287–312

Taylor 1995	P. Taylor, 'Boundaries and Margins: Barnet, Finchley and Totteridge', *Medieval Ecclesiastical Studies in Honour of Dorothy M. Owen*, ed. M.J. Franklin and C. Harper-Bill (Woodbridge, 1995), pp. 259–79
Taylor 2002	P. Taylor, 'Ingelric, Count Eustace and the Foundation of St Martin-le-Grand', *Anglo-Norman Studies XXIV* (Woodbridge, 2002), pp. 215–37
Taylor and Taylor, *Anglo-Saxon Architecture*	H.M. Taylor and J. Taylor, *Anglo-Saxon Architecture*, 3 vols (Cambridge, 1965–8)
Tengvik, *Bynames*	G. Tengvik, *Old English Bynames* (Uppsala, 1938)
Thorpe, *Diplomatarium*	B. Thorpe, *Diplomatarium Anglicum Ævi Saxonici* (London, 1865)
TLMAS	*Transactions of the London and Middlesex Archaeological Society*
ToOED	*Toronto Old English Dictionary*
Urbanism in Medieval Europe	*Urbanism in Medieval Europe: Papers of the 'Medieval Europe Brugge 1997' Conference*, ed. G. De Boe and F. Verhaege, 2 vols (Zollick, 1997)
VCH	*Victoria County History*
Vince, *Saxon London*	A. Vince, *Saxon London: an Archaeological Investigation* (London, 1990)
Vince 1991	A. Vince, 'The Development of Saxon London', *ASNL II*, pp. 409–35
von Feilitzen, *Personal Names*	O. von Feilitzen, *The Pre-Conquest Personal Names of Domesday Book* (Uppsala, 1937)
Watson, *Roman London*	*Roman London: Recent Archaeological Work*, ed, B. Watson, *Journal of Roman Archaeology*, suppl. ser. xxiv (Portsmouth, R.I., 1998)
Watson 2001*a*	B. Watson, 'The Late Saxon Bridgehead', in Watson *et al., London Bridge*, pp. 52–60
Watson 2001*b*	B. Watson, 'The Saxo-Norman Timber Bridge', in Watson *et al., London Bridge*, pp. 73–82
Watson *et al., London Bridge*	*London Bridge: 2000 Years of a River Crossing*, ed. B. Watson, T. Brigham and T. Dyson, MLAS Monograph 8 (London, 2001)
Whatley, *Saint of London*	E.G. Whatley, *The Saint of London* (Binghamton, N.Y., 1989)
Whitelock, *EHD*	*English Historical Documents c. 500–1042*, ed. D. Whitelock, English Historical Documents i, 2nd edn (London, 1979)
Whitelock, *Wills*	*Anglo-Saxon Wills*, ed. D. Whitelock (Cambridge, 1930)
Whitelock 1973	D. Whitelock, 'The Appointment of Dunstan as Archbishop of Canterbury', *Otium and Negotium: Studies ... presented to Olof von Feilitzen*, ed. F. Sandgren (Stockholm, 1973), p. 232–47 (repr. in her *History, Law and Literature in 10th–11th Century England* (London, 1981), no. IV)

Whitelock 1975 — D. Whitelock, *Some Anglo-Saxon Bishops of London*, Chambers Memorial Lecture 1974, University College, London (London, 1975)

William of Malmesbury, *GP* — *Willelmus Malmesbiriensis Monachi De Gestis Pontificum Anglorum Libri Quinque*, ed. N.E.S.A Hamilton, Rolls Series (London, 1870)

Williams 1996 — A. Williams, 'The Vikings in Essex, 871–917', *Essex Archaeology and History* xxvii (1996), pp. 92–101

Williamson, *Herts.* — T. Williamson, *The Origins of Hertfordshire* (Manchester and New York, 2000)

Wormald, *Ideal and Reality* — *Ideal and Reality in Frankish and Anglo-Saxon Society: Studies presented to J.M. Wallace-Hadrill*, ed. P. Wormald (Oxford, 1983)

Wormald, *Law I* — P. Wormald, *The Making of English Law: King Alfred to the Twelfth Century. 1: Legislation and its Limits* (Oxford, 1999)

Wormald 1985 — P. Wormald, *Bede and the Conversion of England: the Charter Evidence*, Jarrow Lecture 1984 (Jarrow, [1985])

Yeo 1986 — G. Yeo, 'Record-Keeping at St Paul's Cathedral', *JSA* viii.1 (1986), pp. 30–44

Yorke, *Kings and Kingdoms* — B. Yorke, *Kings and Kingdoms of Early Anglo-Saxon England* (London, 1990)

Yorke 1985 — B. Yorke, 'The Kingdom of the East Saxons', *Anglo-Saxon England* xiv (1985), pp. 1–36

INTRODUCTION

Only a tiny fraction of the Anglo-Saxon archive of St Paul's has survived into modern times. After the Conquest the London canons focused their attention on a small corpus of mostly forged documents which supported the view that the chapter had an ancient corporate identity independent of the bishop. Other early charters were copied less frequently, but a substantial number of texts were still available for study in the seventeenth century. The most important source by that stage was an *antiquus rotulus*, which seems to have disappeared during the upheavals of the Commonwealth; fortunately it had been seen before that time by the antiquarian scholars Richard James and John Selden, who made valuable extracts from the charters. Other scholars made useful 'facsimile' copies of an original or pseudo-original writ of Edward the Confessor (**28**), which may still have been available in the early eighteenth century (see Plates 1, 2). This edition contains all surviving texts and fragments of texts, analysed within the context of the history of London and of the bishopric.[1]

Also edited here are (i) the writ of Edward the Confessor for the London *Cnihtengild*, preserved in the archive of Holy Trinity Priory, Aldgate (**32**); (ii) the letter of Bishop Wealdhere to Archbishop Berhtwald (Appendix 1, pp. 221–3); and (iii) the will of Bishop Theodore (Appendix 2, pp. 225–8).

1. THE EARLY HISTORY OF LONDON AND ST PAUL'S CATHEDRAL

a. *The Foundation of St Paul's*

When Augustine arrived in England in 597 he may have expected to establish his see in London, which had been the most important city of Roman Britain and the location of a fourth-century episcopal see.[2] As late as June 601 Pope Gregory

---

[1] Previous studies of the early history of St Paul's include: Brooke 1957; Whitelock 1975; Brooke and Keir, *London*, chapter 12. An important new collaborative volume on the history of the cathedral, edited by Derek Keene, is due to appear in 2004.

[2] A bishop of London (with colleagues from York and ? Lincoln) attended a synod in Arles in 314; Haddan & Stubbs, i. 7; J.C. Mann, 'The Administration of Roman Britain', *Antiquity* xxxv (1961),

was outlining plans for the diocesan structure of the new Anglo-Saxon church which assumed that Augustine's see would be in London (Bede, *HE*, i. 29). The pope envisaged two metropolitan provinces, with senior bishops at London and York who would each consecrate twelve suffragans. Political realities required the modification of this scheme and at some point before 604 Augustine installed himself definitively at Canterbury, the principal city of King Æthelberht of Kent, then overlord of south-east England. However, it is possible that Augustine did spend some time based in London, or that he made regular visits there: the eighth-century churchman Boniface was under the impression that the custom of convening regular synods in London dated back to Augustine's time.[3] London's claim to metropolitan status, founded on the 'Gregorian Plan', was to be revived in 798 and on subsequent occasions.[4]

At the beginning of the seventh century, London was the chief city of the East Saxon kingdom, which recognised the overlordship of King Æthelberht. In 604 Augustine consecrated as bishop of the East Saxons an Italian abbot named Mellitus, who had been part of the second wave of missionaries sent from Rome by Pope Gregory in 601. After a period of missionary activity, Mellitus's see was established in London, in a church dedicated to St Paul and built by Æthelberht. Bede notes that the Kentish overlord made generous gifts to the bishop, and provided lands and possessions for the support of his clergy (*HE*, ii. 3). Later tradition at St Paul's identified twenty-four hides north of the City as Æthelberht's donation to the church (see pp. 83–4), and the archive also contains a forged charter attributing to him the grant of Tillingham in Essex (**1**). But this promising start for the church of London was checked by events following the death of the Kentish king in 616 and that of the supportive East Saxon ruler Sæberht at about the same time, for their successors were resolutely pagan; Mellitus and his clergy were driven out of London, and the bishop withdrew temporarily to Gaul (*HE*, ii. 5). The mission in Kent was saved by the sudden conversion of King Eadbald, but the East Saxons remained recalcitrant and the

---

pp. 316–20 at 317; Sharpe 2002, pp. 77–8. An early martyrology mentions another bishop of London called Augul(i)us, who is said in some manuscripts to have been a martyr; he is associated with eight other men, who may have suffered with him. The dating of this episode is obscure (see Sharpe 2002, pp. 122–3).

[3] Campbell, *Essays*, p. 139 and n. 3; Biddle 1989, p. 21; see Tangl, no. 50 (p. 84). There seems no good reason to credit the theory that Augustine established the metropolitan see in London and was never bishop of Canterbury, and that Bede's narrative is a deliberate misrepresentation of the situation, intended to bolster the prestige of Canterbury: see Brooks, *Church of Canterbury*, pp. 11–14.

[4] For the promotion of London's claims by Coenwulf of Mercia, see p. 19 and for the revival of the idea in the twelfth century by Bishops Richard de Belmeis I and Gilbert Foliot, see Morey and Brooke, *Gilbert Foliot*, pp. 151–62.

people of London refused to agree to Mellitus's return (*HE*, ii. 6). The East Saxons remained without a bishop for some forty years, and it may have been even longer before the London see was re-established.

The Saxon cathedral of St Paul's was located on Ludgate Hill, an area of high ground in the west of the walled Roman city, which at that time shelved steeply south to the Thames (see Map 1, p. 5). It was rebuilt at least once in the pre-Conquest period, after a fire in 962 (*ASC*), and probably on other unrecorded occasions. No archaeological traces of the building have been found and there is little hope of future discoveries, for it appears that later terracing in this area has scraped the soil back to the natural gravel; but there is some reason to think that the Saxon cathedral lay slightly to the south of its later medieval successor (Old St Paul's), on the foundations of which Wren built the modern cathedral.[5] Bede's account suggests that Æthelberht built a new church for London, in contrast to the situation in Canterbury where Augustine and its followers refurbished a Roman building. There was a persistent legend, first reported by the antiquary William Camden (1551–1623), that Mellitus's cathedral was built on the site of a Roman temple of Diana, the evidence consisting of a nearby structure called Diana's Chambers and a 'multitude of Oxe heads digged up' when the east part of the cathedral was rebuilt in the time of Edward I.[6] It seems likely that this tradition was ultimately generated from a close reading of a letter of Pope Gregory to Mellitus, incorporated in Bede's history, which includes instructions for converting pagan shrines into Christian churches: the pope explicitly refers to the animal sacrifices of the pagans, and advises Mellitus to tell Augustine to institute Christian feasts where the new converts could slaughter animals for their own food (*HE*, i. 30). A tradition which may possibly have a slightly more substantial foundation concerns the church of St Peter which was built on Cornhill, the area of high ground in the east of the walled city, facing Ludgate Hill across the marshy area of the Walbrook stream. From at least the early fifteenth century St Peter's was claiming to have been the first church founded in London, the see of a Roman archbishop.[7] Modern excavation has

---

[5] Vince, *Saxon London*, pp. 10–11.

[6] See Dugdale, *St Paul's*, p. 3 (citing Camden), and the witty dissection of the legend in J. Clark, 'The Temple of Diana', *Interpreting Roman London: Papers in Memory of Hugh Chapman*, ed. J. Bird, M. Hassall and H. Sheldon (Oxford, 1996), pp. 1–9.

[7] Vince, *Saxon London*, pp. 59–60. In 1417 the City mayor and aldermen confirmed the ancient right of precedence accorded to the rector of St Peter's in the Whit Monday processions, by reason of the ancient foundation of his church. In the late sixteenth century John Stow saw a brass plate in St Peter's claiming that the church had been founded by the first archbishop of London (*A Survey of London*, ed. C.L. Kingford, 2 vols (Oxford, 1908), i. 194); see J. Clark, 'John Stow and the Legendary History of London', *TLMAS* xlviii (1997), pp. 153–5.

shown that St Peter's was built on the site of the basilica associated with the
Roman forum; intriguingly, its chancel is sited directly over a room on the basilica complex that may have been a shrine or cult centre. But there is essentially
no archaeological evidence for occupation of the basilica site between the fourth
century and *c.* 1000, while St Peter's itself is most probably a late Saxon foundation; it may be that the legend arose because some ruins of the basilica complex
still stood at the time that the medieval church was built.[8] Nevertheless, there
may be some significance in the fact that in the later medieval period the bishops
of London held a substantial territorial soke around Cornhill; it has been suggested that this intramural area was probably granted to St Paul's at an early
date, perhaps because it was believed to have been the site of the Roman cathedral.[9] An alternative location for the site of the Roman basilica is in the Tower
Hill area, where excavation has revealed part of a large aisled building, constructed after A.D. 350; it has been argued that this resembles in plan and scale
the late fourth-century cathedral of St Tecla at Milan.[10] One might wish to speculate that the London church of 604–16 was actually connected with one of
these two sites; that it was then abandoned and perhaps destroyed during the
pagan reaction; and that the re-establishment of the see in the later seventh century saw the construction of a new church of St Paul's on Ludgate Hill.

b. *London in the Seventh Century*

Whatever the case, the decision to site the Saxon cathedral in the western part of
the walled city is likely to reflect the new topography of Early and Middle
Saxon London. It is improbable that the Roman bridge, which linked the eastern
part of the city to the Surrey shore, was still in regular use in this period; even if
it was not dismantled by the Romans (a distinct possibility), the maintenance of
the timber decking over the stone piers would have required systematically
organised labour which may not have been available until the time of Alfred and

---

[8] T. Brigham, 'Civic Centre Redevelopment: Forum and Basilica Reassessed', *From Roman
Basilica to Medieval Market: Archaeology in Action in the City of London*, ed. G. Milne (London,
1992), pp. 81–95, at 87, 93–5; Vince, *Saxon London*, p. 68. The basilica was largely demolished
c. 300, but the apse and 'shrine' may have survived for longer (Brigham, p. 95). There is a possible
reference to St Peter's Cornhill in the will of Ælfric, bishop of Elmham (S 1489, *c.* A.D. 1035; see
Whitelock, *Wills*, p. 18).

[9] Taylor 1980, p. 177; see below, pp. 82–3, for a different view about the background to the early
acquisition of intramural property. Other factors may have been relevant: it is possible that the forum
site was granted to the bishopric as a convenient source of worked stone for building purposes.

[10] D. Sankey, 'Cathedrals, Granaries and Urban Vitality in Late Roman London', in Watson, *Roman
London*, pp. 78–82. The alternative interpretation is that the building was a giant *horreum* or state
granary. See also Sharpe 2002, pp. 122–3.

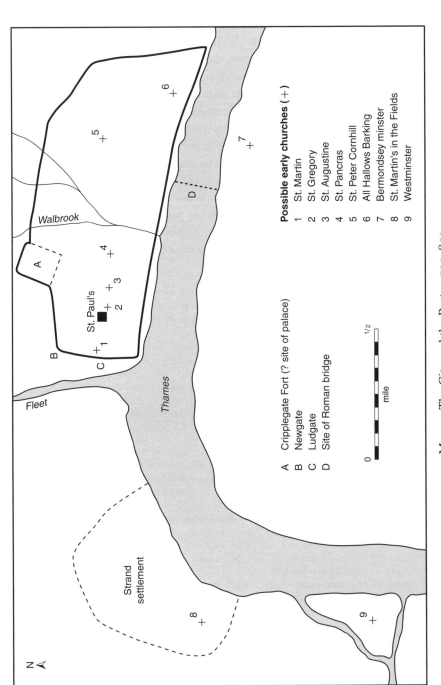

Fleet

Thames

Walbrook

A

St. Paul's

C
B
+1
+2 +3
2   3
+4
4

5
+

6
+

D

7
+

Strand
settlement

8
+

9
+

N

Possible early churches (+)

1   St. Martin
2   St. Gregory
3   St. Augustine
4   St. Pancras
5   St. Peter Cornhill
6   All Hallows Barking
7   Bermondsey minster
8   St. Martin's in the Fields
9   Westminster

A   Cripplegate Fort (? site of palace)
B   Newgate
C   Ludgate
D   Site of Roman bridge

0   1/2
mile

Map 1. The City and the Port c. 700–850

his successors.[11] The population of Roman London had contracted substantially during the fourth century and the city may have been largely abandoned during the fifth.[12] The intramural area has yielded almost no archaeological material from the Early and Middle Saxon periods; the Roman street-pattern does not seem to have survived to any significant degree, and there are extensive layers of dark earth which would be consistent with a picture of minimal occupation between the fourth and later ninth centuries.[13] The focus of settlement had shifted westward outside the walls, to a river-side site in the area of the Strand, which by *c.* 700 was the location of a major trading settlement known as *Lundenwic* or *portus Londoniae*.[14] A seasonal market on the site may have been established as early as the mid sixth century, but it does not seem to have been until the late seventh or early eighth century that settlement began to develop away from the waterfront, eventually expanding to cover some sixty hectares.[15] There was a significant London mint from the seventh century, which probably evolved together with the economic role of the emporium.[16] It was to *Lundenwic*

[11] For the fate of the Roman bridge in the sub-Roman period, see Brigham 2001, p. 51; and for the maintenance of the later Saxo-Norman bridge, see Watson 2001*b*, pp. 73–4. A document from Rochester demonstrates the organisation required to maintain the late Saxon bridge over the Medway: see Brooks 1992*b*.

[12] G. Milne, *The English Heritage Book of Roman London: Urban Archaeology in the Nation's Capital* (London, 1995), esp. pp. 86–8; Vince 1991, pp. 409–11.

[13] B. Watson, ' "Dark Earth" and Urban Decline in Late Roman London', in Watson, *Roman London*, pp. 100–6; Dyson and Schofield 1984, pp. 286–90, 294–5; Vince 1991, p. 410.

[14] The existence of the Strand settlement is a relatively recent discovery, now backed by archaeological evidence from more than thirty sites. For useful overviews, and guides to published material, see R. Cowie and R. Whytehead, '*Lundenwic*: the Archaeological Evidence for Middle Saxon London', *Antiquity* lxiii (1989), pp. 706–18; Milne and Goodburn 1990; Vince, *Saxon London*, esp. pp. 13–20; Vince 1991, pp. 412–19; Blackmore 1997; R. Cowie, '*Londinium* to *Lundenwic*: Early and Middle Saxon Archaeology in the London Region', in Haynes *et al.*, *London Under Ground*, pp. 175–205; Keene 2000, pp. 187–90; Cowie 2001; R. Cowie, 'London', in Hill and Cowie, *Wics*, pp. 87–9. For a prescient discussion of the distinction between *civitas* and *portus* in the London context, see Campbell, *Essays*, pp. 105–6.

[15] The earliest reference to the port is in a Chertsey diploma of *c.* 670 × 674 (S 1165; Kelly, *Chertsey*, no. 1), which mentions a grant of ten hides *iuxta portum Londoniae ubi naues applicant super idem flumen in meridiane parte iuxta uiam publicum*, i.e. on the south bank of the Thames opposite the port. The suggestion that the estate was located at Southwark (see Dyson 1980) requires reassessment now that the port has been located on the Strand. An alternative possibility would be Lambeth, where a Domesday manor with a ten-hide assessment was held TRE by Godgifu, sister of King Edward the Confessor, and TRW by the church of St Mary at Lambeth (GDB 34r; *DB Surrey*, 14:1). St Mary's may have been some kind of collegiate minster founded by Godgifu and endowed with the lands of the manor (Blair, *Surrey*, p. 102). The Lambeth estate is said to have been given by William Rufus to Bishop Gundulf and the Rochester community; it was later exchanged with the archbishop of Canterbury for land at Otford (*ibid.*). Chertsey's sister-minster at Barking is also said to have received a grant of ten hides near the port in this period (S 1246; *supra uicum Londoniae*).

[16] Vince, *Saxon London*, pp. 109–13; Cowie 2001, pp. 203–4.

that Bede would seem to have been referring when he described London in 731 as 'an emporium for many nations which come to it by land and sea'.[17]

A major road from the port entered the walled city at Ludgate, and the cathedral was built upon its intramural extension, close to the gate, at an important road-junction.[18] St Paul's was therefore located within easy access of the extramural settlement, while still enjoying the status of association with the former Roman city. It seems probable that the relative emptiness of the walled city would have facilitated the acquisition of land there by the bishop and his community. Lack of early documentation makes it difficult to identify the cathedral's intramural holdings (the fact that Domesday Book does not cover London is a major disappointment), but there is evidence from the early twelfth century that the bishop then owned territory south of the cathedral precinct, running down to the Thames at St Paul's Wharf, while other records point to a territorial soke in the Cornhill area.[19] Some of this land may have been cultivated, with gardens and orchards being planted among the Roman debris; it is even possible that the community had its home farm at Cornhill.[20] By the tenth century there was a walled enclosure around the precinct, for we find the cathedral being referred to as *Paulesbyrig*.[21] A group of churches clustered around St Paul's have what may be very early dedications, to St Martin, St Gregory and St Pancras; it has been conjectured that some or all of these may have been seventh-century foundations,

[17] *HE*, ii. 3 (*multorum emporium populorum terra marique venientium*). Bede was here supposedly describing London in 604, but it seems probable that his comments refer more precisely to the thriving trading settlement of his own day.

[18] Tatton-Brown 1986, pp. 22–3, and figs. 1, 2 (see Map 1, p. 5). The site was close to an ancient stream, flowing across Newgate (Schofield, *Building of London*, pp. 38–9).

[19] Davis 1925, p. 48; *HMC 9th Report*, Appendix p. 67b; and discussion by Taylor 1980. Note that the area south of St Paul's has produced a high proportion of the very few finds of seventh- to midninth-century date within the walls (Vince 1991, p. 417).

[20] The place-name may derive from a corn-market associated with the site, but it is also possible that it was first coined during a period when there were still arable fields within the walls (Ekwall, *London Street Names*, pp. 186–7).

[21] Vince, *Saxon London*, p. 81; Biddle 1989, p. 23 n. 36. The name is first attested in the tenth century (see S 1486, 1494, and an eleventh-century instance in S 1478). The usage in the privileges of Coenred and Offa (**5a/b**) cannot be taken as proof that the name was current in the seventh and eighth centuries, for these fragments clearly derive from a late forgery. The city itself is *Lundenebyri[g]* in Bishop Theodred's will from *c.* 950 (see Appendix II, and pp. 92–3). Other fortified sites within the walls in the late medieval period were Aldermanbury, possibly a fortified site used as a residence by Æthelred of Mercia in the later ninth century (see further pp. 8, 22); and Lothbury, where the first element (the pers. n. Hlothhere) is the Anglo-Saxon form of a Frankish name, shared by a Kentish king (673–85) and a West Saxon bishop (Leuthere, *c.* 670–6; see **1**). See Ekwall, *London Street Names*, pp. 194–7; Stenton, *Preparatory to ASE*, pp. 35–6.

comparable to a group of churches with similar dedications on a route just outside the walls of Canterbury. But there is no archaeological evidence to support a pre-tenth-century date for these London churches, or indeed for any other London church with the possible exception of All Hallows Barking.[22] There are slightly stronger grounds for speculation that some extramural churches developed from buildings and chapels associated with Roman cemeteries, a pattern observed elsewhere.[23]

It seems probable that there was an early royal and administrative presence within the walled city. A persistent later tradition held that a Saxon royal palace had been situated in the area of the former Roman fort of Cripplegate, a few hundred metres to the north-east of the cathedral.[24] Part of the fort area was later included within the exceptionally important and privileged soke of Aldermanbury ('the fortified place of the ealdorman'), a name which associates the area with the exercise of political power; it is possible that the gatehouse of the fort was utilised as the nucleus of a grand residence.[25] In a very late St Paul's memorandum Aldermanbury is explicitly identified as the site of the palace of the church's founder, King Æthelberht of Kent.[26] At St Albans Abbey it was believed that the church of St Alban Wood Street, which lies within the fort area, was in origin a palace chapel founded by King Offa of Mercia (757–96); the

[22] Brooke and Keir, *London*, pp. 140–1; Tatton-Brown 1986, p. 23; Vince 1991, pp. 427, 429. St Gregory's, immediately south of St Paul's, is perhaps the best candidate for inclusion in a cathedral complex: surviving illustrations show a twelfth-century building (Vince 1991, p. 427), but this was conceivably a replacement of an older church (perhaps destroyed, along with the cathedral, in the fire of 1087). It has been suggested that the early cathedral may have had a *porticus* altar dedicated to St Gregory, from which developed St Gregory's parish (Brooke 1989 p. 35). For All Hallows Barking, see below, p. 21.

[23] Biddle 1989, p. 21: citing evidence for Roman masonry structures under St Bride Fleet Street, St Andrew Holborn, St Martin-in-the-Fields, St Andrew Kingsbury and Westminster Abbey. Vince (*Saxon London*, pp. 60–1) notes that the extramural church of St Martin-in-the-Fields would appear to have been built above a pagan cemetery, and conjectures that the earliest church there may have been a converted pagan temple. See Brooks, *Church of Canterbury*, p. 21, for churches associated with extramural cemeteries in Canterbury.

[24] Page, *London*, pp. 128–9; Biddle 1989, pp. 21–2; Brooke and Keir, *London*, pp. 154–5; Dyson and Schofield 1984, pp. 306–8; Schofield, *Building of London*, pp. 29–31; Taylor 2002, pp. 219–20. The entire walled area may have been an 'elite preserve', with a 'landscape of authority' formed by the St Paul's enclosure and the royal residence (Keene 2000, p. 188).

[25] Dyson and Schofield 1984, p. 307, with map p. 306. For the place-name, see Ekwall, *London Street Names*, p. 13; in the earliest forms of the name the first element is genitive singular, but in the course of the thirteenth century it was transformed into a plural ('aldermen's *burh*').

[26] An account of 1530 gives details of 'Expens and chargis in the clenyng of certeyn olde ruinouse houses and grounde lying in Aldermanbury sumtyme the Palace of Saincte Aethelbert Kyng' (*HMC 9th Report*, p. 44a).

thirteenth-century historian Matthew Paris, citing an eleventh-century source, claimed that the liberties of the former palace site were then preserved by a small house adjacent to the church.[27] An alternative location for the royal residence is south of the fort and nearer to St Paul's, on the site which later formed the precincts of the royal chapel of St Martin-le-Grand, founded in the Confessor's reign by a certain Ingelric, who may have been a royal clerk; it has been argued that when King Edward built a new royal palace at Westminster, some of the privileges and liberties of the intramural residence devolved upon the new royal chapel.[28] New archaeological evidence has been seen to bear out the hypothesis that the north-western part of the city had a continuous association with the business of goverment. It has been shown that the Guildhall, itself the successor of the London husting, is situated in the arena of the Roman amphitheatre just outside the fort, and it has been suggested that this ancient structure was the original site of the London folkmoot, which subsequently assembled just to the south in St Paul's Churchyard, summoned by the cathedral bell.[29] However, there is no archaeological evidence for early occupation of the fort area, and it would be prudent to take into account the possibility that the establishment of a permanent royal residence in the city coincided with the refurbishment of London's defences in the time of King Alfred (see pp. 24–7). In that case, St Paul's may have been the only signficant institution within the walls in the early Anglo-Saxon period.[30]

---

[27] *Gesta Abbatum Monasterii Sancti Albani*, ed. H. Riley, RS (London, 1867), i. 55. St Albans Wood Street has been claimed as mid-Saxon in date on the basis of the simple two-cell plan recovered through excavation, but there were no early finds and the case is far from proven: the church could be eleventh-century (for sceptical notes, see Brooke and Keir, *London*, p. 111 n. 1; Vince, *Saxon London*, pp. 70–1). Its position on a street corner may suggests that it was built to serve an urban population (Vince 1991, p. 427).

[28] Davis 1972, p. 24; and, more recently, D. Keene, 'New Thoughts on the Royal Palace in Pre-Conquest London', presidential address to LMAS in February, 2000 (cited in Taylor 2002). For the foundation of St Martin's, see Taylor 2002, and below, p. 43.

[29] See Biddle 1989, pp. 22–4; Martin 1991, pp. 26–7; Stenton, *Preparatory to ASE*, pp. 29–30; see further below, p. 41. There may be a parallel in Canterbury, where the Roman theatre similarly influenced the later street-pattern, and may have functioned as a place of assembly (Brooks, *Church of Canterbury*, pp. 24–5). For recent excavations at the Guildhall, see G. Porter, 'An Early Medieval Settlement at Guildhall, City of London', *Urbanism in Medieval Europe*, i. 147–52. Here it is noted that the site was a boggy hollow by the later tenth century and that it was levelled and used as an open-air market in the eleventh century. It is possible that the husting originated in association with such a market, rather than as a successor to a relocated folkmoot.

[30] King Sebbi of the East Saxons was living in the city when he died in *c.* 693 or 694, but he had already taken the habit from Bishop Wealdhere at that date, and may have been attached to St Paul's (Bede, *HE*, iv. 11).

c. *The Shaping of the Diocese*

Following the expulsion of Mellitus in *c.* 616, the East Saxon kingdom seems to have remained resolutely pagan until around 654, when Cedd was sent there through the influence of another overlord, Oswiu of Northumbria (*HE*, iii. 22).[31] Cedd founded monasteries within the abandoned Roman fort at *Ythancæstir* (Bradwell-on-Sea) and at Tilbury, but it is not known for certain whether he re-established a substantial ecclesiastical presence in London; he had been trained in the Celtic tradition, where less emphasis was laid on city-based sees than in the churches run by Rome-backed missionaries. He would certainly have been hampered by a shortage of personnel and resources, and it may be that the refoundation of St Paul's was less of a priority than missionary work from Bradwell and Tilbury. Cedd's death in the plague of 664 led to a new period of confusion. Part of the kingdom apostacized; Jaruman, bishop of the Mercians, was apparently successful in enticing a pagan East Saxon king back to the Christian path, but he then departed, leaving the East Saxon kingdom without a bishop of its own (*HE*, iii. 30). Subsequent to this Wine, a former bishop of Winchester who had been ejected by the West Saxon king, was given a seat in London by King Wulfhere of the Mercians and remained there until his death (*HE*, iii. 7). Wine had been trained in Gaul and would therefore have been accustomed to a city-based episcopal organisation; it can be assumed that he took steps to revive the cathedral church at St Paul's church and it seems likely that he introduced into the community those priests and other clerics who had followed him from Wessex. Bede's account of his appointment states that he purchased the London see from Wulfhere for a large sum of money, and this clear accusation of simony has poisoned his later reputation; his name is omitted from the later episcopal lists. But the purchase of preferment was a regular practice in the Frankish church from which Wine had emerged, and we should not dismiss the possibility that he was an effective bishop for London.[32] He was clearly wealthy, and may have used his resources to rebuild St Paul's on a grand scale and to make an important contribution to the ecclesiastical development of the East Saxon kingdom. An interesting characteristic of the earliest surviving East Saxon charters is their close relationship with West Saxon diplomas of the same period; there is certainly a possibility that this connection had its roots in Wine's time (see further, pp. 78–9).

---

[31] For more detail on Cedd and his successors, see below, pp. 106–22.

[32] J.M. Wallace-Hadrill, *Bede's 'Ecclesiastical History of the English People: A Historical Commentary'* (Oxford, 1988), p. 100; Campbell, *Essays*, p. 39.

By the mid 660s the Anglo-Saxon church was in a very fragile condition: at one stage Wine was the only canonically ordained bishop in Britain (*HE*, iii. 28). A major reform was set in motion by Theodore of Tarsus, a papally-appointed archbishop who arrived in England in 669. It was not until *c.* 675 that Theodore was able to consecrate his own choice of bishop for the East Saxon kingdom; Wine may have survived until this time, but there is a possibility that he was succeeded in the early 670s by a shadowy Bishop Hunferth, who is likewise absent from the episcopal lists (see **1** and pp. 109–10). Theodore's candidate was Eorcenwald, a saintly figure who had an existing connection with the London area: he had previously founded minsters at Chertsey in Surrey (where he was abbot) and at Barking in Essex (where his sister was abbess). Eorcenwald was consecrated by Theodore as bishop of the East Saxons in London (*HE*, iv. 6), but it is not clear whether his principal seat was at St Paul's. An episode in Stephanus's *Life of Wilfrid* has Archbishop Theodore summoning Eorcenwald and Wilfrid to London, which implies that the former may have been based outside the city, perhaps in his well-endowed minster at Chertsey.[33] On the other hand, a privilege which Eorcenwald granted to Chertsey in the early years of his pontificate is dated from London (S 1247; Kelly, *Chertsey*, no. 4). After his death Eorcenwald was buried at St Paul's and culted there, but the archive contains no reference to property supposedly acquired during his pontificate; by contrast, the minsters at Chertsey and Barking attribute many grants to Eorcenwald's agency. It is possible that St Paul's did not become the principal episcopal seat of the diocese on a permanent basis until the time of his successor Wealdhere (appointed 693, died 705 × 716), who is the beneficiary of three charters, among them the record of his acquisition of the huge estate at Fulham (**3**; see also **2, 4**). The archive contains a fragment of a spurious privilege in the name of the Mercian king Coenred (**5a**, A.D. 704 × 709), which at least demonstrates that later generations saw Wealdhere's pontificate as an important period in the history of St Paul's. It was during his time that the East Saxon king Sebbi abdicated and took the habit, probably at St Paul's, since he died in London shortly afterwards; he brought with him a large sum of money to be given to the poor (Bede, *HE*, iv. 11). Wealdhere is also likely to have played a part in establishing the cult of Eorcenwald, who was buried in the cathedral,

The documentation associated with Eorcenwald and Wealdhere illustrates the particular problems faced by bishops of London, who frequently found themselves serving two or more masters. Early Anglo-Saxon dioceses were

---

[33] *Life of Wilfrid*, ed. Colgrave, p. 86 (cap. xliii). Campbell (*Essays*, p. 140) notes that Bede seems to have used the term *sedes* to mean a suitable estate for supporting a bishop. In this context, Chertsey may have had advantages lacking at St Paul's.

associated with tribal kingdoms, and in practical terms their boundaries may have fluctuated according to the successes and failures of the local rulers. The London diocese had been established to cater for the kingdom of the East Saxons, which Bede describes as being divided from Kent by the Thames and bordering on the sea to the east, with London as the chief city (*HE*, ii. 3). The core of the kingdom was the later county of Essex, but in the early seventh century the East Saxon kings would also seem to have controlled Middlesex and London, and there is reason to think that their rule also extended to the area of south-eastern Hertfordshire which came to be included in the London diocese.[34] The 'Middle Saxons' who occupied the area around London are now thought to have been a disparate collection of tribes which were given an artificial common identity when Mercian overlordship was imposed on the region in the later seventh century.[35] Also part of the equation is Surrey, the name of which ('southern *ge*' or province) points to an original association with territory north of the Thames (see further below).

In the seventh century the East Saxon kingdom was a second-rank power: but it contained within its territory an overwhelmingly important commercial centre in a strategic location, over which more powerful rulers were anxious to acquire control. The general pattern in the second half of the seventh century is of persistent Mercian encroachment in Middlesex and London, often linked with the recognition of Mercian overlordship by the East Saxon kings; and at the same time a running battle between the kings of Kent, Mercia and Wessex for the control of Surrey.[36] Wulfhere of Mercia (died 674 or 675) enjoyed some degree of lordship over London when he sold the bishopric to Wine in 666: he is also supposed to have made a grant of land there to Barking minster (see S 1246). There is some evidence for a resurgence of Kentish control in London in the time of King Hlothhere (673–85).[37] But after this Mercian encroachment seems to have been inexorable. Wulfhere's successor Æthelred (674–704) gave estates in Middlesex to Barking (S 1246) and to Bishop Wealdhere (2). A diploma of 704 concerning Twickenham in Middlesex describes a joint-grant to Wealdhere by the East Saxon king and a Mercian *comes*, acting with King Æthelred's consent (S 65); this was confirmed by Æthelred's successors Coenred (704–9) and

---

[34] For the diocesan boundaries in this area, see Williamson, *Origins of Hertfordshire*, pp. 79–84.

[35] Bailey 1989; D.N. Dumville, 'Essex, Middle Anglia and the Expansion of Mercia in the South-East Midlands', in his *Britons and Anglo-Saxons in the Early Middle Ages* (Aldershot, 1993), IX, pp. 1–30 at 20–3 (earlier version publ. in Bassett, *Kingdoms*, pp. 123–40).

[36] For a synopsis of the evidence, see Yorke 1985, pp. 31–6.

[37] The joint lawcode of Hlothhere (673–85) and Eadric (sole king 685–6) includes provisions governing the actions of Kentishmen in London, with reference to the presence in the city of the king's town-reeve and the king's hall (Whitelock, *EHD*, no. 30).

Ceolred (709–16).[38] An extract from a document of Coenred's reign shows that by this date a bishop of the Mercian see of Hereford had come into possession of a huge estate on the Thames at Fulham, presumably through the gift of a Mercian ruler (see **3**). Mercian domination of London and Middlesex seems to have been firmly established by the early eighth century, although there are likely to have been power fluctuations during the difficult periods between reigns. Elsewhere north of the Thames the East Saxon rulers appear to have remained in control of their territory, making grants of land in Essex and Hertfordshire to Barking (S 1171, 1246), to the bishops of London (**4, 6**) and to an individual for the foundation of a religious house at Nazeing in Essex (S 65a, 65b).

The history of Surrey in this period is far more complicated. The name 'southern district' may originally to have applied to only to the western part of the modern county, which has an internal organisation similar to that of other *regiones* in the Thames Valley; this territory would seem at some stage to have had a relationship with Middle Saxon tribal areas north of the Thames. By contrast, the land-units of central and eastern Surrey have closer links with Kent and may have had a longstanding historical association with the Kentish kingdom. Before he became bishop, Eorcenwald obtained a privilege for his minster at Chertsey, which demonstrates the flux of power in this area (S 1165, A.D. *c.* 670 × 674 or 675; Kelly, *Chertsey*, no. 1). The minster was first founded, traditionally in 666, under the auspices of the Kentish king Ecgberht, whose control would appear to have extended to the western *regiones* of Surrey. But the privilege records a substantial grant by a subking named Frithuwald, confirmed by his overlord Wulfhere of Mercia; it has been argued that Frithuwald may have been the ruler of a Middle Anglian principality who seized western Surrey and pushed back the Kentish kings.[39] In the following decade the West Saxon king Cædwalla (686–8) rampaged through Surrey and Kent: he was associated with the foundation of minsters at Farnham (Surrey) and Hoo (West Kent) and he made a major grant to Eorcenwald's minster at Barking of an estate at Battersea (S 1246, 1248, 233). His successor Ine (688–726) issued a lawcode in the early years of his reign in which he refers to the advice of 'my bishop Eorcenwald', wording which suggests that part of the territory of the London diocese (presumably Surrey) was then under West Saxon control.[40] But the south bank of the Thames was quickly regained by the Mercians. In Eorcenwald's lifetime the Battersea grant was confirmed by Æthelred of Mercia, possibly in conjunction

---

[38] Æthelred himself does not attest this document, which raises the possibility that it dates from around the time of his abdication in 704. A brief power vacuum could explain why an East Saxon king was here involved in a grant of land in Mercian-dominated Middlesex.

[39] Blair 1989.

[40] The Laws of Ine: Whitelock, *EHD*, no. 32 (p. 399); see discussion in Whitelock 1975, pp. 7–8.

with his invasion of Kent in 691.[41] It is hard to see how this much-disputed territory was considered an integral part of a diocese catering for the East Saxon kingdom. One possible explanation is that western Surrey was treated as part of Eorcenwald's diocese solely because of his prior association with Chertsey, that is, it was a personal link, rather than one that developed because this area was considered to have a connection with the East Saxon kingdom.[42] Tensions following Eorcenwald's death may form the background to a letter written by his successor Wealdhere to Archbishop Berhtwald in 704 × 705 (for the text, see Appendix 1). In veiled language Wealdhere describes a delicate situation, arising out of a series of disputes between the king of the West Saxons (Ine) and 'the rulers of our country' (a circumlocution which may be intended to refer to the Mercians as well as the East Saxons). A peace treaty has been fixed and arrangements have been made for a meeting between the two parties at Brentford, which Wealdhere is anxious to attend, in particular because the kings had promised to endorse an agreement that he had made with 'their bishop' (i.e. Hædde of Winchester). But he is constrained by an archiepiscopal command of the previous year, apparently forbidding contact with the West Saxon ruler until the latter fulfilled a decree on the ordination of bishops (probably a reference to plans for the division of the huge West Saxon diocese, an event which took place c. 705). It has been argued that a (perhaps *the*) major issue of contention between the West Saxons and 'the rulers of our country' was control over Surrey; and that one result of the Brentford meeting may have been the transfer of that province from the diocese of London to that of Winchester.[43] At some point between 708 and 715 the abbot of two Surrey monasteries, at Bermondsey and Woking, obtained a papal privilege guaranteeing a measure of liberty from the relevant bishop: the text states that these houses were situated in the 'province' of the West Saxons.[44] A letter written by a monk of Chertsey between 732 and 745 also indicates that Surrey then formed part of the Winchester

---

[41] For the Mercian invasion of Kent, see S 10 (Kelly, *St Augustine's*, no. 40).
[42] Bede's account of Eorcenwald's foundations locates Chertsey *in regione Sudergeona* and Barking *in Orientalium Saxonum prouincia* (*HE*, iv. 6), which indicates that he recognised a distinction.
[43] Whitelock 1975, p. 11; Yorke 1985, p. 34.
[44] Privilege of Pope Constantine for Bermondsey and Woking: Jaffé no. 2148; BCS 133; Haddan & Stubbs, iii. 276–8. These minsters appear to have been colonies of the great Mercian house of *Medeshamstede* (later Peterborough) and were probably founded during the period when Æthelred of Mercia had ascendancy over Surrey (see Stenton, *Preparatory to ASE*, pp. 185–6; Whitelock 1975, p. 8 n. 5; and for, for the identity of Abbot Headda, 'S. Keynes, *The Councils of* Clofesho, 11th Brixworth Lecture, Vaughan Paper no 38, Univ. of Leicester Dpt of Adult Education, 1994), pp. 40–3). The Mercian origins of the two Surrey minsters may have made it urgent to have had some precise definition of their position with respect to the bishop of Winchester.

diocese.[45] In the later eighth century at least part of the province fell back under Mercian rule, as King Offa annexed Surrey, Sussex and Kent to his kingdom (see S 144, and S 127; Kelly, *Chertsey*, no. 5); control was finally regained by the West Saxons in the aftermath of the 825 battle of Wroughton (*ASC*: see below, pp. 19–20). The diocesan position of Surrey may have retained a degree of ambiguity; even when firmly assigned to Winchester, the western and central areas still fell within London's region, and in the mid tenth century the bishops of London still held important estates in the province, at Wimbledon and Sheen (see pp. 92–3).

d. *Mercian London*

By the early eighth century the Mercian rulers were firmly in control of London and its port. King Æthelbald (716–57) issued an extraordinary series of privileges concerning *Lundenwic*, by which he exempted various ecclesiastics and religious houses from 'the toll (*vectigal*) belonging to me and my predecessors by royal right in the port of London' (*cf.* S 86, 88). Beneficiaries included Ingwald, bishop of London (**7, 8**); the bishops of Rochester and Worcester (S 88, 98); and the abbesses of the Kentish double monastery known as Minster-in-Thanet (S 86–7, 91).[46] These individuals and their churches might own several trading-ships, which would have arrived in the Strand settlement with produce from their own estates and perhaps also luxury goods acquired in the emporia on the Continent which were involved in a trading network with London.[47] Among the merchandise sold at *Lundenwic* would have been slaves: one of the earliest references to the London market appears in Bede's story of a Northumbrian warrior being sold as a slave to a Frisian in London, in the aftermath of the battle of Trent in 678 (*HE*, iv. 22). Written sources indicate that imports from the Continent would have included items such as wine, oil, furs and silk, ivory and metalwork; the archaeological evidence consists primarily of quantities of pottery, much of it from overseas, particularly from Northern France, Flanders and the Rhineland.[48] There is some some evidence for industry within the Strand settlement: huge finds of loom-weights suggest that textile production was important by *c.* 750.[49] The toll-privileges indicate that taxes were collected in the port by

---

[45] Tangl, no. 36; Whitelock 1975, p. 11.

[46] For general discussion of these toll-privileges, see Kelly 1992; Kelly, *St Augustine's*, pp. lxxxv–xc.

[47] For the trading emporia in this period, see Hill and Cowie, *Wics.*; and for London's role, see Cowie 2001; Milne and Goodburn 1990.

[48] Kelly 1992, pp. 14–16; Blackmore 1997, p. 126; Keene 2000, pp. 188–9.

[49] Blackmore 1997, pp. 126–7; Cowie 2001, pp. 203–4.

agents of the Mercian kings (*thelonearii, actionarii*), who may also have exercised rights of pre-emption, as did a later Kentish king in the port of Fordwich (S 29; Kelly, *St Augustine's*, no. 53).

During the reigns of Æthelbald and his successors, the Mercian bishops of Worcester began to build up important holdings in London. The first hint comes in a list of benefactions to the church of Worcester, which attributes to Æthelbald the grant of a tenement between two streets, probably in the City but conceivably in the Strand settlement.[50] Other Mercian churches with less well-preserved archives, in particular the principal Mercian see of Lichfield, are also likely to have begun to acquire property in the London area (see **3** for a bishop of Hereford holding Fulham). For those churches engaged in trade, and for individual merchants, there would have been an advantage in acquiring a plot of land in the Strand settlement or its vicinity, for storing goods and conducting commercial business. A flawed but intriguing document refers to property in *Lundenwic* owned by two brothers with Frankish names, who left it to the abbey of Saint-Denis near Paris: the bequest was subsequently confirmed by King Offa (757–96), who also remitted all the royal tax or toll (*census*) which was due from the property (S 133).[51] There is a strong possibility that other churches were granted rights of exemption in their *Lundenwic* holdings, involving remission of the trading taxes owed to the Mercian kings: in the following century the bishops of Worcester acquired plots of land with special trading exemptions (see S 208, 346, 1628; and below, pp. 22, 25–6). It seems fairly likely that the bishops of London would have had a territorial foothold of some kind in *Lundenwic*, and probably also commercial concessions and privileges, such as a share in the royal toll.

---

[50] *Mon. Angl.*, i. 138: 'curtem unam in Lundonia inter duas stratas, quæ Tiddbertistret et Savinstret [nominantur]'. Both street-names would appear to incorporate an early personal name, Tidberht (see S 1410, 182, 1433) and ? Sebbi (*cf.* the king of the East Saxons, who died in London in 693/4: Bede, *HE*, iv. 11).

[51] This is one of a group of four purportedly 'Anglo-Saxon' documents preserved at Saint-Denis (see also S 1186, 318, 686). Offa's charter, which survives as a twelfth-century pseudo-original, was evidently modelled on an eighth-century English diploma: the scribe is attempting to imitate Insular minuscule; he has incorporated a contemporary witness-list and he dates the grant from Tamworth in Staffordshire, well-known as the site of a royal vill; all the dating indicators are consistent and the text includes the place-name *Lundenwic*, which appears to have fallen out of use in the ninth century. These features do not necessarily mean that the substance of Offa's charter is wholly genuine, but it does suggest that the Saint-Denis scribe had access to some kind of contemporary documentation that mentioned the port of London. See Levison, *England and the Continent*, p. 8 n. 1; H. Atsma and J. Vezin, 'Le dossier suspect des possessions de Saint-Denis en Angleterre revisité (VIII–IX siècles)', *Fälschungen im Mittelalter*, MGH Schriften, xxxiii.4 (Hanover, 1988), pp. 211–36; Kelly 1992.

There are notices of major fires in London in 764, 798 and 801, with the 798 episode claiming many lives; these conflagrations probably affected the Strand settlement, rather than the lightly populated walled city.[52] There is essentially no information about the composition or history of the St Paul's community in the seventh and eighth centuries. It is possible that the original church in the time of Mellitus broadly conformed to the recommendations which Pope Gregory made to Augustine with respect to the cathedral community at Canterbury (Bede, *HE*, i. 27).[53] The bishop and his clergy were to live a communal life, with only the clerics in minor orders being allowed to marry; the revenues of the church were to be divided into three parts, one for the bishop and his *familia*, the second for the clergy and the third to be used for the repair of churches. The evidence from Canterbury indicates that in the seventh and eighth centuries the episcopal community there consisted of priests, deacons and clerks in lesser orders, and the same was probably true of St Paul's.[54] The only member of the early St Paul's community to whom we can give a name was a priest.[55] In the preface to the *Ecclesiastical History*, Bede mentions that Nothhelm ('priest of the church of London') had acted as his intermediary with Abbot Albinus of St Augustine's, Canterbury, relaying information about the Gregorian mission to Kent either in the form of written communications or by word of mouth. Nothhelm added to Albinus's information by travelling to Rome and searching the papal archives for useful documentation. He also corresponded with Bede on matters of biblical exegesis, in response to which the Northumbrian master put together for him two compilations, *In Regum Librum XXX Quaestiones* and *De VIII Quaestionibus*: it would appear that Nothhelm had only limited access to this kind of material at London. Nothhelm was chosen as the archbishop of Canterbury in 735, dying in 739.[56] A later archbishop of Canterbury (Wulfred, 805–32) seems to have been

[52] *Symeon of Durham*, ii. 42, 59, 66. The 801 annal has an obituary for Heahberht, bishop of London, followed by a note: 'et paulo post magna pars vici ipsius repentino igne consumpta est'. The Latin *vicus* is probably a straight translation of *wic* (i.e. *Lundenwic*).

[53] See discussion in Brooks, *Church of Canterbury*, pp. 87–91.

[54] **2** refers to the *monasterialis vita* in the city, and **9** to the *congregatio fratrum*: but these phrases are entirely vague (see Brooke 1957, pp. 10–11).

[55] Gibbs (p. xviii n. 1) notices that Heahstan 'priest-abbot' attests after the bishop in the London contingent at the 803 Synod of Clofesho (S 1431a; BCS 312) and suggests that he may have been attached to St Paul's. But the contingent originally included a second abbot, Plegberht, and there is no proof that either of these was head of the cathedral community. See Brooks and Kelly, *Christ Church*, no. 32.

[56] Brooks, *Church of Canterbury*, p. 99. The date of Nothhelm's visit to Rome is uncertain. Bede mentions that he had received permission to search the archives from 'he who now heads the church as Pope Gregory' (i.e. Gregory II, 715–31). But before his election Gregory had been the librarian of the church of Rome, and it may be that Bede's form of words indicates that it was in this capacity that he had facilitated Nothhelm's researches. See Colgrave and Mynors, *Bede's Ecclesiastical History*, p. 4 n. 3.

from a Middle Saxon family, indeed may even have been related to the earlier Bishop Wealdhere; and it is conceivable that he was attached to St Paul's before moving on to the *familia* of Christ Church. He owned and acquired huge estates in western Middlesex, and is likely to have wielded considerable influence in the London diocese.[57] In that context, it is important to notice that in 808 × 813 Wulfred instituted a reform of the Canterbury community (see S 1265; Brooks and Kelly, *Christ Church*, no. 47). The clergy were to live communally, using a common dormitory and refectory in accordance with 'the rule of monastic discipline'; they were keep the office at the canonical hours; but they could own private property, especially the houses or cells which they had built themselves. It has been suggested that Wulfred was here imposing a rule similar to that of Bishop Chrodegang of Metz, who had transformed his cathedral clergy into a community of canons, and whose ideas were increasingly influential in the Frankish Church in the early ninth century.[58] Chrodegang's *Rule* appears to have formed the basis for the canonical rule observed at St Paul's in the eleventh century (see p. 44). The date at which this observance was adopted is entirely uncertain; there is at least a very good chance that it goes back to the time of Bishop Theodred (*c.* 926–*c.* 951). But it would be unsafe entirely to discount the possibility that elements of canonical organisation were already in place at St Paul's in the early ninth century, perhaps partly inspired by Wulfred's reforms at Canterbury, and possibly also arising from the close contacts between London and the Frankish kingdom.

It became the practice of the Mercian kings to rule their south-eastern possessions at a distance, and to settle most relevant business in ecclesiastical synods and royal councils which often convened in the immediate vicinity of London. A popular venue was Chelsea (S 123, 125, 128, 131, 150–1), but there were also meetings in London itself (see S 168, 170) and at Brentford (S 116, 1257).[59] A spurious charter based on a genuine synodal record provides the information that an ecclesiastical synod met in St Paul's at Pentecost 795, and that it was attended by the Mercian king Offa and his son Ecgfrith, by the archbishop of Canterbury and ten of his suffragans, together with Mercian abbots and nobles (S 132; Brooks and Kelly, *Christ Church*, nos 25, 25A). Offa is supposed to have

---

[57] For discussion of Wulfred's origins and property, see Brooks, *Church of Canterbury*, pp. 132–42. His kinsman and heir, Werheard, owned the estate at Twickenham which had previously been granted to Bishop Wealdhere (S 1414; see S 65 and discussion below, p. 87).

[58] Brooks, *Church of Canterbury*, pp. 154–60. See, however, B. Langefeld ('*Regula canonicorum* or *Regula monasterialis vitae*? The Rule of Chrodegang and Archbishop Wulfred's Reforms at Canterbury', *Anglo-Saxon England* xxv (1996), pp. 21–36), who argues against the idea that Wulfred was influenced by Chrodegang's Rule, and maintains that it would be better to regard Christ Church as a monastic household.

[59] Cubitt, *Councils*, pp. 27–32, 205–10, 306–9. For the political implication of this strategy, see Keynes 1993*b*.

extended the privileges granted to St Paul's by his predecessor Coenred, although it is difficult to believe that the extant fragment derives from a genuine document (5*b*). Several fabricated diplomas from Westminster claim that Offa was a significant benefactor of the community there (S 124, 670, 1122, 1283). The eighth-century bishops of London who followed Wealdhere are little more than a sequence of names (see below, pp. 113–15), but there is a hint of a political row in the Chronicle annal for 796, where it is remarked that Bishops Eadbald of London and Ceolwulf of Lindsey left the country. This was a turbulent year: King Offa died and was briefly succeeded by his son Ecgfrith, who died in his turn a few months later; the Mercian kingdom passed to Coenwulf, a very distant connection. It is possible that Eadbald was closely identified with Offa and his family, and that he opposed Coenwulf's accession. His voluntary exile, leaving the London see effectively vacant, may have given the new Mercian king a useful opportunity to solve two problems at once. In 787 King Offa had engineered a division of the metropolitan province of Canterbury in order to elevate the Mercian see of Lichfield to an archbishopric. This would appear to have caused massive resentment at Canterbury, and may have destabilised the Southumbrian church. On Offa's death, the people of Kent rose in revolt and expelled the Mercian-appointed Archbishop Æthelheard; but this brief period of independence was bloodily quashed by Coenwulf in 798. Against this background, Coenwulf and his advisers had the clever idea of reviving the Gregorian plan and transferring the metropolitan see from Canterbury to London. In 798 the Mercian king wrote to Pope Leo III essentially conceding that the elevation of Lichfield had been a mistake, and hinting broadly that a resolution of the affair could be linked with a promotion for London. The pope refused to be drawn: the archbishopric of Lichfield could be abolished, but the primacy of Canterbury must be respected.[60]

The Mercian domination of southern England crumbled after the death of Coenwulf in 821 and the forced abdication of his successor Ceolwulf in 823. The West Saxon king Ecgberht used his victory in a battle at Wroughton in 825 as a springboard for invasion and conquest of Mercian-controlled areas in south-east England: within the next few years the people of Kent and Surrey, and the South and East Saxons submitted themselves to West Saxon overlordship. In 829 Ecgberht managed to conquer the Mercian kingdom itself, which would probably have brought him control of London and Middlesex. A penny bearing his name and the legend *Lundonia civit.* commemorates this heady but temporary victory.[61] In the following year the Mercian king Wiglaf contrived to

---

[60] For the correspondence, see Whitelock, *EHD*, nos 204–5; Brooks, *Church of Canterbury*, pp. 123–5.

[61] Brooke and Keir, *London*, plate 19.

re-establish himself in Mercia proper, although the south-eastern appendages of
the Mercian empire were definitively lost. He had regained control of Middlesex
and presumably London by 831 (see S 188).[62] This episode had potentially seri-
ous consequences for the London bishops. As far as we can tell, the East Saxons
would appear to have continued to recognise West Saxon overlordship (see **16**);
with London and Middlesex in the Mercian camp, the diocese may have been
split between two masters. After the momentous events of 825–31, the London
bishops rarely attest the diplomas of the Mercian kings; but neither do they
begin to make regular appearances at the court of the West Saxon kings.[63]
Analysis of the pattern of their attestations reveals that during the period of the
Mercian supremacy the London bishops normally attended the great Southumbrian
synods which were convened under the auspices of the Mercian kings and at
which they regulated the affairs of their south-eastern possessions, but that they
were not usually present at smaller councils in the Mercian heartland (generally
attended only by the bishops of Lichfield, Leicester, Lindsey, Worcester and
Hereford). Following the Mercian defeat of the 820s, there is a record of only
one further Mercian-convened synod, duly attended by Ceolberht of London (S
190, A.D. 838): he was also present at two subsequent synodal gatherings, the
later of which took place in London (S 1438, A.D. 839; and S 1194, A.D. 845).
But Ceolberht's subscription is absent from S 188 (A.D. 831), which disposes of
a Middlesex estate (possibly because this was a largely secular gathering); neither he or his successor attested King Berhtwulf's confirmation of the Rochester
toll-privilege (S 88) nor Burgred's 857 grant of a property just outside London
(S 208). It is unclear whether this evidence is sufficient to draw any conclusions
about the political allegiances of the London bishops in the period between the
820s and the 850s: they may have become invisible solely because their diocese
now lay on the periphery of the Mercian realm; or it may be that a territorial
split of the diocese rendered them politically neutral.[64]

---

[62] **9** records the lease of a Hertfordshire estate by St Paul's to a thegn of King Wiglaf; it is unclear
whether it dates from before or after the West Saxon victory of 829–30.

[63] One exception is S 280 (A.D. 838), a diploma of the West Saxon king Ecgberht, attested by
Bishop Ceolberht. It is no doubt significant that this charter, which records a grant to Rochester, is
dated from a royal vill in Surrey, possibly located at Kingston-on-Thames (Blair, *Surrey*, p. 20) and
at any rate on the borders of the London diocese: Ceolberht's presence may reflect a courtesy visit,
rather than his political allegiance.

[64] For a slightly different evaluation of this documentary material, see Keynes 1993*b* pp. 129–30;
idem 1998, p. 8. The archive of Saint-Denis in Paris contains a diploma dated 857 in the name of
Æthelwulf of Wessex, supposedly confirming the abbey's possessions, including its holding in
Lundenwic (S 318). This is a forgery, and a far less convincing one than S 133 (see p. 16 n. 51),
which may have been the source of the reference to the *Lundenwic* property; it cannot be used as
evidence that Æthelwulf controlled London.

e. *The Viking wars and King Alfred's restoration of London*

The archaeological evidence indicates that the Strand settlement went into decline fairly early in the ninth century or perhaps even a little earlier.[65] The bad fires in 798 and 801 may have been one factor; other possible causes were local tidal changes, and on a larger scale, the political upheavals which reduced the capacity of the Mercian kings to protect the market from predators, together with a general decline in overseas trade which also affected the Continental emporia.[66] In the background was the increasing threat of Viking marauders, to whom such undefended trading settlements were an obvious target. The first record of an attack on *Lundenwic* comes from the Chronicle annal for 842, which mentions massive slaughter there and also at Rochester and in the Frankish emporium at *Quentovic* (near Calais). But there is good reason to think that problems began decades earlier: Kentish sources suggest that Viking raids on the south-eastern coasts were already a significant nuisance at the end of Offa's reign (see S 134; Kelly, *St Augustine's*, no. 13), and that by 811 the pirates were building themselves fortified camps on the Kentish coasts (see S 1264, 186).[67] One reaction to these acts of piracy was a retreat from vulnerable sites into more easily defended locations, such as the former Roman walled cities. In Kent the abbess and community of the double monastery at Lyminge were given a refuge in Canterbury, associated with a church dedicated to St Mary (S 160, A.D. 804; Brooks and Kelly, *Christ Church*, no. 34), and there is reason to believe that the exposed community at Minster-in-Thanet was granted a similar retreat in that city.[68] The double monastery at Barking would have been comparably vulnerable, and may have been given a base within the walls of London; it was perhaps at this time that the community acquired its association with the church of All Hallows Barking.[69] The population of the declining port may have started shifting within the walls from the mid century onwards: recent excavations have found evidence pointing to some level of

---

[65] Vince 1991, pp. 417–19; Blackmore 1997, p. 127; Cowie 2001, p. 207.

[66] Cowie 2001, pp. 207–8.

[67] Brooks 1971, pp. 79–80.

[68] Kelly, *St Augustine's*, pp. xxviii–ix.

[69] An eleventh-century hagiographical source from Barking says that the nuns were accustomed to flee to London in difficult times (Colker 1965, pp. 412–13, 416). In the later eleventh century Barking Abbey owned half of the church of All Hallows (already known as 'Barking'), the other half being in the possession of Christ Church, Canterbury (LDB 7v–18r; *DB Essex* 9:7; Kissan 1940a, pp. 65–6; idem 1940b, pp. 214–15; Douglas and Greenaway, *EHD II*, p. 1023). Bombing of the church in 1940 exposed a round Anglo-Saxon arch partly constructed with reused Roman tiles, which looks early and has been tentatively assigned to the seventh or eighth century, although it could well be later (Taylor and Taylor, *Anglo-Saxon Architecture*, pp. 399–400; Schofield, *Building of London*, pp. 21–2). See further Vince, *Saxon London*, pp. 69–70; Brooke and Keir, *London*, p. 137.

intramural occupation from *c.* 850 onwards, rather earlier than the conventional date of 886 for the start of the city's revival.[70] But the *wic* was still functioning in 857, when the Mercian king Burgred granted to the bishop of Worcester 'a very profitable little piece of land' *in uico Lundoniae* (i.e. *Lundenwic*), formerly the property of the king's reeve, which was clearly to be used as a market; the holder was to observe the same system of weights and measures as that used in the port (S 208). The estate was apparently extramural, but was located near the 'west gates' of the city, presumably on the very eastern edge of the *wic*.[71] A complete retreat into the walled area may have been deterred by the vast length of the Roman walls of London, which would have required an extraordinary effort to refurbish and defend. A compromise may have been the construction of smaller fortified enclosures, and it may be that the ninth century saw the construction of the intramural fortifications that gave rise to the names of *Paulesbyrig*, Aldermanbury and Lothbury (see p. 7 n. 21). There are also signs that an effort was made to dig a defensive ditch around the port.[72]

The Scandinavian raids increased in size and ferocity in the middle of the century. In 851 a Viking fleet, estimated (perhaps with understandable exaggeration) at 350 ships, entered the Thames estuary and stormed Canterbury and London (*ASC*). The raiders met the Mercian king Berhtwulf and his army, who may have been engaged in the defence of London, and ignominiously put them to flight. This would appear to have been a devastating and overwhelming defeat. One of the first acts of the next Mercian king, Burgred, who took power in 852, was to request military support from the stronger West Saxon rulers, and this pattern seems to have developed into an effective alliance. Burgred continued to collect the tolls from London (see S 208 from 857), but his grip on the city may have been weak, while London itself may have been slow to recover from the sack of 851. The London mint seems to have been fairly inactive in the 850s, with few coins in Burgred's name being struck. The output increased in the 860s, which saw a novel development: the London moneyers were still minting coins for Burgred, but were also producing limited issues for the West Saxon kings Æthelberht and Æthelred.[73] In the same decade there is some evidence that Bishop Deorwulf was inclining politically towards Wessex. In 860 he was present at a West Saxon assembly, alongside the archbishop of Canterbury, and the bishops of Rochester, Winchester,

---

[70] Clark 1999, p. 38; Blackmore 1997, p. 129.

[71] An identification has been suggested with a site in the Temple area, where excavation has revealed high-status objects from the eighth and ninth centuries (Blackmore 1997, p. 128). The plural 'west gates' could refer to both Newgate and Ludgate, but alternatively it may have meant a single gate in a double-arched gateway (Page, *London*, p. 13; Ekwall, *London Street Names*, p. 36).

[72] Cowie 2001, p. 208.

[73] See Keynes 1998, pp. 8–9, and references cited there.

Sherborne and Selsey; this gathering was attended by no fewer than ten ealdormen and may have had an extraordinary significance (S 327).[74] Seven years later Deorwulf was involved in persuading the West Saxon king Æthelred to make a grant of an estate, possibly at Navestock in Essex; the diploma recording this transaction lies behind a forged charter in favour of St Paul's (see **16**). It is possible that the moneyers' activities and the political veering of the bishop both had the same pragmatic motive. The Mercian ruler was no longer in a position to defend the city in any significant way, so overtures had to be made to the more effective West Saxon kings, already involved in the defence of the Thames estuary through their lordship over Kent and Essex. Perhaps part of the trading toll was now being collected by agents of the West Saxons rulers, which might explain the production of coins of Æthelberht and Æthelred by the London moneyers.

The military situation deteriorated still further from the autumn of 865. At that time a 'great Viking army' landed in East Anglia and proceeded over the next few years to topple that kingdom and also Northumbria, while rampaging across Mercia and attacking the West Saxons from the north. In autumn 871 Scandinavian forces made their way to to London and took up winter-quarters there (*ASC*). The Chronicle remarks that 'the Mercians made peace with the enemy', probably a euphemism for the payment of tribute and the surrender of hostages: the community of the church of Worcester was forced to lease out an estate to raise money for 'the immense tribute of the barbarians, in the year that the pagans stayed in London' (S 1278). The Scandinavians departed in autumn 872, but continued to put pressure on Mercia; in 873/4 they drove out King Burgred and installed a new king, Ceolwulf, and in 877 they split the kingdom, leaving Ceolwulf ruler over western Mercia. Another Scandinavian army wintered on the episcopal estate at Fulham in 878–9.

The position of London at this time is very uncertain, with the scanty historical evidence being interpreted in radically different ways. The conventional view is that the city fell under Danish control in 877 or even before, and remained under occupation until a dramatic reconquest by the West Saxon king Alfred in 886.[75] Balanced against this view is the numismatic evidence. The material is very complex, but seems to indicate that the moneyers normally associated with the London mint were producing coins in the name of Alfred in the middle and later 870s and early 880s, for at least part of that time in combination with coins of the Mercian ruler Ceolwulf.[76] Earlier explanations for this phenomenon

[74] See Keynes 1993*b*, pp. 128–30; *idem* 1998, p. 8.

[75] Brooke and Keir, *London*, p. 19; Stenton, *ASE*, pp. 258–9; and sources cited in Keynes 1998, p. 13 n. 49.

[76] See M. Blackburn, 'The London Mint in the Reign of Alfred', in Blackburn and Dumville, *Kings, Currency and Alliances*, pp. 105–23 at 108–20; Keynes 1998, pp. 15–24.

involved the suggestion that under Danish rule London was a kind of 'open city' where the moneyers were permitted to strike coins for Alfred; or, alternatively, that the London moneyers had decamped to Rochester along with their equipment. More recently it has been proposed that London looked to Alfred for protection soon after Burgred's flight, and that the city actually remained under English control for much of the period between 877 and 886, with only brief periods of Viking occupation. In the course of its description of the complex military campaigns of the early 880s, the Chronicle refers to Alfred and his forces being encamped against the Scandinavian army at London in 883: the circumstances are unclear, but it has been suggested that the episode could be connected to a temporary Viking occupation of the City.[77] The next reference to London is in the annal for 886, which states that 'King Alfred occupied London and all the people that were not under subjection to the Danes submitted to him. And he then entrusted the borough to the control of Ealdorman Æthelred'.[78] A parallel passage in Asser's life of Alfred notes that Alfred 'restored the city of London splendidly . . . and made it habitable again'.[79] The conventional interpretation of the events of 886 is of a triumphal conquest of a Danish-held city, but an alternative view has been proposed, to the effect that Alfred's 'occupation' and 'restoration' are to be connected with a refurbishing of London's defences and the provision of a permanent garrison.[80] The Ealdorman Æthelred to whom Alfred entrusted the city had been in control of English Mercia from c. 880, after the disappearance of Ceolwulf; his non-regal style is a recognition of his submission to authority and lordship of the West Saxon king (he married Alfred's daughter, Æthelflæd, who ruled jointly with him and then in her own right after his death in 911). Although Alfred is said to returned formal control of London to Æthelred, he was still involved in the affairs of the city: in transactions of 889 and 898/9 he is seen acting jointly with Æthelred, and then with Æthelred and Æthelflæd (S 346, 1628). This power-sharing continued in the reign of his son Edward the Elder (see 10).

The years 877–886 must have been very difficult ones for the church of London, whether there was a permanent Danish occupation during that period or a series of temporary occupations. It is possible that the bishop and his clergy evacuated the city during this time, or that they came to an accommodation with the pagan Scandinavians that allowed them to remain in London and carry out at least some of their ecclesiastical functions, as seems to have happened in York.

[77] Keynes 1998, pp. 22–3.
[78] ASC (translation, Whitelock, EHD, p. 199).
[79] Stevenson, Asser, p. 69 (Ælfred . . . Lundoniam civitatem honorifice restauravit et habitabilem fecit); translation, Keynes and Lapidge, Alfred the Great, pp. 97–8.
[80] Keynes 1998, p. 23.

Whatever the case, circumstances must have been straitened, with income curtailed because the church's estates had been ravaged or fallen out of cultivation, and with capital diminished by the necessity of raising tribute or buying protection, and precious church ornaments stolen or melted down. Some improvement may have followed as a result of Alfred's refurbishment of the city. The best-attested area of Alfredian activity is a clear attempt to resuscitate London trade within the walls. In 889 the bishop of Worcester was granted an enclosure to be used for tax-free commercial activity; and in 898 or 899 the archbishop of Canterbury and the bishop of Worcester each received a similar plot associated with a river-mooring at Queenhithe (then *Ætheredshithe*, perhaps named from the ealdorman who was one of the donors, and possibly representing part of the London holdings of the Mercian kings).[81] The records of these donations give important insights into conditions in the city at the end of the ninth century. The 889 diploma includes careful measurements of the enclosure in perches and feet: this is consistent with an urban density of occupation, which made exact dimensions important. While trade in the enclosure would not attract toll, any commercial activity in the street or on the trading shore (*ripa em[p]toralis*) would be liable to pay a toll to the king (the wording would seem to imply that it was Alfred who was ultimately entitled to this tax, rather than Ealdorman Æthelred). The record of the 898/9 transaction, apparently a later memorandum,[82] gives a hint of the difficulties involved in trading from the Thames bank of the City: for it provides a reminder that the riverside wall built by the Romans in the third century was still in place, separating the intramural plots and the moorings on the river. The two properties mentioned lay on either side of a main road (*via publica*) running to the river (probably to a river-gate or a break in the wall); in other directions they were bounded by tracks (*semitae*) and a narrow road. Recent excavations of the Queenhithe area have produced dendrochronological samples which place the construction of the waterfront here to the period *c.* 900;

---

[81] S 346, 1628. I am not convinced by the suggestion that S 346 refers to the same Worcester holding as S 1628 (as suggested in Dyson 1978). The locative detail seems incompatible: while the *Hwætmundestan* property in S 346 ran from a street to the city wall (implying that the street and wall were opposite boundaries), the Queenhithe acre of S 1628 was bounded by a track to the north and a wall to the south, with a road running alongside to the west. Moreover, it is unclear why two documents of different date should refer to the same property, since there is plenty of evidence that Worcester was accumulating multiple properties in London. It has been suggested that the lack of any reference in the Worcester archive to the 898/9 grant might be a difficulty that could be rectified by an equation with S 346 (Dyson 1978, pp. 205–6), but this perception results from a mistaken belief in the survival-rate of Anglo-Saxon documents. On the Queenhithe area, see also Dyson and Schofield 1984, pp. 296–7; Dyson 1990; Vince, *Saxon London*, pp. 21–2.

[82] See Brooks and Kelly, *Christ Church*, no. 100, for discussion of the manuscripts and their significance for the unusual form of the document.

also, and intriguingly, there is some evidence for earlier trading on the river-bank, with activity from c. 850.[83]

It is probable that the bishop of London, like his colleagues at Canterbury and Worcester, acquired or already owned some mooring rights on the city bank of the Thames, probably at St Paul's Wharf.[84] It may even be the case that the bishop and St Paul's also obtained specific trading rights and perhaps a share of the royal tolls in the new intramural markets; a key comparison would be with the situation in Worcester, where Æthelred and Æthelflæd made over to the bishop and his community a share in the lordship of the revived town, together with market tolls and taxes, in return for liturgical services.[85] The revived commercial activity in the Alfredian city was of a different character from that of the defunct emporium on the Strand. Tenth-century archaeological deposits in London have produced very little imported pottery, which would tie in with evidence for a general decline in overseas trade in north-west Europe during this period.[86] For most of the tenth century London's main trading links seem to have been with inland markets along the Thames, with a particular focus on the Oxford region.[87] Much of the new trading activity is likely to have involved agricultural surpluses, with the commercial revival being spearheaded by the efforts and requirements of the great landowning churches. The food-markets at West Cheap would seem to have been laid out in the tenth century, perhaps specifically to sell the produce of the St Paul's estates in the Thames estuary and on the Essex coast.[88] Some of the peculiar features of the post-Conquest chapter economy may have had their origins in this period. Whereas elsewhere the food-rents of leased communal property had generally been commuted to money-payments by c. 1100, at St Paul's the canons continued to receive their food-farms into the fourteenth century; the cathedral bake-house and brewery produced vast quantities of bread and beer, much of which is likely to have been sold in the Cheapside markets.[89]

Other aspects of Alfred's restoration of London are more conjectural. It can be assumed that refurbishment of the military defences was a primary objective. The repair of the Roman walls would have been a huge enterprise, given the

---

[83] Blackmore 1997, pp. 129–30; Clark 1999, p. 38.

[84] For a St Paul's holding here in 1111, see Davis 1925, p. 48; and Taylor 1980, p. 177.

[85] S 223; Whitelock, *EHD*, no. 99.

[86] Vince 1991, pp. 419, 433–4; see R. Hodges, *Dark Age Economics: the Origins of Towns and Trade A.D. 600–1000* (London, 1982), pp. 151–61, for the economic depression of the later ninth century.

[87] Keene 2000, p. 191.

[88] Nightingale, *Mercantile Community*, p. 28.

[89] Brooke and Keir, *London*, p. 176; Brooke 1957, pp. 60–3. For the background to the economic arrangements, see Faith 1994, esp. p. 658.

length of the circuit. It is possible that it was at this time that a regular levy system was set up under which other shires had an obligation to provide labour
for the London defences; there is a reference to such a system in the Chronicle
annal for 1097, and a possible parallel in later arrangements for the maintenance
of the bridge over the Medway at Rochester.[90] Some attention must have been
paid to the old Roman bridge, if only to secure the stone piers into a defensive
structure with the fortification at Southwark, mentioned in the Burghal Hidage.
There is essentially no archaeological evidence for settlement at Southwark
before the eleventh century, which probably indicates that there was not a regularly maintained passage across the bridge in the tenth century.[91] As well as
rebuilding the walls, Alfred and his Mercian colleagues would have had to provide for their regular defence. Once more, the size of the circuit would have
made this a daunting problem. A huge area around the city would have been
obliged to supply fighting men to defend the walls, and the organisation for this
levy may have had an important role in consolidating London's position as the
centre of its region. The citizens of the growing city population are also likely to
have played some role, and one scholar has suggested that the origin of the city
wards lies in self-governing administrative units set up c. 900 to provide for the
defence of the gates and walls.[92] Finally, it has been hypothesised that Alfred
may have constructed a regular street-grid in London, as he is known to have
done at Winchester and in smaller burhs, but this has not been borne out by
excavation results, which would be better compatible with a more organic
growth of street patterns in the second half of the ninth century and in the
tenth.[93]

The Alfredian occupation of 886 did not mark the end of London's difficulties. A document of crucial relevance to the city's position at this time is the so-
called 'Treaty of Alfred and Guthrum', recording an agreement between the

[90] See Stenton, *Preparatory to ASE*, p. 24; and for the documentation on Rochester Bridge, see
Brooks 1992*b*. There is as yet no confirmed archaeological evidence for Alfredian refurbishment of
the walls (Schofield, *Building of London*, p. 24).

[91] See discussion in Watson 2001*a*, pp. 52–3. The assessment of 1800 hides in the Burghal Hidage
suggests that the fortifications required a garrison of 1800 men (which seems excessive, and perhaps
included the levy for manning the bridge).

[92] Haslam 1988, where it is also argued that Alfred and his son Edward the Elder established new
churches and parishes inside the city to cater for the growing population. Most commentators believe
that the wards and parishes developed in the late tenth or early eleventh century (see p. 34).

[93] J. Clark, 'Late Saxon and Norman London: Thirty Years On', in Haynes *et al.*, *London Under
Ground*, pp. 206–22 at 210–18. For the 'planned grid' theory, see, for example, Tatton-Brown 1986,
pp. 25–6; G. Milne, 'King Alfred's Plan for London?', *London Archaeologist* vi (1990), pp. 206–7;
Milne and Goodburn 1990, pp. 630–1; and for the unsupportive archaeological evidence, Dyson
1990, pp. 107–8; Vince, *Saxon London*, pp. 124–6; Vince 1991, pp. 421, 424; Blackmore 1997,
p. 129; Clark 1999; Schofield, *Building of London*, p. 25.

West Saxon ruler and the Viking king of East Anglia: according to this the boundary between the two peoples was to run 'up the Thames, and then up the Lea, and along the Lea to its source, then in a straight line to Bedford and then up the Ouse to Watling Street'.[94] The conventional interpretation would date this treaty to between the Alfredian occupation of London in 886 and the death of King Guthrum in 890, and would see it as marking a boundary between English-held Middlesex and Viking-held Essex. If the new interpretation of the events of 886 is valid (see above, pp. 23–4), then we would need to contemplate revised dating-limits of 880 × 890, or perhaps even 880 × 885.[95] A very different assessment would date the Treaty to a period when London was in Danish hands and Essex still held by the West Saxons: this would involve a reversed understanding of the political complexion of the boundary.[96] Whichever view is correct, there is a general consensus that the Treaty represented only a temporary stage in relations between the English and the Vikings of East Anglia, soon modified by events.[97] A new Scandinavian army arrived in 893 and based itself for at least part of the next few years in Essex. In a dramatic episode in 895 the Danes built a fortress on the Lea, just twenty miles north of London (presumably at or near Hertford). During the summer the citizens marched against them, but were defeated. The economic effect of such a close Danish presence is dramatically demonstrated by Alfred's next move: he ordered his army into camp near London so that the harvest could be brought in under its protection, and not destroyed or seized by the Danes. Eventually the enemy had to abandon their ships, which were triumphantly seized by the men of London and either broken up or brought back to the city for their own use (ASC). Over the next twenty years Essex seems to have been a battleground.[98] Judging from the place-name evidence, only the north-eastern part of the shire, in the Colchester area, saw substantial Danish settlement.[99] But its long coastline and proximity to the Scandinavian kingdom of East Anglia made Essex very vulnerable to infiltration and raids, and at least part of the shire was occupied for long periods. The tide turned in the years after 911. That year saw the death of Ealdorman Æthelred of Mercia, after which the West Saxon king Edward the Elder, son of Alfred, 'succeeded to London and to Oxford and to all the lands which belonged to them'

[94] Keynes and Lapidge, *Alfred the Great*, p. 171.
[95] Keynes 1998, pp. 33–4.
[96] See Dumville, *Wessex and England*, pp. 1–27; and discussion in Williams 1996, pp. 93–4; Keynes 1998, p. 33; Williamson, *Herts.*, pp. 87–90.
[97] See R.H.C. Davis, 'Alfred and Guthrum's Frontier', *English Historical Review* xcvii (1982), pp. 803–10; Dumville, *Wessex and England*, p. 3; Keynes 1998, pp. 33–4.
[98] The history of Viking activity in Essex is surveyed in Williams 1996.
[99] Hart, *Danelaw*, pp. 118, 125 and map 3.1.

(*ASC*).[100] In 912 Edward began campaigning in Essex, consolidating his advances by building fortified burhs; this continued until 917, when the king captured and restored Colchester 'and many people who had been under the rule of the Danes in East Anglia and Essex submitted to him' (*ASC*). This must have been a considerable relief from the perspective of the London bishopric, since for decades a considerable part of the diocese had been frontier territory—occupied, raided and fought over. During this period it is likely that some of the episcopal estates were inaccessible or difficult to cultivate, with consequent effects on the cathedral's income.

f. *St Paul's in the Tenth Century*

There was almost certainly a need for reconstruction and consolidation of the bishopric after this difficult time. The details of the bishops of London are as usual very obscure: there is a notice of the death of Bishop Heahstan in the year 897 (*ASC*), and his successor Wulfsige attests charters between 900 and 909; but thereafter there is a gap in the charter-record and the next two bishops are known only from the episcopal lists. The situation begins to change with the appointment of the formidable Theodred, probably in late 925 or 926. His origins are unknown, but his name is German and he may have arrived from the Continent in order to assist in the reconversion of the newly-conquered Danish areas of England.[101] By fortunate chance his will has been preserved in the archive of Bury St Edmunds (S 1526; see Appendix 2). When the will was drawn up, at some point between 942 and his death in 951 × 953, Theodred was bishop not only of the London diocese, but also over at least the southern part of East Anglia (previously served by a separate diocese which had collapsed in the 860s). It seems likely that this apparent pluralism was a stage in the establishment of a proper episcopal structure for the region, which culminated in the creation of the bishopric of Elmham, probably *c*. 950 × 955.[102] Theodred's will provides valuable insight into the land-holdings of the London bishopric and of the community of St Paul's in the second quarter of the tenth century (below, pp. 90–4). There is also considerable interest in the series of bequests and references to clerics with German names: these men were clearly Theodred's intimate associates, and may

---

[100] The wording here is good evidence for the existence at this date of a recognised London region (Stenton, *Preparatory to ASE*, p. 24). The lands dependent on London and Oxford were presumably the Mercian territory in Middlesex, Hertfordshire, Buckinghamshire and Oxfordshire (J. Blair, *Anglo-Saxon Oxfordshire* (Stroud, 1994), p. 97). Edward assumed control of the rest of English Mercia when Æthelflæd died in 918.

[101] For a more detailed discussion of Theodred's origins and career, see below, pp. 116–18.

[102] Whitelock 1975, pp. 18–20; Campbell 1996, pp. 14–15.

represent some portion of his diocesan clergy. During this period the St Paul's community is likely to have been exposed to ideas and influence from the German Church, and it is conceivable that it was at this time that the community acquired a copy of the 816 *Institutio Canonicorum*, which has been argued to form the basis of a pre-Conquest 'Rule of St Paul' (see below, p. 44). There is no way to discover whether or not Theodred reformed the cathedral community along canonical lines, whether the London clergy already followed some kind of canonical rule (see above, p. 17–18), or whether such reorganisation was delayed until the generation before the Conquest. Nevertheless, it is worth noticing that later generations at St Paul's were to focus on the reign of Æthelstan (924–39) as a significant period in the community's history. There are two post-Conquest forgeries in the name of that king which concern blanket confirmations of lands and liberties: a Latin diploma based on a Chertsey privilege in the name of Edgar (**12**); and a bilingual document supposedly confirming a grant of immunity made by the seventh-century king Sebbi to Bishop Eorcenwald (**13**). Æthelstan's hugely successful reign saw the consolidation of a united English kingdom, with imperial pretensions: he received the submission of formerly independent Scandinavian rulers, and also of the kings of Scotland, Strathclyde and Wales. A number of royal diplomas produced in the central years of his reign (*c.* 928 × 935) are witnessed by huge gatherings, and include subscriptions of these *subreguli*; the St Paul's archive preserves a fragment of one of these charters, connected with a great assembly at Cirencester in 935 (**11**).

From the time of Æthelstan and Theodred comes a document with considerable significance for the history of the city: 'The Ordinance of the Bishops and Reeves of the London District'.[103] This was primarily concerned with the organisation and functioning of a 'peace-guild', which was designed to provide a mechanism for the prevention of theft and other offences and for the policing of the district. The men of the district were grouped into tithings of ten men, which in turn were grouped into hundreds. One of the main purposes of this organisation was to provide a structure for hunting down thieves and confronting their kindred, but there was also a strong social element. Representatives of the hundreds and tithings assembled once a month, and the tithings themselves may have met for a regular feast. Individuals paid a subscription to the organisation, to cover common necessities, and there was provision for the funerals of the guild-members. There are points of contact with the tenth- and eleventh-century gild-statutes from Exeter, Cambridge, Bedwyn and Abbotsbury,[104] and one may

---

[103] Whitelock, *EHD*, no. 37 (pp. 423–7); Brooke and Keir, *London*, pp. 195–6.

[104] Whitelock, *EHD*, nos 136–9. See discussion by G. Rosser, 'The Anglo-Saxon Gilds', in Blair, *Minsters and Parish Churches*, pp. 31–4.

wish to entertain the possibility that the English *Cnihtengild*, which may have come into existence during the reign of Edgar, developed out of the peace-guild of Æthelstan's day (see **32** and discussion there). The particular interest of the 'Ordinance' lies in its implication that the London district already had a special character, which required individual legislation. Its regulations were additional to and supplemented the national lawcodes which Æthelstan had already established; the provisions had to be agreed to and confirmed by 'the bishops and reeves who belong to London, earl and ceorl'. The reference to bishops in the plural would seem to indicate that the London district included areas beyond the boundaries of the London diocese, such as parts of Kent, Surrey and Buckinghamshire (under the respective jurisdiction of the archbishop of Canterbury and the bishops of Winchester and Dorchester-on-Thames).[105] It is also possible that the draftsman intended to refer to those bishops who had property in London and Middlesex, such as the archbishop of Canterbury and the bishop of Worcester.

Theodred remained a significant figure through the reigns of Æthelstan's successors, Eadmund (939–46) and Eadred (946–55), regularly attesting diplomas in a very prominent position; by the time he died in the early 950s he was the senior suffragan bishop in the Canterbury diocese. His successor Brihthelm received a grant of land in Essex from King Eadwig in 957 (**15**), shortly before the division of the kingdom between Eadwig and his brother Edgar. London is assumed to have been reckoned as part of Mercia and thus to have fallen into Edgar's sphere, and there is also reason to think that Edgar also controlled Essex: in 958 he made a grant of land at *Hamme* (East and West Ham) in that shire (S 676). **16** is a spurious diploma in Edgar's name, concerning an Essex estate; its date of 867 was derived from the model, but the forger's inclusion of a subscription of Archbishop Oda provides ostensible dates of 957 × 958 (i.e. within Edgar's reign as king of Mercia). Bishop Brihthelm seems to stop attesting after the division of the kingdom: he may have died in 957 or there may have been other complications (see below, pp. 118–19). At some point between 957 and 959 Edgar appointed as bishop of London the former abbot of Glastonbury, Dunstan, one of the architects of the Benedictine reform movement which was to dominate ecclesiastical affairs in England during the second half of the tenth century.[106] During his tenure of London, Dunstan was responsible for the revival and restoration of the monastery at Westminster.[107] A Westminster

---

[105] Brooke and Keir, *London*, pp. 197–9; Taylor 1995.

[106] For Dunstan's appointment, see Whitelock 1973, p. 233; Brooks 1992a, p. 20; and below, p. 119.

[107] See S 1293; William of Malmesbury, *GP*, p. 178; Whitelock 1975, p. 22; Brooks 1992a, p. 22.

charter, of uncertain authenticity but extant as in a single-sheet version of the late tenth century, refers to a grant by Edgar to the monastery of a five-hide estate between the Tyburn and the Fleet (S 670); this would have represented much of the territory of the defunct port of *Lundenwic*, and would have brought Westminster holdings close to the walls of London.[108] There are signs that Dunstan's patronage of Westminster continued after his appointment as arch-bishop of Canterbury in 958: he granted to the community an estate at Sunbury in Middlesex which he had bought from King Edgar for the sum of 200 man-cuses of gold (S 1447); and Westminster sources mention other estates which he is said to have procured for the community (S 1293, 1295, 1451; and see S 753). The monastery may not have been particularly prominent in the later tenth and early eleventh centuries, to judge by the rare attestations of its abbots during this period, but the existence of a reformed Benedictine house on the outskirts of the city is likely to have some impact on St Paul's and the bishopric.

From the long pontificate of Ælfstan, Dunstan's successor at London, comes an episode which briefly illuminates the condition of the cathedral community. At some stage between 971 and 984 there was an exchange of estates between St Paul's and the monastery at Ely, whereby the London clerics ceded land at Milton (Cambridgeshire) for a more convenient property at Holland on the Essex coast. In its account of this transaction, the *Liber Eliensis* describes the circumstances in which St Paul's acquired Milton. A certain Abbot Thurketel had been expelled from his monastery at *Bedeford* and had petitioned Bishop Ælfstan and his clergy that he might become a member of the community at St Paul's (*ut . . . posset habere communionem et partem in monasterio*), with which he had a prior connection: 'where previously he had purchased himself a place among the priests (*in presbiteratu*)'.[109] But the bishop and all the commu-nity rejected him. At length, depending on the advice and influence of his friends, he made over to St Paul's (*hereditauit*) his estate at Milton, so that he could join the *contubernium* (probably meaning 'confraternity': i.e. he would not have been a full member of the St Paul's community, but would have had a connection with it).[110] This account is full of interesting detail. It is evident that St Paul's was a secular community, a community of priests (unlike, for instance, Winchester Cathedral, which was reformed as a monastic house in 963). The individual priests formed a corporate body, which acted with the bishop in choosing whether to accept new members (the canons were later to claim

[108] M. Gelling, 'The Boundaries of the Westminster Charters', *TLMAS* n.s. xi (1954), pp. 101–4; Vince, *Saxon London*, p. 27 (map). The parish of St Margaret's, Westminster, extended into the *Lundenwic* site and may have succeeded to the lands of an earlier church there (Martin 1991, p. 25).
[109] Blake, *Liber Eliensis*, p. 105; see below, pp. 96–7.
[110] For the translation of *contubernium*, see Gibbs, p. xxxix.

the right to reject applicants without reference to the bishop: see **28**, and p. 44). Membership of the community would have been sufficiently advantageous for it to have been worth Thurketel's while to purchase a place there: the *communio* and *pars* which he hoped to enjoy would have involved sharing in the communal property of the church. In the wider context of the late Anglo-Saxon Church, there is interest in the fact that Thurketel would originally appear to have left St Paul's to become abbot of a monastery at *Bedeford*. The history of this house is obscure, and it was no longer in existence in 1066: perhaps it was a refoundation of Edgar's reign which was suppressed in the period of anti-monastic reaction after Edgar's death in 975 (which may provide a context for its abbot's expulsion).[111] Thurketel can also be linked to another monastery, this time more successful: this is good reason to identify him with the kinsman of Oscytel (archbishop of York, 956–71), who re-established monastic life at Crowland, possibly in Edgar's reign but more probably later.[112]

g. *London c. 950–1016*

Ælfstan's pontificate began with a disaster: in 962 'the great and fatal fire occurred in London and St Paul's minster was burnt and rebuilt in the same year' (*ASC*). There was another great fire in the city twenty years later (ASC *s.a.* 982).[113] These unfortunate events almost certainly had some connection with the increasing population density within the walls. Although the archaeological evidence is not entirely conclusive, it may point an intensification of occupation beginning in the last third of the tenth century and continuing into the early eleventh, by which time most of the major street frontages were occupied.[114] Several wills from *c.* 990 onwards refer to the bequest of urban holdings (*hagas* or *haws*) in the city: testators include a woman with extensive holdings in Hertfordshire, Bedfordshire and Buckinghamshire (S 1497), an archbishop of

[111] An obvious identification is with the county town of Bedfordshire, which was *Bedeford* in GDB, although earlier references point to an original *Bedanford* (*PN Beds.*, p. 11) However, a charter of 798 (S 1258), which is preserved as a transcript of a lost single sheet, refers to a minster at *Bedeford*, which should etymologically speaking be a separate place from *Bedanford*.

[112] D. Whitelock, 'The Conversion of the Eastern Danelaw', *Saga-Book of the Viking Society* xii (1941), pp. 159–76 at 174–5; *HRH*, pp. 30, 41.

[113] The annal for 982 mentions a Viking attack on Dorset before the notice of the London fire, and it has been suggested that the conflagration may possibly have been the result of a raid on the city (Brooke and Keir, *London*, p. 21). But it is far more probable that these were unrelated events; the annalist is unlikely to have given specific details about a minor assault on the Dorset coast (such as the number of ships involved), while dealing so briefly with what would have been a far more shocking attack on a major, well-defended city.

[114] Vince 1991, pp. 420–1, 424, 427; *idem, Saxon London*, pp. 26–30; Keene 2000, pp. 191–3.

Canterbury (S 1488), a major East Anglian landowner[115] and a bishop of
Elmham (S 1489); and the beneficiaries include the abbeys of St Albans, Ely
and (probably) Westminster.[116] Some of the haws were explicitly linked with
rural manors: just before the Conquest Westminster Abbey acquired Staines
(Middlesex), which included a London dependency at *Stæninghaga* (S 1142);
and the name of the parish of Bassishaw derives from *Basinghaga*, pointing to a
link with Basing in Hampshire.[117] The owners of these intramural properties in
some circumstances acquired rights of private jurisdiction over the inhabitants;
this was the origin of the complex and chaotic pattern of private sokes which
was such an important feature of Norman London.[118] The period from *c*. 950
onwards may also have seen important developments in the administrative institutions of the City. The London *Cnihtengild* was probably founded in the reign
of King Edgar (957–75) and invested with responsibility for the defence of the
stretch of the eastern wall around Aldgate; the original *cnihtas* may have been
thegns involved with the city administration (see **32**). By analogy it has been
suggested that the city wards, which had military, judicial and administrative
functions (including in same cases the defence of city gates), may have been
formed at around the same date.[119] There is reason to think that wards and
parishes grew up together, and the evidence seems to indicate that many of the
medieval churches of the City were founded in the late Saxon period.[120]
Overseas trade would also appear to have picked up in the later tenth century.
An exceptionally useful document which appears to date from the reign of King
Æthelred refers to the tolls to be paid at Billingsgate, by the bridge; it gives
details of the duty to be paid by overseas merchants, including men from
Flanders, Normandy, France and Germany.[121] Excavations at New Fresh Wharf

---

[115] Blake, *Liber Eliensis*, pp. 131–2.

[116] The Latin synonym for *haga* was *curtis*: this would have described a dwelling-house with depen-
dencies, forming a single complex (see Bullough 1974, pp. 393–5).

[117] Ekwall, *London Street Names*, p. 94; Dyson and Schofield 1984, pp. 306–7; Schofield, *Building
of London*, pp. 29, 31.

[118] Stenton, *Preparatory to ASE*, pp. 33–5; Brooke and Keir, *London*, pp. 150–7; Martin 1991,
p. 27.

[119] Brooke and Keir, *London*, pp. 162–70 (at 168); Schofield, *Building of London*, pp. 30–1. The
wards were certainly in existence in c. 1130 (see Davis 1925), but there is no firm evidence as to
when they were actually established. Haslam 1988 argues for the creation of at least three of the
wards as early as Alfred's reign.

[120] Vince 1991, p. 429; Brooke and Keir, *London*, chapter 6; Schofield, *Building of London*,
pp. 31–2; Keene 2000, p. 192.

[121] The Customs of London (IV Æthelred): Liebermann, *Gesetze*, i. 232–6; Robertson, *Laws*,
pp. 70–9 (with translation); Schofield, *Building of London*, pp. 31–2 (partial translation). See the
useful map in Vince 1991, p. 432. It has also been suggested that the document may be the result of
an inquest into London tolls in Cnut's reign (Lawson, *Cnut*, pp. 204–6). For an important evaluation
of London's trading links *c*. 1000, see Nightingale, *Mercantile Community*, chap 1.

near Billingsgate have demonstrated major activity on the Thames waterfront at this period, involving the construction of a clay bank strengthened with timber, apparently to raise the waterfront and perhaps to facilitate the unloading of boats; this stretched along the width of at least five properties and may indicate the existence of separate private wharves by the early eleventh century.[122] Eleventh-century documents refer to several such riverside tenements with their own wharves: Chertsey Abbey inherited from a royal priest a *curtis* to which King Æthelred attached a wharf at 'Fish-hithe', which was adjacent to the Queenhithe properties granted to Canterbury and Worcester in 898/9 (S 940);[123] a similar bequest by the city reeve brought an unidentified property and wharf to Westminster Abbey (S 1119); while Edward the Confessor is said to have granted to the Flemish house of St Peter's in Ghent land at *Wermanecher*, with its own landing-place (S 1002).[124]

This growth in London's population and economic importance took place against an increasingly difficult political background. Scandinavian raids on the shores of southern England recommenced in the 980s and intensified in the following decade, eventually culminating in a full-scale Danish invasion and the succession of Cnut as king of all England in 1016.[125] The Anglo-Saxon Chronicle contains a very full account of these years, apparently written retrospectively during the period 1016 X 1023, which has been judged to show a London perspective of the conflict and to have been composed by someone associated with the city, presumably a cleric: in which case the author could well have been a member of the St Paul's community.[126] The first mention of London in this part of the Chronicle narrative comes under the year 992, where there is a reference to a royal decree that all functional warships were to assemble at London: Bishop Ælfstan (probably of London, though there was a contemporary

---

[122] Dyson and Schofield 1984, pp. 302–3; Vince, *Saxon London*, pp. 33–5; Vince 1991, p. 434; Schofield, *Building of London*, pp. 25–7, 29.

[123] Kelly, *Chertsey*, no. 10. Although the Chertsey archive is largely bogus, there is a good chance that S 940 represents a genuine instrument of King Æthelred, with a brief interpolation in which the royal confirmation of the freedom of the *curtis* is extended to cover all the abbey's property. 'Fish-hithe' was located on the boundary between the parishes of St Mary Somerset and St Peter the Less, on the site of the later Trig Lane; the Chertsey holding would appear to have been at 'Broken Wharf' (*ASNL III*, p. 19).

[124] For the location of *Wermanecher*, see Ekwall, *London Street Names*, p. 38 (commenting on an identification made by Page, *London*, p. 132). The diploma is a forgery, but the draftsman does seem to have drawn on a contemporary document for some details.

[125] For an overview of events and discussion of the background, see S. Keynes, 'The Vikings in England c. 790–1016', in *The Oxford Illustrated History of the Vikings*, ed. P. Sawyer (Oxford and New York, 1997), pp. 48–82 at 73–82.

[126] See S. Keynes, 'The Declining Reputation of King Æthelred the Unready', in *Ethelred the Unready*, ed. D. Hill, British Archaeological Reports (Brit. series) lix (Oxford, 1978), pp. 227–53.

namesake at Rochester) was named as one of the leaders of the fleet, which made an unsuccessful attempt to defeat the Danish army in a naval battle. The fleet was an important element of the Anglo-Saxon defence system, and the king was concerned to systematise provisions for building and manning ships, with a royal decree in 1008 that a warship should be provided from every 310 (possibly for 300) hides. This built on earlier arrangements, illustrated by a document of *c.* 1000 which details the responsibility of the estates of St Paul's and the bishopric to provide a certain number of sailors, probably the complement of a single war-ship (see **25**). The first major assault on London came in 994 when Olaf Tryggvason of Norway and the Danish king Swein Forkbeard arrived before the city with ninety-four ships on 8 September and tried unsuccessfully to set it on fire, before giving up and going on to ravage other provinces of south-east England, including Essex (*ASC*). There is no specific reference to further attacks on London until 1009–10, although the rest of the country suffered badly during the intervening period: it is possible that the city defences alone were strong enough to act as a deterrent, but it is probably also significant that London was increasingly the pivot of the English military strategy, a focus for both naval and land-based forces. The English fleet was again mustered in London in 1009. In the winter of that year a Danish army led by Thorkell the Tall based itself in Kent and made frequent raids across the Thames estuary into Essex: it is said to have attacked London on numerous occasions, but never succeeded in taking the city. One element of the city's defences would have been the fortified bridge barring passage along the Thames, for the Danish army later had to leave its ships in Kent and force a land passage through the Chilterns to capture Oxford: it then descended along the Thames valley towards London but, deterred by news that there was an English army collected there, it crossed the river at Staines and apparently made its way back to Kent.

On 12 April 1012 Thorkell's Danish army, then quartered in Greenwich, murdered Archbishop Ælfheah, whom they had captured during an assault on Canterbury in the previous year. The next day (i.e. Easter Sunday), under unknown circumstances, the archbishop's body was taken to London where it was received by Bishops Eadnoth of Dorchester and Ælfhun of London and by the citizens, and reverently buried in St Paul's cathedral.[127] It remained there, the centre of an incipient cult, until its translation to Canterbury in 1023 (see further below, pp. 39–40). At some stage after Ælfheah's murder, Thorkell (reputedly horrified by the event) took forty-five ships and changed

---

[127] A *Passio* of Ælfheah, composed in the late eleventh century at Canterbury, suggests that the citizens of London arranged a truce and redeemed the body with a great sum (see extract edited and translated in Rumble, *Cnut*, pp. 283–4).

sides, entering the service of King Æthelred. It may have been this defection which prompted the Danish king Swein to launch a new and devastating invasion in 1013. His army ravaged the kingdom, subduing Oxford and Winchester, then turned eastwards towards London, which it besieged. The citizens resisted stoutly and refused to surrender because King Æthelred was inside the city, along with Thorkell, and his capture would have been calamitous. After a stand-off, Swein departed and gained the submission of the South-West, subsequent to which he was regarded as king of England: under these circumstances the citizens of London were forced to surrender and give hostages. Æthelred spent some time with the fleet in the Thames, before fleeing to Normandy. He had been preceded by his wife Emma and by his youngest sons Edward and Alfred: the æthelings travelled under the guardianship of Bishop Ælfhun of London, who may have been their tutor.[128]

The eventual full Danish triumph was briefly postponed when Swein died in 1014: while the Danish army recognised his son Cnut, the English sent once more for King Æthelred and the wars began again. During much of this period Thorkell's Danish fleet remained based in Greenwich, requiring huge sums for its support (ASC *s.a.* 1013, 1014). Scandinavian sources indicate that on his return Æthelred was accompanied by Olaf Haraldsson of Norway.[129] A late and probably fictional saga narrative describes in some detail an assault made by the combined forces of the two kings upon Danish-held London, which was initially impeded by the strongly-defended bridge and the associated fortifications at Southwark; Olaf is said to have destroyed the bridge by attaching ropes from his ships to the support posts and then rowing away as hard as possible.[130] If there is any truth in this story, the bridge was quickly repaired, for it played an important part in the complex events of 1016. By that stage Æthelred had based himself in London, while his son Eadmund Ironside attempted to raise forces elsewhere, without a great deal of success: the Chronicle account makes it clear that 'the citizens of London' represented a major fighting force, for at one stage the English army refused to muster unless Æthelred came with the London militia to offer assistance. Events came to a head in the spring. Eadmund joined his father in London, and Cnut approached the city with his whole fleet. At this

---

[128] Emma, and perhaps also the two æthelings, appear to have returned to England at some point; one source puts Emma in London during the siege of 1016 (see Keynes 1991, pp. 175–85). There is no further reference to Bishop Ælfhun, whose successor was consecrated in February 1014 (see pp. 120–1).

[129] Keynes, *Diplomas*, p. 227.

[130] For text, translation and discussion see J.R. Hagland, 'Saxon-Norman London Bridge and Southwark—the Saga Evidence Reconsidered', in Watson *et al., London Bridge*, pp. 232–3 (some sections are translated in Schofield, *Building of London*, p. 33).

juncture King Æthelred died and was buried in St Paul's, and the councillors in London and all the citizens chose Eadmund as king. But a separate assembly that met at Southampton a few days after Æthelred's death declared for Cnut.[131] The latter now besieged London (Eadmund having departed): his fleet approached Greenwich in the second week in May, then made for London, bypassing the bridge by digging a great ditch in the Southwark area and dragging the ships round to the west side. The Chronicle account indicates that Cnut dug an earthwork completely round the city walls and created a blockade; London was briefly relieved by Eadmund, then the Danish blockade was resumed and later lifted. Events elsewhere decided the issue: after the battle of *Assandun* Cnut and Eadmund came to terms and divided the kingdom between them, with Cnut taking Mercia and London. The citizens came to terms with their new Danish ruler and bought peace for themselves; and the Danish army brought their ships to London and took up winter quarters there. The new order proved short-lived; Eadmund died on 30 November and Cnut succeeded to the whole kingdom.[132]

The London diocese saw four bishops during Æthelred's long and eventful reign. Bishop Ælfstan died in 995 or 996. His successor was Wulfstan 'the Homilist', the celebrated prose-writer, who was promoted to the archbishopric of York in 1002. There survive several letters written by and to Wulfstan during his stint at London, of primarily literary interest, except that in one instance he is addressed as metropolitan.[133] A unique record of the naval levy on the St Paul's estates (25) may have been drafted in Wulfstan's pontificate. The bishop was the beneficiary of a bequest of an estate at Barling in Essex which was later in the possession of St Paul's (S 1522); also in his time the community received land at Heybridge in Essex through the will of Ælfflæd, who in addition fulfilled her

[131] *John of Worcester*, p. 484. This is the first recorded instance of Londoners playing a part in deciding the succession (see M. McKisack, 'London and the Succession to the Crown during the Middle Ages', *Studies in Medieval History presented to F.M. Powicke*, ed. R.W. Hunt, W.A. Pantin and R.W. Southern (Oxford, 1948), pp. 76–89 at 76–9; Brooke and Keir, *London*, p. 23).

[132] According to *John of Worcester* (p. 492), Eadmund died in London but was buried at Glastonbury. Cnut is said to have been consecrated king by Archbishop Lyfing in London (Lawson, *Cnut*, p. 82; Diceto, *Abbreviationes*, i. 169).

[133] *The Homilies of Wulfstan*, ed. D. Bethurum (Oxford, 1957), pp. 376–7 (. . . *metropolitano Lundoniae ecclesiae pontificum dignissimo*. . .). See discussion by Whitelock (1975, pp. 25–6), who concludes that 'metropolitan' here probably means 'belonging to a metropolis', rather than having a connection with metropolitan status in the ecclesiastical sense. It may have been in Wulfstan's time that a copy was made, perhaps by a St Paul's scribe, of the manuscript of the Old English translation of Gregory's Pastoral Care, originally sent by King Alfred to Bishop Heahstan: the copy is still extant (BL Cotton Otho B. ii; see Ker, *Catalogue*, no. 175). For a tentative assignment of this manuscript to the London scriptorium, see D.M. Horgan, 'The Relationship between the OE MSS of King Alfred's Translation of Gregory's *Pastoral Care*', *Anglia* xci (1973), pp. 153–69 at 165.

sister's bequest of land at Hadham in Hertfordshire for the use of the bishopric (S 1486; *cf.* **17** and S 1494). The next bishop of London, Ælfhun, may previously have been abbot of a Dorset house. There are signs that he was close to King Æthelred, for the last reference to him is in the annal for 1013, which mentions that he took the Æthelings Edward and Alfred to Normandy, apparently acting as their tutor or guardian. His successor Ælfwig is also likely to have had close ties with the West Saxon royal house: King Æthelred was buried in the cathedral during his time, and Ælfwig was probably a member of the London assembly which hailed Eadmund Ironside as king. The archive preserves the texts of a diploma and a writ in the name of Æthelred, confirming the lands and privileges of St Paul's (**21, 24**): both appear to be late forgeries.

h. *The Anglo-Danish Kingdom*

Bishop Ælfwig's loyalty to Æthelred and Eadmund Ironside may have prejudiced the standing of the London bishopric during Cnut's reign. The Danish king made at least two decisions which had a negative impact on the church of London: at some stage he confiscated the important episcopal estate at Southminster;[134] and in 1023 he gave permission for the miracle-working relics of St Ælfheah to be removed from St Paul's and translated to Canterbury. A post-Conquest narrative from Canterbury, said to be based on an eye-witness account, describes the event as a military operation under Cnut's direction.[135] In the expectation that the citizens would oppose the removal of the relics, the king's housecarls staged diversions at some of the gates to distract attention, while also securing the bridge and the river-banks. Meanwhile two Christ Church monks broke open the tomb at St Paul's, tearing up an iron candelabrum that stood there (presumably to use as a tool), achieving a breach in the masonry exterior and then shifting the stone cover of the interior tomb to expose the saint's remains lying on a convenient plank. As a cover for the relics they pulled off the altar cloth from the main altar of St Paul's (leaving half a pound of gold to pay for it)—the narrative does not mention the reaction of the St Paul's priests. The relics were taken down a narrow street leading to the Thames and there loaded onto a royal longship (probably waiting at the Canterbury wharf at Queenhithe); the ship crossed over to Southwark, from where the saint's body

[134] LDB 10r; *DB Essex* 3: 9. The estate was not recovered until after 1066 (see pp. 48, 104; and **6, 18**). It is possible that the confiscation was connected with non-payment of geld (for the background, see Lawson 1984).

[135] Osbern, *Translatio S. Ælfegi*, edited and translated by A.R. Rumble and R. Morris in Rumble, *Cnut*, pp. 294–315, with discussion pp. 283–93. See also Brooks, *Church of Canterbury*, pp. 291–2; Lawson, *Cnut*, pp. 141–2, 182.

was taken in a solemn procession to Canterbury. One relic of Ælfheah may have been left behind: a 1245 inventory of St Paul's treasures mentions a chasuble 'said to be that of St Ælfheah'.[136] The episode of the translation would appear to have been a huge insult to St Paul's, and it seems unlikely that it would have taken place if the London community had been strong and backed by royal favour.[137] Relations may have improved in the course of the reign, for Cnut would appear to have confirmed the privileges of St Paul's between 1033 and 1035 (27), and may also at some stage have issued a writ confirming Bishop Ælfwig's position.[138] In 1035 Ælfwig was succeeded by Ælfweard, who was abbot of Ramsey and reputedly Cnut's kinsman (see p. 121).

London was immensely important to Cnut, as it had been to Æthelred and Eadmund. Not only was it a strategic hub of communications; it was also the principal mint and port of the kingdom, the key to the markets of Normandy and Flanders.[139] The city's economic significance is illustrated by one of Cnut's first acts as king, the levying of a great tribute to pay off the Danish armies. a total of some £82,500, of which the citizens of London alone paid £10,500 (ASC s.a. 1018). It is possible that the Londoners' share represents punitive taxation, linked with their previous support for Æthelred and Eadmund; and it may be that the translation of Ælfheah's relics was intended to remove a possible focus of rebellion from the city.[140] The loss of mercantile capital may have depressed the London markets for a time, and this would probably have had an effect on the finances of St Paul's; the cathedral itself may have been required to make a huge contribution to the tax.[141] The evidence seems to indicate that there was little Danish settlement in London before 1016, and a minimal trading presence: it has been noticed that only six out of one hundred London moneyers minting for Æthelred had Scandinavian names; and that no Danish merchants are mentioned

---

[136] Simpson 1887, p. 482: 'Casula quae dicitur Sancti Aelphegi est de sameto croceo vividenti plana, ornata aurifrigio bono interhumerali lato, breudato cum lapidibus vitreis, aurifrigiata posteriori subhumerali texto leonibus et avibus tassellis anteriori parvo de filo auri tracto cum perlis'. For the elaborate and costly vestments of Anglo-Saxon England, see Dodwell, AS Art, pp. 170–87.

[137] Brooke and Keir, London, p. 24. It is of course possible that this dramatic account is a fiction, and that the more decorous translation described in ASC D is to be preferred: the theft of relics is a common theme in hagiographical literature (see Rumble, Cnut, pp. 285–9). For the suggestion that Cnut's role in the episode may have been magnified by the author, see P.A. Hayward, 'Translation-Narratives in Post-Conquest Hagiography and English Resistence to the Norman Conquest', Anglo-Norman Studies XXI (Woodbridge, 1999), pp. 67–93 at 70–3.

[138] See Gibbs, no. 18 (Bates, RRAN: Acta of William I, no. 191); and below, p. 121.

[139] Brooke and Keir, London, p. 23.

[140] Lawson, Cnut, pp. 140–2, 181–2; D. Hill, 'An Urban Policy for Cnut?', in Rumble, Cnut, pp. 101–5 at 103–4.

[141] Nightingale, Mercantile Community, pp. 17–22. St Paul's may have lost estates through failure to pay the geld (for the background, see Lawson 1984).

in the earliest version of the 'Customs of London', thought to belong to Æthelred's reign.[142] A case has been made that Cnut's victory resulted in what amounted to a military occupation of London, with a Danish force stationed in the city controlling the walls, and other possible encampments in Southwark and on the road to Westminster.[143] Certainly by the end of Cnut's reign it would appear that London was the chief base for the king's naval mercenaries, the *lithsmen*, a situation that continued until they were disbanded in 1051 (*ASC*).[144] Increasing Danish settlement in the city during the eleventh century is marked by the scatter of churches with Scandinavian dedications, some of them certainly later than Cnut's reign.[145] There was a Danish cemetery in London in 1040, where the body of Harold Harefoot was eventually buried.[146] A stone slab with an Old Norse inscription in Scandinavian runes and Scandinavian-style carving found in St Paul's Churchyard was probably a memorial stone erected for a Danish warrior, possibly set up during the reign of Cnut or his sons.[147] A twelfth-century version of the 'Customs of London' has an addition giving Danish merchants special privileges in the city, permitting them to stay there for a year and to visit markets throughout the kingdom: this seems to reflect a novel development that perhaps began under Cnut.[148] It has been argued that the London court of husting, which regulated commercial business and supervised standards of weight and measures, originated in Cnut's time; the word 'husting' is thought to be of Scandinavian origin.[149] There are also suggestions that Cnut may have been concerned to place Danes in control of the administration of the city and its markets. A follower of Cnut called Osgod Clapa may have had some authority in London, from at least in the final years of Cnut's reign until he was sent into exile in 1046: he attests Cnut's writ for St Paul's after the earls (**27**), and is known to have had a house in Lambeth.[150] There is rather more certainty about the case of Ansgar (or Esgar) the Staller, addressed in an early Westminster

[142] Sawyer 1986, p. 186; Nightingale 1987, pp. 559–60; for the 'Customs of London', see above, p. 34 n. 121.

[143] Nightingale 1987. pp. 567–8. This suggestion is partly based on the spread of churches with Scandinavian dedications; it has been judged 'unprovable but plausible' (Lawson, *Cnut*, p. 182).

[144] Lawson, *Cnut*, p. 178.

[145] Brooke and Keir, *London*, p. 138–42; Sawyer 1986, pp. 191–2.

[146] *John of Worcester*, p. 530.

[147] Brooke and Keir, *London*, plate 30.

[148] Sawyer 1986, pp. 186–7; Lawson, *Cnut*, p. 206.

[149] Nightingale 1987; see Brooke and Keir, *London*, pp. 249–51; Stenton, *Preparatory to ASE*, p. 30. The husting met in the area of the former Roman amphitheatre (see above, p. 9). An eleventh-century date for the husting requires rejection of a potentially tenth-century reference (see S 1809; KCD 793). It has also been suggested that the word husting could be of English origin (Sawyer 1986, p. 192).

[150] Nightingale 1987, pp. 565–6; Brooke and Keir, *London*, p. 193.

writ of Edward the Confessor together with Bishop Ælfweard and all the king's 'burh-thegns' in London (S 1119); in 1066 Ansgar was still in charge in the city, directing preparations for a siege after the battle of Hastings.[151] Other scholars would dispute the theory that Cnut's reign was a particularly crucial period for Danish settlement in and control over London, arguing instead for a longer and more gradual development.[152]

When Cnut died in 1035 he left two potential successors, his sons Harold Harefoot and Harthacnut. The former was chosen as king in England by the powerful Earl Leofric, together with all the thegns north of the Thames and the *scipmen* in London (*ASC*), although Harthacnut was recognised in Denmark. Harold died in London in 1040 and was buried in the monastery at Westminster;[153] Harthacnut succeeded to the English throne, but he himself died two years later, during a wedding-feast at Osgod Clapa's house in Lambeth (ASC *s.a.* 1040, 1042). King Æthelred's son Edward was then chosen king in London. Shortly after his accession he confirmed and extended the privileges of the English *Cnihtengild* over the strategically important ward of Portsoken (**32**), perhaps in a deliberate attempt to promote the power of an English institution in a city which had been dominated by Danes in the previous decades.[154] On the death in 1044 of Bishop Ælfweard, who may have been Anglo-Danish and an appointee of Cnut, the king chose as his successor a Norman, Robert Champart, abbot of Jumièges: his own pro-Norman sympathies had been formed during his exile in the duchy.[155] For the remainder of Edward's reign the London bishopric was held by Normans, apart from a brief period in 1051 when Robert was promoted to Canterbury: in his place the king selected Spearhafoc, abbot of Abingdon, but Robert refused to consecrate him and the bishopric passed instead to William, another Norman and a royal clerk, still in office at the time of the battle of Hastings (for more detail on these bishops, see below, p. 122).

i. *St Paul's on the eve of the Norman Conquest*

The ecclesiastical landscape of London changed considerably during the century before 1066, and with particular speed during the reign of the Confessor.

---

[151] *The 'Carmen de Hastingae Proelio' of Guy, Bishop of Amiens*, ed. C. Morton and H. Muntz (Oxford, 1972), pp. 44 and liii n.3; Harmer, *Writs*, pp. 560–1; Brooke and Keir, *London*, pp. 192–3, 371.

[152] As Lawson, *Cnut*, p. 206.

[153] His body was exhumed on Harthacnut's orders and maltreated, before being buried in the Danish cemetery in London (*John of Worcester*, p. 530).

[154] Nightingale 1987, p. 577.

[155] See Keynes 1991.

Edward lavished patronage on Westminster Abbey, where he intended to be buried, building a huge Romanesque church there which was consecrated on Christmas Day 1065 and is thought to have been modelled on the abbey-church of Jumièges; Bishop Robert may had a hand in its planning before he went into exile in 1052.[156] Edward also chose Westminster as the site of a new royal palace, possibly abandoning an existing royal residence in London (see above, pp. 8–9), and the abbey-church became the ceremonial place of coronation of the kings of England, beginning with Harold and William I. The Confessor's patronage also lay behind a new foundation within the walls, the royal chapel of St Martin-le-Grand, a collegiate church which had and retained close links with the royal court, and which may have inherited some of the liberties of the intra-mural palace.[157] Another important new foundation was Waltham Holy Cross, some twelve miles north of the city, established by Earl Harold as a secular min-ster and dedicated in 1060.[158] In addition to the conventual churches at St Paul's and St Martin, there were already a huge number of small parish churches in London, many of them in origin proprietary churches founded and endowed by individual laymen and clerics.[159] One of these was All Hallows Gracechurch (named from its roof of *græs* or thatch), which was given by its founder Brihtmær to Christ Church, Canterbury, probably between 1052 and 1066 (S 1234; Brooks and Kelly, *Christ Church*, no. 183). This was one of nine churches mentioned in a list of Canterbury properties in London drawn up 1098 × 1108, of which six were given to the Christ Church monks by priests or cler-ics and three by laymen in the course of the eleventh century; these churches and their parishes formed the core of the thirteen parishes that made up Canterbury's London Deanery of the Arches.[160] It has been remarked that the proliferation of private urban churches and parishes in London and elsewhere may reflect the regulatory failure of episcopal authority.[161]

[156] Brooke and Keir, *London*, pp. 295–9; Fernie, *Architecture of Norman England*, pp. 96–8.

[157] Davis 1972, especially p. 24; Taylor 2002; Brooke and Keir, *London*, pp. 310–12, 342. The founder was Ingelric, a clerk in royal service TRW and possibly TRE (see Keynes 1988, pp. 218–20); there is no support for the suggestion that he was a canon of St Paul's, the same man as the Engelric who held land from the bishop in Stepney in 1086 (Taylor 2002, p. 231).

[158] S 1036; Blair 1985, p. 123.

[159] Brooke and Keir, *London*, pp.122–36. By the second half of the twelfth century there are said to have been thirteen greater conventual churches and 126 lesser parish churches in London and its suburbs; within the city the three principal churches were St Paul's, St Martin-le-Grand and Holy Trinity (see William FitzStephen's description of London from *c.* 1170 × 1183: Douglas and Greenaway, *EHD II*, no. 281 (pp. 1024–5)).

[160] The document is edited and discussed in Kissan 1940*a*; see also Kissan 1940*b*. For a translation, see Douglas and Greenaway, *EHD II*, no. 280 (pp. 1022–4).

[161] Brooke 1970, pp. 76–7; Brooke and Keir, *London*, p. 131; Campbell, *Essays*, pp. 146–7.

On the eve of the Conquest St Paul's was a community of canons, but very little detail is known about the organisation and daily life of the chapter. The Exchequer Domesday treats the canons as tenants-in-chief of their lands in Essex and Hertfordshire, indicating that they already had a clear corporate identity separate from the bishop (see discussion below, pp. 103–4). The same impression is given by the writs of Cnut and the Confessor, which may have a genuine basis (27, 28); if the latter is wholly authentic, then the canons may have had a veto on new recruits. There is no direct information about the cathedral hierarchy before the Conquest, although we can be fairly certain that no dean was appointed until after 1066.[162] In the later eleventh and early twelfth centuries, the archdeacon of London wielded an unusual degree of authority in the chapter; this may go back to a pre-Conquest arrangement.[163] The canons are likely to have followed a communal rule of some kind, although its nature remains elusive. The *Constitutions* compiled by Dean Ralph Baldock *c.* 1300 incorporate seven chapters from a set of regulations for canonical living, the *Institutio canonicorum*, issued at the council of Aachen in 816 and ultimately based on the *Rule* of Chrodegang of Metz.[164] This Carolingian work seems to have been little known in Anglo-Saxon England, but an excerpt was made by Wulfstan the Homilist (bishop of London, 996–1002), conceivably from a copy in the St Paul's library that had arrived in the time of Bishops Theodred or Dunstan.[165] The material from the *Institutio* included in the later *Constitutions* of the London chapter has been understood to represent a self-contained pre-Conquest 'Rule of St Paul's'.[166] But there may be reason for scepticism: it has been noticed that the seven chapters are primarily hortatory, giving a general guide to the ideal canonical life, but not including any detailed rules about the daily timetable or the enforcement of discipline.[167]

---

[162] Brooke 1956, especially pp. 236–7. A catalogue of deans in Hutton's notes from the lost *Liber G* (see below, p. 55) includes six names bracketed together as *ante Conquestum*; Brooke suggests that these were perhaps the witnesses of an Old English charter of the late eleventh or early twelfth century, which was misunderstood by the medieval commentator.

[163] Edwards, *Secular Cathedrals*, pp. 250, 253–5.

[164] Simpson, *Registrum Statutorum*, pp. 38–43, with comment pp. lvii–viii (see also GL 25504, 69–73r).

[165] Whitelock 1975, pp 28–30.

[166] Brooke 1957, pp. 11–15, 363; Brooke and Keir, *London*, pp. 339–40; Whitelock 1975, pp. 27–30.

[167] J. Barrow, 'English Cathedral Communities and Reform in the Late Tenth and the Eleventh Centuries', *Anglo-Norman Durham*, ed. D. Rollason, M. Harvey and M. Prestwich (Woodbridge, 1994), pp. 25–39 at 31–2. She argues here that there was minimal interest in monastic and canonical rules in English cathedrals before the mid eleventh century, with the exception of Winchester. A version of the enlarged rule of Chrodegang was in use at Exeter from *c.* 1050; there were also pre-Conquest canons at Wells, York and Hereford, but no early rule survives from these centres (see Brooke 1957, p. 12; J. Barrow, 'Cathedrals, Provosts and Prebends: a Comparison of Twelfth-Century German and English Practice', *Journal of Ecclesiastical History* xxxvii (1986), pp. 536–64 at 552–5).

In more general terms, we can assume that the St Paul's community in the late Anglo-Saxon period had a common refectory and dormitory. Helpful here is a provision in a lawcode of King Æthelred, issued at the Council of Enham in 1008: 'And canons, where there is property, such that they can have a refectory and a dormitory, are to hold their minster with right obedience and with chastity, as their rule directs: otherwise it is right that who will not do so shall forfeit the property'. The Latin version of this lawcode, which was partly drawn up by Wulfstan the Homilist, includes more detail on eating and sleeping communally.[168] The regulation about chastity may have been ignored in laxer times; the St Paul's community c. 1090 included a number of married men, and there is a fairly good chance that a similar situation prevailed before the Conquest.[169] Although the canons were supposed to live communally, they probably owned their own houses or cells, as had been foreseen in the rule which Archbishop Wulfred imposed on Christ Church in the early ninth century (see above, pp. 17–18); there is evidence for this at Waltham and Chester.[170] The members of the community would have been entitled to a share in the common revenues of the chapter, derived from their estates and any tolls and tribute that had been assigned to the church. It is possible that the St Paul's community was already some way along in the transition to a Norman prebendal system, although this was not properly established until the time of Bishop Maurice (see below). A potential insight into pre-Conquest arrangements in London is provided by a reference to the *antiqua institutio* in a privilege of Pope Alexander III (1159–81).[171] This states that all the canons were given a weekly dole of bread and beer and a money payment of ten pence; it also refers to *solandae* ('shoelands'), which would seem to have been small demesne estates carved out of the common lands on a temporary basis and assigned to canons to provide revenue, apparently representing an earlier stage in the development of a system of permanent prebends.[172] There is a possibility that this *antiqua institutio* covered

---

[168] V Æthelred §7 (VI Æthelred § 4); Whitelock, *EHD*, p. 443; *Councils & Synods*, pp. 348–9, 365.

[169] For the post-Conquest period, see Brooke 1951, p. 125.

[170] Blair 1985, p. 124. A document of 1106 refers to a house (*domus*) which Durand, first prebend of Twyford, had built outside the eastern wall of St Paul's (Gibbs, no. 198). The provision of separate dwellings could be a post-Conquest development (as Brooke 1951, p. 119). But the use of the same terminology by Wulfred would be compatible with the suggestion that there was an older traditional of semi-communal living in English secular chapters.

[171] Gibbs no. 225 (*cf.* no. 224); discussed, *ibid.*, pp. xx–xxi.

[172] For the dole of bread and beer, see above, p. 26. For discussion of the meaning of *s(c)olanda*, see Gibbs, pp. xx–xxv; R.E. Latham, 'Some Minor Enigmas from Medieval Records', *English Historical Review* lxxiv (1959), pp. 664–71 at 664–5; C.R. Hart, 'Shoelands', *Journal EPNS* iv (1971–2), pp. 6–11. The twenty-four hides north of the city which the canons claimed to have held since the seventh century, and which would appear to have been known in the tenth as 'the farms of the brethren' (see p. 196), are referred to as *sceolandae* in a writ of Henry I (Gibbs, no. 27).

arrangements already in place in 1066, although it may equally well reflect an agreement hammered out in the later eleventh century. Some canons would have held property in their own right (see p. 106).

An important aspect of their life would have been daily worship in the cathedral. In the Confessor's reign the arrangements at St Paul's were considered worthy of admiration and emulation: when Earl Leofric of Mercia and his wife Godgifu endowed a minster at Stow St Mary in Lincolnshire, they directed that 'service' (*theowdom*) there was to be the same as at St Paul's (S 1478, A.D. 1053 × 1055).[173] The term *theowdom* may have the narrower meaning of 'divine service', or else it might refer more generally to the canonical organisation in London.[174] In the latter case the 'rule' at St Paul's may have been very influential among secular minsters in late Anglo-Saxon Engand. Of the community's intellectual life nothing is known: no surviving pre-Conquest manuscripts can be securely attributed to the London scriptorium (with the possible exception of BL Cotton Otho B. ii: see p. 38 n. 133), although there are tantalising references in the thirteenth-century inventories.[175]

j. *The Norman Period and After*

The St Paul's community, horribly obscure in the Anglo-Saxon period, becomes after the Conquest the best-documented episcopal chapter in western Europe.[176] This change should be understood as a consequence of the massive reorganisation of the chapter and its property which took place in and around the pontificate of Bishop Maurice (1085–1107). During this period part of the communal lands of the community was carved into thirty separate prebends, with the remainder being retained as a common fund; at the same time the first dean was appointed, along with the other officers who made up the conventional hierarchy of the Continental chapter.[177] This reform marked the beginning of a new phase of the history of St Paul's, with the transformation being reinforced by the construction of a new Romanesque cathedral after the Saxon church burnt down in 1087 (*ASC*), an architectural project which seems to have extended well into the

---

[173] Godgifu was also a direct benefactor of St Paul's. The inventory of 1245 mentions a precious chasuble given to the church by *Godiva de Coventria*, while the 1295 version notes that Godgifu's chasuble was *suspensa et fracta*, fit only for making new vestments (Simpson 1887, p. 482).

[174] Gibbs, p. xix; Blair 1985, p. 123.

[175] See Ker 1969, especially nos 1–2, 107–10, 113. This last item was a psalter with a complete English interlineation.

[176] Brooke and Keir, *London*, p. 341.

[177] For the dating of the changes, see Gibbs, pp. xvi–xxxix; Brooke 1951, 1956; *idem* 1957, pp. 17–19.

twelfth century.[178] The St Paul's archive preserves complete lists of the prebendal holders, which permit extensive historical reconstruction of the composition of the chapter.[179] Thus, of the first generation of prebendaries fifteen had French or Continental names (most of these were probably Norman, but they included at least two Lotharingians), and thirteen had English or Anglo-Scandinavian names (with the remaining two, Arthur and Quintilian, less easily classifiable). It is possible that this preponderance of Continental names to some extent reflects pre-Conquest recruitment under Bishops Robert and William.[180] Some of the early prebendaries would seem to have been closely connected with the ruling class of the city, and others were members of the royal court who found it convenient to have a base in London.[181] The St Paul's community remained intensely proud of its pre-Conquest roots, and would seem to have enjoyed a fairly high degree of continuity from the Anglo-Saxon chapter; but nevertheless the large-scale reorganisation of the chapter endowment *c.* 1100 necessarily marked a break in record-keeping, which may have made earlier documentation seem less relevant (see pp. 51–2). There was also some pressure to 'improve' the pre-Conquest muniments and to adapt them to the changed situation. One aspect of this was a spate of forgery. On the basis of models borrowed from Chertsey Abbey, the canons fabricated a privilege in the name of the seventh-century Pope Agatho (Jaffé no. 2114), a grand diploma of King Æthelstan confirming most of the communal lands (**12**), and a related diploma of the Confessor (**29**). Several other spurious diplomas probably came into existence at around the same time (**1, 16, 21, 24**). These documents were frequently copied, and received far more attention than the genuine diplomas in the archive.

The London diocese was well-placed to ride out the storms of the Conquest. It had been ruled by Norman bishops since 1044, with Bishop William (died 1075) surviving until long enough to smooth the transition to the new political regime. There was a significant fillip to the position of the bishopric when the synodal council that met in London in 1075 recognised the ancient right of the London bishop to a seating position immediately below that of the archbishops of

---

[178] R. Gem, 'The Romanesque Architecture of Old St Paul's Cathedral and its Late Eleventh-Century Context', *Medieval Art, Architecture and Archaeology in London*, ed. L. Grant, British Archaeological Association Conference Trans. x (Leeds, 1990), pp. 47–63, especially pp. 51–3; Fernie, *Architecture of Norman England*, p. 130; Schofield, *Building of London*, pp. 41–4. The relics of St Eorcenwald are said to have survived the blaze, and to have been discovered in the ruins by Bishop Maurice and Bishop Walkelin of Winchester; this may have resulted in a new flowering of the cult (see below, pp. 111–12).

[179] See the three St Paul's volumes of Le Neve, *Fasti*.

[180] Brooke 1951, pp. 121–2 (where it is stressed that this is a very approximate analysis); Brooke and Keir, *London*, pp. 342–4.

[181] Brooke 1951, pp. 122–5; Brooke and Keir, *London*, pp. 342–5.

Canterbury and York, a privilege connected with the London prelate's claim to act as dean of the church of Canterbury and the archbishop's second-in-command.[182] The financial position improved after 1066; Bishop William was able to regain the episcopal manor at Southminster, seized long ago by Cnut, and he was also allowed by the Conqueror to purchase extensive new estates in Hertfordshire and Essex, and to build a castle at Bishops Stortford, while the canons took advantage of the unsettled situation in 1066 to invade disputed territory at Navestock and elsewhere (see pp. 103–6). The effect of the Conquest on the chapter's property in London is undocumented. King William built two substantial western fortifications close to St Paul's: Baynard's Castle and Mountfichet's Tower, which may well have encroached upon an area where the cathedral had ancient property interests. There was a 'bishop's ward' south of the cathedral in the twelfth century, which potentially included the Castle area, and a soke known as St Benet's which paid rent to the bishopric; but the scattered documentation is difficult to interpret.[183]

The establishment of the full-scale prebendal system, and the growing corporate confidence of the dean and chapter, required more stringent definition of the canons' rights and privileges: and this would appear to have put some strain on relations with the bishop. In a document that may belong to the very end of his pontificate, Bishop Maurice (1085–1107) expresses repentance for the evils which he had visited on the chapter, and promises to restore the customs and privileges of the canons.[184] A crucial area of the dispute concerned control of 'elections': to the chapter, to the capitular offices and to the individual prebends. The canons claimed the right to control the recruitment of new members—there is a clause to this effect in the writ of Edward the Confessor (**28**), which was much cherished and copied (and which is potentially a forgery from this period). The bishops, on the other hand, were interested in using the chapter as a source of revenue and patronage, and in practice they seem to have had significant powers over recruitment and elections.[185] For large parts of the twelfth century the London bishopric and chapter was under the control of the Belmeis family and their connections.[186] Members of this clan included Richard I de Belmeis (1108–27), Richard II de

---

[182] F. Barlow, *The English Church 1066–1154* (London and New York, 1979), p. 47.

[183] See Taylor 1980, pp. 176–7 (commenting on suggestions made in Page, *London*, pp. 129–30, 173, 176); Davis 1925, pp. 47–8, 56. For the castles, see Schofield, *Building of London*, pp. 38–40 (with map p. 39); Brooke and Keir, *London*, pp. 215–16.

[184] Gibbs, no. 59; Davis 1925, p. 54; Crosby, *Bishop and Chapter*, pp. 318–19.

[185] Brett, *English Church*, pp. 196–7; Brooke and Keir, *London*, pp. 347–9.

[186] See comments by Stubbs in his edition of Diceto, *Abbreviationes*, pp. xxi–xxxviii; and Brett, *English Church*, pp. 190–1; Crosby, *Bishop and Chapter*, pp. 321–30; Morey and Brooke, *Gilbert Foliot*, pp. 43–7, 205–6; Brooke and Keir, *London*, pp. 345–7. There is an interesting reassessment of the evidence in Whatley, *Saint of London*, pp. 26–36.

Belmeis (1152–62) and Gilbert Foliot (1163–87); various nephews and cousins turn up as canons and cathedral officers. It was against the background of the struggle for autonomy that the canons produced their first cartularies, which privileged the forged charters that supported their position (see pp. 51–3). The most significant figure from this period was the historian and polymath Ralph Diceto, dean 1180-(? 1199 × 1201) and perhaps another Belmeis relative.[187] He undertook an ambitious survey of the communal lands of the chapter, and compiled two registers (both now lost), probably as part of a major overhaul of the archive; he is also remembered for his statute of residence, which tackled the problems of absenteeism and pluralism by specifying a minimum period of residence on the part of the prebendaries in order to qualify them for a share in the common fund.[188]

At the end of the medieval period, the bishops of London enjoyed a high status, but could draw only a fairly mediocre income; by contrast, the canons were immensely wealthy.[189] As a secular chapter St Paul's escaped relatively unscathed from the attentions of Henry VIII and Thomas Cromwell, but faced catastrophe during the period of the Commonwealth. In October 1642 the cathedral was closed and the property of the dean and chapter was sequestrated; the canons were dispersed, many of them choosing to withdraw from London.[190] A substantial part of the archive fell into the hands of the chairman of the sequestrators, before being rescued by William Dugdale (see pp. 56–9). The fabric of the cathedral suffered more than most from the neglect and hooliganism of these years. An elegant Italianate refurbishment by Inigo Jones had been in progress when the Civil War brought an end to building work, leaving St Paul's with great areas of scaffolding holding up the walls and roof. In 1649 the Army turned the cathedral into cavalry stables and there was massive vandalism. Later Parliament sold off the scaffolding, which led to partial collapse of the roof and walls. By the time of the restoration and the re-establishment of the chapter in 1660 the cathedral was a disaster zone. Money was raised for further rebuilding and refurbishment, but all this activity was negated by the Great Fire of 1666.[191]

---

[187] For Diceto, see Stubbs in Diceto, *Abbreviationes*, pp. lv–lxxii; Gransden, *Historical Writing*, pp. 230–6; and below, pp. 52–3. His death is usually dated to 1202, but see D. Greenway 'The Succession to Ralph de Diceto, Dean of St Paul's' *Bulletin of the Institute of Historical Research* xxxix (1966), pp. 86–95.

[188] For the background to the residency question, see Edwards, *English Secular Cathedrals*, chapter 1; and for St Paul's in particular, see Brooke 1957, pp. 51–3; Brooke and Keir, *London*, pp. 350–2.

[189] Brooke 1957, pp. 58–65.

[190] *VCH London*, i. 417–18; E.F. Carpenter, 'The Reformation: 1485–1660', in Matthews and Atkins, *St Paul's Cathedral*, pp. 100–71 at 168.

[191] J. Lang, *Rebuilding St Paul's after the Great Fire of London* (Oxford, 1956), prologue; Schofield, *Building of London*, p. 169 (illustration of Jones's design).

2. THE HISTORY OF THE ARCHIVE

Only a relatively small number of pre-Conquest documents have survived from St Paul's, and it is particularly sad that there were important losses in fairly recent times.[1] The sealed original or pseudo-original of Edward the Confessor's writ (**28**) was still available in the seventeenth century and may even have survived into the early eighteenth century, while three medieval cartularies with copies of pre-Conquest charters (*Libri B, C, G*) disappeared after the 1650s. But the greatest loss was a medieval roll, possibly dating from the late thirteenth century, which contained copies of at least twenty-eight pre-Conquest texts, the great majority of them not witnessed elsewhere; this roll seems to have vanished during the period of the Commonwealth. We are remarkably fortunate that earlier in the seventeenth century it had been studied by Richard James and John Selden, who made extensive extracts from the charters (see Bodleian, James 23, pp. 32–6; London, Lincoln's Inn, Hale 84, 93r–94r); it may also have been seen slightly later by a third scholar, who made notes on Anglo-Saxon formulas in St Paul's documents (BL Lansdowne 364, 134rv). There was further stroke of luck in the fact that William Dugdale gained access to *Liber B* in the middle of the seventeenth century, and used it the basis for his edition of St Paul's texts in the *Monasticon Anglicanum* and in his history of the cathedral.

This background of relatively late losses, mitigated by antiquarian activity, determines the character of the present edition. The only document for which there is a very large number of medieval witnesses is the important writ of the Confessor (**28**), which was of primary importance to the chapter: but here the preferred manuscript is a painstaking seventeenth-century facsimile of the lost original. The surviving medieval cartularies of St Paul's contain copies of a small number of complete texts, many of them forgeries, which had particular resonance for the medieval canons (**1, 12, 16, 21, 23, 26, 28, 29, 31**). Dugdale's printed works preserve full texts of a further three documents, which arguably derive from the lost *Liber B* (**13, 22, 27**). But the bulk of the documents edited here are extracts made in the seventeenth century from the lost roll: some reasonably substantial (for example, **7, 8, 10**), some very brief indeed (as **2, 3, 4, 6A, 11**).

Little can be said about the history of the St Paul's muniments before the twelfth century, although it should be noted that the survival of apparently genuine

---

[1] There are important studies of the history of the archive in Gibbs, Introduction; Yeo 1986; and Ramsay in Keene, forthcoming. For a partial catalogue of the St Paul's muniments, see *HMC 9th Report* (the prospective new catalogue mentioned in Yeo 1986, p. 31 n. 13, did not materialise).

documents from the later seventh century onwards would seem to indicate that the frequent fires which swept the city and cathedral, and the vicissitudes of Danish occupation and other military actions, did not have an entirely cata-strophic effect on the early archive. We do known that, from at least the early twelfth century until the sixteenth or seventeenth, the muniments were stored in the cathedral treasury, and responsibility for their care was assigned to the sac-rist, acting as the treasurer's deputy.[2] The organisation of the prebends under Bishop Maurice (1082–1107) would have required some research into the earlier archive, and it seems possible that this generated a separate compilation which was the precursor of the earliest extant cartulary in the archive (GL 25504, *Liber L*), dating from the second quarter of the twelfth century (see below). In addition, it would appear that several supposedly pre-Conquest diplomas were actually fabricated in this period. These include a pancarta in the name of King Æthelstan (**12**), which was based on a forgery from Chertsey; a related papal bull modelled on a genuine Chertsey privilege (Jaffé no. 2114); general confir-mations of St Paul's lands by Æthelred and Cnut (**21, 26**); and diplomas of Edgar and Edward the Confessor which can be linked with post-Conquest land-disputes (**16, 29**).

The pattern of preservation and fabrication does suggest an intriguing premise. It is noticeable that essentially all the known documents which seem to reflect genuine pre-Conquest title-deeds relate to estates which were controlled in 1086 by the bishop, as opposed to the canons.[3] There is good reason to think that the lands allocated to the support of the chapter had been to a large extent separated from the bishop's holdings as early as 1066, and perhaps even by *c.* 1000 (see pp. 82, 93–4, 100, 104). The separate management of these two sec-tions of the endowment could conceivably have affected the custody of the muni-ments. One might wish to speculate that the pre-Conquest title-deeds of the canons' lands were destroyed or otherwise lost, so that it was only the bishop's early title-deeds which were available to the medieval compiler of the roll so fruitfully studied by James and Selden, which is the source of most of our knowledge of the pre-Conquest land-charters of the London Church. Some level of destruction of the

---

[2] Yeo 1986, pp. 30–1, 39–40. The first reference to the treasury as a depository is in a document from the time of Bishop Richard de Belmeis I (1108–27).

[3] **2** (Ealing in Fulham); **3** (Fulham); **6** (Southminster); **14** (Shopland); **15** (Orsett); **17** (Hadham); **19** (Orsett); **20** (? Crondon in Orsett). Two documents deal with land no longer controlled by the London Church in 1066 (**4, 9**); the first is a grant to the bishop. One forged charter may relate to Southminster (**18**). **7** and **8** cover grants of privileges to the bishops, rather than land. The only exception to the pattern is **10**, dealing with land at Islington, held by the canons in 1066/1086. But Islington may have been reckoned under the bishop's share of the endowment *c.* 1000 (see **25** and p. 100); and there was later a manor at Barnsbury in Islington, reckoned under the episcopal manor at Stepney (see p. 199).

records prior to *c.* 1125 is certainly suggested by the failure of William of
Malmesbury to discover any substantive details about the Anglo-Saxon bishops
(see p. 107). The devastating fire of 1087 may have been a crucial event,
although the survival of a number of writs of William I for the chapter would
seem to rule out that possibility. It is tempting to speculate further, to the effect
that the lack of genuine pre-Conquest title-deeds prompted the canons to fabri-
cate a set of documents for their most important estates in the late eleventh or
early twelfth century; and also led them to borrow models from the monastery at
Chertsey, founded by St Paul's own St Eorcenwald (see further, pp. 75–7).

GL 25504, the earliest extant cartulary, is conveniently referred to as *Liber L*,
the classification under which it appears in an inventory of the St Paul's muniments made in 1447 (see below). By that date it had acquired a spurious antiquity, being attributed to the time of William the Conqueror. The compiler has
included only a selection of early documents, for the most part recent forgeries.
He has left two precisely-calculated gaps, which strongly indicates that he was
using as his exemplar an existing compilation of early documents. It would
appear that already by the early twelfth century the chapter's archivists had chosen to highlight a relatively small selection of early documents, and were paying
less attention to the bulk of the pre-Conquest archive.

There was a major overhaul of the muniments in the time of Dean Ralph
Diceto (1180–(1199 × 1201)), who undertook a survey of the St Paul's manors
and churches in 1181.[4] The 1447 inventory refers to two cartularies that were
associated with Diceto, his 'greater register' (*Liber B*), which included a copy of
the 1181 survey, and his 'lesser register' (*Liber C*). The latter is wholly lost, and
of the former only a single bifolium survives, conceivably written by Diceto
himself. This includes a list of contents, with one section headed *De cartis per
ordinem positis vel notatis tali signo* +: evidently some effort had already been
made to order and categorise the muniments, conceivably by Diceto himself.[5]
Some reconstruction of *Liber B* can be attempted, on the basis of the 1447
inventory and of use made of the volume by William Dugdale (see further
below, pp. 62–4). From this it appears that there was a selection of pre-Conquest
material similar to that in the earlier *Liber L*, with the probable addition of three
documents, all in Old English (**13, 22, 27**).

Diceto's 'lesser register', the lost *Liber C*, is more obscure. The 1447 inventory
has a tantalisingly oblique guide to its contents, which indicates that there were
some pre-Conquest texts: a charter covering Barling and Chingford occurring on

---

[4] For Ralph's activities at St Paul's, see Stubbs's introduction to Ralph Diceto, *Abbreviationes*,
pp. lx–lxi; and for his survey, see Hale, *St Paul's Domesday*, pp. 107–19.
[5] Gransden, *Historical Writing*, p. 234 n. 124; Yeo 1986, pp. 36–7.

fol. 40 is probably **29**; a charter for twelve *mansiones* at Navestock found on fol. 46 is probably **16** (with the error *xii* for *xv*); and another text on the same folio which concerned Laver and Cockhampstead is likely to have been **23** (GL 25511, 98r–99v). William Dugdale used *Liber C*; he refers to a copy of **31** that he found there, on fol. 65v; and he reproduces a text of William I's 'coronation-day' charter from fol. 69r.[6] But the cartulary seems to have disappeared by the end of the seventeenth century, when its binding was being used to cover a fifteenth-century volume of statutes.[7]

In the early thirteenth century thirteen St Paul's charters were submitted for confirmation, and were copied into Cartae Antiquae Roll 1.[8] The selection included three writs of William I, but nothing from the pre-Conquest period. The absence of the writ of Edward the Confessor (**28**) may have an important bearing on its history and authenticity (see p. 210).

Another cartulary, known as *Liber A* or *Liber Pilosus* (GL 25501) was begun in 1241, with contemporary documents being added on a fairly regular basis from 1244 until the fourteenth century. The all-important writ of Edward the Confessor (**28**), which had not been included in *Liber L*, is given pride of place at the beginning of the main cartulary, while the same selection of pre-Conquest texts as in *Liber L* appears here, in a slightly different order, in a continuation of the main cartulary datable to 1241 × 1244. The scribe seems to have been using an existing compilation which was not *Liber L*, but may perhaps have been *Liber B*. The fact that the pre-Conquest texts were not originally included in the main cartulary gives the impression that the chapter's early charters, with the apparent exception of **28**, were no longer valued as highly as they had been in the previous century.

The later thirteenth century may have seen further initiatives in the custody of the muniments. New reference marks were added to some documents.[9] Extant from this period is a roll containing copies of some thirty royal writs and charters of the eleventh and twelfth centuries, including **28**; the scribe has added some press-marks in the left-hand margin, which may indicate that he was copying from the originals (GL 25272, formerly D. &. C, A Box 69: see below, p. 66). There seems to be a fair chance that the lost roll seen by Selden and James, with copies of a substantial number of pre-Conquest charters, was produced at around the same time. Both rolls would seem to have shared the feature of

---

[6] *St Paul's*, p. 5 (reference to **31**), p. 190 (charter of William I); *Mon. Angl.*, p. 305 (charter of William I). See further below, pp. 102–3.

[7] Now GL 25502; see Gibbs, p. xv; Yeo 1986, p. 35. The notes supposedly taken by Matthew Hutton from *Liber C* are from the volume of statutes.

[8] *The Cartae Antiquae Rolls 1–10*, ed. L. Landon, Pipe Roll Society (London, 1939), pp. 1–5. A copy of a charter of Henry I was added to a later roll (pp. 12–13).

[9] Yeo 1986, p. 37.

having been written on both sides, and they seem each to have contained around the same number of texts. It is possible that these were the two rolls referred to in the 1447 inventory: 'duo rotuli notabiles de antiquis priuilegiis ecclesie et diuerse carte regum in lingua Latina et Saxonica de maneriis et libertatibus ecclesie'; or else that they formed part of another group of six 'antiqui rotuli de antiquis cartis regum et libertatibus ecclesie' (GL 25511, 58v, 68r). Use of rolls for record-keeping seems to have become more popular in the thirteenth century, following the example of the royal government, and the St Paul's archivists may have been influenced by Exchequer practice.[10] The roll format was much less convenient than the codex for recording documents to which frequent reference would need to be made, although it had short-term advantages for continuous copying of contemporary documents. It is probably significant that both the lost roll and the extant roll were repositories of ancient documents which were no longer of day-to-day significance, unlike the documents which were being added to *Liber A* at this period. A note in *Liber A* adds a further perspective. The copy here of **31** (Latin), which was made in the period 1241×1244, is followed by a note that an English version of the text followed in the scribe's source. There is an addition by another medieval scribe, to the effect 'quam [cartam] inuenies in quodam rotulo bullato'.

The register known as *Liber I* (GL 25516) was compiled in the early four-teenth century, probably under the auspices of Ralph Baldock, dean of St Paul's and bishop of London (1304–13). This includes surveys of the documentation of individual manors, with running references to Æthelstan's pancarta (**12**), and a full text of **16** at the beginning of the section on the manor at Navestock. The separate treatment of **16** may indicate the continued survival of the pseudo-original (see next).

In 1447 Dean Thomas Lyseux commissioned a massive inventory of the muniments of the Chapter, which still survives.[11] This comprises a list of loose documents in the order in which they were stored and also in alphabetical order, together with an analysis of the contents of individual cartularies and other bound volumes. Among the loose documents was a sealed vernacular charter of King Edward, presumably **28** (GL 25511, 60v). No other pre-Conquest single-sheet is specifically mentioned, although it is possible that there were other charters still extant but concealed within the general references to separate

---

[10] See the useful study of the use of rolls in M.T. Clanchy, *From Memory to Written Record: England 1066–1307* (London, 1979), pp. 105–13.

[11] GL 25511 (formerly St Paul's D. & C., WD 11) is a contemporary fair copy of an original draft represented by GL 25511A (formerly St Paul's, D. & C., WD 11a). For the contents of the inventory, see *HMC 9th Report*; Hale, *St Paul's Domesday*, pp. xvi–xvii; Holtzmann, *Papsturkunden*, i. 173–9.

collections of manorial records: the best candidate is the Navestock diploma (**16**), apparently copied separately into *Liber C* in the twelfth century and into *Liber I* in the fourteenth, and also available in the lost *Liber G* (see below). The inventory refers to fifteen cartularies, with a classification based on the size of the individual volumes, beginning with *Liber A* and continuing to *Liber N*, with in addition a *Liber AB* and a *Liber Goedmanni*. Of these only five currently exist: *Libri A, I* and *L* (see above, and discussion below, pp. 61–2, 64–7); *Liber K* (the record of a thirteenth-century decanal visitation); and the *Liber Goedmanni* (the chapter act book for 1411–48).[12] The details of the contents are sometimes vague, but it would appear that there were pre-Conquest documents copied into six of the cartularies listed in 1447: the three extant volumes, *Libri L, A, I*; the two registers of Ralph Diceto, *Libri B* and *C* (see above); and also in *Liber G* (see next paragraph). It is possible that the compilation of the inventory coincided with a reorganisation and renumbering of the muniments.[13]

The lost *Liber G* is described as [*liber*] *de placitis et breuibus* (GL 25511, 116v–120r). It would appear to have included a list of manors, and to have continued with a selection of early documents: folio 2 contained a charter relating to fifteen hides at Navestock (i.e. **16**), a charter of Cnut confirming all the lands of St Paul's (**26**) and a confirmation of land at Laver and Cockhampstead (**23**). In the seventeenth century the cartulary was seen by Dugdale, who noted that it included the text of a privilege of Coenred of Mercia (with a double folio reference, 1r and 5r, which might mean that there were two copies); presumably this was the same document as the privilege of Coenred on the lost roll, from which Richard James made a brief extract (see **5**).[14] Dugdale reproduces two documents from *Liber G*, a narrative about a legendary 'first foundation' in the time of King Lucius of the Britons, cited from fol. 12r and corresponding with an entry in the 1447 inventory: *Item de prima fundacione ecclesie S. Pauli 12* (GL 25511, 118r); and a tract on the number of canons, cited from 8or.[15] It is possible that a further notice in the inventory, *Item que Ethelbertus dedit ecclesie xxiiii hidas* (no folio given), was another 'historical' narrative (GL 25511, 118r). Towards the end of the century *Liber G* was also seen by Matthew Hutton, who extracted from it a list of deans that would seem to have been compiled no earlier than the mid fourteenth century; this may indicate that the manuscript itself was produced in the later fourteenth or early fifteenth century.[16]

---

[12] *Liber K* is now GL 25514 (edited in Hales, *St Paul's Domesday*); and the *Liber Goedmanni* is now GL 25513. See Yeo 1986, pp. 34–5.

[13] Yeo 1986, p. 38.

[14] Dugdale, *St Paul's*, p. 4.

[15] Dugdale, *St Paul's*, pp. 177, 255; *Mon. Angl.*, pp. 298, 346

[16] Brooke 1956, p. 232.

St Paul's was a secular foundation, and so its endowment and archive were not seriously affected by the Henrician reformation. Its situation in the capital meant that its muniments were easily accessible to the first generations of anti-quarian scholars. The writ of Edward the Confessor (**28**), still extant as a sealed original or pseudo-original, attracted particular attention, particularly from members of the nearby College of Arms, who had a special interest in seals. A notebook associated with John Guillim, Rougecroix Pursuivant (died 1621), includes a careful facsimile of the writ, with details of its attachment and a drawing of the damaged seal (PRO, DL 42/149, 113r; see Plate 2). An almost identical but less competent facsimile was included almost a century later in a manuscript work compiled by John Anstis the Elder, the Garter king of Arms who died in 1744 (BL Stowe 666, 67v); his source may have been a copy, rather than the original writ. Partial facsimiles by two other scholars of the period, John Glover (died 1588) and Nicholas Charles, Lancaster Herald (died 1613), were probably taken independently from a lost common exemplar (Oxford, the Queen's College, 88, 186v; BL Cotton Jul. C. vii, 198v). More general interest in the St Paul's muniments was shown by Richard James (1592–1638), employed as librarian by Sir Robert Cotton and then by his son, whose papers include extracts from pre-Conquest diplomas under the heading *Rotulus antiquus ecclesiæ sancti Pauli* (Bodleian, James 23, pp. 32–6). The antiquary John Selden (1584–1654) made notes from the same source (Lincoln's Inn, Hale MS 84, 93r–94v). See below, pp. 67–70, for discussion and an attempted recon-struction of the lost roll.

The archive came under enormous threat during the period of the Commonwealth. Nationally, the lands of the archbishops and bishops were con-fiscated in October/November 1646 and those of the deans and chapters in April 1649; Parliament decreed that their deeds and registers were to be collected in a single repository in London.[17] The first registry was set up in Gurney House in Old Jewry; the records seem to have been kept in very poor order, but it was possible for new owners of former episcopal and chapter lands to carry out searches there for documentation. In 1654, by which time the sale of church lands appears to have been halted, the records were moved to the excise office in Broad Street where they were kept in dreadful conditions; a contemporary peti-tion speaks of documents being 'trodden under foot'. The church records were still in Broad Street when the sale of church lands was declared void on 7 December 1660. The re-established bishops and reconstituted chapters were understandably eager to regain their deeds and registers in order to prove title,

---

[17] For the next section, see D. Owen, 'Bringing Home the Records: the Recovery of the Ely Chapter Muniments at the Restoration', *Archives* viii (1967–8), pp. 123–9; Yeo 1986, pp. 32–3.

but there was considerable confusion. At some point in 1661 the records were moved to a chapel in the east end of St Paul's, before being transported to Lambeth Palace after the archbishop of Canterbury took on the responsibility for them. It appears that the historian William Dugdale must have been engaged to sort at least part of the contents of the registry, for an entry in his diary for 21 November 1664 records the payments which had been made to him by a large number of bishoprics 'towards my recompence for sorting the old Evidences of the Bishops, which were brought up to London in the times of the late troubles, and confounded together, by mixing with the other.'[18] London is mentioned in the list of bishoprics, and Dugdale indicates that the Dean of St Paul's had been instrumental in gathering the monies due to him. The implication is that some St Paul's records passed into the London repository.

However, certain passages in Dugdale's autobiography and in his introduction to the second edition of his history of St Paul's show that a considerable part of the chapter archive was not given up to the central registry, but passed instead into the hands of the lawyer who was appointed by Parliament to chair a committee managing the possessions of the cathedral; it seems possible that it was only the most important current records which were sent to the London repository. The relevant passage in the autobiography (which was written in the third person in around 1680) runs:

'In which Time of his Residence in London [1655–6], meeting casually with Mr. John Reading, a Nottingham-shire Gentleman, who having formerly been Clerk of the Nisi-Prius, for the Midland Circuit, (and with whom before the Rebellion he had been acquainted) he Friendly invited Mr. Dugdale to his House at Scrivener's-Hall (near Silver-Street) with Promise to show him some Old Manuscript Books, Original Charters and other Ancient Writings, who coming thither accordingly, he brought forth Five Ancient Manuscript Books in Folio, which were Leiger-Books of the Lands anciently given to the Cathedral of S. Paul in London, and freely lent them to him until the next ensuing Michaelmas Term, thus intimating that he should have the Use of many more upon his next Return to London.

'But in Michaelmas Term, when Mr. Dugdale came to restore those Books so lent, he found that Mr. Reading was dead, and had constituted one Mr. Williams (a Barrister at Law of the Temple) his Executor. Addressing himself therefore to the said Mr. Williams, and desiring a Sight of the rest, he very civilly brought him to Scriveners-Hall, and there shewing him many other Old Manuscript Books, Original Charters, and very Ancient Writings in Bags and Hampers, all

---

[18] *The Life, Diary and Correspondence of Sir William Dugdale, Knight*, ed. W. Hamper (London, 1827), pp. 117–18.

relating to that great Cathedral, he freely lent them to him, to carry to his own Lodging, they amounting to no less than Ten Porters Burdens. Having them therefore in his private Custody, and bestowing Pains to sort them into Order, he made Extracts from them, of what he found Historical in Reference to that Church.'[19]

In his introduction to the second edition to the history of St Paul's, Dugdale records his satisfaction at his role in preserving the muniments, and gives some more relevant detail about John Reading:

'Nor do I account it other than the like Providence, that I was the chief Means of Preserving all those Venerable Chartularies, and Records, belonging to this Ancient and Famous Church; which, upon that sacrilegious and ravenous Seizure of the Deans and Chapters Lands throughout this whole Nation, by that Long Parliament, coming to the Hands of one Mr. John Reading, Chair-man of the Committee for ordering the Possessions thereof, were by him casually communicated to me. Whence, having reduced them out of no little Confusion, and extracted what I have said in my ensuing Discourse of this Cathedral, I kept them in my Hands, during the whole Time of the late Usurpation, and soon after his Late Majesty was most happily restored, did faithfully deliver them unto the then worthy Dean, Dr. Barwick; by whom being carefully laid up, they are still preserved for the Benefit of After-Ages.'[20]

The first edition of Dugdale's history of the cathedral was published in 1658, and was presumably worked up from the records then in 'his private Custody'; many of the same texts edited in the appendix to the history subsequently appeared in the section on St Paul's in the third volume of the *Monasticon*, published in 1673. Dugdale made extensive use of *Liber B*, the 'greater register' of Ralph Diceto, as a source for pre-Conquest charters. His texts of Pope Agatho's privilege and of three post-Conquest charters were taken from the thirteenth-century cartulary, *Liber A*, and he also consulted *Liber C*, Diceto's 'lesser register' (see pp. 52–3 above) and another lost cartulary, *Liber G* (p. 55 above). In addition he cites a relic-list from an unspecified 'ancient manuscript in St Paul's', and an enrolment of a writ of William I.

Dugdale evidently had access to an important part of the medieval archive, but he does not seem to have come across the medieval roll that had been studied so productively by James and Selden. There is some reason to believe that this roll, together with other important muniments, also escaped the central

---

[19] The autobiography was first published in the second edition of Dugdale's *History of St Paul's*, with Edward Maynard's continuation describing Dugdale's death and burial (pp. iv–xvii). The autobiography was also printed in Ellis's 1818 edition, with explanatory notes from Anthony Wood's manuscript, and in Hamper's *Life*.

[20] *St Paul's* (2nd edn), p. xxvii.

repository and resided in other hands during the difficult years of the suppression. The compiler of a substantial note-book, now partly preserved as BL Lansdowne 364, seems to have been in a position to take notes from some of the St Paul's muniments, including *Liber A*, and his researches evidently extended into the 1640s and perhaps later. Towards the end of the notebook is a memorandum headed: 'A noat of such writings as I sent up in a chest from Tewin [Herts.] to my Uncle Dr <Layford, ? Layfield> at London March 29 1659 [*altered from* 1658]' (fol. 136r).[21] These documents include a number of 'rowls' relating to individual St Paul's prebends, 'a bundle of severall accounts in Parchment', a series of dean's registers (14th–16th centuries), a 'Rentall antiquæ fabricæ', a 'Liber de statu Ecclesiæ sancti Pauli' and 'Gabriel Duns account of St Paul's'. The notetaker seems to have had a close personal association with the chapter, and it seems possible that some of the muniments available to him had been retained by a former prebendary when the chapter was dissolved and its members dispersed. Among the documents which he studied were a number of pre-Conquest texts, from which he extracted brief formulas (fol. 134rv), and he also provides a list of early place-names said to have been taken from the community's privileges (fol. 145v): see further below, pp. 71–3. Some of his extracts correspond with charters on the lost roll used by James and Selden, and it is possible that this roll was among the documents available to him. The fate of the records sent from Tewin to London in 1659 is unclear. None of the registers of the medieval deans has survived, and it has been suggested that they perished in the Great Fire of 1666.[22] An alternative possibility is that through some mischance the collection of material from Tewin did not rejoin the main archive after the restoration in 1660.

In general the re-established cathedral archives seem to have survived the 1666 fire with only minor losses, due to the heroic salvage efforts of the clerk of works, John Tillison.[23] After the rebuilding of the cathedral the chapter house became the main repository, until the construction of a muniment room *c.* 1773; subsequently the records were divided between the two locations. Toward the end of the seventeenth century the muniments were studied by Matthew Hutton, who found that the storage system was very haphazard, perhaps still reflecting the adhoc arrangements after the Great Fire (BL Harl. 6955–6956). Hutton was able to make extracts from *Liber B*, which was Dugdale's main source for the

---

[21] The name of the recipient is unclear. Edward Layfield was a prominent member of the chapter at the time, a nephew of Archbishop Laud who served as archdeacon of Essex and prebendary of Harlesden; he died in 1680 (Le Neve, *Fasti 1541–1857*, pp. 9, 36). In 1710 a charity was set up in Tewin in accordance with the will of a Rev. Charles Layfield (*VCH Herts. III*, p. 487).

[22] Yeo 1986, p. 34.

[23] *Ibid.*

pre-Conquest period, and also from *Liber G*; but both volumes seem to have disappeared soon afterwards. Other cartularies and single sheets vanished in the later seventeenth or eighteenth centuries; these may have included the sealed writ of Edward the Confessor (**28**).[24] Some attempts were made to sort and catalogue the records in this period, but an effective reform had to await the nineteenth century and the efforts of Archdeacon William Hale (1842–70) and Canon W. Sparrow Simpson, appointed librarian in 1862.[25] In Sparrow's time the records were transported from the old muniment room to a gallery adjoining the cathedral library. An account of the muniments by H. Maxwell Lyte was published by the Historical Manuscripts Commission in 1883.[26] During the twentieth century problems of storage space and preservation became increasingly apparent and in 1980 it was agreed that the St Paul's records should be transferred to the Guildhall Library.

3. THE MANUSCRIPTS

Summary (see also previous section)

The only pre-Conquest charter from St Paul's which was very frequently copied in the later medieval period was the important writ of Edward the Confessor (**28**), which was still extant as a sealed original or pseudo-original in the seventeenth century and may even have survived into the eighteenth. It was copied into the St Paul's cartularies and into at least two medieval rolls; moreover, it was submitted for confirmation and enrolment in 1316 with other St Paul's documents, and the resulting Inspeximus charter was subsequently confirmed and enrolled on seven further occasions. The original writ was examined and reproduced, sometimes in facsimile, by antiquarian scholars from the sixteenth to eighteenth centuries.

A group of seven royal charters, most of them general grants of privileges and confirmations of the abbey's lands (**1, 12, 16, 21, 23, 26, 29**), together with the memorandum of a private grant (**31**), was copied into the mid-twelfth-century cartulary known as *Liber L* (GL 25504) and then, shortly after 1241, included as an addition in the later and grander cartulary, *Liber A* (GL 25501); the latter also includes a copy of **28** at the beginning of the original compilation. This same group of eight charters and at least three extra pre-Conquest documents (**13, 22, 27**) also appeared in the lost twelfth-century cartulary *Liber B*, which was used

[24] Yeo 1986, pp. 35–6; below, pp. 207–9.

[25] Yeo 1986, pp. 41–3.

[26] *HMC 9th Report*, part 1, appendix 1–72; see Yeo 1986, p. 43.

by Dugdale as a source for the *History of St Paul's* and *Monasticon Anglicanum*. The texts of two post-Conquest documents in Old English, edited here in Appendix 3, were copied in *Liber L*, but not *Liber A*. There were also pre-Conquest documents in three other medieval cartularies, *Libri C, I* and *G* (pp. 52–5).

In the early seventeenth century Richard James and John Selden made extracts from a substantial number of pre-Conquest texts copied onto an 'ancient roll' which has since disappeared (Bodleian, James 23, pp. 32–6; London, Lincoln's Inn, Hale 84, 93r–94r: see **2–11, 14–15, 17, 20, 24, 30**). The notebook of another scholar, who seems to have had access to part of the archive during the period of the Commonwealth, preserves fragments of several more charters (BL Lansdowne 364: see **18, 19, 20**).

A document of *c.* 1000 which concerns the naval obligations of the London bishopric (**25**) is preserved in a collection of Anglo-Saxon legal material, compiled *c.* 1125–1130 (CCCC 383). The manuscript is discussed in the commentary to the text (p. 193).

a. *GL 25504 (formerly St Paul's D. & C., WD 4;* Liber L) [C]

This is a composite register, of which the earliest part (fos 5–30) is a cartulary written by a single scribe in a large, careful bookhand, probably in the second quarter of the twelfth century.[27] The notice in Dean Lyseux's 1447 inventory exaggerates its antiquity: 'Contenta in quodam antiquo et notabili registro de tempore Willelmi conquestoris, clauso cum uno nodulo' (GL 25511, 126v). *Liber L* contains the texts of the chapter's standard corpus of eight purportedly pre-Conquest charters (see above), followed by a few royal charters in the names of Williams I and II and Henry I, and then by a collection of deeds and lists of sureties for various of the community's estates. The scribe left blank spaces between some of the texts: the whole of fol. 11r (between the texts of **23** and **21**), and from line 10 of 14r to line 13 of fol. 15v (between the last Anglo-Saxon document and the first post-Conquest charter). The precision of the second gap could indicate that he was copying from an existing manuscript source rather than from the charters themselves. It is possible that the gaps represent vernacular documents which the scribe chose not to copy out: the first gap may correspond to the text of **22**, which is related to **23** and was associated with it in the slightly later *Liber B* (see below). Other omitted texts may have been **13** and **27**, two further Old English documents which would seem to have been copied with the same group of charters in *Liber B*. In *Liber L* the pre-Conquest

---

[27] Davis, *Cartularies*, no. 596; *HMC 9th Report*, part i, Appendix pp. 60–9.

documents appear in roughly chronological order (with **16** classified according to its donor rather than its date) between fos 5v and 14r. The sequence begins with **1** and continues with the privilege of Pope Agatho (Jaffé no. 2114); then come six royal charters (**12, 16, 23, 21, 26, 29**) and one private document which refers to Edward the Confessor (**31**). Further on in this section of the manuscript there is a collection of post-Conquest deeds, concluding with one of the two post-Conquest documents edited in Appendix 3; the second of these appears later in the manuscript, in an a section written by a different but apparently coeval scribe (fos 31–60). In general the texts of *Liber L* seem to be very good indeed. The forms of personal names and place-names show no signs of corruption, and the scribe carefully reproduced runic letters. The compiler of the cartulary (or the compiler of its source) appears to have been interested only in documents which were directly in favour of the St Paul's community.

b. *St Paul's D. & C*, Liber B [D]

The entry for *Liber B* in Dean Lyseux's 1447 inventory runs: 'Tabula contentorum in maiori registro de Diceto decani, signata cum littera B, 20 folio in rubrica post tabulam: Isti sunt cottarii A.D. 1181' (GL 25511, 95r). The list of contents, arranged alphabetically, refers to several pre-Conquest documents on fos 20 and 21: there was a charter of Edgar for Barling etc. (i.e. **29**), a charter of Æthelred for Laver etc. (**23**), and one of Edgar for Navestock (**16**); and there are also collective references to this section of the manuscript (e.g. 'Cartae regum et episcoporum de privilegiis et beneficiis, 20'). This cartulary was the source of a number of the pre-Conquest texts printed by Dugdale in his history of the cathedral, first published in 1658, and in the third volume of the *Monasticon* (published 1673). It was subsequently seen by Matthew Hutton (1639–1711), who made notes from this and other St Paul's manuscripts in *c*. 1699.[28] The register seems to have been lost or dismembered at some point in the eighteenth century, and all that now survives are two leaves among the Rawlinson papers in the Bodleian Library, bound into Rawlinson B. 372, fos 3–4.[29] This bifolium would appear to have been used as a book-binding: it gives some impression of the dimensions of the volume (355×250 mm), and indicates that it was written in two columns in a large bookhand. It has been suggested that the scribe may have been Diceto himself.[30]

---

[28] Hutton's notes from *Liber B* are now BL Harl 6956, 82v–85v; they do not include extracts from any pre-Conquest texts. See Yeo 1986, p. 35; and for Hutton's career, see *DNB*.

[29] Edited by Hale, *St Paul's Domesday*, pp. 109–17. For Rawlinson's acquisitions from St Paul's, see Yeo 1986, p. 36. Kemble appears to claim to have taken some of his texts from 'Reg. B' in the archive of the dean and chapter (see KCD vol vi, p. xxv), but his source was actually *Mon. Angl.* The same is true of the texts edited by Thorpe, who cites the foliation to *Liber B* mentioned by Dugdale.

[30] Yeo 1986, p. 37.

The contents of the bifolium include a brief list of the *capitula* of the whole register which, in conjunction with the information derived from the inventory and from Dugdale and Hutton, make possible a general reconstruction. The first part of the register contained the inquisition into the communal estates of the chapter, commissioned by Dean Ralph in 1181 (see p. 52). This was followed by a list of donors, and then a *capitulum* with a double title: *Qui Reges Anglorum immunitatem indulserunt. De cartis per ordinem positis vel notatis tali signo +.* Later sections covered churches founded outside London and within the city, the lands of the canons, and the payments due to the canons on three specified feast days. There can be little doubt that this volume was put together on the initiative of Dean Ralph in his early years of office (a later medieval hand added the words *Domesday Radulphi de Diceto* in the upper margin of the first folio of *Liber B*, which survives in Bodl. Rawl. B. 372). It seems to have had a companion volume in *Liber C*, also lost, which is described in the 1447 inventory as the 'lesser register of Ralph Diceto' (see above, pp. 52–3).

The pre-Conquest charters printed by Dugdale in the *History of St Paul's* and the *Monasticon* would appear to have been taken from the third section. The sequence of texts in both works begins with **1**, which has a marginal citation of '*Liber B*, fol. 20r'. For the privilege of Pope Agatho, which comes next, Dugdale had to turn to *Liber A*, which would tend to confirm that the *Liber B* texts were limited to royal and episcopal charters. This papal privilege is followed in the *History* by the brief *Vita sancti Erkenwaldi*, which is wrongly identified as coming from *Liber B*, 20r; in the *Monasticon* this reference is corrected to (BL) Cotton Claud. A. v, p. 135.[31] The fourth item is **12**, said to be from *Liber B*, 20r. This is followed by **13** in both Old English and Latin versions, with the citation *ib[idem]*, presumably indicating that it was also from *Liber B*, 20r. After this come **16** (*ib. 20b*), **22** (no source), **23** (*ib. 21a*) and **21** (no source), **26** (*ib. 20b*), **27** (no source), **29** (*ib. 21b*), and **28** (no source).

The implication of the marginal notes is that all these texts were taken from *Liber B*. There may, however, be a slight problem. Four of the ten charters are not given an explicit source, and two of these (**22, 27**) are documents which are found only in Dugdale's works, and not in *Liber L* or *Liber A*; the third charter peculiar to Dugdale (**13**) is given a marginal *ibid*, but no folio number. It is possible that Dugdale found these three documents in another of the muniments he examined, for example *Liber C* or *Libr G*. Assuming that he did not, the

---

[31] The modern editor of the *Vita* interprets this correction as an indication that Dugdale's text was based on both manuscripts (Whatley, *Saint of London*, pp. 2–3, 7). He considers that the places where Dugdale's version diverges from that in BL Cotton Claud. A. v may in certain instances represent actual manuscript variants, although he concedes that some may be printer's errors or Dugdale's own emendations.

approximate sequence of pre-Conquest texts in *Liber B* was: (fol. 20r) **1, 12, 13** (?); (fol. 20v) **16, 25, 27** (?); (fol. 21r) **22** (?); **23** (?); (fol. 21v) **29, 28** (?). Two vernacular texts (**22** and **27**) are followed by Latin translations, apparently Dugdale's own. There is a possibility that the Latin version of **13** is also Dugdale's work (see discussion p. 167). Although Dugdale does not give the text of **31**, and indeed cites *Liber C* in his only reference to the document (see p. 214), the 1447 inventory notes a charter for Weeley on fol 19 of *Liber B*, which would have immediately preceded the group of texts which Dugdale quoted.

The texts in the first edition of *St Paul's* were essentially reproduced in the *Monasticon*, with some generally minor variants; some of these may be authorial corrections and improvements, while others would appear to be corrections of printer's errors, especially in the case of Old English documents, where the use of a special font seems to have caused confusion. The second edition of *St Paul's* (published 1716 but compiled much earlier) also has a fair number of variants, some of them clear corrections and others perhaps printing errors. In this edition, variants from all three volumes have been given where the document survives only in Dugdale's works (**13, 22, 27**). In the case of documents preserved in medieval copies, only the variants in the *Monasticon* have been noted, to avoid overburdening the apparatus.

c. *GL 25501 (formerly St Paul's D. & C., WD 1:* Liber A) [E]

This is the largest of the early registers: hence its classification at the head of the series.[32] It was also known as the *Liber Pilosus*, apparently because its original covering was untanned leather; part of this, with writing on its flesh side, has been bound into the back of the volume. The earliest section of the manuscript (original fos 1–38) is a general cartulary begun in 1241, possibly as the result of the appointment of a new dean; the preliminary rubric runs: 'In hoc libro continentur transcripta omnium cartarum, cyrographorum et aliorum diuersorum scriptorum inuentorum in thesauro ecclesie sancti Pauli London' anno Domini. mccxl. primo'. The compilation took place in stages, with additions being made into the fourteenth century. A single scribe was responsible for fos 1–38 [original foliation]. Subsequently a second scribe, working 1241 × 1244, added another three folios (38*–40). Then from 1244 onwards the cartulary seems to have been regularly updated with the addition of groups of contemporary

---

[32] Davis, *Cartularies*, no. 597. See Gibbs, *St Paul's*, pp. xl–xli, for a description, and p. xi for classification of the registers according to size.

documents. The first section was edited by Marion Gibbs, who also calendared the contents of fos 38*–40.[33] The cartulary proper was foliated, but is now preceded by seventeen un-numbered pages: in this edition I have provided both the actual and the original foliation.

28 was copied at the beginning of the 1241 cartulary. The rest of the pre-Conquest charters in the manuscript were added between 1241 and 1244 in the first continuation, on fos 38*–39r: it is the same selection of documents as in *Liber L*, but in a slightly different order. The copying is poor, with personal names and place-names modernized or botched; and witness-lists have either been dropped or very much abbreviated, with the occasional substitution of a note such as *Ipsa nomina sunt in carta* (after **16**) or *et alii in carta* (after **12, 23**). In the list of estates in **12** Drayton has been replaced by Norton, and in **29** the donor has been altered from Æthelred to Alfred: this is probably poor copying rather than deliberate tampering. The principal value of *Liber A* lies in occasional references to the existence of a vernacular version of a Latin charter. After **12** comes the note 'Sequitur carta regis eiusdem in Anglico sermone de verbo in verbum' (possibly a mistaken reference to **13**); after **23** 'Hec eadem carta est in Anglico sermone de verbo ad verbum' (perhaps a mistaken reference to **22**); and after **31** 'Sequitur carta eiusdem Eadgiue in Anglico sermone de verbo ad verbum'.[34] The fourth instance is a little more complex; **21** (transformed into a charter of Alfred) is followed by the text of **26** and then by a note 'Sequitur carta predicti Aluredi Regis in Anglico sermone, de verbo ad verbum, sicut prescriptum est'. This should presumably be understood as a reference to a vernacular version of **21**, unless the scribe has become very confused and is referring to **27**, a writ of Cnut (see further discussion in the commentaries to the individual charters). These notes would seem to indicate that the scribe who copied these texts into *Liber A* was working from an existing collection, not from the original muniments. If he did not understand Old English, and was indeed referring to **13, 22** and **27** in his asides, then he may well have been using the material in *Liber B*.

In the early seventeenth century Richard James made a series of extracts from a St Paul's register under the heading 'Ex registro Radulphi de Diceto ex archivis sancti Pauli' (Bodleian, James 25, pp. 155–63). The heading would suggest that he was making use of one of the two registers associated with Dean Ralph: either his 'greater register' (*Liber B*) or his 'lesser register' (*Liber C*), as described in the 1447 inventory of Dean Lyseux (GL 25511, 95r, 98r); but

---

[33] *Early Charters of the Cathedral Church of St Paul, London*, ed. M. Gibbs, Camden Third Series lviii (London, 1939): cited here as Gibbs. She calendars the first continuation on pp. 279–80.

[34] A second hand has added a further note to this reference to a vernacular version of **31**: 'quam inuenies in quodam rotulo bullato. . .' See further above, p. 54.

Marion Gibbs has established that James was here copying from *Liber A*.[35] The extracts include a transcript of **28**.

d. *GL 25272 (formerly St Paul's, D. & C., A Box 69)* [F]

This is a roll headed 'Carte libertatum ecclesie sancti Pauli', which contains copies of around thirty royal writs of the eleventh and twelfth century.[36] It is ostensibly made up of two membranes, but the first has been extended or repaired, apparently before writing. It is written on both sides, with a copy of Edward the Confessor's writ (**28**) appearing at the top of the dorse. The rather artificial hand was originally identified as twelfth century, but is now securely dated to the late thirteenth century; the same scribe added a document of 1272 to *Liber A*.[37] Given the dating of the content, it may be that the scribe was copying an existing roll or codex; in one place there is a note that a charter also existed in Old English, followed by the beginning of the text and then a long gap. The scribe (or the scribe of his exemplar) may have been working from the original documents, for he sometimes provides press-marks in the left-hand margin. The language of **28** and of the two post-Conquest writs in Old English has been modernised, and the Confessor's writ has in addition been damaged by wear due to its position on the roll; its variants are not noted in this edition. See further discussion of this roll above, pp. 53–4.

e. *GL 25516 (formerly St Paul's, D. & C., WD 16,* 'Liber I') [P]

This register was compiled in the early thirteenth century and can be associated with the activities of Ralph Baldock, canon, dean of St Paul's and later bishop of London (1304–13), although there are later additions.[38] The first section comprises surveys and visitations from 1283, 1290, 1295 and 1298, including inventories of church ornaments and treasures. This is followed by surveys of individual manors and their documentation, including notes on the Domesday entries and details of initial donation. There are running references to the pancarta of King Æthelstan (**12**), with a summary version of the charter on 136r, and also references to **29** under Barling and Chingford. The Navestock section is preceded by a copy of **16** (73r), which may represent a text ultimately copied

---

[35] Gibbs, pp. ix–x.

[36] Davis, *Cartularies*, no. 598; *HMC 9th Report*, pp. 48–9; Gibbs, p. xliii n. 3. See Davis 1925 for some discussion of the content of the roll, with the erroneous twelfth-century dating. It is difficult to cite an exact number of texts, because some are only notes and others are incomplete.

[37] See Gibbs, p. xliii n. 3.

[38] *HMC 9th Report*, part i, App. p. 70.

from the pseudo-original, although the place-name and personal names have been modernized. The section on the glebeland at Lambourn (Berkshire), which passed into the possession of St Paul's after the Conquest, includes an Old English document from the later eleventh century describing the dues owed to the church there (40v). This is followed by a note identifying the document as a charter of Cnut, granting the property to St Paul's; this impression was evidently based on a misreading of the text (see below, p. 101).

f. *PRO Ch.R. 9 Edw. II, m. 12* [G]

An Inspeximus charter of Edward II dated 6 February 1316 includes the text of **28** (also Gibbs nos 11, 16, 21, 29, 46, 51). The original charter is not longer extant, but there is a copy on the Charter Roll for that year (9 Edw. II, m. 12, no. 37). The 1316 Inspeximus was confirmed with some additions by Edward III at Walton, 25 June 1338 (Ch.R. 12 Edw. III m. 8), and there were further confirmations by Richard II and succeeding rulers, each confirming the charter of his predecessor:

1. PRO Ch. R. 12 Ric. II, m. 22 (18 Nov., A.D. 1388);
2. Pat. R. 2 Hen. IV, pt 2, mm 29-8 (20 Nov., A.D. 1400);
3. Pat. R. 1 Hen. V, pt 4, mm 3-2 (1 Dec., A.D. 1413);
4. Pat. R. 2 Hen. VI, pt 3, mm. 15-14 (20 Jan., A.D. 1424);
5. Ch. R. 5–20 Hen. VI. no. 12 (same date);
6. Conf. R. 5, no. 10 (2 Rich. III);
7. Conf. R. 11, no. 9 (2 Hen. VII);
8. Conf. R. 16, no. ii (3 Hen. VII).

None of the original Inspeximus charters have survived. Edward III's Inspeximus was incorporated into the statutes of St Paul's, and is thus contained in GL 25520 (formerly St Pauls WD 20) and in Cambridge, University Library, Ee. v. 21: see the edition in Simpson, *Registrum statutorum*. A copy of Henry IV's Inspeximus of 1400 is to be found in BL Harl. Roll I 1.[39]

g. *Oxford, Bodleian Library, James 23, pp. 32–6* [H]

Richard James (1592–1638) was successively librarian to Sir Robert Cotton and to his son, Sir Thomas Cotton.[40] In his lifetime his publications were predominantly of sermons and poems, but a much broader picture of his scholarly and antiquarian interests is provided by forty-six books of manuscript notes which were acquired for the Bodleian Library in 1676, and which include the fruits of

---

[39] The roll was reported missing in July 2002. See Davis, *Cartularies*, no. 606; Gibbs, p. xliv, n. 1.

[40] For James, see *DNB*, and C.G. Tite, *The Manuscript Library of Sir Robert Cotton* (1994).

what appears to have been more than one visit to the St Paul's archive.[41] The most significant set of notes is a series of extracts from pre-Conquest diplomas, under the heading *Rotulus antiquus ecclesie sancti Pauli*, evidently taken from the same medieval roll that was studied by John Selden at around the same time.[42] James gives extracts from some eighteen pre-Conquest documents (**30, 17, 20, 24, 16, 22/3, 3, 2, 10, 4, 11, 6, 14, 15, 8, 9, 5**), and also refers to **27** and **28**. There is some overlap with the extracts made by Selden, but on the whole it would appear that the two scholars were taking notes from only a selection of the documents on the lost roll. James seems to have retained the order of texts in his exemplar, merely jotting down what caught his attention. All the indications are that he was a generally faithful copyist; Gibbs has compared his notes from *Liber A* with the texts in the cartulary and concluded that, while he omitted witness-lists and changed punctuation, he did not usually modify spelling or distort by capricious omission.[43] He also made an effort to reproduce Anglo-Saxon letter-forms, most noticeably in his extracts from **24** and **23**. A proposed reconstruction of the lost roll appears below, pp. 69–70.

h. *London, Lincoln's Inn, Hale 84, 93r–94r* [I]

John Selden (1584–1654) was an eminent and highly prolific antiquary, and an avid collector of medieval manuscripts. Much of his library and some of his papers passed to the Bodleian Library soon after his death. Other papers were retained by one of his executors, Matthew Hale (1609–76) and some of these were given when he died to the library of Lincoln's Inn (now represented by MSS Hale 11–13, 34, 84 and 86). Professor Simon Keynes has recently discovered that one of the Lincoln's Inn notebooks contains extracts from a *Rotulus cartarum in archivis ecclesie Pauline*, which would appear to have been the same roll seen by Richard James (MS Hale 84, fos 93–4).[44] There are three pages of notes, written in an often illegible secretary hand. The extracts are on the whole more substantial that those made by James, although there is also a series of very brief notes (see **19**b, **20**c). Selden expands upon James's extracts from **8, 10** and **17**; and provides one complete new text (**7**). He seems to be copying fairly accurately, as far as can be determined from the truly dreadful script, but he is given to adding English parentheses. He usefully

---

[41] James studied *Liber A* (Bodleian, James 25, pp. 155–63; see above, pp. 65–6), and various other St Paul's muniments: see Gibbs, pp. vii–viii.

[42] These were first studied and edited by Gibbs, pp. vii–x, 1–8.

[43] Gibbs, pp. ix–x.

[44] See Keynes 1993a for Selden and his manuscripts.

distinguishes between the texts on the face and those on the dorse, which makes possible a reconstruction of the lost roll (see next section).

i. *Reconstruction of the lost roll used by James and Selden*

The medieval roll with copies of pre-Conquest documents is the saddest loss to the archive. There is no certain trace of it after the time of James and Selden, although it may have been available to the St Paul's student responsible for BL Lansdowne 364, who seems to have had access to part of the archive during the period when the chapter was suppressed under the Commonwealth (see next section). Selden's notes show that the roll was written on both sides, as is the extant roll GL 25272 (formerly St Paul's, D. & C., A Box 69), which was produced in the later thirteenth century and which may represent transcripts of single sheets, including the original or pseudo-original of **28** (see above, p. 66). It is conceivable that the lost roll came into existence at around the same time (see pp. 53–4). The existing toll consists of two membranes sewn together, and contains the texts of around thirty documents; the lost roll may have been on a similar scale or even larger. Between them, James and Selden refer to some twenty-two pre-Conquest charters, plus the privilege of Pope Agatho. Their notes allow a hypothetical reconstruction of the sequence of texts.

Face

1) Both James and Selden begin with **17**.

2) Selden mentions a charter for Orsett (**19b**), and then another charter dated 986, probably for Crondon in Orsett (**20c**). James also has an extract from the 986 diploma (**20b**). Presumably the Orsett charter (**19**) preceded that for Crondon (**20**).

3) At this point Selden mentions a charter concerning *Sciredesforde* (**30**). James jotted an extract from the same diploma in the margin of his notebook opposite **17**; Selden probably gives a better idea of its location on the roll.

4) Selden now refers to Pope Agatho's privilege for St Paul's (Jaffé no. 2115; see pp. 75–6).

5) At this stage, both James and Selden give extracts from a royal writ, James from that of Æthelred (**24**), Selden from the closely related writ of Edward (**28**). James's note after the text of **24** suggests that Cnut's writ (**27**) was also to be found on the roll (what caught James's attention was the detail that **24, 27** and **28** all shared the same difficult abbreviation for *biscopes*). It can probably be assumed that the three writs occurred together in this location.

6) Selden now refers to Edward's confirmation of Agatho's privilege (**29**). This seems to connect naturally with the papal privilege and the three royal writs granting general privileges and immunity.

7) James gives instead an extract from a spurious charter concerning Navestock (**16**), and then part of two witness-lists, apparently from **23** and **22**. It is possible that these texts were located on the dorse.

Dorse

8) At this point the two antiquaries again both cite the same charter (**3**). Selden precedes the reference with a useful note *In dorso*.

9) James then mentions another early grant (**2**).

10) Both scholars give a long extract from **10**.

11) After this Selden seems to have omitted several texts noticed by James (**4, 11, 6, 14, 15**).

12) Both mention **8**. Selden follows it with the text of another toll-charter (**7**). This is his last extract.

13) James refers to **6A** and **9**, then concludes with extracts from a spurious charter (possibly two charters) recording a general grant of immunity by Coenred of Mercia, confirmed by Offa (**5a/b**).

j. *PRO DL 42/149* [J]

This is a collection of sketches of seals, with copies of some documents and notes on heraldry. An inscription on fol. 5 associates the volume with John Guillim (1565–1621), who served as Rouge Croix Pursuivant in the College of Arms; most of the notes are said to be in his handwriting, with additions made by Joseph Holland of Devonshire. The notebook was acquired by the office of the Duchy of Lancaster on 19 November 1810, at the Gough's sale at Leigh and Sothebys (inscription, 5v). Among the drawings are facsimiles of two St Paul's writs, **28** (see Plate 2) and William I's confirmation of the twenty-four hides said to have been granted by King Æthelberht (Bates, *RRAN: Acta of William I*, no. 187). Guillim has made a very good attempt at reproducing the script of the original (or pseudo-original) of **28**, and his text forms the basis of the current edition. The seal was broken and probably worn; his reproduction may be in part fanciful (see pp. 208–9). An almost identical, but less reliable, facsimile appears in a manuscript work on seals by John Anstis the Elder, who died in 1744 and was also associated with the College of Arms (BL Stowe 666; see below). The similarity is so great that it seems likely that Anstis was copying Guillim's work, or that both men were using the same intermediate exemplar.

k. *Oxford, The Queen's College, 88* [K] *and BL Cotton Jul. C. vii* [L]

A manuscript work on seals and heraldry by Robert Glover of Ashford in Kent (1544–88), now in the library of The Queen's College, includes a copy of the

PLATE I

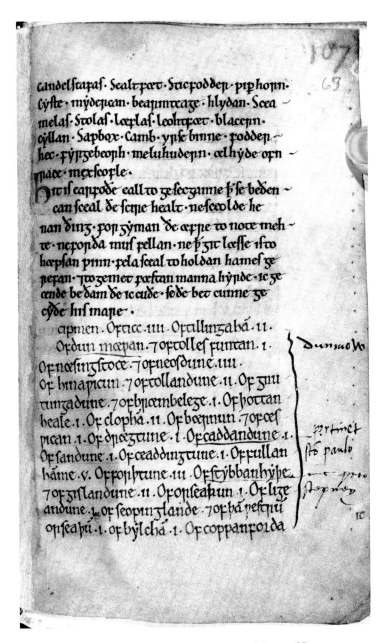

candelſtaƿaſ · ſealtƿæt · ſticƿoddeꞃ · piphoꞃn ·
cyſte · mydcꞃican · beaꞃꞃmtꞃæᵹe · hlydan · Scea
melaſ · ſtolaſ · læꝼlaſ · leohtꝼæt · blaceꞃn ·
cyllan · ſapbox · camb · yſeꞃ binne · ꝼoddeꞃ
hec · ꝼyꞃᵹebeoꝛh · meluhudeꞃn · ælhyde oꞃn
ꝼace · meꞃſcoꝼle ·

Hit iſ eaꞃꝼode eall to ᵹeſecᵹanne ꝥ ſe beden
can ſceal de ſcꞃe healt · ne ſceolde he
nan dinᵹ · ꝼoꞃ ᵹyman de æꝼꞃe to noꞇe meh
ꞇe · neꝼoꞃda muſ ꝼellan · ne ꝥ ᵹꞇ læſſe iſ to
hæꝼſan pꞃꞃꞃ · ꝼela ſceal to holdan hameſ ᵹe
ꝼeꞃan · 7 to ᵹemeꞇ ꝼæſtan manna hyꞃde · ic ᵹe
cende be dam de ic cuðe · ſe de beꞇ cunne ᵹe
cyðe hiſ maꞃe ·

cꞃmen · Oꝼꞇicc · iiii · Oꝼꞇillinᵹabá · ii ·
Oꝼdun mæꝼan · 7 oꝼꞇolleſ ꝼunꞇan · i ·
Oꝼ næſinᵹſtoce · 7 oꝼneoſdune · iiii ·
Oꝼ hꞃnaꝼicꞃꞃ · 7 oꝼꞇollandune · ii · Oꝼ ᵹꞃꞃ
ꞇinᵹadune · 7 oꝼbꞃꞃcꞃmbeleᵹe · i · Oꝼhoꞇꞇan
heaſe · i · Oꝼ clophá · ii · Oꝼ bꞃꞃꞃnun · 7 oꝼcœſ
ꝼican · i · Oꝼ dꞃꞃᵹꞇuine · i · Oꝼcaddandune · i ·
Oꝼ ſandune · i · Oꝼ ceaddinᵹꞇuine · i · Oꝼꝼullan
háme · v · Oꝼꝼoꞃꝰꞃune · iii · Oꝼſꞇybbanhyꝥe ·
7 oꝼᵹꞃſlandune · ii · Oꝼoꞃſeaꝥun · i · Oꝼ liᵹe
andune · i · oꝼ ſeopꞃꞃᵹlande · 7 oꝼ ꝥá ꝼeꞇꞃꞃꞃ
oꞃ ſeaꝥú · i · oꝼ bylehá · i · Oꝼcoppanꝼoꞃda

Cambridge, Corpus Christi College, 383, fol. 107r (**25**)

PLATE 2

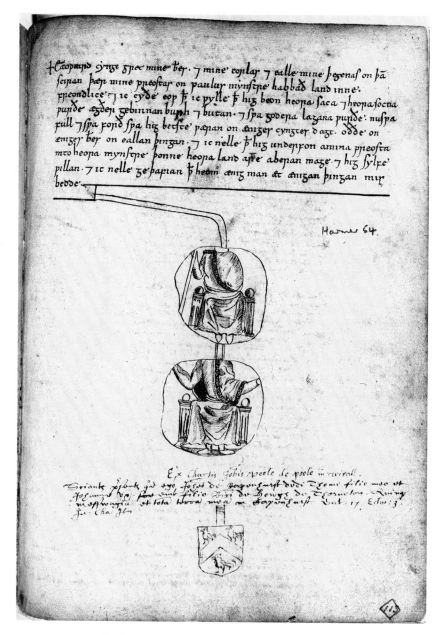

London, Public Record Office, DL 42/149, fol. 113r (**28**)

broken seal of King Edward's writ (**28**), with a transcription in partly imitative script. It has the heading 'A Saxon Charter of King Edward the Confessor' and a concluding note 'with this very seale broken just in this manner'. The same heading and note accompany a similar facsimile in a notebook compiled in about 1611 by Nicholas Charles, Lancaster Herald, who died in 1613 (BL Cotton Jul. C. vii). Charles's text is rather better than Glover's and certainly not copied from it, so it would appear that both men were making use of an existing copy of the writ and seal, presumably dating from the mid sixteenth century. The two manuscripts also have a copy of the same writ of William I (Bates, *RRAN: Acta of William I*, no. 187) that appears in Guillim's notebook (see previous section). There is some possibility that all three scholars (together with the rather later John Anstis: see below) were all drawing upon the same intermediate transcription of the original (see the commentary to **28**).

1. *BL Lansdowne 364, 134r* [M]

This volume is a bound collection of originally loose notes by a single seventeenth-century scholar. On the recto of the first folio is a large signature, J. Franklin, and the date 1684; Franklin was the St Paul's archivist at this date. It is not at all clear whether Franklin was the original note-taker. The only real clue to the latter's identity appears on fol. 136r, which is headed: *A noat of such writings as I sent up in a chest from Tewin* [Herts.] *to my Uncle Dr* <?*Layford, Layfield*> *at London March 29 1659* [altered from 1658] *belonging to St Paul's Church* (see above, p. 59). The volume now consists of 145 folios, with several additional separate sheets folded and bound inside the back cover. This is clearly only a selection of the available manuscript notes; the original pagination ran to p. 586, and there is a later foliation to 310. Fols 4–7v contain an unpolished narrative history of St Paul's down to the immediately post-Conquest period. This shows an awareness of several of the church's charters that were preserved in the cartularies (presumably these were derived from *Liber A*, for fols 125–30 consist of notes from this volume). The bulk of the notes are extracts from and paraphrases of fairly modern records relating to the recent history of St Paul's and the individual prebends, including a quantity of accounts and leases from the sixteenth and earlier seventeenth century.

It proves difficult to date this collection of notes. Gibbs (p. viii) suggested that the compiler was working for the cathedral chapter in around 1632. Some details would indeed support the view that he was active in the decade before the chapter was suppressed under the Commonwealth. A list of deans (fol. 32rv) seems originally to have ended with the name of John Donne and the date 1622; after this, and perhaps added subsequently, is the name of Thomas Wynniffe and

the date March 1641. Wynniffe was appointed dean in 1631 and made bishop of
Lincoln in December 1641. There are numerous references to individual prebendaries, who seem to represent the penultimate and ultimate office-holders before
the events of the 1640s. However, the notes also mention documents as late as
1646 (fol 41r), and the memorandum on St Paul's muniments cited above (fol.
136r) shows that the note-taker was still active in 1658/9. One possible explanation, which takes into account the information in the memorandum, is that the
compiler of BL Lansdowne 364 had access during the 1640s and 1650s to a part
of the St Paul's archive which was not surrendered to the parliamentary commis-
sioners, and which did not therefore come into the hands of the Mr Reading with
whom Dugdale had dealings (see discussion above, pp. 57–9). Although the
notetaker was interested in the remote history of the chapter, he was more concerned with contemporary documentation, especially leases and other agreements. It is conceivable that he was a member of the chapter who took part of
the archive away with him when he and his fellows were dispersed, and who
spent some time researching the material in order to clarify the tenurial situation
of the prebendal lands in the years before the upheavals of the Commonwealth,
perhaps with his eye fixed on some future restoration.

The notebook is full of interest and deserves fuller study, but in the present
context two entries rate particular attention. On fol. 134r, under a heading
Formulae Fundationum cum Anathemat' Fundatorum, appears a series of very
brief extracts from eight pre-Conquest charters, consisting mainly of anathemas
and formulas claiming spiritual motivation. The first two extracts are from a
charter of Edgar granting seventy hides to St Paul's (**18**), which is otherwise
unknown, and a diploma of Æthelred dated 982, which is conceivably related to
a text mentioned by Selden (**19**). Next comes an anathema, apparently from a
text dated 986; again there is a possible connection with a text on the lost roll
seen by James and Selden (**20**). The remaining extracts are less useful. There is
another anathema, of the standardised form first devised in the early 960s and
associated with the charter-scribe known as 'Edgar A': it is possible that the
source was **17**, a diploma of Edgar on the lost roll. A third detached anathema
corresponds with that in **21**, and that is followed by a dispositive phrase also
seen in **26**, both documents being forgeries found in the main cartularies: it is
possible that the formulas in fact derive from the (lost) models used for the fabrication. Next follows a brief motivation clause, either from **12** or **29**, followed
by four words from the corresponding clause in **3**. The final extract is a further
motivation clause, which cannot be linked with any extant document: 'de ecclesiæ Pauli ut illic habitantes serui Domini pro meis peccatis interueniant, pro
redemptione animæ meæ atque parentum meorum'. It is not possible to ascer-
tain the source of these extracts, but it may have been the case that the notetaker

had access to the roll used by James and Selden, or else to a separate compilation of early documents.

Also of interest is a list of fourteen estates on 145v, under the heading is *Privilegia et Terræ concessae*.[45] The list runs:

1. *Manerium de Fulanham* (i.e. Fulham, *cf.* **3**)
2. *Manerium de Tyrranham* (perhaps for Tillingham, *cf.* **1**)
3. *Gillingas* (i.e. Ealing, *cf.* **2**)
4. *Gillanduna* (i.e. Islington, *cf.* **10**)
5. *Hæmela* (i.e. Hemel, *cf.* **4**)
6. *Heddaham* (i.e. Hadham, *cf.* **17**)
7. *Willaham* (bis)
8. *Mealduna* (Maldon, Essex, or Malden, Surrey)
9. *Scopingland* (i.e. Shopland, *cf.* **14**)
10. *Horscada* (i.e. Orsett, *cf.* **15**)
11. (?) *Berfled*
12. *Berlingas* (i.e. Barling, *cf.* **29** and S 1522)
13. *Bacanuella*.

The forms of the place-names are early, and several of the estates correspond with charters on the lost roll. It seems possible that they were taken from the same source as the formulas on 134r.

m. *Bodleian, Dodsworth 10, 8r* [N]

Among the papers of Roger Dodsworth (died 1654) is a copy of **1**, from an unspecified source. It was clearly not taken from the slightly abbreviated version of the texts in *Liber A*. Not surprisingly, the closest links are with the printed text in the *Monasticon*, which derives from *Liber B*. It is however clear that the *Monasticon* text was not based directly on this transcript, and it seems likely that Dugdale generated his version directly from *Liber B*.

n. *BL Stowe 666* [O]

John Anstis the Elder (1669–1744) was Garter King of Arms, and a prolific antiquary. His manuscripts came into the possession of Thomas Astle in 1768, and now form part of the Stowe collection in the British Library. They include a two-volume manuscript work on seals entitled *Aspilogia sive de Iconibus scutariis gentilitiis commentarius*, with additions by Thomas Astle, now Stowe 665 and 666. Anstis included many drawings and fascimiles of ancient documents,

---

[45] First printed by Gibbs, p. viii n. 2.

including a Christ Church writ (S 1088) and the Confessor's writ for St Paul's (**28**). The facsimile is discussed below, pp. 208–9. It is very similar indeed to the facsimile in the notebook of John Guillim (PRO DL 42/149; see above), an earlier member of the College of Arms, which may indicate that it was copied from Guillim's notes or from a common intermediate exemplar, rather than directly from the original or pseudo-original of **28b** (see pp. 70–1).

4. THE AUTHENTICITY OF THE CHARTERS

Assessing the authenticity of texts in the St Paul's archive presents peculiar problems. When a charter is preserved only in the form of a brief extract, analysis is a matter of gauging probabilities. It seems very likely indeed that the diplomas which were the source for extracts such as **2, 3, 4, 6, 9, 14** and **15** were genuine and contemporary: one can point to the contemporary formulation, the ancient form of the place-names and personal names, and the acceptable historical context. Even here we may suspect some interference, for example in the hidage in the Fulham grant (**3**); and it is possible that the full texts would have had worrying internal contradictions. Other fragments are less convincing: neither the formulation nor the detail of **18** is easily compatible with a diploma of Edgar; and the extracts from supposed grants of privileges by Coenred and Offa (**5**) are intrinsically suspicious. Sometimes too little survives for any valid judgement: thus the dating clause printed here as **11** derives ultimately from a genuine diploma of Æthelstan, but it may have been attached to a later fabrication (compare S 434–6).

In the case of longer extracts and full texts, we are on stronger ground. The ship-toll privileges (**7, 8**) and the Islington charter (**10**) carry conviction because they are closely related to reliable documents preserved in other archives. Other charters are instantly recognisable as late forgeries, such as the blanket confirmations of lands and privileges in the names of Æthelstan (**13**), Æthelred (**21**) and Cnut (**26**): there are no acceptable examples of documents of this type from Anglo-Saxon England. It proves particularly difficult to assess the authenticity of writs surviving only as later copies, for these brief and stereotyped texts were easily adapted and multiplied by forgers. Four writs are printed in this edition, three from St Paul's (**24, 27, 28**) and the *Cnihtengild* writ from Holy Trinity, Aldgate (**32**). This last seems more likely than not to be acceptable. The Confessor's writ for St Paul's (**28**) survived in single-sheet form into the early modern period and was reproduced in facsimile in several antiquarian notebooks; some details raise the possibility that this was a pseudo-original, forged rather later than its implied date. The writ of Æthelred (**24**) is very unlikely indeed to be authentic, while Cnut's writ (**27**) has some persuasive features.

Two pairs of forgeries in the archive are especially interesting. The creators of **1** and **16** modelled their texts on genuine early diplomas which no longer survive. In the case of **1** the exemplar was a very early text, datable to 670 × 676: the forger used the witness-list and some of the formulation of this lost diploma to concoct a charter in the name of Æthelberht of Kent, which had the useful double function of providing a title-deed for an important estate and of commemorating the ancient origins of St Paul's. The fabrication of **16** was less painstaking: to create a diploma in the name of Edgar the forger simply reproduced much of the formulation of a diploma of 867, substituting the names of Edgar and Oda for those of the original donor and archbishop, and altering the dispositive section to make this a grant to St Paul's (it is possible, although not certain, that the exemplar also concerned the same estate). Both **1** and **16** were already in existence when *Liber L* was compiled in the second quarter of the twelfth century. **16** was perhaps forged in connection with post-Conquest disputes about the Navestock manor after the Conquest, but it is more difficult to put a date to **1**. Alongside these two texts one may wish to consider **22** and **23**, Æthelflæd's grant of Laver and Cockhampstead and the supposed confirmation of this by King Æthelred, the latter also copied into *Liber L*. There may be some kernel of genuine documentation here, but the texts have been burdened with impossible witness-lists, indicating some degree of interference. These estates were not held by St Paul's in 1066 or subsequently, but both are mentioned as having been 'restored' by King William I in his spurious 'coronation-day' diploma, along with Navestock and other estates (Bates, *RRAN: Acta of William I*, no. 183; see pp. 102–3): there was clearly a post-Conquest claim of some kind, which may have led to falsification or 'improvement 'of the documentation.

Two further related fabrications are the confirmations of St Paul's lands by Æthelstan (**12**) and Edward the Confessor (**29**). Again both documents were already in existence when *Liber L* was compiled in the second quarter of the twelfth century. It has been recognised that these two texts are closely related to diplomas in the the archive of Chertsey Abbey—S 752 in the name of King Edgar, and S 1035 in the name of the Confessor; and it has been pointed out that St Paul's and Chertsey must therefore have colluded in the production of fabricated documents.[46] There is good reason to think that it was the Chertsey texts which provided the inspiration for the St Paul's forgers: **12** appears to be a poor adaptation of S 752, and **29** is probably a later concoction on the basis of **12**. A further facet of the collaboration between the two houses was the creation at St Paul's

---

[46] Whitelock, *EHD*, p. 371. I am currently preparing an edition of the Chertsey charters for this series.

of a privilege in the name of Pope Agatho addressed to Bishop Eorcenwald (Jaffé no. 2114; BCS 55), which is evidently based on the Agatho privilege for Chertsey (Jaffé no. 2115; BCS 56).[47] This privilege and Eorcenwald's journey to Rome are referred to in S 752 and 1035 (and therefore also in the derivative St Paul's versions, **12** and **29**). It is probable that one motive for fabrication at St Paul's was a desire to co-opt the Chertsey tradition of papally-derived immunity from episcopal interference. The St Paul's Agatho privilege explicitly forbids Eorcenwald to seize any of the rights and property of the community, and also includes a clause which was evidently supposed to relate to the issue of recruitment to the chapter, but which is actually a spectacularly poor adaptation of two passages in the Chertsey privilege. The latter first has a provision making the election of a new abbot the sole responsibility of the Chertsey community, followed by a passage giving the monks the controlling decision over the choice of who was to be consecrated priest or deacon. The compiler of the St Paul's privilege appears to have borrowed several formulas and to have combined them without really understanding them; while his intention would seem to have been to confirm the chapter's right to select a new priest for their number when one had died, the passage actually seems to be claiming the right to elect the bishop.[48] Control over chapter lands and recruitment were burning issues in the later eleventh and early twelfth centuries, as the canons struggled to assert their claims of autonomy (see above, pp. 48–9). There seems to be a very good chance that the St Paul's privilege was forged against the background of the establishment of the prebendal system in the time of Bishop Maurice, who was to apologise for his conduct and promise to restore the chapter's rights and privileges. It is also probable that **12** and **29** were fabricated at the same time, as the canons took steps to produce impressive title-deeds for those estates which remained communal lands after the prebends had been hived off.

The pattern of authenticity and fabrication among the St Paul's muniments has a very interesting aspect. If we exclude the writs, then the charters granting land and/or privileges fall into two main categories. On the one hand are the texts which most likely represent authentic and contemporary documentation. These include fourteen records of transactions involving land (**2, 3, 4, 6, 6A, 9, 10, 14, 15, 17, 19, 20, 30**) and two 'ship-toll' charters (**7, 8**). As has already been noted (see p. 51), essentially all those estates which can be identified (and which still belonged to the London Church after the Conquest) formed part of the

---

[47] Anton, *Studien*, p. 65 n. 62. The Chertsey privilege is likely to be fundamentally authentic (*ibid.*, p. 61 n. 59, p. 68 n. 71, p. 69 n. 73, p. 121 n. 188).

[48] It is of course possible that such was indeed the forger's intended meaning; for the background in relation to monastic sees, see Knowles, *Monastic Order*, pp. 627–9.

bishop's holdings in 1066/1086, as opposed to the endowment allocated for the support of the chapter. The only real exception is **10**, which covers land at Islington. This was a St Paul's manor in 1066, but seems to have been reckoned under the bishop's lands *c.* 1000 (see **25**, and p. 156); there is an added complication that part of Islington later came under the bishop's manor at Stepney (see p. 199). The second main category of charters is the archive is formed by those documents which cannot be accepted in their present form, or which are clear fabrications. These include five land-charters (**1, 16, 18, 29, 31**), a will and its confirmation (**22, 23**), three wholesale confirmations of the lands of St Paul's (**12, 13, 21**) and a grant of privileges (**5**). With the exception of **18**, all these documents were preserved in the St Paul's cartularies and (not surprisingly) deal with the estates and privileges of the chapter.

There would appear to be a connection between the non-survival of genuine early title-deeds for the canons' lands, and the production of a string of forgeries (including the general confirmations), which probably took place in the late eleventh or early twelfth century. One possibility is that the pre-Conquest muniments of the chapter were at some stage stored separately from the bishop's charters, as a consequence of the early division of the endowment (see pp. 51–2), and that they were destroyed or mislaid. This would provide a context for the fabrication of replacements after the Conquest, and the use of models from Chertsey. It may also explain why the St Paul's community was so energetic in seeking confirmations of its lands and privileges from the Anglo-Norman kings. But it is also possible to suggest other scenarios. The chapter may have been dissatisfied by its pre-Conquest muniments (some of which may have named the bishop as beneficiary) and may simply have replaced them with forgeries that presented a more eligible picture. Once the fabrications were in existence, the genuine muniments may have been neglected or deliberately destroyed.

Note on the formulation of early charters from the London diocese. It is now accepted that the Anglo-Saxon Latin charter descends from the late Roman private deed.[49] The earliest surviving examples date from the 670s, leading to suggestions that the introduction of such written records was due to the influence of Archbishop Theodore (669–90).[50] But a fairly good case can be made that charters were being produced in England before Theodore's time; the lack of surviving earlier examples can perhaps be explained by the use of papyrus, which is far less durable than parchment in a damp climate.[51] One good reason to extend the

---

[49] Levison, *England and the Continent*, pp. 224–33; Chaplais 1965, 1968.

[50] Stenton, *ASE*, p. 141; Whitelock, *EHD*, p. 375.

[51] See P. Chaplais, 'Who Introduced Charters into England? The Case for Augustine', *JSA* iii.10 (1969), pp. 526–42 (repr. in Ranger, *Prisca Munimenta*, pp. 88–107); Kelly 1990; *eadem, St Augustine's*, pp. lxxiii–v.

prehistory of the Anglo-Saxon charter is the fact that the diplomas produced in
the 670s and 680s already show distinct regional characteristics; Kentish charters
are recognisably different from their counterparts in West Saxon and West Mercian
archives. In the seventh century, beneficiary production seems to have been the
norm, with charters often being drawn up by monastic scribes, but it can also be
assumed that bishops and their secretaries had an important role to play.

The early diplomatic of the London diocese is represented by several fragments
from St Paul's (**2, 3, 4, 6**) and by charters preserved in the archives of Barking
(S 1171, 1246), Chertsey (S 1165, 1247), Canterbury (S 65, 100), Winchester
(S 235, from Farnham minster) and Westminster (S 1248, from Barking). These
documents have a distinctive character. There is a particularly strong inter-
relationship between the formulation of S 1165 and S 1171, from Eorcenwald's
two foundations at Barking and Chertsey, and also links with the Farnham
diploma (S 235), where Eorcenwald is one of the witnesses: it has been suggested that the London bishop drafted all three diplomas.[52] He would also have
been responsible for the three documents in his own name (S 1246–8). On a
more general level, the charters of the London diocese share some wording and
elements of formulation in with West Saxon diplomas of the same period; the
common features have been identified as a persistent 'humility formula'; the dispositive verb *decrevi*; the inclusion of a blessing; and similar themes in the
anathema.[53] The formulation of the brief fragments from St Paul's can be linked
with other East Saxon charters, and more generally with some West Saxon texts:
the wording of the dispositive section in **2** has elements in common with S 1171;
the dispositive verb in **3** is *decreveram*, and there are links with several West
Saxon diplomas of the same period (S 1164, 1169, 1245); the proem of **6** is
almost identical to that of S 1248 (the wording of **4** poses rather more difficulty). It has been pointed out that Eorcenwald had a close connection with the
West Saxon kings (he is described by Ine as 'my bishop'); the inference would
seem to be that responsibility for shaping the character of East Saxon diplomatic
could be laid at the door of the most celebrated and influential early bishop of
London.[54] This seems a very plausible suggestion, but it is possible to propose
an alternative version of events—Eorcenwald's predecessor, Wine, had previously been bishop of Winchester, and when he arrived in London in 666 he is
likely to have been accompanied by clerics from his former see (see above,
p. 10). It can be assumed that over the course of the eighth century the diplomatic of the London diocese developed away from the 'West Saxon' model,

---

[52] Chaplais 1968, pp. 328–30 (pp. 78–81); Wormald 1985, p. 9.
[53] Wormald 1985, pp. 9–11, 30; for a summary guide to West Saxon diplomatic, see Edwards,
Charters, pp. 309–13.
[54] Wormald 1985, pp. 9–11.

but there is almost no material for analysis. Of the two 'ship-toll' privileges, **7** has certain features in common with the earlier model, while **8** shares some technical formulation with a related Kentish document; there is some possibility that the shared elements of the general formulation of the 'ship-toll' privileges of Æthelbald's reign reflect the practice of the London scriptorium.

5. THE ESTATES OF THE BISHOPRIC OF LONDON AND ST PAUL'S

The patchy pre-Conquest archive is of limited value in tracing the accumulation of the landed endowment of the bishops of London and the St Paul's community. In partial compensation, there are two pre-Conquest documents which throw some light on the church's holdings in the middle of the tenth century and *c.* 1000: the will of Bishop Theodred (S 1526: edited below, Appendix 2) and a document relating to the naval levy on the St Paul's estates (**25**). The Domesday survey provides information about the lands of the bishop and chapter in Middlesex, Essex, Hertfordshire, Bedfordshire and Surrey. London itself is not covered in Domesday, but this omission is in part rectified by a survey of the London lands of St Paul's, compiled *c.* 1130.[1] After the Conquest the estates of the St Paul's are very well-documented indeed; there is, for instance, an almost complete catalogue of the cathedral prebends and their holders from about 1086, and valuable evidence about the exploitation of the communal manors.[2] Questions arise concerning the extent to which this later material can be extrapolated backwards to fill in gaps in our knowledge of the Anglo-Saxon endowment.

Evaluation of the evidence is far from straightforward, and some general issues need to be addressed at once. In the first place, recent discussion has tended to assume the essential stability of the St Paul's endowment; in particular, it has been suggested that it may be possible to identify certain substantial estates as ancient endowment, in the continuous possession of the bishopric from as early as the seventh century.[3] The present discussion takes a more sceptical attitude towards this material, and will stress the evidence for a relatively volatile episcopal estate. Thus it seems significant that, of the nine estates

---

[1] GL 25504, 47r–50v; edited and discussed in Davis 1925 (possibly a revision of an earlier survey: see Martin 1991, p. 29).

[2] Brooke 1951; Faith 1994.

[3] The St Paul's endowment has been the special study of Pamela Taylor: see her unpublished Ph.D. thesis, 'The Estates of the Bishopric of London from the Seventh Century to the Early Sixteenth Century' (London, 1976); and Taylor 1980, 1990, 1992, 1995, 2002; and her chapter in Keene, forthcoming. I am very grateful to Dr Taylor for her comments.

mentioned in connection with St Paul's in Theodred's will (datable to *c*. 950), only six would appear to have been still in the possession of the church when **25** was compiled *c*. 1000, and only five of these still belonged to the bishop and chapter in 1086 (William I having recently restored Southminster). At one stage the pre-Conquest archive at St Paul's would have included a quantity of documentation illustrating the complex interplay of forces shaping the endowment, in the form of (mostly vernacular) wills, private charters, deeds of sale and exchange, records of dispute settlements and of the everyday management of the estates and their produce. Only a few Anglo-Saxon archives preserve this type of material in any significant quantity (most notably Christ Church, Worcester and Bury St Edmunds); for the most part it has simply disappeared. Such documents supplement the inflexible and sometimes misleading testimony of royal diplomas, and without them it can be very difficult to produce a realistic picture of the growth and management of the endowment. An additional problem at St Paul's is the possible destruction of the portion of the pre-Conquest archive that related to the acquisition of the lands allocated to the canons; the charters which seem to reflect genuine early landbooks essentially relate to the episcopal holdings (see pp. 51–2, 76–7).

It seems useful to give some consideration here to the general patterns of ecclesiastical landholding in Anglo-Saxon England. One point to bear in mind is that pre-Conquest endowments were not built up solely through the largesse of kings and other landholders, with any losses due to unscrupulous seizure (although that is often the impression given by later sources).[4] Church lands were actively managed: isolated or inconveniently distant estates might be sold or exchanged for more desirable property, with a view to consolidating holdings or acquiring land suitable for specialised exploitation. For instance, between 971 and 984 the bishop and St Paul's exchanged a recently-acquired estate at Milton in Cambridgeshire for one at Holland in Essex, close to land already in the church's possession (see below, pp. 96–7). Holland belonged to St Paul's in *c*. 1000 (see **25**), but would appear to have been alienated before 1066. In addition, land might be purchased: as early as 704 × 709 the bishop of London bought an estate at Fulham from the bishop of Hereford (**3**); and his successor also handed over a substantial sum of silver for another, unidentified property (**6A**). Some land would have passed to the church as a result of bequests and gifts, and these estates would not always have been conveniently placed for exploitation. Milton was a donation, while Bishop Theodred gave St Paul's land at Southery in North Norfolk; both possessions appear to have been disposed of quickly. It is probably correct to recognise, as a general principle, that churches

---

[4] For a fuller discussion of these issues, see Kelly, *Abingdon*, pp. cxxxi–liii.

would seek to consolidate their lands: which means that larger holdings may in certain cases represent a series of piecemeal acquisitions, rather than single big donations.[5]

Furthermore, arrangements for the exploitation of estates could lead directly to losses. Some of the church's lands would have been farmed in demesne, but other properties would be let out to tenants, perhaps for a limited period (a typical Worcester lease in the tenth century lasted for 'three lives', i.e. those of the original lessee and two heirs), perhaps on a longer-term basis. The only evidence from St Paul's for a pre-Conquest lease comes from the ninth century, when the bishop and community leased out land at Braughing in Hertfordshire to a thegn in return for a down-payment and an annual rent (**9**); the tenant was given the right to pass on the estate to members of his kindred, and only if his family died out was the land to return to ecclesiastical possession. This arrangement was beneficial to the tenant, who could in many ways regard this land as his hereditary property: there was always a risk that the church would lose its rights over the property. Further problems might arise when the church was the beneficiary of a deferred bequest, which seems to be a fairly common arrangement in Anglo-Saxon England. Æthelflæd, widow of King Eadmund, promised St Paul's the reversion of an estate at Hadham, but the church had to wait until after the deaths of her sister and brother-in-law before it received the property (**17**; S 1494, 1486). A deferred bequest of Lisson Green seems to have gone astray when the testator's widow married another man (see p. 103). A pair of difficult diplomas in the archive may relate another bequest that was not fulfilled or was subsequently upset (**22, 23**). Promises of reversion, other gifts that were challenged by the family of the donor, long leasehold arrangements: transactions of this type meant that St Paul's would have had fluctuating claims on various estates which were not really under its control.

Other ambiguities could affect the endowment of an episcopal church. A bishop could own property in his own right as well as controlling the episcopal estate (as did Theodred); there was a danger that the church lands might be diverted to the bishop's kindred, through beneficial leasing or by becoming confused with the heritable lands. Land at Twickenham was granted to Bishop Wealdhere in 704 (see S 65); in the next century it was in the possession of a priest who may have belonged to Wealdhere's family, and who in turn passed the estate to Christ Church, Canterbury (S 1414; see further, pp. 18, 87). The eleventh-century Bishop Ælfweard may have despoiled St Paul's in order to benefit the monastery at Evesham, where he had been abbot (see p. 121). A particularly vexing question concerns the relationship between the episcopal

---

[5] See the general comments in Clarke, *English Nobility*, pp. 55–60.

endowment and the lands of the independent minsters within the diocese. There is evidence from elsewhere that bishops, particularly in the eighth and ninth centuries, were anxious to exert control over the local minsters and that in some cases this involved absorbing their lands into the episcopal estate. The evidence from London is sparse, but it is probably significant that the document relating to the lease of land at Braughing by the bishop and chapter (**9**) provides for the ultimate reversion to a minster dedicated to St Andrew (perhaps at Braughing); it is possible that this land had been taken over by the bishop from an originally independent local church (see further below, p. 89).

The second important debate concerns the date at which the St Paul's community began to control its own lands, without reference to the bishop. Unique among cathedral chapters, the canons of St Paul's are treated as tenants-in-chief in respect of their lands in the Domesday surveys of Essex and Hertfordshire. There have long been suggestions that this situation reflects an unusually early separation of assets between the bishop and the St Paul's community, perhaps already in operation in the time of Bishop Theodred in the mid tenth century, possibly even earlier. The evidence for these claims requires careful treatment, for there are important issues of definition. At Canterbury, which has a very large and well-preserved pre-Conquest archive, it is clear that certain estates were already being allocated for the maintenance of the Christ Church community *c.* 800; there are diplomas from the early ninth century which show an archbishop donating land to, and exchanging estates with, his cathedral community. But it is also clear that the archbishops still had overall control of these allocated lands at the time of the Domesday survey, although soon afterwards Christ Church began to operate more independently, a pattern seen in other chapters in the twelfth century. The situation with regard to the St Paul's community was evidently different in 1086, but it is a moot point whether the London church was simply in advance of the general development or whether the arrangement had more ancient roots. An important question is whether the chapter had suffecent corporate identity to act as an independent body in the pre-Conquest period, making its own decisions about property.[6]

a. *The original endowment*

The establishment of an episcopal seat in London in 604 almost certainly entailed the donation of some portion of land for the maintenance of the church and community. The walled city was sparsely populated, perhaps essentially

---

[6] There is a very useful survey of these issues in Crosby, *Bishop and Chapter*. See also above, pp. 44–6.

deserted in the seventh century: there is a possibility that St Paul's acquired at this stage quite substantial intramural areas which were used for orchards and gardens. The community may also have had an early territorial footing in the developing extramural port settlement of *Lundenwic*.

Post-Conquest sources from St Paul's ascribe to the first founder, Æthelberht of Kent, the grant of twenty-four hides to the north of the walled city, an area apparently roughly corresponding to territory represented by the canons' Domesday manors of Rug Moor, Tottenham (Court), St Pancras, Islington, Hoxton, and *Stanestaple*.[7] The earliest documentary evidence for this claim of ancient endowment consists of two writs in the name of William I: he orders that the twenty-four hides given to St Paul's by King Æthelberht be quit of shire and hundred and all other customs; and, more expansively, he makes it known that these lands, given by Æthelberht when he founded the church, were to be exempt from danegeld and all other gelds, from military service and other burdens.[8] A writ in the name of William II is apparently a reiteration of the second, longer writ, but does not have a specific reference to Æthelberht; nor does a writ of Henry I again ordering that these twenty-four hides be free of gelds, customs and services, as stipulated by the writs of his father and brother.[9] If these documents are genuine, then they show that the canons were already claiming by the 1080s that these lands constituted ancient endowment and were therefore entitled to special privileges.[10] But such a claim could have the status of a useful myth, based on Bede's statement that Æthelberht bestowed lands and possessions upon the bishopric of London (Bede, *HE*, ii. 3); it need not have a basis in reality.[11]

---

[7] Gibbs, p. xxiv; GDB 127v–128r; *DB Middx* 3:19–29; see comment in Keynes 1993a, p. 315. This area was later carved into several prebends, including Moorfields, St Pancras, Camden and Islington. There seem to have been fluctuating ideas about the exact location and extent of these twenty-four hides, for instance on the issue of whether Stoke Newington should be included: see, for example, Lansdowne 364, 6r.

[8] Bates, *RRAN: Acta of William I*, nos 187–8 (pp. 610–13); Gibbs, nos 11, 16 (pp. 14, 17). Bates notes that the briefer writ could belong to William II, but ascribes it to the Conqueror on the grounds that St Paul's was very active in obtaining writs from William I to support its property and liberties. The shorter writ was extant as an original or pseudo-original in the sixteenth or seventeenth century, when facsimiles were included in various antiquarian compilations, alongside comparable copies of **28** (see pp. 70–1, 73).

[9] Gibbs, nos 8, 27 (p. 13, 23).

[10] Some of the claims are likely to be exaggerated. If these twenty-four hides were free of geld (as indicated in Gibbs no. 16), it is difficult to explain why there are Domesday entries for several manors here.

[11] Bede's reference to Æthelberht's generosity also covered the bishoprics of Canterbury and Rochester. St Augustine's in Canterbury forged charters in Æthelberht's name supposedly granting estates which had actually been acquired and built up in later centuries (S 2–4; Kelly, *St Augustine's*, nos 1–3). The episcopal community at Rochester also produced a spurious diploma of Æthelberht (S 1; Campbell, *Rochester*, no. 1).

The only pre-Conquest document which explicitly touches on the history of these lands is the Islington charter of 903 (**10**), which shows that ten hides in the area had been granted by King Coenwulf of Mercia (796–821) to a layman as hereditary property, and that this estate was still in lay hands in the early tenth century. Another factor which needs to be taken into account is the question of whether Æthelberht of Kent would have been in a position to make a grant of land in Middlesex; and it is also questionable whether a grant made in the early seventh century would have persisted over the subsequent decades when the clerics were expelled from London. On the whole, it seems best to take a sceptical view. There may well have been valid traditions that the London church had ancient possessions to the north of London, and some of this territory may even have been held on a fairly continuous basis since the restoration of the London bishopric in the second half of the seventh century; but the block of lands represented by the twenty-four hides of the eleventh century and later is more likely to reflect centuries of consolidation than a single ancient grant. There is one possible pre-Conquest reference to this area which may be illuminating. The document relating to the naval levy on the episcopal estate *c.* 1000 (**25**) mentions a place called *Hinawicun*, 'the (dairy-)farms of the religious community'. An earlier identification with Wickham St Paul's in Essex is untenable, and there is reason to think that the place referred to here was located between Neasden and Islington, and thus in the approximate area of the 'twenty-four hides' (see p. 196). The use of the plural form would suggest that there were several farms here which contributed to the supplies of the chapter.

Æthelberht is also said to have granted to Bishop Mellitus land at Tillingham in Essex for his monastery at St Paul's. The charter to this effect is an egregious forgery, partly based on a document of the early 670s which is unlikely to have had any connection with Tillingham (**1**). However, it has been argued that this estate may indeed have been a very ancient possession of the see.[12] The factors of location and size have been cited: the Domesday assessment of twenty hides has been thought to point to 'a large and primitive holding', and the estate's proximity to the seaboard has also been seen as significant. More pertinent is the fact that the Tillingham manor is in the same general area as the site of the Saxon Shore fort of Othona, the *Ythancæstir* where Bishop Cedd established a minster in the mid seventh century (i.e. at Bradwell-on-Sea; Bede, *HE*, iii. 22; see above, p. 10). It has been argued that the lands surrounding the fort must have formed part of the ancient holdings of the bishopric. Another detail, of uncertain relevance, is the reference by Bede to a second minster founded by Cedd, at Tilbury, where the first element of the place-name is apparently the

[12] Hart, *Danelaw*, pp. 208–9.

same fairly rare personal name Til(l)i. Tillingham is mentioned in the will of Bishop Theodred, where it is one of four estates which he bequeathed to the St Paul's community for its maintenance; at least one of the other estates mentioned in this context was Theodred's personal property, and the overwhelming likelihood is that all four places belonged to him, rather than representing existing possessions of the see (see below, p. 91). It is worth bearing in mind that we have no evidence that a minster founded by Bishop Cedd would necessarily continue to be regarded as episcopal property after his death: indeed, the converse may be the case, for there is evidence from elsewhere of minsters being associated with their founder and his family or followers rather than with the bishopric. A third minster linked with Cedd was Lastingham in Northumbria, which he founded after becoming bishop of the East Saxons and left to his brother to organise; he evidently visited Lastingham regularly and indeed died there in 664 (Bede, *HE*, iii. 23). Rather than considering Bradwell minster and its endowment in terms of episcopal property, it may be more valid to see it (at least in the seventh century) as an independent ecclesiastical institution within the London diocese. Episcopal control over independent minsters was a burning issue in the eighth and earlier ninth centuries (see the commentary to **9**), and it is possible that the Bradwell at some stage became an episcopal possession: but it cannot simply be assumed that this happened. Many early minsters failed to survive for economic or political reasons, with the devastation of the ninth-century Viking raids and occupations apparently providing the coup de grâce in many instances. It is highly unlikely that the Bradwell community would have been able to remain at the site during the late ninth and early tenth centuries; the minster was too exposed to sea raids, and the Danish occupation of parts of Essex would have made it very difficult for the brethren to cultivate or draw income from its estates. It may have been the case that communal life ceased at Bradwell during this time, and that its estates subsequently came into royal or other secular possession. This scenario would provide a route for the land to have passed to Theodred as his personal property, and then to have been given by him to St Paul's.[13] 'Chich' (St Osyth), another of the estates which Theodred bequeathed to St Pauls', may also have been the site of an early minster abandoned in the ninth century (see p. 195).

---

[13] At the time of the Domesday survey the area of the Roman fort and the surviving early church at Bradwell were not included in the St Paul's Tillingham estate. There were two small manors in the area, both assessed at 1.5 hides: one held TRE by Thorkell and later by the Norman abbey of St Valéry (LDB 21r; *DB Essex*, 14:6), identified as the manor of East Hall in Bradwell; and the other held by Wulfmær TRE and later by Hugh de Montfort (LDB 53v; *DB Essex*, 27:12), identified as the manor of Battails in Bradwell (see *VCH Essex*, i. 392–3). Tilbury, the site of Cedd's other minster, was also in lay ownership TRE and afterwards.

Another of the great Domesday estates of the see which has been argued to have been part of Æthelberht's foundation grant is Stepney, immediately east of London.[14] The first documented reference is in **25** from *c.* 1000, where the levy from the estate is stated to have been two sailors. The episcopal manor of Shepney was assessed at fifty hides in the Domesday survey, and included Hackney and perhaps also a detached area at Clerkenwell, to the west of the twenty-four hide block claimed by the canons as Æthelbert's donation.[15] Taken together, Stepney and the chapter lands would represent a St Paul's holding that virtually encircled the city to the north and east. The argument runs that land in the Stepney area was in a highly strategic location in relation to the city, and that Æthelberht would be a more likely donor of a block of territory here than any later ruler; but the grounds for this assumption are unclear. There is no decisive evidence to show that the core of the Stepney estate was necessarily an ancient land-unit, rather than an aggregation of smaller holdings (one of them the Bromley estate which was assessed separately in **25**). The place-name indicates that the settlement from which Stepney developed would have been at one stage associated with a certain Stybba; the focus was 'Stybba's landing-place', probably located on the gravel at Ratcliff Cross.[16] It is debatable whether land to the east of London could be regarded as strategic in the middle Saxon period, when the focus was on the Strand settlement and the walled city was essentially deserted; and it should also be noted that later kings and sub-kings were not slow to grant important estates in the London area to other religious houses.[17] While there is a possibility that Æthelberht or (rather more probably) some other early ruler granted a large estate at Stepney to the bishop of London, there is no real evidence to support the suggestion (and no sign of any claim to that effect in the St Paul's sources). In fact, one piece of evidence militates against the suggestion that the London church had continuous possession of Stepney from the seventh century. Bishop Theodred's will (which is discussed below) appears to list all the significant episcopal estates *c.* 950; it refers to *Lundenbyri(g)*, which has been understood to include extramural property at Stepney, but is more likely to refer specifically to the area within the walls (i.e within the *burh*).

[14] Taylor 1980, 1990; and Taylor in Keene, *St Paul's Cathedral* (forthcoming).

[15] GDB 127rv; *DB Middx*, 3:1–11; see Taylor 1990 for the Clerkenwell identification.

[16] *VCH Middx*, xi. 13; *PN Essex*, pp. 149–50. The personal name may also occur in Stebbing, a village in Essex near Great Dunmow: see *DEPN*, p. 440, and also in the bounds in S 683.

[17] Compare, for instance, Barking, which acquired substantial areas in Middlesex from King Æthelred of Mercia, as well as a huge estate at Battersea from Cædwalla of Wessex and land *iuxta* London from Wulfhere of Mercia, according to an early list of donations in S 1246. Commenting on this material, Hart suggests that Wulfhere's donation, ostensibly of a single hide, was actually of fifty hides (*ECEE*, p. 142).

b. *The endowment between Eorcenwald and Theodred*

St Paul's assiduously promoted the cult of Bishop Eorcenwald (*c.* 675–93), but did not credit him with obtaining any lands for the church. By contrast, Eorcenwald's minsters at Barking and Chertsey remembered receiving generous gifts (see S 1171, 1246, 1248; and S 1165); one wonders whether the bishop was more energetic in building up the endowments of his personal foundations than in soliciting gifts for the community at St Paul's (see above, p. 11). There is far more information about acquisitions under Eorcenwald's successors, Wealdhere and Ingwald. The former was granted three substantial estates in western Middlesex: ten hides in the area of Ealing by Æthelred of Mercia, specifically to support the *vita monasterialis* in the city of London (**2**); fifty hides at Fulham by a bishop of Hereford, for which Wealdhere made a payment (**3**); and thirty hides at Twickenham in a joint grant by the East Saxon king and a Mercian *comes* (S 65; Brooks and Kelly, *Christ Church*, no. 9). This pattern of donation reflects Mercian domination of western Middlesex in this period. Another East Saxon king granted land in Hertfordshire, probably in the Vale of St Albans (**4**). Of the places named here, only Fulham and Ealing remained in the possession of the London Church in the later Anglo-Saxon period.[18] In the early ninth century the thirty-hide Twickenham estate formed part of the *patrimonium* of a priest named Werhard, who bequeathed it to Christ Church in Canterbury (S 1414; Brooks and Kelly, *Christ Church*, no. 64).[19] It would appear from the charter (S 65) that Twickenham was a personal grant to Wealdhere, rather than to the bishopric; he may have alienated it, or bequeathed it to a member of his family.[20] The Hertfordshire estate at *Hæmele* (*cf.* Hemel Hempstead) cannot be matched with the later holdings of the bishop and chapter, and would seem to have been lost or deliberately alienated, perhaps as part of a process of retrenchment.

Bishop Ingwald was granted a vast area of seventy hides at *Deningei* on the Essex seaboard by the East Saxon king Swæfred (**6**). The place-name ('marsh-island of the *Dæningas* tribe') survives in Dengie, a village just south of Tillingham; it also gave its name to Dengie hundred.[21] Some or all of the land granted to Ingwald still belonged to the bishopric in the mid tenth century, for it

---

[18] In later records Ealing was reckoned under the manor of Fulham (*VCH Middx*, vii. 144).

[19] Christ Church had lost Twickenham by 1066, but continued to assert its claim in a series of forged charters (S 132, 477, 515, 537). Twickenham became part of the seventy-hide manor of Isleworth, held by Earl Ælfgar TRE; this included land at Isleworth claimed by Barking as an early possession (S 1246).

[20] It has been suggested that Wealdhere, Werhard and Werhard's kinsman Archbishop Wulfred were all members of the same Middlesex kin-group (Brooks, *Church of Canterbury*, pp. 141–2).

[21] *PN Essex*, pp. 213–14; *DEPN*, p. 141.

is clearly to be connected with the episcopal estate at *Denesige* mentioned in Bishop Theodred's will. There were two large Domesday manors in the Dengie area belonging to St Paul's: the bishop's thirty-hide estate at Southminster and the canons' twenty hides at Tillingham, the latter apparently acquired through a personal bequest by Bishop Theodred.[22] The name 'Southminster' was already current in *c.* 1000 (see **25**), and is thought to have been coined to distinguish a church built there from Bradwell minster to the north; by 1066 Dengie village was in other hands, which suggests some reorganisation of the area, possibly linked with the seizure of Southminster by Cnut (see below).[23]

Apart from a brief note by Richard James which is apparently taken from a document concerning Ingwald's purchase of an unnamed estate (**6A**), there is no further record of land-acquisition in eighth century. But the survival of two charters granting remission of toll on trading-ships to Bishop Ingwald is a reminder that the London Church is likely to have drawn at least part of its income from commercial business, linked with the great emporium at *Lundenwic* on the Strand (**7, 8**; and see above, pp. 6–7). Almost nothing at all is known of the history of the London church during the reigns of the powerful Mercian overlords Offa (757–96) and Coenwulf (796–821). Offa was remembered at Canterbury and elsewhere as a predator on ecclesiastical lands, in part in the interests of building up a network of royal minsters that were intended to remain the hereditary property of his family. But he seems to have been responsible for founding and promoting the monastery at St Albans, perhaps providing it with a London base at the church of St Albans Wood, associated with a royal palace in the Cripplegate Fort area (see above, pp. 8–9). Coenwulf is known to have made a grant of land at Islington to one of his *comites* (see **10**); this land was later reckoned as part of the ancient endowment of St Paul's, perhaps tendentiously (see above, pp. 83–4), and one might wish to argue that the donation represented a deprivation of the London Church. But there seems to be no general context for the Mercian kings to wish to damage the interests of St Paul's, and far more reason for them to try to underpin the support of an episcopal see in such an important location. The reigns of Offa and Coenwulf seem to have coincided with a precipitate decline in status of the local East Saxon kings, which altered and possibly limited the pattern of donations for the London Church; but any losses in this area could have been balanced by generosity of the much wealthier

---

[22] LDB 10rv, 13r; *DB Essex* 3:9, 5:5.

[23] *PN Essex*, p. 225; the first reference cited there is incorrect, since the charter in question was concerned with Minster-in-Thanet, also known as 'Southminster' in the ninth century. Thorkell held 2.5 hides at Dengie TRE (LDB 21rv; *DB Essex*, 14:7); he was also the owner of land in the area of St Peter's chapel at Bradwell. A second Dengie estate of the same size was held by Siric TRE (LDB 24r; *DB Essex*, 18:22).

Mercian kings who regularly visited the city. There is simply no evidence to assess the situation.

Equally, there is no way to assess the impact on St Paul's of the events following the West Saxon victory over the Mercians at Wroughton in 825, which may have left the London diocese partitioned (see pp. 19–20). The only St Paul's record from the period is 9, according to which the bishop and the St Paul's community made a grant to Sigeric, a thegn of the Mercian king Wiglaf, of ten hides at Braughing in Hertfordshire; the beneficiary was empowered to bequeath the land to his family (*genus*), but when his relatives (*propinqui*) had died out, the land was to pass to the church of St Andrew (? at Braughing). Sigeric paid a large sum for the land, and undertook to pay a yearly rent in money and kind. This is effectively a tenancy agreement, but one particularly favourable to the tenant (since the land would be very difficult to regain). It is possible that the bishop and the St Paul's community were exploiting land which had previously belonged to a minster at Braughing which had come under episcopal control. There was certainly a minster-church there by *c.* 1000, which was perhaps a revival of an earlier house (S 1497; Crick, *St Albans*, no. 7). By this time any links between St Paul's and Braughing seem to have been severed, although the territory remained within the London diocese (see p. 153).

It would be highly unsafe to take the Navestock diploma of 867 (**16**) as evidence of a genuine donation to St Paul's at that date, attributed to the tenth-century king Edgar only through some innocent error. The charter as it stands is a forgery, and the wording of the reference to the beneficiary is completely unconvincing: it seems very clear that the forger's model was a diploma in favour of a different beneficiary and that the reference to St Paul's is a substitution. It is also impossible to be certain that the model was actually a diploma for Navestock. **16** is best treated as a fabrication based on a ninth-century diploma found in the archive and co-opted for the purpose; the forgery may be connected with eleventh-century disputes over Navestock (see p. 173). All that can be concluded is that land there was in the possession of the bishop and chapter *c.* 1000, since Navestock is mentioned in **25**.

St Paul's and its lands are likely to have been severely affected by the Viking raids, which intensified from the second quarter of the ninth century onwards. The church may have lost a significant source of income as commerce contracted, and far more than that during the periods of Danish occupation of the City. Its estates would have been raided and perhaps devastated: little is likely to have remained at Fulham after the Danish army over-wintered there in 878–9. The situation may have begun to improve when Alfred of Wessex entered London in 886 and began refurbishments, but Essex remained a zone of conflict until 917. Some insight into the massive economic disruption caused by this continuing warfare is provided by the annal for 895 in the Chronicle: at this point the Danes had established themselves in a fortress on the Lea, only twenty miles above London, and King Alfred found it necessary to position his English army near the city to give Londoners the chance of taking in the harvest without being attacked (see p. 128). There was also the question of tribute: in 872, when the Danes were camped in London, the church at Worcester had to lease out part of its estates to pay the immense tribute (S 1278). The effect on a front-line church, with its lands devastated and occupied, is likely to have been very much greater, and it seems probable that the London church was deeply impoverished at the beginning of the tenth century. The privilege of Æthelstan confirming St Paul's properties (**12**) cannot be used as evidence here, since it is a forgery of *c.* 1100.

c. *The will of Bishop Theodred*

A far more reliable source of information is the will of Bishop Theodred, preserved in the archive of Bury St Edmunds (and edited below in Appendix 2, pp. 225–8). The will is datable to between 942, when the bishop acquired one of the estates mentioned in the text (*cf.* S 483), and the death of the testator between 951 and 953. When the will was drawn up Theodred was bishop of an area which appears to have covered not only the traditional area of the London diocese but also the southern East Anglian diocese of Dunwich, which had foundered in the ninth century. The temporary merging of the two dioceses can be seen as a first step in the re-establishment of an episcopal structure in areas that had been settled by the Danes (see above, p. 29). It is clear from the will that the bishop was a major local land-owner in his own right: he bequeathed three estates in Cambridgeshire and (?) Norfolk to the king, and various estates in Suffolk to members of his own family. Theodred made diverse bequests to St Paul's, which are listed immediately after the bequests to the king. First come the portable goods: the bishop's two best chasubles with all the things that belong to them, a chalice and one cup, his best mass-book and the best of his own collection of relics.[24] Then Theodred gives details of four estates which he intended to bequeath to St Paul's, specifying that the slaves working on them were to be freed for the sake of his soul. Firstly the estate at 'Chich' (St Osyth) on the Essex coast, as *beodlande* (i.e. to provide food for the community from its income). Next the estate at Southery in Norfolk, with its fishing

---

[24] A thirteenth-century St Paul's inventory refers to relics donated by Bishop 'Theodore' which were preserved in the cover of an ancient gospel-book (see below, p. 118). This may be a reference to Theodred's bequest.

(a supply of fish was essential to any religious community); the estate at Tillingham in Essex as the property (*are*) of the community; and finally the estate at Dunmow, also in Essex. It has been suggested that these four estates represented all the lands held by the St Paul's community (as distinct from the bishopric) in the mid tenth century, and that they were already in the possession of the cathedral when the will was drawn up: thus 'this section of the will is better regarded as an acknowledgement of their existing rights that as a grant *de novo*'.[25] This argument is very unlikely to be correct.[26] The bequests to St Paul's appear in the will between two passages concerned with the distribution of estates which are evidently Theodred's personal property, while the wording of the text does not include a single detail that indicates that the bequests to St Paul's were confirmations. One of the four estates, Southery in Norfolk, had been granted to Theodred in 942 as his personal property, with the right to bequeath it as he pleased (S 483).[27] The suggestion that Tillingham was an ancient possession of the see is not backed by any reliable evidence (see above, pp. 84–5). Similarly, the argument that 'Chich' (St Osyth) was an early episcopal estate is purely speculative (see pp. 85, 195).

If these four estates were, as seems most probable, bequests of personal property to St Paul's, then it would follow that they are unlikely to represent the whole of the lands available for the maintenance of the community: rather, these estates would be an extension of existing provision for this purpose.[28] It is of some interest that only one of the four places was under the control of the canons in 1066. A possibility that should be borne in mind is that the provisions of the will were not fully implemented. If they were, then Southery was probably the first to be detached from the community's possession, in line with the principle that governed the disposal of distant estates in favour of less vulnerable and more convenient properties. Southery is not mentioned in **25** from *c.* 1000, and by 1066 the manor was in the possession of Bury St Edmunds, with an assessment of two carucates (LDB 209r): since the landbook was also preserved in the Bury archive, it seems probable that an exchange had taken place between the two communities (analogous to the perhaps contemporary exchange of a Cambridgeshire property with Ely Abbey, discussed below). The other three estates of the will head the list of *scipmen* in **25** (for the details, see p. 195);

[25] Hart, *Danelaw*, p. 213.

[26] Taylor 1992, p. 290.

[27] Hart argues that it was the custom of the bishop to give to the chapter such lands as he had acquired outside his diocese (*Danelaw*, p. 213 n.); but there is nothing to substantiate this suggestion (Taylor 1992, p. 290 n. 16). Note that Norfolk may conceivably have been part of Theodred's diocese at this time (*cf.* Campbell 1996, p. 44).

[28] Taylor 1992, pp. 290–1.

but Dunmow had slipped from the church's possession by 1066. At the time of the Domesday Survey, 'Chich' (St Osyth) was an episcopal manor, with Tillingham the only one of the four estates of the will that was still controlled by the chapter.

After detailing the bequests to St Paul's, Theodred goes on to cover the land-grants to his relatives, to the church at Mendham (possibly a family minster) and to the abbey of Bury St Edmunds. This section seems to complete the disposal of his bookland: subsequently he is concerned with bequests of money and other goods, and of future arrangements with respect to the episcopal estates under his control. Pious bequests involve the grant of five pounds to every episcopal see (probably for distribution to the poor, or liturgical commemoration) and five marks of gold to the archbishop. More particularly, Theodred provides for the distribution of ten pounds within his diocese (*bishopriche*) 'in London and outside London',[29] and ten pounds in his diocese at Hoxne in Suffolk: clearly the London and southern East Anglian dioceses had not been merged in any formal sense and were still regarded as separate entities, although headed by a single bishop. Theodred goes on to name six episcopal estates: Hoxne, 'London' (*Lundenbyri*), Wimbledon and Sheen in Surrey, Fulham in Middlesex and 'Dengie' (*cf.* Southminster) in Essex. He mentions these in the context of his wishes for the disposal of the stock (*erfe*) which he has added to these estates: what he found on the estates was to remain there, but the stock which he had acquired was to be divided into two, with half for the 'minster' and half for his soul. In addition, the slaves were to be freed. Exceptionally, the estate at Fulham was to be left as it stood, unless anyone should decide to free the slaves.

Almost certainly that these six named places represent the principal demesne estates of the London and southern East Anglian dioceses in the middle of the tenth century.[30] It is of some interest that the latter was apparently supported only by the estate at Hoxne; lack of resources may have been a significant factor in the delay in re-establishing the East Anglian dioceses in the tenth century.[31] Fulham and 'Dengie' (Southminster) had been acquired by the bishops of

---

[29] The translation of *biscopric* causes difficulties here. In *Wills* and *EHD*, Whitelock initially translated the word as 'episcopal demesne', but later preferred the more neutral 'bishopric' (*Councils & Synods*, pp. 79, 80). Taylor used the translation 'episcopal demesne' as the basis for a restrictive interpretation, taking the *biscopric* outside London as an explicit reference to Stepney (Taylor 1992, p. 290 n. 15). But the sums mentioned are fairly substantial, and assuming that they were intended for the relief of the poor it would seem most probable that the distribution was for the whole diocese, not just as Taylor assumes (in the London context) within the City and in Stepney.

[30] Taylor 1992, pp. 290–1.

[31] The see would seem to have been transferred to Elmham in the second half of the tenth century (Campbell 1996, p. 15). The priests at Hoxne are mentioned in a will of 1035 × 1040 (S 1489). Hoxne was an episcopal manor in 1066 (LDB 379r; *DB Suffolk*, 18:1).

London in the eighth century (**3, 6**). It has been suggested that the estate at *Lundenbyri* included extramural property represented by the episcopal lands at Stepney, identified as possible ancient endowment (see above, p. 86);[32] however, the place-name incorporates the element *byrig* and should probably be understood as a specific reference to the area within the walled city. Neither of the two Surrey estates (Wimbledon and Sheen) were held by the bishops of London in 1066; and their absence from **25** suggests that they had been alienated by *c.* 1000, possibly in line with a general tendency to dispose of land outside the diocese proper (although **25** refers to two other Surrey estates, the land in Bedfordshire, and possibly also to places in Suffolk). The 'Wimbledon' property may have been exchanged with or sold to the archbishop of Canterbury, for part of the later parish there was a member of the archbishop's great Domesday manor of Mortlake.[33] Sheen (later Richmond) was associated with the royal manor at Kingston-on-Thames in post-Conquest sources.[34]

It is very unlikely that these five estates comprised the whole of the endowment allocated for the support of the bishop and his household. The provisions in the will are concerned with the distribution of stock and the freeing of slaves, and would only apply to the larger demesne estates—the bishops would almost certainly have owned additional properties which were leased out to tenants, in return for food-rents and money payments. It is argued below that the naval assessment list of *c.* 1000 (**25**) falls into two parts, with the first eighteen places named representing the endowment of the chapter, and the final fifteen estates being associated with the bishop and his household. Some of the 'episcopal' estates named in **25** can be shown to have been acquired in the half century after the production of Theodred's will (such as Orsett, Holland and Shopland), but others may have been existing possessions which were held by tenants when Theodred's will was drawn up. It is possible that such a background may account for the 'invisibility' of any Stepney holdings in the middle of the tenth century.

To conclude, Theodred's will names the principal demesne estates of the bishopric, and mentions several bequests to St Paul's: but it is not a comprehensive overview of the holdings of the bishop and cathedral community in the mid tenth century. The document indicates that at some level the lands of the bishop and of St Paul's were already being managed separately. The cathedral community

---

[32] Taylor 1992, p. 290 n. 15.

[33] GDB 30v–31r; *DB Surrey* 2:3; *cf.* Blair, *Surrey*, p. 25; Taylor 1992, p. 297. The only Surrey holding of the London Church in Domesday Book, the canons' eight-hide manor of Barnes, was a dependency of Mortlake.

[34] Blair (*Surrey*, pp. 99–100) argues that Sheen fell within the *parochia* of an early minster at Kingston.

might hold an estate as its own property (*are*; see the Tillingham bequest), but other lands might be held on different terms, which is the implication of the reference to *beodland* in the bequest of 'Chich'. It may be significant that 'Chich' was classed with St Paul's estates in **25**, but was an episcopal manor in 1066; the community might have had full title to lands held as *are*, but a lesser claim to *beodland*. This distinction indicates that there was not yet a firm division between episcopal and chapter lands, although there would seem to have been some development in this area. Finally, the volatility of the endowment should be stressed: two of the five demesne estates had been alienated by *c.* 1000, and two of the four estates bequeathed to the community no longer belonged to the London Church in 1066.

d. *Bequests and grants c. 950–c. 1000*

Some patchy details of acquisitions during the following half century can be extracted from the fragmentary texts in the St Paul's archive, and from more complete documents preserved elsewhere. There is little evidence for direct royal donations. In 957 Theodred's immediate successor, Brihthelm, was given ten hides at Orsett in Essex by Edgar, then king of the Mercians (**15**). A generation later, perhaps in 982, there was a royal grant of another Orsett estate to a deacon named Werenberht (**19**); this would seem to have passed into the hands of the bishop before *c.* 1000, and to account for the reference to two separate Orsett estates in **25**. In 986 King Æthelred granted an area of woodland as an appurtenance to the second estate, either to Werenberht or to St Paul's (**20**). Two spurious texts credit Edgar with the grant of Navestock and a seventy-hide property, possibly at Southminster (**16, 18**).

Shortly before Theodred's death, Ælfgar, ealdorman of Essex, had stipulated in his will that the inheritor of his estate at Heybridge in Essex was to pay an annual food-rent to the community at St Paul's (*then hird at Paulesbiri:* S 1483, A.D. 946 × *c.* 951). Later his two daughters remembered the London Church in their wills. Æthelflæd, the second wife of King Edmund, left the estate at Hadham in Hertfordshire which she had acquired from King Edgar (**17**) to her brother-in-law, Ealdorman Brihtnoth, and her sister Ælfflæd, on condition that after their deaths it passed to St Paul's in London as episcopal property (*into Paulusbyrig æt Lundænæ to bisceophame*; S 1494, A.D. 975 × 991). Ælfflæd survived her husband, and in her own will she fulfilled her sister's bequests with regard to Hadham, granting it to St Paul's minster as episcopal property (*to biscophame*; S 1486, A.D. 991 × *c.* 1000; for the dating, see below, p. 177). She also bequeathed the Heybridge estate to St Paul's for the use of the community (*tham hirede to brece*), again apparently at the request of a relative.

The terminology of these wills repays attention. Ælfflæd apparently considered 'St Paul's minster' as an appropriate designation for both bishop and community: she specified that one estate was to be used for episcopal purposes and the other to support the community. Neither Hadham nor Heybridge figures in **25**, possibly because Ælfflæd's will had not yet taken effect when it was drawn up. At the time of the Domesday survey Hadham was indeed an episcopal manor, while Heybridge belonged to the canons.

Two other wills of the period mention bequests to the bishops of London. Æthelric of Bocking granted land at Rayne (*be westan*) in Essex to St Paul's for the bishop, to pay for lights and preaching (*into sancte Paule tham bisceope togeleohtenne and thar on Godes folce cristendom to dælenne*), and also two hides at an unidentified place which were held by a rent-paying tenant (S 1501; Brooks and Kelly, *Christ Church*, no. 136). In addition, he bequeathed certain pieces of property specifically to Bishop Ælfstan (who died in 995/6), probably as a personal bequest, since he also requested the bishop's protection for his widow. This property consisted of woods and fields to the east of the road which Æthelric gave to the bishop *into Coppanforde* (? for the estate at Copford), plus an enclosure at Glazenwood. The wording indicates that the bishop already owned Copford, and that the bequest was of appurtenances to be added to the estate, rather than of Copford itself. The will was drawn up at some point between 962 and the death of Bishop Ælfstan (probably later rather than earlier), but it was not immediately implemented, for an attempt was made to confiscate Æthelric's property after his death. Eventually the will was confirmed by King Æthelred, at some point between 995 and 999 (S 939; Brooks and Kelly, *Christ Church*, no. 137). It is possible that not all the bequests were fulfilled, and it may be that the personal bequests to the late Bishop Ælfstan fell by the way.[35] St Paul's did not yet hold the estate at Rayne when **25** was drawn up *c*. 1000, although it was an episcopal estate in 1066.[36] Copford is mentioned in **25**, perhaps because bishop Ælfstan's existing holding there had passed to the episcopal estate after his death. There is some interest in the provision that the bishop was to use the revenue from Rayne to pay for lights and preaching in the cathedral; at St Paul's the bishop continued to have a responsibility for cathedral costs well into the twelfth century, although elsewhere such burdens had been shouldered by the chapter by this time.[37]

---

[35] An early list of Christ Church estates, which can plausibly be associated with the year 1002, does not mention the property which that church was to have inherited from Æthelric (S 914: see discussion in Brooks and Kelly, *Christ Church*, no. 140).

[36] LDB 10r; *DB Essex*, 3:8.

[37] Edwards, *Secular Cathedrals*, pp. 120–4.

In a will precisely dated 998 and preserved in the Westminster archive, Leofwine son of Wulfstan bequeathed an estate at Barling in Essex to *minum hlaforde Wulfstane bisceope* (S 1522); the land was probably initially Wulfstan's personal property, but it later passed into the endowment of the bishopric and was allocated to St Paul's before the Conquest. Once more it does not figure in **25**, no doubt because it was not acquired by the church until after *c.* 1000. A charter in the name of Edward the Confessor was subsequently forged to provide a better title-deed for the estate (**29**).

Finally, it is necessary to consider **22**, the bequest of four hides at Laver and two at Cockhampstead, both in Essex, by a woman named Æthelflæd to St Paul's, for the maintenance of the community; **23** purports to be King Æthelred's consent to the bequest. Something is seriously wrong with the witness-lists of the two texts; **23** may be an outright forgery, but **22** could have a genuine basis. Neither Laver nor Cockhampstead was among the lands of the bishopric *c.* 1000 or in 1066, but they are mentioned in the forged 'Coronation Day' charter of William I among a number of estates said to have been stolen in the reigns of his predecessors (see pp. 102–3); there was evidently a disputed claim which led to falsification of documentation.

A passage in the *Liber Eliensis* describes the circumstances behind the acquisition by St Paul's of an estate of five hides at Holland on the coast of Essex. A certain Abbot Thurketel was expelled from his house at 'Bedford' and petitioned Bishop Ælfstan and his clergy that he might become a member of the community at St Paul's, with which he had a prior connection: 'where previously he had purchased himself a place among the priests'.[38] However, the

---

[38] Blake, *Liber Eliensis*, p. 105: 'In eadem villa habuit etiam Thurchetelus abbas iiii hydas et dimidiam. Qui eo tempore, quo expulsus erat de Bedeford, petiit ab episcopo Lundoniensi, nomine Ælfstano, et a clero, ut cum eis posset habere communionem et partem in monasterio ubi prius in presbiteratu emerat sibi locum, sed episcopus cum toto clero recusavit eum. Tandem vero usus consilio et patrocinio amicorum hereditavit sanctum Paulum de iiii hydis et dimidia, quas habuit apud Mideltune, ut in illorum contubernio esse posset. Quod cum factum fuerat, ipse, quamdiu vixerat, tenuit eandem terram de fratribus, hoc est de clero, dans eis quotannis inde xx solidos. Post mortem vero ipsius utebantur ipsi clerici illa terra, sed cum iniuriosa difficultate. Qui cum multas iniurias paterentur ibi, concupivit tandem Brihtnothus abbas eandem terram ab eis vel ad censum vel ad mutationem, si forte habuisset tantundem terre, que prope esset eis, infra comitatum. Interea contigit quod avia Ædgari regis, nomine Eadgiva, cum moreretur, dimisit cuidam nobili matrone, que dicebatur Ælftreth, v hydas in Estsexe apud Holand, quas ipse emerat a Sprowe pro xx libris. Tunc predicta matrona, scilicet Ælftreth, dedit illam terram sancte Ætheldrethe. Æthelwoldus vero episcopus et Brihtnothus abbas totusque cetus monachorum de Ely tradiderunt eandem terram sancto Paulo et clero Lundunensi pro iiii hidis e dimidia de Middeltune. Dederunt etiam pecuniam pro pecunia, superhabundabant tamen apud Holande c oves et lv porci et duo homines et v boves subiugales'.

bishop and all the community rejected him. At length, depending on the advice and influence of his friends, he made over to St Paul's (*hereditauit*) an estate of four and a half hides which he had at *Mideltune* (probably Milton in Cambridgeshire) so that he could join the *contubernium* (probably meaning 'confraternity': i.e. he would not have been a full member of the St Paul's community, but would have had a connection with it).[39] Thurketel retained possession of the estate, but paid to St Paul's a rent of twenty shillings a year. After his death, the community kept the estate, but apparently only with difficulty, probably due to its distance from the rest of its endowment. It happened that Abbot Brihtnoth of Ely was anxious to acquire Milton, either by purchase or exchange. Eadgifu, the grandmother of King Edgar, had bought five hides at Holland in Essex from a man named Sprow for £20; this property she bequeathed to a woman named Æthelthryth, who in turn gave it to Ely. The Holland estate was adjacent to the St Paul's land at 'Chich' (St Osyth) on the Essex seaboard, and was an acceptable exchange for the troublesome Cambridgeshire property. The transaction was thus effected, with the assistance of Ely's patron, Bishop Æthelwold of Winchester; the stock of the two estates was simply exchanged, and the Ely chronicler carefully notes an excess at Holland which comprised 100 sheep, 60 pigs, two slaves and five oxen. The exchange must have taken place between the foundation of the monastery at Ely *c.* 971 and the death of Bishop Æthelwold in 984: Holland is mentioned in **25** from *c.* 1000. The episode provides an illuminating glimpse of the St Paul's community in the later tenth century (see discussion above, pp. 32–3), and probably represents one of many such transactions between the London Church and other religious houses in the pre-Conquest period.

e. *The* scipmen *list* (**25**)

This unique document, copied in the twelfth century into a legal manuscript of presumed St Paul's provenance, consists of the word *scipmen* followed by a list of places and associated numbers; it would appear to be a record of the naval levy on the estates of the London Church *c.* 1000. There is detailed discussion of the purpose of this list, with details of the individual estates and their identifications, in the commentary to **25**. Analysis here will be confined to the general implications for the history of the endowment.

---

[39] For the translation of *contubernium*, see Gibbs, St Paul's, p. xxxix. Gibbs's identification of Mideltune as Milton Ernest, Bedfordshire, cannot be correct (see Blake, *Liber Eliensis*, p. 105 n. 2). The Cambridgeshire Milton was an Ely manor in 1066, which would fit the general details of the narrative (GDB 201v).

This is a translation of the document, with numerals inserted to facilitate discussion of the estates:

Seamen: from (1) 'Chich' [St Osyth] four; from (2) Tillingham two; from (3) Dunmow and from (4) Tolleshunt one; from (5) Navestock and from (6) Neasden four; from (7) *Hinawicun* and from (8) Tollington two; from (9) *Gnutungadene* and from (10) Bromley one; from (11) Tottenham [Court] one; from (12) Clapham two; from (13) Barnes and from (14) Chiswick one; from (15) West Drayton one; from (16) Caddington one; from (17) Sandon one; from (18) *Ceaddingtune* one; from (19) Fulham five; from (20) *Forthtune* three; from (21) Stepney and from (22) Islington two; from (23) Orsett one; from (24) Laindon one; from (25) Shopland and from (26) 'western' Orsett one; from (27) Belchamp [St Paul's] one; from (28) Copford and (29) Holland one; from (30) Southminster five; from (31) Clacton two; from (32) Hadleigh and from (33) *Codanham* one.

There seems good reason to think that **25** refers to all, or essentially all, of the estates held by and the bishopric of London and the St Paul's community *c.* 1000 (there is some possibility of wholly exempt estates). It has not previously been noticed is that the list appears to fall into two parts—the first eighteen entries refer to places for the most part linked with the cathedral community, while the remaining fifteen consist of estates primarily associated with the bishopric. The list begins with three estates in Essex ('Chich', Tillingham and Dunmow) which Theodred had given to St Paul's. Of the next fifteen places, no fewer than eight are documented as belonging to the cathedral community after the Conquest.[40] Three places are unidentified; one of these (*Hinawicun*, 'the farms of the religious community') may refer to land north of London which was an ancient demesne estate of the canons (see pp. 84, 196). Bromley (10) is likely to be Bromley-by-Bow, which was to be reckoned as part of the bishop's Domesday manor at Stepney; but it seems probable that this was the portion of the manor held by the canons for their supplies (see pp. 197, 199). These first eighteen entries have a rough geographical distribution, with some blurring (possibly the result of the scribe's misleading 'pairing' of similarly-sized estates): thus the list begins with Essex manors, moves on to Middlesex, slips across the Thames to Surrey and then back to Middlesex, and ends with two properties in Hertfordshire and one unidentified place (see Map 2).

---

[40] Navestock (5); Neasden (6); Tottenham Court (11); Barnes (13); Chiswick (14); West Drayton (15); Caddington (16); Sandon (17)

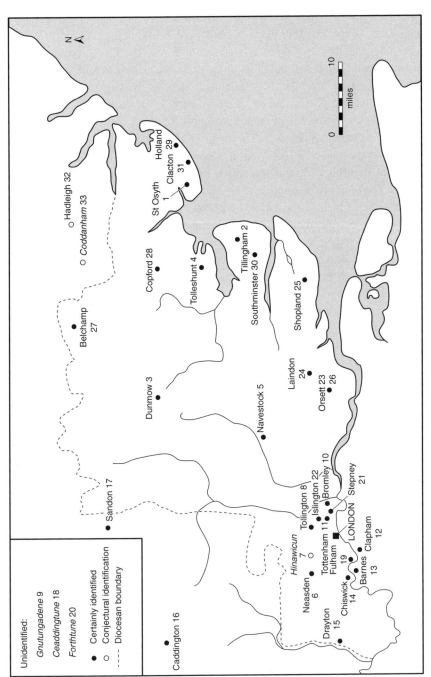

Unidentified:
Gnutungadene 9
Ceaddingtune 18
Forthtune 20

● Certainly identified
○ Conjectural identification
--- Diocesan boundary

Caddington 16

Drayton 15
Neasden 6
Hinawicun 7
Chiswick 14
Tottenham 11
Fulham
Barnes 13
Clapham 12
LONDON
Stepney 21
Tollington 8
Islington 22
Bromley 10
Sandon 17
Navestock 5
Dunmow 3
Laindon 24
Orsett 23 26
Belchamp 27
Southminster 30
Tillingham 2
Shopland 25
Copford 28
Tolleshunt 4
Hadleigh 32
Coddanham 33
St Osyth
Holland
Clacton 29
31
1

0 10 miles

Map 2. St. Paul's Naval Assessment c. 1000

The final fifteen entries would appear to have a separate geographical arrangement. Three of the first four places named were in Middlesex (the fourth is not
identified), and the next seven estates are in Essex; the identification of the
remaining two is disputed, but they can be plausibly located in Suffolk, near the
Essex border (see Map 2). This section of the the list begins with Fulham,
a huge and ancient possession, and the third entry is Stepney, the bishop's other
great Middlesex manor. Six of the following twelve places are listed as episcopal
property in Domesday Book.[41] The main Domesday manor at Islington (22)
belonged to the canons in 1066, but it is possible that **25** refers to the five-hide
holding at Barnsbury in Islington which was reckoned as part of Stepney (see
p. 199). The only real disruption to the pattern comes in the case of Belchamp
St Paul's (27), which was associated with the chapter by 1066 (there is no valid
pre-Conquest documentation). To put this minor discrepancy into perspective, it
is pertinent to remember that 'Chich' was a St Paul's estate in c. 950 (albeit in
the category of *beodland*) and an episcopal manor in 1066. Some adjustment of
holdings between bishop and cathedral in the years between c. 1000 and the
Conquest seems a reasonable assumption. Generally, the evidence seems to bear
out the suggestion that **25** treats the lands of St Paul's and of the bishopric in
separate sections, each with its own geographical organisation. This would be
compatible with a high degree of separation between the two endowments as
early as the turn of the tenth century.

f. *The endowment between c. 1000 and 1066*

The documentary evidence for acquisitions between c. 1000 and 1066 is very
limited. The bequests of Hadham and Heybridge by Ælfflæd may have taken
effect in the first years of the new century (S 1486; see pp. 94–5, 177). At some
stage the canons gained possession of Barling, which had been a personal
bequest to Bishop Wulfstan in a will dated 998 (S 1522; see p. 96); the fabrication of a charter in the name of Edward the Confessor concerning Barling and
Chingford (29) may give some indication of the date at which these places actually passed to St Paul's. There is a memorandum of a grant by Eadgifu and her
husband of Weeley in Essex, supposedly with the permission of King Edward,
although the Domesday picture is confused (31; see p. 215). A fragmentary text
concerning a grant by King Edward of an unidentified place to a thegn could
perhaps reflect another pre-Conquest donation (30).

The fortunes of St Paul's may have fluctuated wildly during this period. King
Æthelred and by his son Eadmund Ironside used London as an important base,

---

[41] Orsett (23) and 'western' Orsett (26); Laindon (24); Copford (28); Southminster (30); Clacton (31).

and Æthelred was buried in St Paul's (see pp. 37–8). It is possible that the London Church flourished under royal and aristocratic patronage at this time, and it is also likely to have benefited from the expansion of trade and urban life which took place in the later tenth and early eleventh century; the church's intra-mural properties would probably have increased in value, although the increased rents may have been offset by the huge tributes exacted in Æthelred's reign to pay off the Danish invaders. But an association with King Æthelred could have been a liability under the succeeding Anglo-Scandinavian regime. Cnut seized the great estate at Southminster, which was the largest episcopal manor in Essex, and this was not regained until after 1066 (LDB 10r; *DB Essex* 3:9). He also did St Paul's the disservice of removing the relics of St Ælfheah, already a magnet for the valuable pilgrim trade (see pp. 39–40).

A minor red herring is provided by an Old English document copied into GL 25516, on fol. 40v. This is a record of the dues rendered to the church at Lambourn in Berkshire, which in its present form dates from the reign of William I or later, and which makes no explicit reference to St Paul's.[42] The document is followed by a note: 'Carta supradicta Cnutonis regis Anglie et Dacie, qui ecclesiam sancti Michaelis de Lambourne contulit Deo et ecclesie sancti Pauli London' et ad victum decani qui pro tempore fuerit. Scripta est carta circa medium ueteris missalis de Lambourne'. The scribe who wrote this note was clearly under a mis-apprehension, no doubt due to his unfamiliarity with Old English: a passage which referred to the pasture of 'two cows with the king's [cows]' (...*twa ky mid thæs kinges*...) appears to have been read as *knud thæs kinges*.[43] All the witnesses that can be identified appear in Domesday as holders of land TRW; in addition, two of these are referred to in the text, in such a way as to indicate that the document was wholly drawn up after the Conquest. Robertson tentatively identifies the very last witness, Ælfwine *b'*, with Ælfwine, bishop of Winchester 1032–47, who was con-temporary with Cnut, and suggests that this name may have been taken over from an earlier document. But this must be regarded as wholly speculative: an episcopal subscription is unlikely to have been tacked on after the subscriptions of local priests and thegns; and *b'* could well be an abbreviated byname, as in the previ-ous two subscriptions. Lambourn was a St Paul's estate in the twelfth century, but would appear to have been a post-Conquest acquisition; it was a royal manor in 1066 and 1086.[44] It was not instituted to the dean until the later thirteenth century.[45]

---

[42] Robertson, *Charters*, pp. 240–1, with notes pp. 490–3.

[43] As noted by Gibbs, p. xxxi n. 1. The same error was made by the nineteenth-century editor, J. Footman (see Robertson's edition, note 5).

[44] GDB 57v; *DB Berks.*, 1:29.

[45] Gibbs, no. 7, and p. xxxi.

Some level of grievance about losses and encroachment in the years up to 1066 is suggested by the forged 'coronation-day charter', supposedly granted by King William on Christmas Day 1066, which was in existence by the early twelfth century and purports to restore to St Paul's a number of estates which had been unjustly seized by certain men in the time of William's predecessors.[46] The lands in question are:

1. *Navestock* (Essex; fifteen hides). Navestock was a possession of the church of London in *c.* 1000 (**25**). The two Navestock manors which the canons held in 1086 had been divided up between various free men in 1066; some of this land was annexed by St Paul's after William's arrival, and other portions were said to be held *ex dono regis* (see p. 173). **16** is a fabricated charter for this estate, no doubt produced in order to support the canons' claims.

2. *Laver* (Essex; four hides) and *Cockhampstead* (Herts.; three hides). These estates are said to have been bequeathed to St Paul's by Æthelflæd in the time of King Æthelred (see **22, 23**, neither authentic in its present form), but they were not in the canons' possession in 1066 or subsequently. The monks of Christ Church in Canterbury may also have had some claim on Laver (see further, p. 191). Æthelflæd's bequest may have been thwarted or reversed.

3. *Runwell* (Essex; six hides). The Essex Domesday mentions three Runwell manors, one of eight hides held by St Paul's, and another two with a total assessment of five hides which were held TRE by Leofstan and Eadgifu, but were later annexed by Engelric and subsequently transferred to Count Eustace.[47] It is possible that St Paul's had a claim on the lands held by Count Eustace.

4. *Islington* (Middx; nine or eight hides). Land here had been held by the London Church *c.* 1000 (**25**); the reference appears among estates associated with the bishops rather than the canons, and may refer to Barnsbury in Islington, which was later reckoned as part of the episcopal manor of Stepney (see p. 199). The canons held two Islington manors TRE/TRW, with a total assessment of four hides, while the Barnsbury manor was reckoned at five hides.[48] The Middlesex Domesday refers to two further manors there, each of half a hide and each held TRE by a man

---

[46] Bates, *RRAN: Acta of William I*, no. 183. The forger makes an egregious error in naming as co-donor Queen Matilda, who was not in England at this date.

[47] LDB 13v, 31v; *DB Essex* 5:9, 20:53–4.

[48] GDB 127r, 128r; *DB Middx*, 3:2, 22–3.

of King Edward.[49] The overall total of ten hides would be equivalent to the assessment of the estate at Islington mentioned as a lay possession in a diploma of 903 (**10**). It is possible that the canons were laying claim to the whole of a larger estate which had been broken up between 903 and 1066.

5. *Lisson Green* (Middx; two hides). In Domesday this manor appears under a heading *Terra in elemosina data*; it is said to have been held TRE by Edward, son of Swein, a man of King Edward, and TRW by Eadgifu from the king.[50] St Paul's records point to a dispute arising from a deferred bequest. According to the canons' version of events, the original holder, Edward, a citizen of London, had promised them the estate, swearing on the altar of St Paul's in King Edward's reign and again in William's time; the land was to revert to the canons after the death of his wife, Eadgifu, who was to pay a yearly render of ten shillings. She subsequently married Otto the Goldsmith, who thwarted the bequest. The dispute continued into the twelfth century.[51]

In assessing the state of the St Paul's endowment in the years leading up the the Conquest, it is also useful to consider the writs of Cnut and Edward, which arguably have an authentic basis (**27, 28**). Both documents confirm that the priests of St Paul's were to enjoy sake and soke over their lands; in neither case is there a reference to the bishop, although in **27** Bishop Ælfwig appears among the witnesses. These writs would be compatible with the argument that the London chapter had separate control over its own lands in the decades before 1066. There is a distinct contrast here with a comparable document confirming the privileges of the monks at Christ Church in Canterbury, who are associated with the bishop in a similar writ of the Confessor.[52] In 1057 × 1060 the priests at Hereford were also the beneficiaries of a writ confirming their rights over their lands, which would seem to show them acting independently of their bishop (S 1101).

g. *The endowment in Domesday Book*

The Domesday account of the landed property of the London Church is particularly complex, and only the general outline will be summarised here.[53] In 1066

---

[49] GDB129v; *DB Middx*, 9:3, 23:1

[50] GDB 130v: *DB Middx*, 25:1.

[51] GL 25504, 47rv; *HMC 9th Report*, i. 65b; Gibbs, p. 136 n. 1; Round 1891.

[52] S 1088 (Harmer, *Writs*, no. 33). This is an original writ, of which all but the first three lines have been erased and rewritten, but enough survives to show that the first version of the text concerned a confirmation of sake and soke. See also S 1089.

[53] There is a useful overview of this material in Taylor 1992, pp. 303–11; and see Faith 1994, p. 658.

the principal estates of the bishop and chapter were located in Middlesex, Essex and Hertfordshire; the canons also held single manors in Surrey (Barnes) and Bedfordshire (Caddington). In the Essex and Hertfordshire surveys, there is a separate heading for the lands of the canons (*Terrae canonicorum S. Pauli in Exsessa; Terra S. Pauli Lundon'*), especially noticeable in the case of Hertfordshire, where the entries for the holdings of bishop and chapter are widely separated. In the Middlesex Domesday the lands of the St Paul's clergy are considered together with the episcopal estates, under the same heading (*Terra Episcopi Londoniensis*), which is the usual pattern for the treatment of the lands of a cathedral church; but even here there is evidence of separate treatment, with the bishop's holdings considered first and the canons' manors later.[54] The Domesday entries would appear to indicate that, at least in Essex and Hertfordshire, the canons were recognised as tenants-in-chief of their own lands, operating separately from the bishop and his household, a precocious instance of a pattern which became the norm in the later eleventh century. There is no firm evidence about the date at which such a division of assets took place. The fact that the Middlesex lands were still not wholly separated in 1086 (this was probably also true of the holdings in the city) might suggest that the process was fairly recent and was still continuing, in which case this novel development in London could be ascribed to the influence of the Norman bishops who held the see from 1044. But the fragmentary early evidence about the endowment discussed above (notably the *scipmen* list) could be considered to support that argument that the separate treatment of the canons' lands was already a reality in the tenth century, if not before (see pp. 82, 93–4, 98–100).

The Conquest seems to have had a generally beneficial effect on the endowment of the London Church. The bishops, relatively poor in 1066, were big gainers. In 1066 the episcopal estate was weighted towards Middlesex, the location of the two great manors at Stepney and Fulham; Bishop William also held some sixty hides in Essex, but had been bereft of the great manor at Southminster since the time of Cnut; while his assets in Hertfordshire amounted only to the 7.5-hide Hadham manor acquired in the early eleventh century (see **17**; S 1486).[55] King William restored Southminster, and in addition he granted Bishop William the manor at Little Warley, because it had formerly belonged to St Paul's, and he ruled in the bishop's favour in the case of two disputed estates at Layer Marney. Even more significantly, Bishop William appears to have been

---

[54] Pinder 1991, p. 11 (where it is noted that the repeated rubric for 'Ossultune Hundred' may have been intended to mark the division).

[55] GDB 127rv, 133v; LDB 9r–11r; *DB Middx* 3:1–13; *DB Essex* 3:2–4, 8, 10, 12–16; *DB Herts* 4:2.

permitted and perhaps encouraged by the king to acquire substantial areas of land in Essex and Hertfordshire, which are categorised in Domesday Book as Bishop William's 'fee' (*feudum*) and are listed separately from the bishop's 'lands' (*terrae*), which were the manors already held in 1066.[56] These may have included estates, for example at Hadham, to which St Paul's had some kind of ancient claim (see p. 177). Bishop William was also allowed to build a castle at Bishops Stortford.

The Domesday lands of the canons were slightly more widely dispersed than the episcopal estate, comprising about eighty hides TRE in Essex, about fifty in Middlesex and eighteen in Hertfordshire. as well as small manors in Surrey and Bedfordshire.[57] The St Paul's clergy made relatively few new acquisitions in William's reign. The principal gains were in Hertfordshire, where the canons took over ten hides at Kensworth and ten at Caddington, which had belonged to Leofwine Cild; they also held a separate manor of Caddington just over the Bedfordshire border, again associated with Leofwine TRE.[58] Elsewhere the canons seem to have taken the opportunity to press their claims to disputed territory. In Essex they are said to have annexed a total of three hides and forty acres at Navestock, receiving another five hides less twenty acres there by the king's gift; the forgery of **16** may be connected with claims to these lands (see pp. 75, 102, 173). The canons also annexed a half hide at Barling, and somehow acquired a small manor at *Lea* (Lee Chapel), which had been held by a woman TRE; they also found themselves in possession of a half-hide at Norton Mandeville, said to have been given to them after King William's arrival by a woman named Godgifu, although they had no documentation to back this claim.[59] The canons' known losses in the decades after 1066 seem to have been minimal. One hide of

---

[56] On this see Round in *VCH Essex*, i. 339–40 and *VCH Herts.*, i. 278–9; Taylor 1990, p. 19; *eadem* 1992, pp. 305–7. In 1086 Bishop Maurice also held St Andrew's church at Ilchester in Somerset, previously a Glastonbury possession (GDB 91r), and a small manor in Wimborne Minster in Dorset, held TRE by Ælfric Dod (GDB 77v). It is to be assumed that these were personal possessions.

[57] ESSEX: Chingford (6 hides); Belchamp St Paul's (5 hides); Wickham St Paul's (3 hides less one virgate); Tillingham (20 hides and 6 acres); Runwell (8 hides); Heybridge (8 hides); The Naze (27 hides); Barling (2.5 hides less 15 acres). See LDB 12v-13r; *DB Essex*, 5:2–5, 9–12. Note also a one-hide manor at Wanstead, held by St Paul's TRE, but listed under the lands of the bishop (LDB 9v; *DB Essex* 3:5). MIDDLESEX: Fulham, i.e. Chiswick (5 hides); Willesden (15 hides); Harlesden (5 hides); Tottenham Court (5 hides); St Pancras (4 hides); Islington (2 + 2 hides); Stoke Newington (2.5 hides); Hoxton (1 + 3 hides); *Stanestaple* (4 hides); West Drayton (10 hides). GDB 127v–128v; *DB Middx* 3:14, 17–18, 20–8, 30). HERTFORDSHIRE: Ardeley (6 hides); Luffenhall (2 hides); Sandon (10 hides). See GDB 136r; *DB Herts.*, 13: 3–5. SURREY: Barnes (8 hides); GDB 34r; *DB Surrey* 13:1.

[58] GDB 136r; *DB Herts.* 13:1–2. Caddington is mentioned in **25**, and so would seem to have been linked with the London Church *c.* 1000 (see p. 198).

[59] LDB 12v-13v; *DB Essex* 5:1, 6–8, 12.

the community's six-hide manor at Chingford in Essex was seized by Peter de Valognes and was not recovered (see below, p. 212). The loss to Peter de Valognes is mentioned in a document of the late eleventh century which lists five minor *invasiones* inflicted on the St Paul's estates.[60] The canons' complaints also covered Lisson Green in Middlesex, which was a thwarted bequest (see p. 103), one hide at Navestock, apparently seized after 1086, and a half hide at Heybridge.

The chapter's lands were not yet divided into permanent prebends, but there are signs that a rudimentary prebendal system was already developing, at least in Middlesex (see also above, pp. 45–6, on *solandae*). In 1086 three canons held land which was part of the lordship of St Paul's: Gyrth held two hides in Twyford; Ralph two hides in Rug Moor; and and Walter one hide at St Pancras. Other canons held land on different terms: Durand held two hides at Twyford from the king TRW; while in 1066 the canon Sired owned half the five-hide manor at Barnsbury in Islington in his own right, with the remainder held by the canons for their supplies (this was episcopal land in 1086, part of the manor of Stepney). Within the next few years, the full-fledged prebendal system was put into place by Bishop Maurice: the records show that Ralph was reckoned as the first prebendary of Rug Moor, and Durand the first prebendary of Twyford.[61]

The Domesday evidence is consistent with a picture of an endowment in a condition of change and development. At the time of the Conquest the lands allocated to the canons were roughly equal in extent to the lands of the bishop; by 1086 the latter had been substantially increased as a result of Bishop William's acquisitions in Essex and Hertfordshire. In Essex and Hertfordshire the holdings of the bishop and canons had been divided up by 1086; but they were still partly inter-twined in Middlesex, and probably also in London itself.[62] Some proto-prebends evidently existed by 1086, and it was in the following decades that an organised prebendal system was established. One trigger may have been the burning down of the Anglo-Saxon cathedral in 1087: the consequent drain on the funds of the London Church may have accelerated trends towards wholly separating the two endowments.[63] But the divorce may have been fairly gradual: as late as the middle of the twelfth century the bishop was still partly responsible for the running expenses of the cathedral.[64]

---

[60] GL 25504, 47rv (old fol. 43); *HMC 9th Report*, i. 65b; see Round 1891.

[61] Brooke and Keir, London, p. 343; Gibbs, pp. xxiii–iv.

[62] Gibbs, p. xviii n. 2.

[63] See Crosby, *Bishop and Chapter*, pp. 318–20.

[64] Gibbs, p. xviii n. 2, pp. xxxv–vii, and nos 61, 219.

6. THE BISHOPS OF LONDON

Details of the careers of the earlier bishops of London/the East Saxons can be retrieved from Bede's *Ecclesiastical History*, but very little information is available about the Anglo-Saxon successors to Eorcenwald. William of Malmesbury, writing in the twelfth century, complained: '[the rest] lie under a cloud of obscurity, and not even their burial sites are known'; and simply gave a list of names, with a little extra detail on Theodred (d. 951 × 953).[1] There are various collections of Anglo-Saxon episcopal lists which can be collated with each other and with the information from William and from John of Worcester to provide a fairly reliable sequence of London bishops.[2] It is possible to supply precise or approximate dates for pontificates by analysing the bishops' attestations to charters, and further deductions can be made from collections of obituaries. A few additional sources flesh out the picture: an extant letter of Bishop Wealdhere (Appendix 1); the will of Bishop Theodred (Appendix 2); an occasional reference in the Anglo-Saxon Chronicle (particularly useful for the eleventh century). But in general the level of information about the bishops of London is depressingly low, largely because so little has survived from St Paul's: even as important a figure as Theodred remains shadowy, his dates approximate.[3]

1. **MELLITUS**, bishop 604–*c.* 616. A former abbot and one of the group of reinforcements sent to Augustine by Gregory in 601, Mellitus was consecrated bishop of the East Saxons in 604 and his seat established in London, after plans to establish the archiepiscopal see in the city were abandoned (Bede, *HE*, i. 29, ii. 3; see above, pp. 1–2). Some years later Mellitus travelled to Rome to discuss the English mission with Pope Boniface IV (608–15); while in Rome he attended a synod of Italian bishops, and brought back to England with him a copy of the synodal *acta*, as well as various letters addressed to Archbishop Laurentius and other English recipients (*HE*, ii. 4).[4] After the death of East Saxon king Sæberht in *c.* 616 Mellitus was driven out of the kingdom. He first travelled to Kent and later to Gaul, where he stayed for a year; he then returned to England, but was unable to re-establish himself in London because the people

---

[1] *GP*, § 73 (pp. 144–5).

[2] For a summary of the material, see *Handbook of British Chronology*, ed. E.B. Fryde, D.E. Greenway, S. Porter and I. Roy, 3rd edn (London, 1986), pp. 209–10; and discussion of problems in the London list in Page 1965, pp. 91–2.

[3] There is a superb summary of the evidence in Whitelock 1975. See also the study of the succession between 850 and 950 in O'Donovan 1973.

[4] The synod, which is otherwise unknown, apparently took place in 610 (it is dated 27 February, in the eighth year of Emperor Phocas and the thirteenth indiction).

there refused to receive him. When Laurentius died on 2 February 619 Mellitus was appointed his successor at Canterbury. Bede notes that he suffered from gout but was mentally active: 'he was noble by birth but nobler still in loftiness of spirit'. He died on 24 April 624 and was buried in the monastery of SS Peter and Paul (St Augustine's) at Canterbury (*HE*, ii. 6–7). London and the East Saxon kingdom remained without a bishop for some decades.

2. **CEDD**, bishop *c.* 653–? 664. Cedd was trained at the monastery in Lindisfarne, where he would have learned Irish observances (Bede, *HE*, iii. 22–3). He was one of small group of priests who travelled south from Northumbria to evangelise the Middle Angles in *c.* 653; subsequently he was sent by the Northumbrian king Oswiu on a mission to the East Saxons (then under Northumbrian overlordship). After a successful beginning he returned to Lindisfarne, where he was consecrated bishop of the East Saxons. His two principal foundations in the diocese were at Bradwell-on-Sea (*Ythancæstir*) and at Tilbury, where he set up communities following a monastic rule. He baptised the new king Swithhelm in the East Anglian royal vill at Rendlesham (*HE*, iii. 22). It is not known whether he re-established the minster community at St Paul's in London (see pp. 10–11). Cedd retained strong links with Northumbria, which he regularly revisited on preaching journeys; he founded a monastery at Lastingham, which followed the religious practices of Lindisfarne, and he died and was buried there after catching the plague (*HE*, ii. 23). This probably took place shortly after the 664 synod of Whitby, which Cedd had attended and where he had foresworn Irish customs (*HE*, iii. 25–6). After his death some of the East Saxons reverted to paganism; in response King Wulfhere of Mercia, the new overlord of the kingdom, send Jaruman, bishop of the Mercians, on a temporary mission to re-establish the Christian faith in the East Saxon kingdom (*HE*, iii. 30).

3. **WINE**, bishop 666–(*c.* 670 × *c.* 675). Wine was an Englishman who had been consecrated in Gaul. He was bishop of Winchester for some years, was expelled by the West Saxon king Cenwealh and then took refuge with the Mercian king Wulfhere and bought the see of London from him, remaining there for the rest of his life (*HE*, iii. 7). While bishop of Winchester he consecrated Chad, with the assistance of two British bishops; at the time he was the only bishop of Britain who had been canonically ordained (*HE*, iii. 28). His subscription as bishop of London occurs in S 68 (A.D. 664), the 'foundation-charter' of the monastery at *Medeshamstede* (the later Peterborough): while the diploma is clearly a post-Conquest fabrication, the witness-list is intriguing and was conceivably constructed from early records. Wine is not mentioned in the episcopal lists for London—his name may have been dropped as a result of Bede's explicit accusation of simony. The purchase of preferment was not unusual in the Frankish

Church, where Wine had been trained, and the circumstances of his acquisition of the London diocese do not necessarily mean that he was a bad bishop. Wine was accustomed to city-based sees, and he is more likely then Cedd to have been responsible for the revival of Mellitus's episcopal seat in London. There is a very good chance that he brought with him to London a personal entourage of clerics who had followed him from Winchester when he was expelled, and that these men either joined an existing community at St Paul's (if one had been re-established by Cedd) or else themselves rebuilt the church originally founded by Mellitus.[5] The earliest surviving charters from the London area date from shortly after Wine's time, and share many diplomatic features with West Saxon charters of the same generation (see pp. 78–9). It has been suggested that it was Wine's successor Eorcenwald who represents the link between the two diplomatic traditions, but it could also be the case that the original connection began when Wine transferred from Winchester.[6] Wine did not attend the synod of Hertford, convened in 672 or 673 (*HE*, iv. 5); he was either dead by that time, or was *persona non grata* with the new archbishop Theodore, perhaps on account of his simony (Theodore's hostility may explain why Bede was so unusually ready to blacken the name of a bishop). According to an apocryphal tale from Winchester, Wine resigned his see three years before his death and entered a monastery in Winchester to do penance for his sin of simony.[7]

4. ? **HUNFERTH**, ? bishop *c.* 670. There is some possibility that Wine was succeeded at London by one Hunferth. A bishop of that name is the only episcopal witness to the very early Chertsey diploma, S 1165 (Kelly, *Chertsey*, no. 1), which predates the death of Wulfhere of Mercia in 674 or 675. There is no other contemporary reference to a Hunferth, so Whitelock suggested that the name represents a corruption of Wynferth/Wynfrith, the bishop of Lichfield who was appointed in 672 and and deposed by Archbishop Theodore at some point before 676.[8] But the case for the existence of a separate Bishop Hunferth is supported by a detail of which Whitelock was unaware—a Bishop Hunferth is mentioned twice in the spurious Tillingham landbook in the St Paul's archive (**1**), which was partly modelled on a lost diploma of the early 670s. The canons are known to have borrowed Chertsey documents as models for their own forgeries, and so

---

[5] There is a parallel in the career of Bishop Wilfrid, a contemporary of Wine who was also consecrated in Gaul; during his vagabond life after he was expelled from his see, Wilfrid was accompanied by his clergy and companions (*Life of Wilfrid*, caps. xxv, xxix, xxxiii–iv, xl, l, lv (pp. 50, 56, 66–70, 80, 102, 120)).

[6] For the identification of the diplomatic parallels and the suggestion of Eorcenwald's responsibility, see Wormald 1985, and above, pp. 78–9.

[7] Whitelock 1975, p. 5 n. 2, citing the Winchester writer Thomas of Rudborne (*Anglia Sacra*, i. 192).

[8] Whitelock, *EHD*, p. 480 n. 1; see Bede, *HE*, iv. 3, 6.

one might wonder whether the reference here could be influenced by S 1165; but the balance of probability is that this is an independent reference to Hunferth, for **1** includes some early formulation which does not seem to have been borrowed from the Chertsey diploma. There seem to be grounds for suggesting that there was a bishop named Hunferth who had authority over western Surrey and perhaps the whole East Saxon diocese in the early 670s. Perhaps he was Wine's successor, and it may be that he was similarly wiped from the record because he did not find favour with the new reforming archbishop Theodore. See further discussion in the commentary to **1**, below p. 136.

    5. **EORCENWALD**, bishop *c.* 675–693. His unusual name incorporates the Frankish element *Eorcen*, and may associate him with the Kentish royal dynasty.[9] Before his appointment as bishop he founded a monastery at Chertsey, over which he was abbot (see S 1165, 1247), and a second monastery at Barking, where he set up his sister Æthelburh as abbess (see S 1171, 1246, 1248). Bede's rather sparse information about Eorcenwald appears to have been derived from a Barking source, but may have been supplemented by details provided by Nothhelm, the London priest who was one of his most important collaborators.[10] Bede notes that Archbishop Theodore consecrated Eorcenwald as bishop of the East Saxons at London, apparently after the synod of Hertford in 672 or 673 (*HE*, iv. 6); the date usually cited is 675.[11] It is possible that Eorcenwald retained Chertsey as his principal episcopal seat, in preference to St Paul's (see p. 11). There is good reason to accept the tradition at Chertsey and Barking that he made a journey to Rome in *c.* 678 (see S 1246, 1247); the extant Chertsey privilege in the name of Pope Agatho may be fundamentally authentic, and is the model for the fake St Paul's version (see above, pp. 75–6). Eorcenwald had a close relationship with the West Saxon kings Cædwalla (686–8) and Ine (688–726). He secured a grant from Cædwalla for Barking of land at Battersea (S 1246, 1248), and witnessed a charter of that king concerned

---

[9] Whitelock 1975, p. 5: *cf.* King Eorcenberht of Kent (640–64) and his daughter St Eorcengota of Faremoutier (*HE*, iii. 8). Eorcenwald's sister, Æthelburh, shares her name with the daughter of King Æthelberht of Kent, wife of Edwin of Northumbria and later abbess of Lyminge. Bede mentions a Frankish *patricius* named Eorcenwald, the Neustrian mayor of the palace (*HE*, iii. 19). Later hagiographical tradition claimed that Ss Eorcenwald and Æthelburh were the descendants of a King Offa, either of the East Saxons or the East Angles (Whitelock 1975, p. 5 n. 5). There is no obvious candidate for this role, although there is evidence that one later East Saxon ruler was so-called (see **4**). Yorke (*Kings and Kingdoms*, pp. 55–6) has argued that Eorcenwald and his sister may have been members of the East Saxon royal house, perhaps from a branch that descended from a marriage alliance with the Kentish dynasty.

[10] Bede used a lost life of St Æthelburh, referred to as *liber* or *libellus* (*HE*, iv. 7–8). For Nothhelm see above, p. 17.

[11] The source is *John of Worcester* (p. 128), but the date may not be based on any reliable information (see the editors' note, *ibid.*, p. 129).

with the foundation of a Surrey minster at Farnham (S 235, A.D. 688).[12] Ine refers to him as 'my bishop' in his lawcode, issued between 688 and Eorcenwald's death, which probably took place in 693.[13] It seem probable that Eorcenwald's relationship with the West Saxon rulers was a consequence of the fact that his diocese included western Surrey, which was gradually moving permanently into the West Saxon orbit. What is less clear is whether western Surrey had previously been reckoned as a part of the diocese of the East Saxons, or whether this was a novel development of Eorcenwald's pontificate and arose from the fact that he had an existing connection with Chertsey before his appointment was bishop. After his day Surrey was detached from the London diocese and shifted under the control of Winchester (see pp. 13–15).

Eorcenwald died on 30 April, probably in 693, and became the centre of an important cult at St Paul's. Bede mentions in passing both ante-mortem and post-mortem miracles, and more particularly the fact that a focal point of Eorcenwald's cult was the horse-litter in which he was carried when ill, which was believed to have curative powers (*HE*, iv. 6). There was continung commemoration in the Anglo-Saxon period: Eorcenwald is the only saint associated with London in a pre-Conquest list of saints' resting-places, and his name appears in a number of pre-Conquest calendars.[14] Bishop Maurice may have deliberately revived the cult in the aftermath of the fire which destroyed the cathedral in 1087. According to the *Miracula S. Erkenwaldi*, probably composed between 1140 and 1145 by Arcoid, nephew of Bishop Gilbert 'the Universal' (1128–34), the pre-Conquest shrine of Eorcenwald was located behind the main altar, and consisted of a wooden reliquary or *theca* covered with an ancient linen cloth (*pallium*) and resting on a stone plinth; the reliquary probably contained a sealed lead coffin.[15] Bishop Maurice and Bishop Walkelin of Winchester are said to have inspected the smouldering ruins of the church three days after the fire in 1087, and to have discovered the shrine untouched by the flames. Maurice began to build a new Romanesque cathedral, placing Eorcenwald's relics in the crypt to await the (long-delayed) completion of the choir. He may have commissioned a new Life of the saint, represented by a fairly brief text

[12] Note also S 233, a spurious confection relating to a minster at Hoo in Kent, which was a daughter-house of *Medeshamstede* (Peterborough). The forger has made use of some genuine seventh-century documentation, and includes several conjoined witness-lists, the earliest of which is associated with a grant by Cædwalla: this incorporates a subscription of Eorcenwald, after that of Archbishop Theodore.

[13] Whitelock, *EHD*, no. 32; *cf.* Whitelock 1975, p. 8.

[14] Whitelock 1975, p. 6; D.W. Rollason, 'Lists of Saints' Resting-Places in Anglo-Saxon England', *Anglo-Saxon England* vii (1978), pp. 61–93 at 90; Whatley, *Saint of London*, pp. 58–9.

[15] Whately, *Saint of London*, pp. 59–60, 120–8; and for the date and authorship of the *Miracula*, see chapter 3.

known as the *Vita S. Erkenwaldi*, which is argued to have been drawn up between 1087 and 1125.[16] This depends largely on Bede's account of the bishop's career, but has some interesting information about his demise. Eorcenwald is said to have died at Barking, after which his remains were disputed between representatives of Barking, Chertsey and Saint Paul's. The latter prevailed, because the citizens of London came to carry off the corpse (assisted by a timely miracle). One of the intended functions of the *Vita* may have been to present Eorcenwald as the city's own saint, and to persuade the citizens to contribute towards the costs of the new cathedral. The composition of the *Miracula* in the 1140s may have had a similar background; the saint was finally translated into the new choir and the citizens were invited to contribute towards a new silver shrine.[17] The thirteenth-century St Paul's inventories include a reference to a 'very ancient psalter of St Eorcenwald';[18] perhaps this was associated with the shrine, as the Stonyhurst Gospel was associated with the tomb of St Cuthbert.

6. **WEALDHERE**, bishop *c.* 693 to (705 × 716). Bede mentions Wealdhere only in the context of the saintly death of King Sebbi, who took the religious habit from his hands before his death in 693 or 694 (*HE*, iv. 11).[19] Wealdhere may have been more active than Eorcenwald in securing the interests of St Paul's. As bishop, he was the beneficiary of three charters preserved as fragments in the St Paul's archive (**2, 3, 4**), covering estates at Ealing and Fulham in Middlesex, and also land in the Vale of St Albans, in Hertfordshire; the first of these transactions was explicitly intended to support St Paul's (*ad augmentum monasterialis uitæ in Londoniæ*). The Ealing property was granted by the Mercian king Æthelred, while Wealdhere purchased Fulham from the (presumably Mercian) bishop of Hereford: only the Hertfordshire estate was granted by an East Saxon king. A fourth diploma, dated 704 and preserved in the Christ Church archive (S 65), concerns land at Twickenham and was a joint-grant by the East Saxon king and a Mercian *comes*, the latter acting with the permission of the Mercian king Æthelred. It would appear that Mercian control over Middlesex was becoming

---

[16] *Ibid.*, pp. 13–23. Whatley's dating of the *Vita* depends on the observation that the text seems to have been known to William of Malmesbury, who used it for the *GP*, the first version of which was completed in 1125; this rules out a suggested attribution to Arcoid (as Brooke and Keir, *London*, p. 356). Whatley argues that Goscelin of Saint-Bertin was drawing on an earlier life of Eorcenwald when he wrote a life of Æthelburh in 1087 (for this see Colker 1965), and cites stylistic evidence to prove that Goscelin himself was not the author of the exiting *Vita*.

[17] *Ibid.*, pp. 61–6.

[18] Ker 1969, p. 59 (no. 107): 'Psalterium sancti Erkenwaldi vetusissimum est cum pater noster et credo in fine et quibusdam oracionibus nichil valet'.

[19] A Wealdhere *pr'* attests a diploma of King Æthelred of Mercia dated 692 (S 75); but he may have been a *princeps*, and is anyway likely to be the same man as the Wealdhere *miles* attesting two dubious Evesham diplomas of 709 (S 79, 1174).

more confident during Wealdhere's pontificate. There is a remote possibility that Wealdhere obtained a charter of privileges from the Mercian king Coenred, although the extant fragment does not look trustworthy (see **5a**). Political pressures also came from other directions. An original letter from Wealdhere to Archbishop Berhtwald refers guardedly to conflict between the West Saxons and 'the rulers of our country', which was to be resolved at a meeting at Brentford; the dispute may have been over Surrey, which was detached from the London diocese at around this time (see Appendix 1, and discussion above, pp. 13–15). In 705 Wealdhere took part in a synod of Southumbrian bishops, and witnessed there a grant by King Ine to the monastery at Glastonbury (S 248). He attested a grant by the East Saxon king of an estate at Nazeing in *c.* 700 (S 65b).[20] He was no longer in office by 716, when his successor Ingwald took part in a synod held at *Clofesho* (see below).

7. **INGWALD**, bishop (705 × 716)–745. He can perhaps be identified the priest named *Igguald* who attested S 65b in *c.* 700. He was appointed bishop in or before 716, when he attended a synod at *Clofesho* (S 22; spurious, but with a witness-list taken from a genuine record). Bishop Ingwald is the beneficiary of four fragmentary charters in the St Paul's archive, one recording a grant of a very large estate in on the Essex seaboard, associated with the later episcopal manor of Southminster (**6**), another concerning his purchase of an unnamed property (**6A**), the remaining two concerned with remission of toll on the bishop's ships at the port of London (**7, 8**). He is mentioned by Bede only in the context of the latter's round-up of the English bishops in office in 731 (*HE*, v. 23), but the annals added to the Moore manuscript of the *Historia Ecclesiastica* include a notice of his death in 745.[21] He attended a synod in 736 or 737 at which the dispute outlined in S 1429 was resolved, and he was one of the witnesses to a diploma granting toll-privileges in the London port to the church of Worcester (S 98).

8. **ECGWULF**, bishop 745–(765 × 772). He attended the synod of *Clofesho* in 747, and was probably present when Archbishop Jænberht was consecrated in 765.[22] His subscription appears in the witness-lists of a toll-privilege issued in London in 748, and of a later confirmation of another toll-privilege (S 91, 143, A.D. 759 × 764; Kelly, *St Augustine's*, nos 50, 52). He died in or before August 772.

---

[20] His subscription also appears in a spurious Peterborough diploma dated 680 (S 72). Another problematic appearance is in the witness-list of a diploma in the name of his predecessor (S 1248); conceivably his subscription was part of a later confirmation.

[21] Colgrave and Mynors, *Bede's Ecclesiastical History*, p. 572.

[22] Haddan & Stubbs, iii. 362; S 107 (spurious).

9. **WIGHEAH**, bishop (765 × 772)–(772 × 781). His only appearance is as a witness to S 108, dated 15 August 772 (Brooks and Kelly, *Christ Church*, no. 18).

10. **EADBERHT**, bishop (772 × 781)–(786 × 789). He attended a synod held at Brentford in 781 (S 1257) and another church council in 786 (BCS 250; Whitelock, *EHD*, no. 191). In 787 the Canterbury diocese was divided and a new archiepiscopal see established at Lichfield. London remained in the Canterbury sphere.

11. **EDGAR**, bishop (786 × 789)–(789 × 793). His only appearance is at a Chelsea synod convened in 789 (S 130, 131).

12. **COENWALH**, bishop (789 × 793)–(793 × 796). He was present at a Chelsea synod in 793 (S 136) and at one held at *Clofesho* between 793 and 796 (S 139).

13. **EADBALD**, bishop (793 × 796)–(796 × 798). Eadbald does not attest any extant charter, but he is mentioned in episcopal lists. The *ASC* annal for 796 states that Bishop Ceolwulf (of Lindsey) and Bishop Eadbald left the country. Ceolwulf seems to have died in the same year (*ASC* D, E), but nothing is known of Eadbald's fate or of the reasons for this temporary or permanent exile; it is possible that he was caught up in the politics of the Mercian succession. King Coenwulf tried to take advantage of the London vacancy by persuading the pope to agree to the transfer of the archiepiscopal see from Canterbury to London (see p. 19).

14. **HATHUBERHT**, bishop (796 × 798)–(*c.* 800 × 803). He attested charters in 798 and 799 (S 153, 155), and his subscription appears in an endorsement added to an earlier charter between 799 and 801 (S 106, 1186a).

15. **OSMUND**, bishop (*c.* 800 × 803)–(805 × 811). He attended the important *Clofesho* synod of 803, which formally abolished the archbishopric of Lichfield and also made a sweeping resolution on lay lordship of minsters (S 1431a, 1431b: Brooks and Kelly, *Christ Church,* nos 32, 33). He also attended a synod at *Aclea* in 805 (S 40, 161).

The witness-list of S 1431a contains group-attestations from every Southumbrian see: the subscription of each bishop is followed by subscriptions of (usually) six other clerics, who would have been his supporters at the synod. The resolution was evidently produced in multiple copies, and two versions with minor variants survive at Canterbury. These two manuscripts have a major discrepancy in the subscriptions of the London contingent. In the earliest version, Bishop Osmund is accompanied by only five supporters, instead of the normal six: Heahstan, priest-abbot; Wigheard, Tidhun and Freothored, priests; and an unstyled Æthelhelm. The second manuscript (a later single-sheet copy of a separate exemplar) omits the last four names, but supplies a sixth (Plegberht, abbot) who was probably part of the original contingent. It has been suggested that

Abbot Heahstan may have been head of the St Paul's community, but there is no evidence for or against this: there would have been other religious houses in the diocese whose heads could accompany the bishop.[23] However, there is a fairly good chance that one or more of the men in Bishop Osmund's entourage were attached to St Paul's.

16. ÆTHELNOTH, bishop (805 × 811)–(816 × 824). A copy of his profession to Archbishop Wulfred survives in the Canterbury archive.[24] His attestations are to S 167 (? A.D. 811), S 170 (from a council held at London in 812), S 173 (A.D. 814) and S 180 (A.D. 816). He attended a synod at Chelsea in the latter year.[25]

17. **CEOLBERHT**, bishop (816 × 824)–(845 × 860). His profession to Archbishop Wulfred was preserved at Canterbury.[26] He attested a number of documents emanating from the *Clofesho* synod of 824 (S 1433–7), plus S 190, S 280 (both A.D. 838), S 281 (A.D. 839) and the confirmation of S 1438 at the *æt Astran* synod of 839. His last appearance is in the witness-list of S 1194 (A.D. 845, 8 November), a charter covering an exchange of land in Middlesex which was issued in London, probably at an ecclesiastical synod that had been convened there. Ceolberht's pontificate saw major political changes in southern England, as the Mercian hegemony crumbled and Essex fell under West Saxon control: these events, and their effect on the London diocese, are discussed above, pp. 19–20). At some point between 827 and 840 Ceolberht and the St Paul's community leased an estate to a thegn of the Mercian king Wiglaf (see **9**).

18. **DEORWULF**, bishop (845 × 860)–(867 × 896). His profession to Archbishop Ceolnoth was preserved at Canterbury.[27] He attests a Rochester charter of the West Saxon King Æthelberht (S 327, A.D. 860) and is also mentioned in the spurious Navestock charter (**16**), which is apparently based on a

---

[23] Gibbs, p. xviii n. 1. Whitelock (1975, p. 15) argues against a suggestion that Heahstan should be identified with Alcuin's correspondent of the same name.

[24] Richter, *Professions*, no. 7. It was the custom for newly-consecrated bishops to make a profession of obedience to the archbishop of Canterbury, and these promises were recorded at Christ Church. There are thirty extant professions from the pre-Conquest period, all but one from the ninth century. Some of the texts share elements of wording and formulation, probably because in these instances the professions were drafted at Christ Church: thus Æthelnoth's profession is very similar to the promises made by contemporary bishops of Lichfield and Hereford (see Brooks, *Church of Canterbury*, p. 166).

[25] Haddan & Stubbs, iii. 579.

[26] Richter, *Professions*, no. 13. This text was probably drafted at Canterbury; it shares common features with professions by bishops of Rochester, Leicester, Elmham and Lichfield (Brooks, *Church of Canterbury*, p. 166).

[27] Richter, *Professions*, no. 23. This has no textual links with other surviving professions, and it is possible that Deorwulf drafted the document himself, as he seems to claim (*cartulam mee confessionis et desponsionis componens*).

diploma of 867 in the name of King Æthelred of Wessex. He does not subscribe any extant Mercian diploma, and may have chosen to switch allegiance to the West Saxon rulers (for the background, see above, pp. 22–3).

19. **SWITHWULF**. He is named in the episcopal lists as Deorwulf's successor. His only appearance is in S 200 (A.D. 851), a Crowland forgery with a concocted and chronologically impossible witness-list partly based on pre-Conquest documentation.[28]

20. **HEAHSTAN**, bishop (867 × 896)–897. His death in 897 is noted in the *Anglo-Saxon Chronicle*. BL Cotton Otho B. ii is a later copy of the translation of Gregory's Pastoral Care which Alfred sent to Heahstan in the early 890s. The copy was produced *c.* 1000, possibly in the London scriptorium.[29]

21. **WULFSIGE**, bishop (897 × 900)–(909 × 926). He attests a number of the diplomas of King Edward the Elder between 900 and 909 (S 360, 1443, 1205, 368, 370, 372–4, 1286, 275–8, 381–3). No royal charters survive from the last decades of Edward's reign, which makes it nearly impossible to sort out episcopal dates for the period. In some episcopal lists Wulfsige's name follows that of Æthelweard.[30]

22. **ÆTHELWEARD**. He is known only from the episcopal lists.

23. **LEOFSTAN**. He is known only from the episcopal lists.[31]

24. **THEODRED**, bishop (909 × 926, possibly 925 × 926)–(951 × 953). Theodred's name is German, which suggests that he was of Continental origin. His will mentions other clerics with German names, to whom he grants much of his ecclesiastical apparatus (S 1526; see Appendix 2, and discussion, pp. 29–30, 90–4): Gosebriht, who had bequeathed him a massbook; another Theodred, possibly one of the two men of that name who held the revived see at Elmham between *c.* 970 and 995;[32] also Odgar and Gundwine. There is no reference to any other, English-named cleric, and the implication is clearly that Theodred's most intimate associates, at least during the later part of his career, were of foreign origin. Other evidence suggests that German clergy were coming to England during the reign of Æthelstan, and there were close contacts between the Anglo-Saxon and German churches.[33] At some stage in his career, perhaps

[28] O'Donovan 1973, p. 97. There was a contemporary Swithulf at Rochester (outside dating limits 867 × 896, attests S 321, 1276), which raises the possibility of confusion; but the witness to S 200 is firmly identified as bishop of London.

[29] See p. 38 n. 133. For the background to the distribution of copies of the translation of the Pastoral Care, see Keynes and Lapidge, *Alfred the Great*, pp. 124, 294 n. 1.

[30] O'Donovan 1973, p. 97.

[31] Page 1965, pp. 91–2; O'Donovan 1973, p. 97

[32] Campbell 1996, pp. 14–15.

[33] Stenton, *ASE*, p. 444; M. Wood, 'The Making of Æthelstan's Empire: an English Charlemagne?', in Wormald, *Ideal and Reality*, pp. 250–72, esp. pp. 259–65.

before becoming bishop or perhaps later, Theodred travelled to Italy, for his will mentions two chasubles which he had purchased in Pavia. This was one of the greatest markets in Europe, with a particular reputation for Byzantine silks, and it stood on one of the main pilgrim routes from north-west Europe to Rome.[34]

Theodred was in England in 926, from which date he attests royal diplomas on a regular basis. Almost no royal charters survive from the period between c. 909 and 926 (see above, and pp. 157–8). There are two exceptions: a Burton charter of 925 with an abbreviated witness-list reflecting a Mercian gathering, with attestations of the bishops of Lichfield, Dorchester, Worcester and Hereford (S 395; Sawyer, Burton, no. 2); and a curious document from St Augustine's which is associated with the day of King Æthelstan's consecration, 4 September 925 (S 394; Kelly, St Augustine's, no. 26). The latter is attested by the arch-bishop of Canterbury and seven bishops, all of whom were presumably present at the ceremony. There is no bishop of London, although the consecration appar-ently took place at Kingston-on-Thames, on the borders of the London see.[35] This strongly suggests that Theodred was appointed between September 925 and 926, when he began attesting charters. Under his rule the London see became more prominent than it had been for centuries, probably largely as a result of his personal standing. From the beginning he attested in a prominent position, a pat-tern that became firmly established in documents from c. 935 onwards, when the subscriptions of Ælfheah of Winchester and Theodred usually headed those of the other suffragans: it also became the normal practice of charter-scribes to expand the subscriptions of these two men with an identification of their sees. According to William of Malmesbury, Theodred accompanied King Æthelstan en route to the Battle of Brunanburh in 937.[36] By the time he drew up his will he was a very wealthy man, with a personal landed endowment centred on Suffolk, which also included estates in Norfolk, Cambridgeshire and Essex. He had been granted one Norfolk estate by King Eadmund in 942 (S 483). Apart from bequests to the king and Queen Eadgifu, and to St Paul's, he left property to a minster at Mendham in Suffolk, to Glastonbury Abbey (the cen-tre of monastic reform in England, under Abbot Dunstan) and to 'St Edmund's church' (i.e. what was to become the abbey of Bury St Edmunds). In Bury

---

[34] Dodwell, AS Art, pp. 149–53.

[35] Also missing was Bishop Frithestan of Winchester, who may have been at odds with King Æthelstan (see comment in The Liber Vitae of the New Minster and Hyde Abbey, Winchester, ed. S. Keynes, Early English MSS in Facsimile (Copenhagen, 1996), p. 20); plus the bishops of Ramsbury and Rochester (where there may have been vacancies), and the bishops of the more distant sees of Cornwall and Hereford.

[36] GP, § 73 (p. 144).

tradition, Theodred was associated with the translation of the martyred King Edmund's relics to the site of the later abbey: he may indeed have helped revive the cult.[37] As well as endowing religious houses, Theodred was concerned to benefit his kindred: most of his Suffolk estates were left to his nephews Osgot and Offa, and to a second kinsman named Osgot, Ealdulf's son.[38] The will shows that Theodred was at that point also acting as bishop in Suffolk, in the territory of the southern East Anglian see of Dunwich which had been extinguished by the Viking assaults of the ninth century. This area was evidently regarded as separate from the London diocese, and had its own see at Hoxne in Suffolk. It seems reasonably certain that this arrangement was a stage in the re-establishment of episcopal organisation in East Anglia (see above, pp. 29, 92).

Theodred's last subscription is found in a diploma of 951, and his successor begins to subscribe in 953 (no charters survive from the intervening year). He and Eorcenwald were the only pre-Conquest bishops who were remembered in St Paul's in the later medieval period. William of Malmesbury notes that Theodred's tomb was situated near the window of the cathedral crypt and that it was visible to passers-by.[39] Theodred's bequests to St Paul's included his best relics (possibly acquired at Pavia, along with his vestments). An inventory of the abbey's treasures compiled in 1245 mentions a high-quality Old Testament written in 'ancient English script', the front cover of which contained the relics given to the church by 'Bishop Theodore' (while the back cover contained a list of the reign-lengths of kings from *Alwredus* (? Alfred) onwards).[40] There seems to be a fair chance that the relics in question were those given by Theodred (his name having become slightly corrupted), rather than a separate set donated by (Arch-)bishop Theodore.

25. **BRIHTHELM**, bishop (951 × 953)–(957 × 959). In the 950s several English sees (London, Wells, Selsey and Winchester) were occupied by bishops named Brihthelm; one of these was briefly appointed to Canterbury in 959,

---

[37] See D.N. Dumville, *English Caroline Script and Monastic History: Studies in Benedictinism, A.D. 950–1030* (Woodbridge, 1993), pp. 35–8

[38] Theodred's family connections will be explored further in the forthcoming edition of the charters of Bury St Edmunds by K. Lowe and S. Foot.

[39] *GP*, § 73 (p. 144).

[40] 'Item alia pars bibliae consimiliter Anglicae litterae sed melioris, in cuius custodia prima continentur reliquiae quas Theodorus Episcopus contulit ecclesiae, in secunda quot annis Alwredus Rex et successores sui vixerunt; et dicitur liber Hugoni Episcopi [probably Hugh de Orivalle, 1075–1084]. Finit in Job': printed Simpson 1887, p. 496. This inventory was reproduced with additions in 1255: see edition and discussion of the section concerning books in Ker 1969, p. 49. Ker suggests that the notes of English kings from Alfred onwards in London, Lambeth Palace 8, fos 151v–152r, may be from this source.

before being demoted in favour of Dunstan. It seems likely that fewer then four individuals were involved, and that at least two sees were held in plurality: but debate continues over possible interpretations.[41] Bishop Brihthelm of London was the beneficiary of the 957 diploma of which **14** is an extract. Later in that year the kingdon was split between King Eadwig and his brother Edgar, with Edgar becoming king of the Mercians. London was traditionally part of the Mercian realm and one would have expected Brihthelm of London to start attesting Edgar's diplomas: but he does not. It is possible that he died or retired in 957, or that he sided with Eadwig for political reasons, a circumstance that may have some connection with the proliferation of Brihthelms in this period.

26. **DUNSTAN**, bishop (957 × 959)– ? 959. The celebrated Dunstan, former abbot of Glastonbury, was in charge of the see of London before his elevation to Canterbury in 959. He had gone into exile after falling out with King Eadwig, but was recalled by Edgar after the division of the kingdom in 957 and appointed bishop, apparently at first not to any particular see: but on the eve of Edgar's succession to the whole kingdom in 959 he was acting as bishop of both Worcester and London.[42] Dunstan's name is omitted from the episcopal lists for London, perhaps due to sensitivity about the issue of pluralism. He attests a Peterborough diploma of 959 explicitly as bishop of London (S 681), and is included as one of the holders of the London see by William of Malmesbury and John of Worcester.[43] Westminster tradition claimed that Dunstan refounded the monastery there while bishop of London, and S 1293 is a spurious diploma to that effect (see also S 670, and above, pp. 31–2).[44] When Edgar became king of the whole of England after Eadwig's death in October 959, he installed Dunstan at Canterbury. It is possible that Dunstan retained London for a few more years.

27. **ÆLFSTAN**, bishop (959 × 964)–(995 × 996). There was a contemporary Ælfstan at Rochester during this period, which means that there is a potential for confusion between his subscriptions and those of Ælfstan of London: although it is argued that it is generally possible to distinguish between them.[45] The picture is

---

[41] See Whitelock 1973, pp. 233–6; Brooks, *Church of Canterbury*, pp. 238–9, 376 n. 107; P. Wormald, 'The Strange Affair of the Selsey Bishopric, 953–963', in *Belief and Culture in the Middle Ages*, ed. R. Gameson and H. Leyser (Oxford, 2001), pp. 128–41.

[42] See Whitelock 1973, p. 233, for evidence that Dunstan was not immediately associated with a particular see. He attests six diplomas of 958 as bishop, in one case alongside Cenwald of Worcester, which shows that his immediate appointment was not to Worcester. However, given the uncertainty about Brihthelm's position after the 957 division, it is possible that Dunstan was attesting in 958 as bishop of London.

[43] *GP*, § 73 (p. 145); *John of Worcester*, pp. 406, 407n.

[44] Whitelock 1975, p. 22.

[45] Keynes, *Diplomas*, p. 179 n. 99. It is noted here that Ælfstan of London generally attests in the same relative position, either before of after Æthelwold of Winchester.

rather hazy at the beginning of Edgar's reign. Both Ælfstans attest a diploma of
964 (S 725), but it is impossible to say whether the single Ælfstan attesting several diplomas between 959 and 964 was the bishop of London or of Rochester. It
was probably the case that Dunstan relinquished London on his appointment to
Canterbury, and that his successor was consecrated soon after: but it is possible
that there was a delay.[46] Ælfstan had an exceptionally long and obscure pontificate, which saw at least two disasters: St Paul's burned down in 962 and London
in 982 (ASC). His last years coincided with a renewed Viking onslaught, and a
nearly-successful attempt to burn the city in 994 (ASC). In 992 one of the Bishops
Ælfstan was named as a leader of a naval expedition against the Danes (ASC).
The bishop of London was a beneficiary under the will of Æthelric of Bocking
(S 1501; see p. 95). There was a confused tradition at Evesham that King
Æthelred granted the monastery there to a Bishop Æthelstan, probably an error
for Ælfstan (of London or Rochester).[47] The London Ælfstan attests until 995.

28. **WULFSTAN**, bishop 996–1002. Wulfstan 'the Homilist' was bishop of
London for several years before he was promoted to York in 1002. He may have
had family connections with the East Midlands, and he was buried at Ely.[48] He
was consecrated bishop of London in 996 (ASC F). Collected among his works
is a small group of letters written by or to Wulfstan as bishop of London, all in
homiletic vein (see above, p. 38). The list of chasubles in the 1245 inventory of
St Paul's treasures begins with a casula Wulfstani, which might possibly have
been associated with the bishop.[49]

29. **ÆLFHUN**, bishop (1002 × 1004)–(1013 × 1014). He may previously
have been abbot of Milton Abbas in Dorset.[50] During his pontificate the remains
of Archbishop Ælfheah, captured and murdered by the Vikings, were brought to
London and buried in St Paul's church, where they became the centre of a fledg-
ling cult (ASC s.a. 1012; see p. 36). Between 1009 and 1012 the body of
St Edmund is supposed to have been transferred from Bury to St Gregory's
church in London for safekeeping; it was later claimed at Bury that Ælfhun tried
to purloin the relics.[51] In 1013 Ælfhun escorted the æthelings Edward and

[46] Brooks 1992, p. 21.

[47] Whitelock 1975, p. 23 n. 3. There is reason to think that King Æthelred was deeply hostile to
Ælfstan of Rochester in the 980s (Keynes, Diplomas, pp. 178–9), which would make it likely that
the London bishop was the beneficiary of any grant of Evesham (unless Æthelred gave Evesham to
the Rochester Ælfstan as compensation).

[48] A. Orchard in Blackwell, p. 494.

[49] Simpson 1887, p. 482. The next item on the list is the chasuble given by Godgifu of Coventry
(see p. 46 n. 173), which would suggest that the list began with the oldest of the community's
vestments.

[50] HRH, p. 56; Robertson, Charters, pp. 375, 384–5.

[51] Memorials of St Edmund's Abbey, ed. T. Arnold, RS, 3 vols (London, 1890–6), i. 43

Alfred to Normandy (*ASC*); he may have been their tutor (see pp. 37, 39). He seems to have resigned his bishopric or died before February 1014, when his successor was consecrated.[52]

30. ÆLFWIG, bishop 1014–35. He was consecrated at York on 16 February 1014 (*ASC* D). King Æthelred died in London in 1016 and was buried at St Paul's; his son Eadmund (Ironside) was elected to succeed him by the witan at London. The following sequence of events included Cnut's siege of the city, a subsequent treaty between Cnut and Eadmund which left Cnut master of Mercia and London, and the death of Eadmund. Bishop Ælfwig attests King Cnut's charters on a fairly regular basis between 1018 and 1035, but he may have been generally out of favour with the king as a result of his support for Eadmund; during his pontificate Cnut seized the episcopal estate at Southminster and also ordered the transfer of the valuable relics of St Ælfheah to Canterbury (see above, pp. 39–40). But the Danish king may have relented before his death: a writ of 1033 × 1035 confirming the lands and privileges of St Paul's (**27**) may be authentic; while a post-Conquest writ of William I or II confirms to Bishop Maurice all the property and rights enjoyed by his predecessors *Ælfinius* (i.e *Ælfwig*) and William, wording which would seem to imply the existence of a writ or similar document in favour of Ælfwig.[53] It is possible that the charter mentioned in the writ lies behind a spurious Latin diploma in Cnut's name, ostensibly confirming the lands of St Paul's (**26**).

31. ÆLFWEARD, bishop 1035–July 1044. Ælfweard had previously a monk of Ramsey and abbot of Evesham.[54] He retained the abbacy after his appointment to London, and continued to benefit its monks: for instance, by sending them books, on both sacred and grammatical subjects. He is said to have been a kinsman of King Cnut, and was one of the delegates who went to Flanders in 1040 to ask Harthacnut to become king; during the voyage he saved the ship in a storm with a well-judged prayer to St Ecgwine. It seems that Ælfweard had to resign his see when he became ill, apparently with leprosy (reputedly the result of an injudicious attempt to filch relics from the tomb of St Osyth). He went to Evesham but the monks there refused to receive him, so he travelled to Ramsey where he was welcomed; as a result he transferred his gifts from Evesham to Ramsey.[55]

---

[52] It has been suggested by Keynes (*Diplomas*, p. 67), that Ælfhun was briefly reinstated, because he appears to attest S 934 from 1015. But the reading in the MS of S 934 is more likely to be *Alfuii* than *Alfun* (see Kelly, *Abingdon*, p. 538).

[53] Gibbs, no. 18 (p. 18); Bates, *RRAN: Acta of William I*, no 191. Cnut is the likeliest donor of such a writ, but the document in question could date from the last two years of Æthelred's reign.

[54] Whitelock 1975, pp. 32–4; *HRH*, p. 47. See also S 1423, an Evesham lease of 1016 × 1023.

[55] *Chronicon Abbatiæ Rameseiensis*, ed. W.D. Macray, RS (London, 1886), pp. 148–50, 157–8, 198; *Chronicon Abbatiæ de Evesham*, ed. *idem*, RS (London, 1863), pp. 36–7, 81–5, 314.

32. **ROBERT OF JUMIÈGES**, bishop 1044–51. Robert Champart was a prior of St Ouen in Rouen, who in 1037 was made abbot of Jumièges. He became an associate of Edward the Confessor during the latter's exile in Normandy, and it was to Edward's favour that he owed his appointment to London and his disastrous promotion to Canterbury in 1051.[56]

33. **SPEARHAFOC**, bishop 1051. He was a monk of Bury St Edmund's, and abbot of Abingdon from *c.* 1051, and is reputed to have been the king's goldsmith; his selection by King Edward as bishop of London may have been dictated by the political necessity of promoting an Englishman instead of a Norman.[57] At the time Robert of Jumièges, newly appointed as archbishop, was in Rome to collect his pallium; on his return he refused (apparently with papal approval) to consecrate Spearhafoc, who was expelled from the see and fled abroad. The fugitive was accused of despoiling the bishopric, as well as stealing the precious materials he had been given to make a crown for King Edward.[58]

34. **WILLIAM**, bishop 1051–75. William was a Norman clerk of King Edward, apparently appointed under the influence of Robert of Jumièges.[59] He efficiently maintained the interests of the bishopric after the Conquest (see pp. 47–8).

[56] See Barlow, *English Church*, pp. 44, 46–50, 85–6.
[57] Kelly, *Abingdon*, p. ccxvi; Barlow, *English Church*, pp. 47–8; *HRH*, p. 24.
[58] *Chron. Abingdon*, i. 463.
[59] Barlow, *English Church*, pp. 49–50, 81–2, 219–20.

LIST OF CHARTERS

CHARTERS OF ST PAUL'S

1. Æthelberht, king [of Kent], grants land at Tillingham, Essex, to Bishop Mellitus and St Paul's minster. [A.D. 604 × 616]

2. Æthelred, king of the Mercians, grants ten hides at Ealing, Middlesex, to Wealdhere, bishop [of London]. [A.D. 693 × 704]

3. Tyrhtel, bishop [of Hereford], grants fifty hides at Fulham, Middlesex, to Wealdhere, bishop of London. A.D. 701 [? for 704 × 709]

4. Offa, king of the East Saxons, grants land in the district called *Hæmele* [Hertfordshire], to Wealdhere, bishop [of London]. [*c.* A.D. 704 × 709]

5. (*a*) Coenred, king of the Mercians, renews the liberty granted by King Æthelberht to St Paul's minster. [A.D. 704 × 709]

(*b*) Offa, king of the Mercians, extends the liberty of St Paul's. [A.D. 757 × 796]

6. Swæfred, king of the East Saxons, grants seventy hides in the district called *Deningei* [Essex] to Ingwald, bishop of London. [A.D. (705 × 716) × 745]

6A. Extract from a charter connected with Ingwald, bishop of London. [A.D. (705 × 716) × 745]

7. Æthelbald, king of the Mercians, grants remission of toll on one ship to Ingwald, bishop of London. [A.D. 716 × 745]

8. Æthelbald, king of the Mercians, grants remission of toll on one ship to Ingwald, bishop of London. [A.D. 716 × 745]

9. Ceolberht, bishop of London, and the brethren of St Paul's church lease ten hides at Braughing, Hertfordshire, to Sigeric, *minister* of Wiglaf, king of the Mercians, with reversion to St Andrew's church. [A.D. 827 × 829 or 830 × 840]

10. King Edward, with Æthelred and Æthelflæd of Mercia, at the request of Æthelfrith, *dux*, renews a charter of Coenwulf, king of the Mercians, granting ten hides at Islington, Middlesex, to Beornnoth, *comes*. A.D. 903

11. Part of a dating clause and witness-list from a diploma of King Æthelstan. A.D. 935

12. King Æthelstan confirms for St Paul's minster: ten hides at Sandon with *Rothe* (? Roe Green in St Peter's) and eight hides at Ardeley with Luffenhall, Hertfordshire; ten hides at Belchamp St Paul's with Wickham St Paul's, eight at

Heybridge and twelve at Runwell, Essex; thirty hides at *Eduluesnæsa* (The Naze, Essex); ten hides at West Drayton, Middlesex; eight hides at Barnes, Surrey; and ten hides at Neasden with Willesden, Middlesex. [A.D. 924 × 939]

13. King Æthelstan confirms the privileges of St Paul's minster, first granted in the time of King Sebbi. [A.D. 924 × 939]

14. King Eadred grants twelve hides at Shopland, Essex, to Eawynn, a nun. A.D. 946

15. King Eadwig grants ten hides at Orsett, Essex, to Bishop Brihthelm. [A.D. 957]

16. King Edgar grants fifteen hides at Navestock, Essex, to St Paul's minster. A.D. 867 [for 957 × 958]

17. King Edgar grants forty hides at [Hadham, Hertfordshire], to Æthelflæd, widow and nun. A.D. 969

18. King Edgar grants seventy hides to St Paul. [A.D. 957 × 975]

19. (*a*) Extract from a diploma of King Æthelred. A.D. 982

(*b*) Extract from a diploma [? of King Æthelred] in favour of Werenberht, deacon, possibly concerning land at Orsett, Essex [A.D. 971 × 992]

20. Extracts from a diploma or diplomas of King Æthelred. A.D. 986

21. King Æthelred confirms the lands of St Paul's minster. [A.D. 978 × 995/6]

22. Æthelflæd bequeaths four hides at Laver, Essex, and two at Cockhampstead, Hertfordshire, to St Paul's minster. [*c*. A.D. 1000]

23. King Æthelred confirms Æthelflæd's bequest to St Paul's minster of four hides at Laver, Essex, and two at Cockhampstead, Hertfordshire. [*c*. A.D. 1000]

24. King Æthelred grants judicial privileges to the priests of St Paul's minster. [A.D. 978 × 1016]

25. List of contributions required from St Paul's estates for the manning of a ship. [*c*. A.D. 1000]

26. King Cnut confirms the lands given by himself and his predecessors to St Paul's minster in London. [A.D. 1016 × 1035]

27. King Cnut grants judicial and financial privileges to St Paul's minster. [A.D. 1033 × 1035]

28. King Edward grants judicial and financial privileges to the priests of St Paul's minster. [A.D. 1042 × 1066]

29. King Edward renews the liberties of St Paul's minster, with particular reference to eight hides at Barling and five at Chingford, Essex. [A.D. 1042 × 1066]

30. King Edward grants one hide at *Sciredesforde* to Fræwine, *minister*. [A.D. 1042 × 1066]

31. Eadgifu and her husband grant land at Weeley, Essex, to the brethren of St Paul's church, with the permission of King Edward. [A.D. 1042 × 1066]

THE LONDON *CNIHTENGILD*

32. King Edward declares that his men in the gild of the English *cnihtas* are to have their sake and soke, within the city and without, and to be entitled to as good laws as they enjoyed in the days of Kings Edgar, Æthelred and Cnut. [A.D. 1042 × 1044]

CONCORDANCE

No.	Sawyer (1st edn)	Sawyer (rev. edn)	Birch	Kemble	Harmer, *Writs*	Gibbs, *St Paul's*
1	5	5	8	982		
2	1783	LStP 1				J7
3	1785	LstP 2				J6
4	1784	LStP 3				J9
5	1786, 1790	LStP 4, 7				J17, J18
6	1787	LStP 5				J11
7		103a				
8	1788	103b				J14
9	1791	LStP 8				J16
10		367a				J8
11	1792	LStP 9				J10
12	453	453	737	1127		
13	452	452	735–6	1126		
14	1793	LStP 10				J12
15	1794	LStP 11				J13
16	337	337	1210	1259		
17	1795	LStP 12				J1
18		LStP 18				
19		LStP 14, 17				
20		LStP 16				
21	941	941		1311		
22	1495	1495		972		
23	908	908		1300		J5
24	945	945			52	J3
25		1458a				
26	978	978		1320		
27	992	992		1319	53	
28	1104	1104		887	54	
29	1056	1056		913		
30		LStP 18				(p. 1 n.)
31		1243a				(p. 280)
32	1103	1103			51	

SIGLA

In this edition the siglum A is reserved for originals. My attention was drawn to the text in GL 25516 (MS P) at a late stage and it is therefore listed out of chronological order. Certain printed works are the sole witness to lost manuscript sources and are cited in the apparatus (see § iv below).

i. *Principal Manuscripts of the Charters of St Paul's*
B. CCCC 383 (s. xii)
C. GL 25504 (*Liber L*) (s. xii^1)
D. St Paul's, D. & C., *Liber B* (s. xii^{ex}; *lost*)
E. GL 25501 (*Liber A*) (s. xiii^{med})
F. GL 25272 (s. xiii^2)
G. PRO Ch.R. 9 Edw. II, m. 2 (Inspeximus, A.D. 1316)
H. Bodleian, James 23 (s. xvii^1)
I. London, Lincoln's Inn, Hale 84 (s. xvii^1)
J. PRO DL 42/149 (s. xvii^1)
K. Oxford, The Queen's College, 88 (s. xvi/xvii)
L. BL Cotton Jul. C. vii (s. xvii^1)
M. BL Lansdowne 364 (s. xvii^{med})
N. Bodleian, Dodsworth 10 (s. xvii^{med})
O. BL Stowe 666 (s. xviii^1)
P. GL 25516 (s. xiv^1)

ii. *Manuscripts of* **32**
Q. Glasgow, University Library, Hunter U. 2. 6 (s. xiv/xv)
R. London, Corporation of London Records Office, Letter Book C (s. xv)
S. London, Corporation of London Records Office, *Liber Dunthorne* (s. xv)

iii. *Manuscripts of Theodred's Will (Appendix 2)*
T. Cambridge, UL. Ff. 2. 33 (s. xiii^2)
U. BL Add. 14847 (s. xiv)

iv. *Printed Works*
MA. R. Dodsworth and W. Dugdale, *Monasticon Anglicanum* (London, 1655–73)
SP1. W. Dugdale, *A History of St Paul's Cathedral in London* (London, 1658)
SP2. W. Dugdale, *A History of St Paul's Cathedral in London*, 2nd edn with author's corrections (London, 1716)

NOTE ON THE METHOD OF EDITING

The underlying principle of this edition has been to provide texts that are as close as possible to the original versions, while still accessible to the modern reader. Where a text is preserved in multiple manuscripts, the best version has been used as the basis for the edition, with variants noted in the apparatus; but where there are better readings in other manuscripts, these have generally been transposed to the main text. In order to avoid over-burdening the apparatus, only the more significant variants are given for the Latin texts; thus, for example, medieval spelling variants such as *mihi/michi* and *statio/stacio* have not usually been noted. The apparatus for the vernacular documents is more comprehensive. One document (**28**) survives in a very large number of copies; in this case only the principal witnesses are collated here.

Evident corruptions and misreadings are usually corrected in the text, with the manuscript reading given in the apparatus. Standard abbreviations have been expanded silently. Modern punctuation has generally been supplied for all texts, with the exception of **25** and of the letter of Bishop Wealdhere (Appendix I). The capitalization of the exemplar(s) has been replaced throughout with modern capitalization: that is, capitals have been supplied for all personal names and place-names, and have been provided at the beginning of sentences. Old English documents and shorter passages have been translated (except in the case of **13**, which is a bilingual Old English/Latin document).

THE CHARTERS

THE CHAPTERS

1

Æthelberht, king [of Kent], grants land at Tillingham, Essex, to Bishop Mellitus and St Paul's minster. [A.D. 604 × 616]

C. GL 25504 (*Liber L*), 5v: copy, s. xii[1]
　　Rubric: Priuilegium Æðelberti Regis 'anno gracie circa .dcx.' [*addition by a medieval annotator*]
D. St Paul's D. & C., *Liber B*, 20r: copy, s. xii[ex] (lost)
E. GL 25501 (*Liber A*), 56v (original foliation 38v): copy, s. xiii[med]
M. BL Lansdowne 364, 124r: incomplete copy, s. xvii[med]
N. Bodleian, Dodsworth 10, 8r: copy, s. xvii[med]
　　Rubric: Diploma regis Ethelberti factum Melito episcopo sancti Pauli London'
Ed.: a. Dugdale, *St Paul's*, p. 181, from D (SP1)
　　　b. *Mon. Angl.*, iii. 299, from D (MA)
　　　c. Dugdale, *St Paul's* (2nd edn), App. p. 5, from D (SP2)
　　　d. Dugdale, *St Paul's* (3rd edn), p. 288, from D
　　　e. Kemble 982, from *Mon. Angl.*
　　　f. Haddan and Stubbs, pp. 59–60, from Kemble
　　　g. Simpson, *Registrum statutorum*, p. 380, from C
　　　h. Birch 8, from Kemble, *Mon. Angl.* and Haddan and Stubbs
　　　i. Pierquin, *Recueil*, pt 3, no. 1, from Birch
Listed: Sawyer 5; Hart, *ECE*, no. 1
Edited from C, with variants from E, N and MA (*Mon. Angl.*)

[a]In Christi nomine.[b] Æðelbertus[c] rex Deo inspirante, pro animę suę remedio, dedit episcopo Mellito[d] terram quę appellatur Tillincgeham[e] ad monasterii sui solatium, scilicet monasterii[f] sancti Pauli apostoli doctoris gentium. Et ego rex[f] Æðelbertus[g] ita firmiter concedo tibi pręsuli Mellito[d] potestatem eius habendi et possidendi, ut inperpetuum in monasterii utilitate permaneat. Si quis uero contradicere temptauerit hanc donationem, anathema et excommunicatus sit ab omni societate christiana usque ad satisfactionem. Qua de re ego episcopus Mellitus, una cum rege Æðelberto,[h] Hunfredum[i] episcopum subscribere rogaui.

Signum manus Hunfredi[j] episcopi.[k]
Signum manus Letharii episcopi.
Signum manus Æbane.[l]
Signum manus Æþelpaldi.[m]
Signum manus Æscpine,[n] et aliorum multorum.

---

[a] Carta Regis Æthelberti facta ecclesiæ S. Pauli de manerio de Tillingham *rubric in* MA (*possibly from lost* Liber B)　　[b] In nomine Christi E　　[c] Ethelbertus E, N, MA
[d] Melito N　　[e] Tyllingham E; Tillingeham N, MA　　[f] *Word omitted* N　　[g] Adelbertus E; Edelbertus N; Ethelbertus MA　　[h] Edelberto E, N; Ethelbert MA　　[i] Humfredum E, N

^j Humfredi N; Hunfridi MA   ^k *Subscriptions run across the page* C, E; *crosses supplied*
after the subscriptions MA   ^l Abbane N; Abbanæ MA   ^m Ethelpaldi N   ⁿ Espine N;
Æspine MA

1 is a fabrication, which functions as a title-deed for the manor of Tillingham while also celebrating the early foundation of St Paul's. It was one of the small collection of mostly suspect pre-Conquest documents which was copied into the main St Paul's cartularies in the twelfth and thirteenth centuries (MSS C, D, E). One of these is now missing (MS D, *Liber B*), but was the source for the texts in *Mon. Angl.* and Dugdale's *History of St Paul's*; it seems likely that Dugdale normalised some of the proper nouns and supplied the subscription crosses. The antiquarian extract in BL Lansdowne 364 (MS M) breaks off after the anathema; it was certainly not copied from MS E, but was conceivably taken from C or D. The exemplar for Dodsworth's text (MS N) seems most likely to have been MS D.

The forger has modelled the text in part on a charter of the early 670s. This is most clearly signalled in the witness-list, which includes subscriptions of Bishop Leuthere of Winchester (670–6) and of an obscure Bishop Hunferth. There is another subscription of the latter in S 1165 (Kelly, *Chertsey*, no. 1), a grant to the minster at Chertsey in Surrey, which belongs to the period before the death of King Wulfhere of Mercia in 674 or 675 (see also S 1181, a forgery based on S 1165). Dorothy Whitelock, commenting on the Chertsey diploma and unaware of the second subscription in **1**, conjectured that the name Hunferth in S 1165 was a corruption of a different name and proposed an identification with Wynferth, appointed bishop of the Mercians in 672 (*EHD*, p. 480 n. 1). But the repetition of the same name in **1**, in a witness-list with other affinities with S 1165, would seem to suggest that Hunferth was a separate individual, perhaps a bishop of London active between Wine (666–?) and Eorcenwald, who was appointed *c.* 675 (see above, pp. 109–10). The *Æb(b)ana* who attests **1** may be the *Ebbus* of S 1165, and Æthelwald is perhaps the Mercian *subregulus* of that name who subscribes the same charter. Roy Hart has conjectured that the final witness, Æscwine, may be the king of Wessex who ruled between 674 and 676 (*ECE*, p. 8). If so, the position of his name would suggest that he had confirmed the charter (i.e. the original diploma used by the forger of **1**), as Wulfhere of Mercia did S 1165. For the historical context in Surrey in the 670s, see above, pp. 13–15.

Some aspects of the formulation of the text may also demonstrate dependence upon a model of the later seventh century. The brief royal style (*rex Deo inspirante*) has a glancing but not conclusive resemblance to the styles of contemporary West Saxon kings (compare S 231, 234, 235 and *cf.* S1169, and Edwards, *Charters*, p. 308); for the close relationship between charters from Wessex and the London diocese in this period, see Wormald 1985, pp. 9–11, and above, pp. 77–9. The phrase *ad monasterii sui solatium* recalls *ad solacium seruorum Dei* in a West Saxon charter from the time of Ine (S 1176, A.D. 708; *cf.* also S 1171, *ad augmentum monasterii tui*). The use of the second person in the reference to the beneficiary is generally an early feature (compare, for example, S 8, 45, 1165, 1167–8, 1171; and see Edwards, *ibid.*, pp. 134–5). The statement of powers could be an adaptation of an early formula (compare S 1164, 65, 1177, 1799–1800, and see Edwards, *ibid.*, p. 232; Kelly, *St Augustine's*, p. lxxx n. 30); the same may be true of the anathema (compare S 1165, 1171, which both include the phrase *ab omni societate christiana*). A rogation clause is a regular feature of seventh-century English charters, occasionally incorporating a reference to a specific witness (see, for example, S 9, 19, 20, 1167); the usual formula is *ut subscribere(n)t rogavi*. It is possible that the short verbal invocation was also taken from the model; its only other appearance is in S 260 (Kelly, *Malmesbury*, no 12; A.D. 758), but it is not incompatible with an early date (compare S 9, 11: *In nomine saluatoris*). The forger appears to have altered slightly the structure of his source, so that the dispositive section begins with a narrative sentence, before switching to the first person; and he has inserted references to Æthelberht, Mellitus and St Paul's (the last in a particularly clumsy phrase): his inspiration was no doubt Bede's statement that Æthelberht bestowed lands and possessions on his new foundation (*HE*, ii. 3). Later St Paul's tradition dated Æthelberht's grant to the year 610 (see, for example, the addition to the rubric in MS C, and BL Lansdowne 364, 8r).

Tillingham was bequeathed to St Paul's by Bishop Theodred (died 951 × 953) to be 'the property (*are*) of the community' (S 1526: see Appendix 2 for the text of the will). It seems most likely that the estate formed part of his own patrimony, and that the bequest marks the first acquisition of the estate by St Paul's, although it has also been argued that Tillingham was an early possession of the bishopric, and that Theodred's bequest was essentially a transfer of the property from the bishop to the chapter (see discussion above, pp. 84–5). One possibility is that Tillingham had an early association, not with St Paul's, but with the minster founded by Cedd at *Ythancæstir* (Bradwell-on-Sea), just north of Tillingham (Bede, *HE*, iii. 22). Coincidentally (or perhaps not), Cedd's second minster in the East Saxon kingdom was at Tilbury, which has the same first element (a personal name *Tilli* or *Tylli*) as Tillingham; there may have been an earlier connection between the two places (for the place-names, see *PN Essex*, pp. 173, 229). Tillingham appears among the estates of the church of London *c.* 1000 in a document relating to a naval levy (**25**), and it is listed among the lands of the canons in Domesday Book, with an assessment of twenty hides and six acres (LDB 13r; *DB Essex*, 5:5). It was the only one of the estates bequeathed to St Paul's by Theodred which remained in the possession of the canons at the time of the Domesday survey.

2

Æthelred, king of the Mercians, grants ten hides (manentes) *at Ealing, Middlesex, to Wealdhere, bishop [of London].* [A.D. 693 × 704]

H. Bodleian, James 23, p. 33: extract, s. xvii[1]
Ed.: Gibbs, p. 4 (J7)
Translated: Whitelock, *EHD*, p. 488 (no. 61)
Listed: Sawyer 1783 (LonStP 1); Gelling, *ECTV*, no. 190

In nomine Dei summi. Ego Ethelredus rex Merciorum cum consensu et licentia sapientum meorum do tibi Waldherio episcopo aliquam partem terræ in loco qui dicitur Gillingas, id est 10 manentium, ad augmentum monasterialis vitæ in civitate Londoniæ.

This is an extract by Richard James from a text on the lost St Paul's roll (see above, pp. 67–70). The source seems more likely than not to have been an authentic charter. It fits what is known of the historical context: Mercian overlordship over Middlesex seems to have been well-established by *c.* 700 (see above, pp. 12–13); King Æthelred of

Mercia is said to have granted an estate at Isleworth to the minster at Barking (S 1246); and in the year of Æthelred's retirement his *comes* Pæogthath made a joint-grant with an East Saxon king to Bishop Wealdhere of land at Twickenham (S 65). **2** is such a brief extract that it is impossible to divine whether Æthelred's grant of Ealing was attested or confirmed by the current East Saxon king. The dating limits are provided by Wealdhere's appointment in 693 and Æthelred's abdication in 704. As far as it goes, the formulation of the extract seems generally compatible with the implied date. The verbal invocation recurs in a nearly coeval charter from the kingdom of the Hwicce (S 1177, A.D. 704 × 709) and in an Evesham charter dated 718, perhaps for 727 (S 85), both of which seem to be essentially genuine; it was used occasionally from the eighth century to the eleventh. The use of the second person to refer to the beneficiary is a common feature of seventh-century diplomatic (compare, for example, S 8, 45, 1165, 1167–8, 1171; and see Edwards, *ibid.*, pp. 134–5), and the dispositive verb in the present tense would also be acceptable in an early text (compare S 1165, 1171). The earliest surviving original from the East Saxon kingdom (S 1171; probably A.D. 690 × 693) provides a parallel for the construction *in [loco] qui dicitur*, the assessment in *manentes*, and the phrasing of the final clause (compare *ad augmentum monasterii tui* in S 1171): for the unit of assessment, see also S 65a, 65b from Barking. The clause *cum consensu et licentia sapientum meorum* may be a little awkward. Other early diplomas have similar consent-clauses (for example, **3, 6** and S 65), but the only close parallels for this wording are in two Kentish documents from the ninth century (S 293, 344, and *cf.* S 286, 1438).

The beneficiary is Bishop Wealdhere, but the land was intended to support 'monastic life' in the city of London. In this instance the word *monasterium* and the corresponding adjective *monasterialis* do not necessarily refer to a regular monastic community, but should perhaps be associated with the more general sense of the Old English word *minster*, used to refer to a range of types of religious community (see S. Foot, 'Anglo-Saxon Minsters: a Review of Terminology', in *Pastoral Care before the Parish*, ed. J. Blair and R. Sharpe (Leicester, 1992), pp. 212–25). There is some reason to believe that Wealdhere was more active than his predecessor in building up the St Paul's endowment (see p. 87). The ten hides were in the area known as *Gillingas* ('Gilla's people'), which was the origin of the place-name Ealing, now attached to an area west of the City on the north bank of the Thames (see *PN Middx*, pp. 90–1). *Gillingas* was originally a tribal name, and in the seventh century it probably referred to an area far more extensive than the later Ealing, perhaps including the whole south-western corner of the later Ossultone Hundred, north and south of the important Roman road between London and Silchester (Bailey 1989, p. 117). In the Domesday survey Ealing would have been reckoned under the episcopal manor of Fulham (GDB 127v; see Bailey, *ibid.*; *VCH Essex*, vii. 123). Wealdhere subsequently purchased fifty hides at Fulham from a bishop of Hereford (**3**), and in 704 was granted a great estate at Twickenham, a little further west along the Thames (S 65).

3

Tyrhtel, bishop [of Hereford], grants fifty hides (manentes) *at Fulham,
Middlesex, to Wealdhere, bishop of London.* A.D. 701 [? for 704 × 709]

H. Bodleian, James 23, p. 33: extract, s. xvii[1]

I. London, Lincoln's Inn, Hale 84, 93r: extract, s. xvii[1]
Ed.: Gibbs, pp. 3–4 (J6), from H
Translated: Whitelock, *EHD*, p. 488 (no. 62)
Listed: Sawyer 1785 (LonStP 2); Gelling, *ECTV*, no. 192

(*a*)
Edited from H

In nomine Domini nostri Iesu Christi. Ego Tyrhtelus episcopus aliquantulam terræ partem Waldario London' episcopo pro sua placabili pecunia proferre[a] largirique decreueram, cum consensu et licentia Sigehardi regis Eastseaxonum et Conredi[b] regis Merciorum, quatenus hæc emolumenta ecclesiæ libenter collata peccatorum meorum piacula purgare et indulta supernæ pietatis remedia adipisci valeam. Possessio autem huius terræ .l. manentium sunt in loco qui dicitur Fulanham etc.

    [a] *Perhaps for* conferre   [b] *For* Coenredi

(*b*)
Edited from I

Anno 701, indict[ione] 14. Ego Tyrhtelus episcopus ⟨gives⟩[a] 'Waldario episcopo Londonensi'[b] Fulanham; consensu et licentia Sigeheardi regis Eastsaxonum et Ceonredi regis Merciorum. ⟨The kings subscribe⟩.[a]
[c]Id est his ⟨testibus⟩[d]
Ego Alricus comes consensi.
Ego Eadberhtus comes consensi.
Ego Sceafthere comes consensi.
Ego Westheah comes consensi.
Ego Seaftuwine consensi.
Ego Cuthred comes consensi.
[...........][e]

    [a] *Selden's interpolated comment*   [b] *Added above the line*   [c] *The following subscriptions*
    are written in the margin and linked with previous paraphrase by a line   [d] *Reading uncertain*
    [e] *The last line is difficult to make out (it is not a full subscription)*

The two extracts are were taken respectively by James and Selden from the lost St Paul's roll (see pp. 67–70). They are clearly from the same document, which is probably fundamentally authentic (although it should be noted that the Fulham manor was one of the most important estates of the bishopric in the later Anglo-Saxon period and after the Conquest; there would have been considerable interest in the title-deed, and perhaps some pressure to revise the details). Selden's paraphrase of the grant (*b*) appears at the end of the first page of his notes, linked with a collection of subscriptions jotted into the margin: the latter are almost certainly those of witnesses to Bishop Tyrhtel's grant (as pointed out in Keynes 1993*a*, p. 307).

The date attached to the transaction in Selden's paraphrase is not without difficulty. The incarnation year 701 agrees with the given indiction, but is not compatible with the internal reference to Coenred of Mercia, who is said by Bede (*HE*, v. 24) to have succeeded King Æthelred after the latter's abdication in 704. However, there is some possibility that Coenred did enjoy a measure of authority before 704, perhaps as an associate-ruler with Æthelred: some manuscripts of the *Anglo-Saxon Chronicle* include a notice that Coenred took control of the Mercian kingdom in 702, which could be significant—or could be a simple doublet of the 704 entry (see Whitelock, *EHD*, p. 170 n. 1). King Sigeheard and his brother Swæfred (see **6**) succeeded their father Sebbi after his abdication in the 690s (Bede, *HE*, iv. 11; Yorke 1985, pp. 20, 22); they seem to have co-operated with the contemporary Mercian kings, who were probably *de facto* rulers of the Middlesex area at this time (see pp. 12–13). In 704 Swæfred made a joint-grant to Bishop Wealdhere of land at Twickenham, in association with a *comes* of King Æthelred (S 65); the grant was not attested by Æthelred, and perhaps coincides with the period of his abdication. The *comites* who appear to have attested **3** may have been Mercian noblemen, or a mixture of Mercians and East Saxons. Sceafthere and Eadberht occur in the witness-list of S 75 (A.D. 692), a fabricated Worcester charter which is partly based on some early records, while Cuthred, Eadberht and Sceftwine are found among the witnesses to S 65 (the first in a primary witness list headed by King Coenred, the other two in a witness-list associated with a confirmation by Coenred's successor, Ceolred: see Brooks and Kelly, *Christ Church*, no. 9).

The formation preserved in the extract by James seems generally acceptable. The invocation is an extremely common formula, used throughout the Anglo-Saxon period. The dispositive section follows the pattern of contemporary royal diplomas in the West Saxon/East Saxon tradition (see pp. 77–9). The dispositive verb *decreveram* recalls *decreuerim* in S 1164 (A.D. 670 × 676; Kelly, *Shaftesbury*, no. 1), while a formulation *conferre largirique* is found in two early diplomas from Malmesbury (S 1245, 1169; Kelly, *Malmesbury*, nos 1, 4). A consent-clause was a common feature in East Saxon charters from this period (compare **4**, **6**, and S 65); the nature of the transaction would presumably have required royal consent. The language of the following motivation clause is rather elevated (for the use of *emolumentum* in this context, see S 231, 1251a; Kelly, *Malmesbury*, nos 6, 9). The final sentence of the extract picks up the reference to land earlier in the charter; the wording here has some resemblance to that of S 25 (Kelly, *St Augustine's*, no. 11), which begins with an invocation and continues: *Possessio quedam est terre*. Of particular interest is the statement that Bishop Wealdhere has handed over a sum of money in return for the Fulham estate: for discussion of the sale of land in early Anglo-Saxon England, see Campbell 1989 (see also **6A**). However, it is a potential difficulty that there are no parallels for the phrase *pro sua placabili pecunia* until the ninth century (see S 186, 196, 214; and the confirmation of S 1172 by Ceolwulf of Mercia).

The detail of the transaction is surely based on a contemporary record. The donor (or, rather, vendor) is the contemporary bishop of Hereford, who apparently owned a very large estate in Middlesex; this is presumably a reflection of Mercian overlordship in the area. Fulham was one of several properties in western Middlesex acquired by Bishop

Wealdhere at around this time; he had already been granted land at Ealing (2) and a thirty-hide estate at Twickenham (S 65). Fulham was close to Brentford, which was the venue for several councils in the eighth century and probably the location of a Mercian royal vill (Bailey 1989, p. 117; Sawyer 1983, p. 291; see Appendix 1, and S 116, 1257). In 878 a Danish army camped at Fulham, and probably remained there over the winter (*ASC*; see above, p. 23); excavation on the site of the later episcopal palace has revealed fortifications of late Roman date, which may have been refurbished by the Scandinavians (Vince, *Saxon London*, pp. 83–4). Fulham is mentioned in the will of Bishop Theodred as one of the demesne manors of the bishopric of London (S 1526: for the text see Appendix 2, with discussion above, pp. 90–4), and it appears with a quota of five men in a document of *c.* 1000 relating to the St Paul's naval levy (25). The Domesday assessment totalled fifty hides TRE: forty were held by the bishop before the Conquest, five by two of his freemen (with no alienation rights) and five by the canons from the king (GDB 127v; *DB Middx*, 3:12–14). The coincidence between the Domesday assessment and the assessment in the charter is not necessarily an encouraging feature. It is fairly unusual for an assessment to remain static between the eighth and eleventh centuries, and this might indicate that the text had been tampered with (note also that land at Ealing was included within the Fulham manor at the time of the Domesday survey: see 2).

4

Offa, king of the East Saxons, grants land in the district called
Hæmele [*Hertfordshire*] *to Wealdhere, bishop* [*of London*].
[*c.* A.D. 704 × 709]

H. Bodleian, James 23, p. 34: extract, s xvii[1]
Ed.: Gibbs, p. 5 (J9)
Translated: Whitelock, *EHD*, pp. 488–9 (no. 63)
Listed: Sawyer 1784 (LonStP 3); Gelling, *ECTV*, no. 160

In nomine Domini nostri Iesu Christi salvatoris. Licet sermo sacerdotum et decreta regalium sanctionum inconcussa stabilitate per sæcula durent, attamen quia plerumque tempestates et turbines sæcularium rerum etiam portas ecclesiæ pulsant ... .[a] Ego Offa Rex Eastsaxonum aliquam terræ partem in pago quæ[b] dicitur Hæmele tibi Vualdario episcopo Lond' etc.

[a] *The proem would have continued with a statement about the need to record grants in writing* (*compare* 6) [b] *For* qui

Richard James made this extract from a text on the lost St Paul's roll (see pp. 67–70). The source-document was apparently a charter in the name of Offa, the son of King Sigehere of the East Saxons, a saintly youth who travelled to Rome in 709 with Coenred, the former king of Mercia, and there received the tonsure (Bede, *HE*, v. 19;

for Coenred, see **5**). By Bede's account, Offa was not yet king on his departure; but it is possible that he did have a regal position of some kind, perhaps as his father's sub-king within a province of the East Saxon kingdom (see Yorke 1985, pp. 7–8, 25–6; *eadem, Kings and Kingdoms*, pp. 49–50; and for discussion of the preoccupations which led Bede to deny a royal status to certain individuals, see J. Campbell, *Bede's Reges and Principes*, Jarrow Lecture 1979 (Jarrow, [1980]) (repr. in Campbell, *Essays*, pp. 85–98)). An alternative possibility is that the charter which lies behind **4** did not actually refer to Offa as king, and that the royal style was supplied by a later revisor of the text; for an earlier grant by an East Saxon nobleman, a royal kinsman who was not styled king, see S 1171 (probably A.D. 690 × 693). Since **4** is only a brief extract from a longer charter, it would be unwise to draw any conclusion from the lack of reference to Mercian approval or confirmation of Offa's grant to Bishop Wealdhere. However, it may be the case the the land concerned was still an integral part of the East Saxon kingdom, at a time when Middlesex was slipping under Mercian control (see above, pp. 12–13).

There survives one other diploma which has been attributed to Offa of the East Saxons. S 64 purports to record the grant to the church of Worcester by Offa, 'king of the Mercians', of several properties in Warwickshire and Worcestershire; it cannot be genuine as it stands, but some early document evidently underlies the text. The dating is impossible for the celebrated Offa of Mercia (757–96), since the witnesses include Ecgwine, bishop of Worcester from *c.* 693 to 717, and three sons of the Hwiccean king Oshere, who lived in the late seventh century (Sims-Williams, *Religion and Literature*, p. 35 n. 99): so it has been suggested that the donor was actually Offa of the East Saxons. This would solve the dating problem (and in the context of questions about Offa's status it is interesting that the donor of S 64 is referred to as both *rex* and *subregulus*), but the suggestion raises the additional question of the plausibility of the East Saxon Offa being in a position to grant away property located in the kingdom of the Hwicce. At first this may seem extremely unlikely; but it is perhaps scarcely more unlikely than that a bishop of Hereford should own an estate at Fulham in Middlesex, which is the implication of **3**. Mercian domination of parts of the East Saxon kingdom in the previous generation could provide a context for some level of interchange of property (for this see above, pp. 12–13), and the well-recorded personal association between Offa and Coenred of Mercia could also be relevant. Offa's very name suggests a possible link with Mercia: it stands out from the general pattern in the East Saxon dynasty, which there an overwhelming preference for names alliterating in S, and it accords with the naming patterns of the Hwiccean royals, who had a predilection for names alliterating in O. (Worcester tradition, as reflected in a dubious diploma (S 55), claimed that the celebrated Offa of Mercia was of Hwiccean descent; he was moreover named from the legendary Offa of Angeln, a supposed ancestor of the Mercian royal line.) It has been suggested that the mother of Offa of Essex may have been a Hwiccean princess (see Finberg, *ECWM*, pp. 180–3), but the evidence is fairly tenuous (see Yorke 1985, p. 20 n. 107).

The formulation of **4** is probably acceptable (it has no resemblance to that of S 64, which in its received form seems to follow a Mercian pattern), although there are some difficulties. The verbal invocation is extremely common in the late seventh and early eighth centuries (see, for example, S 1164, 1171, 1248). The same is true of the general theme of the proem, which would (in its complete form) have dwelt on the desirability of making written records. Proems of this type are very common in early diplomas of the West/East Saxon tradition (for which see Wormald 1985, pp. 9–11; and above pp. 77–9): see, for instance, **6** and S 65, 1248. But the wording here is slightly unusual. The more common pattern for such proems is that seen in **6**, which points out that, although oral testimony was sufficient proof of canonical decrees and synodal statutes, yet written records were an important bastion against the vicissitudes of time. It is usual to refer simply to *sermo* (as S 65), although later Kentish charters have *sermo catholicorum* (S 123) and *sermo sapientum* (S 176–7), and a slightly dubious Muchelney diploma of 702 refers to *sermones fidelium personarum* (S 244). There is no obvious early parallel for the reference here to 'the testimony of priests and the decrees of royal sanctions' as the alternative to written records. But some very similar wording is found in a selection of tenth-century documents. Two diplomas from the reign of Edward the Elder have a proem beginning *Quamvis verba regum et procerum decreta*, which has a final section: *tamen plerumque tempestates et turbines secularium rerum regnorum statuta pulsantes* (S 374, 1286). A standard formula first seen in charters of the 940s, which begins *Quamvis decreta pontificum et verba sacerdotum*, also includes the phrase *tamen plerumque tempestates et turbines secularium rerum* (see S 493, 497, 501, 506–7, 525, 528). Moreover, a later variant of this formula incorporates the idea of storms striking at the doors of the church (S 713; Kelly, *Abingdon*, no. 97; *portas ecclesiae pulsant*), while a second variant speaks of them 'striking the fragile course of human life' (S 687). It was a commonplace in Anglo-Saxon diplomatic to reuse and rework formulation from older diplomas, so it is not necessarily suspicious that the closest parallels to the wording of the proem in **4** are to be found in charters from the middle of the tenth century. But it is worth noting the possibility that the source of this extract was a diploma that had been partly revised some time after its ostensible date. By contrast, the brief passage from the beginning of the dispositive section looks genuinely early. At this time the East Saxon kings were usually styled *rex Eastsaxonum* or *rex Eastsaxanorum* (see **6**; and S 65, 65b). The use of the second person to refer to the beneficiary is compatible with an early date, as is the assessment in *manentes* (see **2**). The spelling of the bishop's name is the same in S 65 and in his letter to Archbishop Berhtwald (see Appendix 1, pp. 221–3).

The district-name *Hæmele* has been preserved in Hemel Hempstead, in the Vale of St Albans; in Domesday Book the latter appears as *Hamelamestede*, where the second element is OE *hamstede*, 'homestead' (GDB 136v; *DB Herts.* 15:10). The name has been connected with OW *hamel*, perhaps referring to the broken, hilly character of the local terrain (*PN Herts.*, pp. 40–1). In 1066 the manor at Hemel Hempstead was assessed at ten hides and held by two brothers who were Earl Leofwine's men, and it later passed into the possession of the Count of Mortain; there is no evidence of any St Paul's interest in this manor. It may be that the property covered in **4** lay elsewhere within the old district of *Hæmele* (although it is also possible that the estate was alienated or lost by the bishop at some stage). The medieval parish was very large, and may have included the Gaddesdens to the north (Williamson, *Herts.*, p. 121; *VCH Herts.*, ii. 216). Bailey (1989, p. 111, 119, and see map p. 116) notes that the *Hæmele* district would seem to have represented the extreme north-western part of the territory of the East Saxons, and suggests that it may have originated as a Romano-British territorial unit associated with *Verulamium* (St Albans).

5

(a) *Coenred, king of the Mercians, renews the liberty granted by King
Æthelberht to St Paul's minster.* [A.D. 704 × 709]

(b) *Offa, king of the Mercians, extends the liberty of St Paul's.* [A.D. 757 × 796]

H. Bodleian, James 23, p. 36: extract, s. xvii[1]
Ed.: Gibbs, p. 8 (J17, J18)
Listed: Sawyer 1786, 1790 (LonStP 4, 7); Gelling, *ECTV*, nos 193, 200

(a)

Ego Ceonred rex Merciorum diligenter perscrutari coepi quid animæ meæ utile
facerem ut salvus fiam in die Domini, et ecce ad mentem mihi veniebat quod
ecclesia sancta quæ sita est in Londonia et noto notamine Paulesbyri dicitur
maiori servitute premeretur quam ab Æthelberto rege pio permissum sit, qui
hanc ecclesiam fundavit et perhenni libertate sublimavit. Nunc ergo volo ut
predicti regis sanctio publice innovetur et firmissime conservetur.

(b)

Ego Offa Merciorum rex deuotus monasterium quod celebri uocabulo Paulesbiri
iuxta linguam huius insulae vocitatur æterna libertate pro animæ meæ salute
amplifico.

Richard James made these extracts from a text or texts on the lost St Paul's roll (see
pp. 67–70). It seems most probable that the source was a a single document, a grant by
Coenred with a confirmation by Offa. Dugdale saw a copy of Coenred's privilege, for he
remarks that he could not find any benefactor of the church between (Bishop) Eorcenwald
and (King) Æthelstan, apart from 'Kenred, who onely granted this immunity, i.e. thereto that
it should be in all things as free as he himself desired it to be in the Day of Judgement'
(*St Paul's*, p. 4). He cites as his source the lost *Liber G*, with two folio references (1r, 5r), which
may mean that there were two copies of the document in that cartulary (see discussion above,
p. 55). Dugdale evidently knew nothing of any separate document in the name of Offa.

James's extracts almost certainly derive from a fabricated diploma, probably composed
at the end of the Anglo-Saxon period or in the first decades after the Conquest. Early
Anglo-Saxon kings did on occasion bestow exemptions and immunities upon churches in
their kingdoms, but such documents tend to be both more generally applicable and more
specifically detailed. In 699 the Kentish king Wihtred (*c.* 691–725) freed the churches and
monasteries of Kent from all public tribute (S 20; Kelly, *St Augustine's*, no. 10; Brooks and
Kelly, *Christ Church*, no. 7; note that S 22 is a ninth-century forgery). Shortly afterwards
King Ine granted a similar exemption from secular burdens to the churches and monasteries
of Wessex (S 245; Kelly, *Malmesbury*, no. 8). Later in the eighth century King Æthelbald
issued a grant of privileges to the minsters and churches of Mercia (S 92, A.D. 749) and
also seems to have confirmed Wihtred's grant to the Kentish houses, as did King Offa in
792 (S 134; Kelly, *St Augustine's*, no. 15). Early privileges supposedly making a grant of
general liberty to individual churches are inevitably forgeries: thus S 246 is a Glastonbury
fabrication based on S 245. It is of interest that the St Paul's document is allocated to

Coenred of Mercia (*c.* 704–9), a contemporary of Wihtred and Ine, both of whom issued genuine privileges at around this time. Coenred's piety was celebrated by Bede (*HE*, v. 13), and his retirement to Rome in company with the East Saxon Offa provided a local link (*HE*, v. 19; for Offa see **4**); he could have been selected by a forger on the basis of his saintly reputation. But there is independent evidence that Coenred did indeed wield some degree of control over Middlesex (see S 65, and above, pp. 12–13). One might conjecture that Coenred was inspired by the example of Wihtred and Ine, and that he granted the same freedoms to the Mercian churches as had recently been bestowed upon the Kentish and West Saxon houses; and that the existence of a genuine privilege with a more general application could lie behind the choice of Coenred as a donor in the St Paul's forgery.

However, it must be stressed that the wording of the extract gives little sign of being derived from an early document. Coenred's sudden revelation that St Paul's was more heavily burdened than in the time of King Æthelberht, is intrinsically suspicious. Some of the vocabulary and phrasing is almost certainly later. Thus the word *notamen*, 'name', may be a tenth-century coinage (its earliest use in a charter is in S 546, A.D. 949); while the phrase *celebri vocabulo* is common from the second half of the tenth century onwards. Explicit references to place-names being in the English/Saxon tongue are technically possible in an early diploma (see, for instance, S 100), but are far more frequent in documents from later Anglo-Saxon England; no precise parallel presents itself for the phrase *lingua huius insule*. The only other references to the place-name *Paulesbyri*[*g*] are in documents from the tenth and eleventh centuries (S 1486, 1494, 1478), and it is extremely unsafe to cite **5** as evidence for the use of this name as early as the eighth century. The second extract, the single sentence in the name of King Offa, repeats the language of Coenred's grant. There is some possibility that an earlier version of **5** mentioned Offa of Essex, Coenred's contemporary and close associate, rather than the later Offa of Mercia (for Offa of Essex, see **4**).

The most interesting feature of these two brief extracts is the complete absence of any reference to freedoms associated with Bishop Eorcenwald. In *c.* 1100, the canons of St Paul's co-opted the Chertsey tradition that Eorcenwald had acquired for the community a papal guarantee of its lands and liberties, and created their own dossier of privileges and royal diplomas to support this claim (see **12, 29**, and pp. 75–6). These documents prioritise Eorcenwald's contribution and do not mention Æthelberht of Kent. It is possible that **5** is representative of an alternative tradition which emphasised the grants and privileges of the original founder (see also **1**).

6

Swæfred, king of the East Saxons, grants seventy hides (cassati) *in the district called* Deningei [*Essex*] *to Ingwald, bishop of London.* [A.D. (705 × 716) × 745]

H. Bodleian, James 23, p. 34: extract, s. xvii[1]
Ed.: Gibbs, pp. 5–6 (J11)
Listed: Sawyer 1787 (LonStP 5); Hart, *ECE*, no. 7

In nomine Domini nostri Iesu Christi salvatoris mundi. Ea quæ secundum decreta canonum ac statuta synodalia salubriter definiuntur, quamvis sermo solus ad testimonium sufficeret, attamen ob incertam futurorum temporum conditionem firmissima scripturarum syngraphia et cautionum cyrographis sunt roboranda. Qua de re ego Suebredus rex Eastsaxonum, cum gratia Dei et cum consilio episcoporum meorum et consensu principum et sapientum nostrorum, pro spe remunerationis æternæ seu etiam pro expiatione nostrorum piaculorum et pro amore omnipotentis Dei, Ingualdo episcopo Londoniæ quandam partem terræ iuris mei .lxx. cassatorum in regione qui dicitur Deningei etc.

This is an extract made by Richard James from a text on the lost St Paul's roll (see pp. 67–70). The donor was the son and successor of King Sebbi of Essex, who began his reign as joint-king with his brother Sigeheard, probably in the early 690s (Bede, *HE*, iv. 11; see **3**). He should be distinguished from the Swæfheard (*Suebheardus*), also a son of Sæbbi, who ruled in Kent for a period between 692 and 694 (see S 10, 11, 233; Kelly, *St Augustine's*, pp. 196–7). Two other archives preserve documents in the name of Swæfred. In S 65 (A.D. 704) he grants land in Twickenham in Middlesex to Bishop Wealdhere of London, in association with a *comes* of King Æthelred of Mercia: the estate and charter later passed into the possession of the archbishops of Canterbury (Brooks and Kelly, *Christ Church*, no. 9). Among a recently discovered collection of early documents from the minster at Barking are the records of two grants of land in Essex by Swæfred to a beneficiary named *Ffymme*, intended for the foundation and endowment of a short-lived minster at Nazeing in Essex (S 65a, 65b); these charters are undated, but seem to belong to the period *c.* 700. There is no evidence for the date of Swæfred's death, and so **6** is datable only to the span of Bishop Ingwald's inconveniently long pontificate ((705 × 716) × 745); the likelihood is that it belongs to the earlier part of that dating range. During this period the Mercian kings dominated the former East Saxon province of Middlesex, but it is possible that the East Saxon kings were still acting independently in the rest of their kingdom (see above, pp. 12–13). This extract makes no reference to Mercian consent (although it may have been the case that full text of the charter included a subscription or confirmation in the name of a Mercian king).

The formulation can be accepted as contemporary. The verbal invocation is typical of this period, and there is no significance in the fact that it is not precisely paralleled until the ninth century; the earliest Anglo-Saxon charter-scribes were particularly inclined to introduce minor variants into essentially similar invocations. The theme of the proem is the need to record donations in writing to supplement verbal testimony, a common preoccupation at this period, especially in charters from Wessex (see **4** and comments); there is almost identical wording in the proem of S 1248 (A.D. 693), a diploma originally in the name of Bishop Eorcenwald covering land at Battersea in Surrey, and there are also links with S 65, Swæfred's charter for Bishop Wealdhere (see further Wormald 1985, pp. 9–11). The inclusion of a consent-clause seems fairly routine in early charters from the East Saxon kingdom (compare **2**, **3**; and S 1171, 65), and may be a reflection of the political instability of the region. Swæfred gives a multiplicity of motives for making the grant, which is unusual but not likely to be intrinsically suspicious; a motivation clause also occurs after the superscription in S 65a, and the charter in the name of Bishop Tyrhtel (**3**) also dwells on the divine benefits to be expected from his generosity. The unit of assessment is the *cassatus* rather than the more usual *manens:* there is a reassuring parallel in S 65.

Once more the land is identified by a district name. This survives in the modern place-name Dengie, which is a hamlet just south of Tillingham and Bradwell-on-Sea. The meaning of the name has been much debated (see *PN Essex*, pp. xxii–xxiii, 213–14; *DEPN*, p. 141; Cox 1976, p. 20), but later forms suggest the first element is a personal name Dene (sometimes with connective *-ing*) and that the second is *ieg*, 'island'. Evidently the seventy hides granted in **6** covered a very substantial area, perhaps stretching as far west as Danbury, near Chelmsford (it should be noted that the huge size of the land-grant is not unusual at this date; thus the abbess of Barking was originally given seventy-five hides in Essex in S 1171, although that figure was later altered in the charter). Land at *Denesige* is mentioned in the tenth-century will of Bishop Theodred in such a way as to suggest that it formed part of the episcopal patrimony (S 1526: see Appendix 2 for the text, and discussion above, pp. 90–4); Theodred decreed that the estate was to be left as he found it, and the rest (the increase or profit) was to be split between the minister and his soul (presumably to pay for masses or be given as alms). By the end of the century the bishop's Dengie estate seems to have been known as Southminster, which is the name that appears in **25**, a document from *c.* 1000 outlining the naval levy due from the St Paul's lands; there is no reference here to Dengie. It has been suggested that the name 'Southminster' was coined to distinguish this estate, with its minster, from Tillingham (with the minster at Bradwell) immediately to the north in the same peninsula (*PN Essex*, p. 225; also Hart, *Danelaw*, p. 209): see now discussion above, pp. 84–5. It is possible that the source of the fragment here edited as **18** was a fabricated charter in the name of King Edgar covering the same seventy hides, perhaps forged in order to associate the new name with the estate. The Domesday entry for Southminster states that the bishop's manor there had been confiscated by Cnut, but recovered by Bishop William after the Conquest; it was assessed at thirty hides, and apparently carried 1000 sheep (LDB 10r; *DB Essex* 3:9).

6A

Extract from a charter connected with Ingwald,
bishop of London. [A.D. (705 × 716) × 745]

H. Bodleian, James 23, p. 35: extract, s. xvii[1]
Ed.: Gibbs, p. 7 (J15)
Listed: Sawyer 1789 (LonStP 6)

—Signum manus Eaba þendri—Signum manus Eaba Haligreding—Tunc Ingualdus episcopus terram supradictam comparavit pretio argenti, id est cannarum .xxx.

This very brief extract appears among the notes made by Richard James from the lost St Paul's roll (see pp. 67–70); the punctuation is his. It is to be assumed that the two subscriptions came from an early land-charter, to which the note about Ingwald's purchase of the estate may have been an endorsement or an addition. The reference to the bishop is the only indicator of date. The objective form of the subscriptions (*Signum manus*) is compatible with the early eighth century, although such formulation continued in use in Anglo-Saxon diplomas until the middle of the ninth century (for the historical background, see Chaplais 1968, pp. 326–7 (pp. 76–7); Edwards, *Charters*, p. 312; Kelly, *St Augustine's*, p. lxxxv). The uncompounded personal name Eaba is of a type that was far more common in the early Anglo-Saxon period than later (Redin, *Personal Names*, p. 92). James's attention was presumably drawn to these subscriptions because the two namesakes are distinguished by the use of bynames. *Haligreding* would appear to be a patronymic in *-ing*, although the name Haligred does not seem to be otherwise attested; the oldest bynames are of this type (Tengvik, *Bynames*, p. 139). *Thendri* is more difficult and may have been mistranscribed. Just possibly there is a connection with the place-name Tendring in Essex, which is of uncertain etymology but has early forms *Tendringa* and *Thendring*; one possible root for this is a version of OE *tender*, 'tinder', which might also function as a nickname (*DEPN*, p. 463; although see Gelling, *Signposts*, p. 121, for the suggestion that *Tendring* derives from a stream-name in *-ing*).

The text would appear to state that Ingwald purchased the land for a sum of silver, 'that is, thirty *cannae*'. The primary meaning of the word in classical Latin is 'reed' or 'something made from a reed' or 'wind-pipe', although there is an alternative meaning of 'small vessel' (Lewis and Short). The *Dictionary of Medieval Latin from British Sources* notes that in some late medieval sources *canna* refers to a linear measure, of land or cloth, and suggests that this may be the meaning here. But a more satisfactory reading would connect the word with the price paid for the estate, the *pretium argenti* (as in James's marginal note: *cannæ moneta*). Gibbs comments: '*canna* is a general word for weight or measure' (p. 7 n. 1). It may be that *canna* here means something like 'ingot' or '(silver) bar', and that it is connected to the form in which the metal was shaped for transport or trade, before being worked into a precious object. In the later seventh century Abbot Hedda of *Medeshamstede* (later Peterborough) purchased an estate by handing over a miscellaneous collection of property, including slaves, a massive gold brooch and two horses *cum cannis duabus* (S 1804); that reading is most probably a mistake for *canis*, '(with two) dogs'.

7

Æthelbald, king of the Mercians, grants remission of toll on one ship to Ingwald, bishop of London. [A.D. 716 × 745]

I. London, Lincoln's Inn, Hale 84, 94r: extract, s. xvii[1]
    Rubric: Idem de eodem (*cf.* **8**)
Ed.: Kelly 1992, p. 25
Listed: Sawyer 103a

In nomine Domini 'Dei'[a] saluatoris nostri Iesu Christi. Ego Ædilbaldus rex Merciorum, pro eterno remedio anime mee necnon et pro pio amore saluatoris mundi, aliquam partem iuris mei omnipotenti largitori bonorum omnium donare decreui.[b] Idcirco Ingualdo episcopo Londonie ciuitatis unius nauis tributa[c] in propriam possessionem iure perpetuali in eternum dono, ut absque aliquo mutabilitatis scrupulo habeat, nec de ea aliquis regum successorumque meorum uel cuiuscumque gradus absque tua uoluntate aliquid sibi usurpare presumat, sed mihi in munus perpetuum in beata requie feliciter conseruetur. Si quis*d* proinde hanc donationem a me saluberrime tractatam augere, defendere, adunare uoluerit, augeat Dominus partem eius in libro uite; sin autem aliter, quod minime credo, contigerit ut aliquis, maligni spiritus instinctu ac diabolica fraude deceptus, hanc eleemosynam meam minuere uel uiolare presumpserat,*e* sciat se in presenti seculo a participatione sacratissimi corporis et sanguinis Christi fore suspensum et in nouissimo die sciat se separatum a Deo et tenebris exterioribus destinandum.*f*

+ Ego Edilbaldus rex donator ad confirmationem donationis mee, pro ignorantia literarum, signum saluatoris crucis expressi.

+ Ego Wilfrid et Ego Obba consentio et subscribo.

a Added above line   b ? decreuit I (reading unclear)   c ? For tributum   d Or qui
e For presumpserit   f The subscriptions are written as part of the text, not in a column

For commentary on this charter, see that on **8** (pp. 150–2).

8

Æthelbald, king of the Mercians, grants remission of toll on one ship to Ingwald, bishop of London. [A.D. 716 × 745]

H. Bodleian, James 23, p. 35: extract, s. xvii[1]
I. London, Lincoln's Inn, Hale 84, 93v–94r: extract, s. xvii[1]
   Rubric: De tributo uel uectigali unius nauis.
Ed.: a. Gibbs, pp. 7–8 (J14), from H
     b. Kelly 1992, pp. 25–6, from H and I
Listed: Sawyer 103b (previously 1788); Gelling, *ECTV*, no. 194
Edited from H, with variants and final section from I

In nomine Dei patris et summi salvatoris. Quia unicuique homini in hac mortali vita degenti*a* incertus est cursus atque finis vitæ temporalis, ob quam causam ego Aethilbaldus*b* rex Merciorum, pro remedio æternaque salute animæ meæ, tibi Ingualdo episcopo civitatis Londoniæ unius nauis uectigal atque tributum, quæ mihi antea iure competebant, post omne subsequens tempus, quamdiu christianæ religionis status permanserit, perpetualiter concedo, ita ut cuicunque volueris hæredum successorum tuorum uel quorumlibet hominum hoc ipsum de tuo iure perdonare liberam habeas potestatem. Hoc et de aliis similiter antea navibus secundum oportunitatem rerum ac temporum ipsa predicta conditione pro supernæ scilicet mercedis amore et pro vestrorum suffragiis orationum facere curavi. Proinde igitur precipio, in nomine Dei patris omnipotentis, omnibus meis ducibus, prefectis, thelonariis,*c* cæterisque publicis dignitatibus ut hæc donatio mea, mihi a Deo data illique redonata,*d* per presentes ac subsequentes[e] illæsa firmaque perduret, et ad augmentum huiusce donationis hoc addo, ut navis ista vel veterata vel confractione collisa,[f] ut alia et alia in huius donationis locum et conditionem construatur et habeatur.[g] Si quis uero, quod absit, diabolica instinctus fraude, hanc donationem meam uiolare uel minuere temptauerit, sciat se in presenti seculo a participatione corporis et sanguinis Christi suspensum et in ultimo iudicio eternas sine fine penas passurum.

+ Ego Ædilbaldus rex in hanc cartulam pro confirmatione donationis mee signum sancte crucis nostri saluatoris impressi.

[a] degente I   [b] Eþilbaldus I   [c] theloneariis I   [d] I *omits* illique redonata   [e] ? *Supply* tempores   [f] conlisa I   [g] H *ends here*

7 and **8** are excerpts from two documents on the lost St Paul's roll studied by James and Selden (see above, pp. 67–70). In this instance, Selden's notes (MS I) are much fuller: he gives substantial extracts from both charters, while James (MS H) provides only a shorter extract from **8**.

7 and **8** form part of a group of seven charters in the name of King Æthelbald of Mercia (716–57) granting remission of ship-toll to ecclesiastical beneficiaries: see also S 86, 87, 91 from Minster-in-Thanet (Kelly, *St Augustine's*, nos 49–51); S 88 from Rochester (Campbell, *Rochester*, no. 2); and S 98 from Worcester. All but S 87 have a connection with London, the site of a major emporium; three (S 86, 88, 98) refer specifically to London tolls, one (S 91) was issued in London, while the two St Paul's examples are in favour of Bishop Ingwald (for a discussion of the background, see Kelly 1992; and above, pp. 15–16). Only two of these seven documents can be satisfactorily dated: S 88 belongs to 734 and S 91 to 748. S 87 may have been issued in the first year of Æthelbald's reign; S 86 may be coeval with S 88; **7**, **8** and S 98 predate 745, the year of Bishop Ingwald's death, but have no reliable *terminus post quem*, other than the beginning of Æthelbald's reign. There is good reason to believe that these privileges were generally drawn up by the beneficiaries; similarity of formulation can be explained by the use of a small number of common models (see Kelly, *St Augustine's*, pp. lxxxv–xcvi; for an alternative view, see Scharer, *Königsurkunde*, pp. 195–211). The lack of precise dating clauses in the Worcester and St Paul's examples may also be due to the factor of beneficiary production; the Kentish privileges tend to have dating clauses, as do Kentish land-charters, while those from the Mercian area omit them, in line with regular current practice in the drafting of land-charters (see further, Kelly, *ibid.*, pp. lxxxix–xc).

7 has none of the specific technical formulation usually associated with Anglo-Saxon toll-privileges (such as the references to toll-collectors and the 'ship-wreck clause' which are found in **8**). The draftsman may have made use of the formulation normally employed for land-charters, possibly because no model for a ship-toll privilege was at that stage available at St Paul's. Our meagre evidence about the diplomatic tradition in London in this period indicates the continuing influence of the 'Saxon' formulation associated with Bishop Eorcenwald (see above, pp. 77–9, and the commentary to **4**). Features in **7** which recall that formulation are the dispositive verbs *donare decrevi* in the motivation formula (compare S 1248: *impendere decrevi*; and S 65: *donare decrevimus*); and the paired blessing and anathema. The unremarkable verbal invocation recurs in S 86 and 88, but can also be compared to those in S 1171, 1248, 65. In other respects **7** diverges from the 'East Saxon' pattern, and it is possible that the draftsman had to improvise to a certain extent. There is no proem, although its absence is partly rectified by a motivation clause after the superscription; possibly this reflects influence from the current Mercian diplomatic tradition (compare S 89, 94). The formulation of the anathema is partly reproduced in **8**. Æthelbald's subscription identifies him as the grantor (*donator*), a feature of some very early charters (compare S 8, 235, 1165, 1246). The formulaic reference to his illiteracy shows awareness of the late antique tradition, where literate and illiterate witnesses were distinguished (for the background, see Chaplais 1968, pp. 326–7 (pp. 76–7); and above, pp. 147–8). The two other subscriptions in the vestigial witness-list are those of the laymen Oba and Wilfrid, who can probably be identified with men who shared Æthelbald's exile before 716 (*cf.* Felix, *Life of Guthlac*, caps 39, 40, 45 (pp. 122, 124, 139)). The former (also Ofa, Oua) attested Æthelbald's diplomas throughout the reign, and was the pre-eminent Mercian noble in the 740s: in S 90 (A.D. 742) he is styled *patricius*. The absence of his subscription from Æthelbald's last diploma (S 96) probably indicates that he died before the king. Wilfrid attests from 716 × 717, with a style *dux* in S 102, but he would appear to have died or retired by the 730s or 740s: it is just possible that he is the Abbot Wilfrid who was Felix's informant (Felix, *Life of Guthlac*, prologue (pp. 64, 175)). The subscriptions of these two men would be compatible with a relatively early date for **7**.

8 shares some of its formulation with S 91 (Kelly, *St Augustine's*, no. 51), a ship-toll privilege in favour of Abbess Eadburg of Minster-in-Thanet, which was issued in London (*in civitate Lundonia*) in May 748. The relationship lies primarily in the technical wording of the dispositive section: both include a clause providing for the transfer of the privilege to a new vessel in case of decay or shipwreck (a detail which shows that the toll-exemption was connected with a particular ship, perhaps branded in some way: see discussion in Kelly, *ibid.*, p. lxxxviii). The two texts diverge in the proem and sanction, which supports the argument for beneficiary production: it seems that the draftsmen were using similar models, which they adapted in their own way, retaining the technical details. S 91 includes some formulation particularly associated with Kent (Kelly, *ibid.*, p. 177); the injunction directed at various royal officials is longer than in **8**, and contains some vocabulary that may be borrowed from a Frankish toll-privilege (Kelly 1992, p. 19). In the case of **8**, a St Paul's origin is indicated by the sanction, which partly reproduces the anathema of **7**. There are no precise parallels for the verbal invocation or the brief proem. The statement of powers is shared with S 91: the implication is that this is a grant to Ingwald in his personal capacity, which he can pass on to his successors or to any other individual. If this formulation reflected reality, it would seem that Ingwald himself owned a fleet of trading ships: for Æthelbald states that he has previously made the same concession in respect of other ships (**7** may represent an earlier instance). But it is probably difficult to separate Ingwald from his office here: the sequence of charters to the abbesses of Minster-in-Thanet were clearly benefiting the house, rather than the individual abbesses.

The survival of the small group of toll-privileges from St Paul's, Minster-in-Thanet and other houses is fairly miraculous, given that the exemptions themselves are unlikely to have remained effective much after the collapse of Mercian power in the early ninth century and the coeval decay of *Lundenwic*. These may be survivors of a much larger corpus of such documents. Many questions remain unanswerable (see, generally, Kelly 1992). In the Frankish kingdom, beneficiaries of toll-privileges seem to have carried their documents on trading journeys and to have presented them to the toll-collectors en route. It is difficult to believe that a similar system operated in eighth-century England, where written records do not seem to have been routinely used for administrative purposes. However, the Rochester toll-privilege (S 88), which survives as a later single-sheet copy, was folded into a remarkably tiny package, perhaps for ease of transport; while the translation of the Worcester privilege (S 98) into the vernacular was perhaps intended to make it more functional. It is possible that the toll-privilege was presented once to a relevant official and then stored in the church's archive until the exemption was challenged, or until a change of regime made it necessary to repeat the procedure. For everyday proceedings there may have been a practice of physically marking a ship as exempt (as suggested by the 'ship-wreck clause' in **8** and other later toll-privileges, transferring the exemption to a new ship in case of disaster). Another question concerns the limited period during which the Anglo-Saxon privileges were produced: seven of the ten extant examples are in the name of King Æthelbald (**7, 8** and S 86–8, 91); one of these was confirmed by his successor King Offa (S 143); and two were issued by a Kentish king between 762 and 764 (S 29, 1612). It seems probable that churches continued to be granted commercial privileges and exemptions, but that changing procedures meant that these were implemented according to a different system which bypassed the need for written records.

9

Ceolberht, bishop of London, and the brethren of St Paul's church grant
ten hides (manentes) *at Braughing, Hertfordshire, to Sigeric*, minister
of Wiglaf, king of the Mercians, with reversion to St Andrew's church.
[A.D. 827 × 829 or 830 × 840]

H. Bodleian, James 23, pp. 35–6: extract, s. xvii[1]
Ed.: Gibbs, pp. 7–8 (J16)
Listed: Sawyer 1791 (LonStP 8); Gelling, *ECTV*, no. 165

Regnante inperpetuum Domino nostro Iesu Christo. Ceolberht episcopus London' civitatis et congregatio fratrum ecclesiæ sancti Pauli apostoli rogati fuimus a quodam homine, qui nominatus est Sigric et minister Wiglavi regis Merciorum, ut aliquam partem terræ propriæ hæreditatis ecclesiæ sancti Pauli apostoli Christi illi donaremus pro mercede pecuniæ suæ, id est 4^{or} milia argenteis, et huius terræ sunt .x. manentes in loco qui dicitur Breahingas, et nos cogitavimus commodare ei petitionem suam hoc modo, ut habeat Sigric illam terram cuius proprium fruendi ac possidendi et tradendi in genus suum cuicunque voluerit, et nunquam in alienigenum. Et iterum ultra, postquam deficient propinqui eius, quod tunc redeat et detur illa terra ad ecclesiam sancti Andreæ apostoli Christi, quamdiu fides catholica in hac terra permanebit. *^{a}þ is þæt gafol .c. peningas. et .xxx. dægþina on herfeste.^{a}* Ego Sigric rex orientalium Saxonum consensi et subscripsi etc.

$^{a…a}$ *OE passage: 'This is the rent: 100 pennies and thirty (? days' expenses) at harvest-time'.*

This is an extract by Richard James from a document on the lost St Paul's roll (see pp. 67–70). In the brief Old English passage ($^{a...a}$) he has made an attempt to reproduce Insular letter-forms, presumably from his exemplar (**e, f, g, r, s**).

This is a rather unusual transaction. Sigeric, a thegn of the Mercian king Wiglaf, here acquires land at Braughing from the bishop and community, in return for a substantial payment of four thousand silver coins plus an annual rent consisting of a money payment and some other payment in connection with the harvest. (OE *dægwine* was used to gloss Latin *diarium, diurnum* and *expensum* and is thought to mean 'a day's wages or expenses' (*ToOED*); here there may be a connection with the provision of supplies to the community at harvest-time.) The land is to remain within Sigeric's line (*genus*), and if the family dies out the estate is to be returned and then given in perpetuity to a church dedicated to St Andrew. The Hereford archive contains a document of approximately the same date which seems to be outlining a comparable transaction (S 1270, A.D. 840 × 852); there the bishop of Hereford and the episcopal community grant a three-life lease of land in Frome to an ealdorman in return for a ring worth fifteen mancuses, with a specified reversion to a minster at Bromyard. Both documents are couched in the first person plural, and use the term *congregatio ecclesie*. In S 1270 the bishop and his community can be understood to be leasing out land previously attached to a formerly independent minster which had devolved into episcopal possession; the specification of the final reversion was perhaps intended to circumvent restrictions on the full alienation of church land (see Sims-Williams, *Religion and Literature*, pp. 169–76, for the absorption of minsters into the episcopal estate in the Midlands *c.* 800; and Brooks, *Church of Canterbury*, pp. 174–206, for the situation in Kent). It is possible that **9** had a similar background, and that the Braughing estate originally formed part of the endowment of the minster dedicated to St Andrew which enjoyed the final reversion. The latter canot be readily identified (see Levison, *England and the Continent*, p. 262, for early dedications to St Andrew). There is a chance that it was located at Braughing itself, perhaps as an earlier incarnation of the minster there which was one of the beneficiaries of the will of Æthelgifu at the end of the tenth century (S 1497; Crick, *St Albans*, no. 7). The later parish-church at Braughing was dedicated to St Mary (*VCH Herts.*, iii. 315). In Domesday Book a five-hide manor at Braughing appears among the lands of Count Eustace of Boulogne (GDB 137v; *DB Herts.* 17:15); it had previously been held by two thegns, a man of King Edward with four hides, and a man of Asgar the constable with one; they could not sell because the land was *in elemosina*. It would appear that the Braughing property remained in private hands. For its later history, see *VCH Herts.* iii. 308. This area of eastern Hertfordshire formed part of the London diocese, and was known as the Deanery of Braughing (Williamson, *Herts.*, pp. 79–84). It has been suggested that the leasing transaction recorded in **9** may be connected with the breakup of a territorial estate based at Braughing (*ibid.*, pp. 107–10).

The dating limits for **9** are provided by the two reigns of King Wiglaf of Mercia, who was briefly ousted by Ecgberht of Wessex between 829 and 830 (*ASC*). The dates of Bishop Ceolberht cannot be fixed with any certainty (see p. 115), but the attestation of the East Saxon king Sigeric is potentially helpful in narrowing down the limits. A King Sigeric of the East Saxons went to Rome in 798 (*ASC* F); the implication is that he abdicated and left for good (as did so many earlier kings), though this may be a mistaken impression. The next (and the last known) East Saxon king is

Sigered, who attended a Mercian synod in London in 811 and appears as *rex* in the witness lists of two charters emanating from the meeting (S 165, 168, and *cf.* S 167); in charters of 812 and 823 he is styled *subregulus* (S 170, 187). The King Sigeric of the St Paul's charter may have been his successor, perhaps the Rome-bound Sigeric returned and back in power, more probably a later namesake. It has been suggested that both Sigerics of **9** were the same man, styled *minister* in the text and *rex* in the witness-list (Yorke 1985, p. 24), but this seems unlikely. There was a precedent for the description of a client-king as a thegn in a Mercian charter (S 155), but that was an instance where a pejorative impression was intended; it would surely be unnecessarily cruel to call the beneficiary of **9** a thegn (and 'a certain man'), and fairly pointless if he was to be a king in the witness-list.

10

King Edward, with Æthelred and Æthelflæd of Mercia, at the request of Æthelfrith, dux, *renews a charter of Coenwulf, king of the Mercians, granting ten hides* (cassati) *at Islington, Middlesex, to Beornnoth,* comes. *A.D. 903*

H. Bodleian, James 23, pp. 33–4: extract, s. xvii[1]
I. London, Lincoln's Inn, Hale 84, 93v: copy, s. xvii[1]
    Rubric: De Gisladuna — dors.
Ed.: a. Gibbs p. 4 (J8), from H
        b. Keynes 1993*a*, p. 310, from H and I, with translation, pp. 310–11
Listed: Sawyer 367a
Edited from H and I, with variants from S 367, 371

Regnante imperpetuum et mundi monarchiam gubernante altithroni ⟨patris⟩[a] sobole, qui celestia simul et terrestria[b] moderatur. Illius incarnationis anno .dcccciii., indictione vero .vi., contigit quod Æþelfriðo[c] duci omnes sui[d] hæreditarii libri ignis vastatione combusti perierunt. Tali igitur necessitate cogente, predictus dux Eadwardum regem rogavit[e] Æþelredum quoque Æþelfledamque,[f] qui tunc principatum potestatemque[g] gentis Merciorum sub predicto rege tenuerunt, omnes etiam senatores Merciorum, ut ei consentirent et licentiam darent alios sibi[d] libros rescribendi. Tunc illi omnes unanimiter[h] devota mente consenserunt, ut alii ei libri scriberentur eodem modo sicut[i] priores scripti erant, in quantum eos memoriter recordari potuisset. Si vero quoslibet recordari minime potuisset, tunc ei ista cartula in auxilio et affirmatione fieret, ut nullus eum contentiose cum aliis libris affligere valuisset, nec propinquus nec alienus, quamvis aliquis homo de vetustis libris aliquem[j] protulerit,[k] quem prius fraudulenter vel[l] hora ipsius incendii vel aliquo[m] tempore per furtum abstraxisset. Novimus ⟨quoque⟩[n] quod omnia quæ in hoc mundo contingere solent, aliquando vero tardius, aliquando vero citius,[o] ex memoria mortalium delapsa [p]in oblivionem devenire,[p] nisi in scedulis literarum karacteribus adnotantur.

Quapropter in hac cartula innotescere ratum atque gratum satisque commodum duximus de illa videlicet terra^q æt Gisladune .x. cassatorum quod eam ⟨Ceonulfus⟩^{r} rex inclitus Merciorum suo fideli Beornoþo comiti condonavit sibi suisque 'post se' perhenniter heredibus liberam, cum omni utilitate possidendam, signoque alme crucis suam munivit prerogativam ac fideliter firmavit, cum silvis, pratis ac paschuis^s omnibusque utilitatibus perpetualiter possidendam.^{t}

+ Eadwardus rex

+ Æþelred

+ Aþelfled

+ Þilfere^u bisceop   [*Dorchester or Lichfield*]

+ Þerferd^v bisceop   [*Worcester*]

+ Plegmund archiepiscopus   [*Canterbury*]

+ Þimund^w bisceop   [*Dorchester or Lichfield*]

+ Eadgar bisceop   [*Hereford*]

+ Æþelperd

+ Osferd^x

+ Orlaf^y

+ Aþelun abb' + subscripsi.

---

^{a} patri H, I; patris S 367, 371 (*correctly*) ^{b} terrena S 367, 371 ^{c} Æthel- H ^{d} *Word omitted* S 367, 371 ^{e} rogavit Eadweardum regem S 367, 371 ^{f} et Æþelfledam S 367, 371 ^{g} et potestatem S 367, 371 ^{h} unanimiter omnes S 367, 371 ^{i} quo et S 367, 371 ^{j} aliquem de vetustis libris S 367, 371 ^{k} H *ends here* ^{l} in S 367; vel S 371 ^{m} alio quolibet S 367, 371 ^{n} quodque I; namque S 367, 371 ^{o} aliquando citius aliquando uero tardius S 367, 371 $^{p...p}$ deueniunt S 367, 371 ^{q} *At this point the common material in* 10 *and* S 367, 371 *comes to an end, and the three texts continue with details specific to each* ^{r} Cronulfus I; *a corruption of the name* Coen[w]ulfus ^{s} *A spelling for* pascuis ^{t} *The subscriptions run across the page (as in* S 367) ^{u} *For* Þilferð ^{v} *For* Þerferð ^{w} *For* Þigmund ^{x} *For* Osferð ^{y} *For* Ordlaf

---

This text derives from a diploma on the lost St Paul's roll, which was studied by James and Selden (see above, pp. 67–70). Only Selden's version (MS I) includes the particular detail on Islington (see Keynes 1993a). Two other documents closely related to **10** are preserved in other archives: an original from Christ Church, Canterbury (S 367; Brooks and Kelly, *Christ Church*, no. 101), and a copy in the Glastonbury archive (S 371). The text common to all three charters tells how the hereditary landbooks of Ealdorman Æthelfrith were all destroyed in a fire. The ealdorman petitioned King Edward (the Elder), together with Æthelred and Æthelflæd, who 'then' ruled the Mercian people under the king, and all the great men of Mercia, for permission for new landbooks to be drawn up as replacements. They gave their agreement. New landbooks were to be written 'in the same way as the originals had been written, in so far as he [Æthelfrith] could remember them'. Where his memory failed, he was to use 'this charter' (i.e. the base text found here and in S 367, 371) as his proof of ownership. No-one (kinsman or stranger) was to bring forward any of the older charters, if by chance they had been rescued from the fire or stolen at some other time. At this point the common text slips into the first person plural: it is to be presumed that it is expressing the sentiments of King Edward, the Mercian rulers and all those who witness the text. 'We' realise that earthly matters slip from the memory of mortal men, unless written down: and so it is thought right to refer in this charter to 'that land...' Here the three charters diverge, all giving details of separate estates; it appears that the common text was adapted into several versions to cover separately each estate for which the documentation had been lost. S 367 has a sentence towards the end mentioning thirty hides at 'eastern' (later Monks) Risborough in Buckinghamshire, which Athulf had given to his daughter Æthelgyth, followed by vernacular bounds; in the same position in S 371 is a simple reference to twenty hides at Wrington in Somerset (this text may have been revised at Glastonbury, with the name of Wrington being substituted for that of a different estate).

The charter preserved at St Paul's concerned ten hides at Islington, previously given by King Coenwulf of Mercia (796–821) to his *comes* Beornnoth; the specific passage appears to be repeating some details of the lost charter. Several men named Beornnoth witnessed the diplomas of the Mercian kings in the early ninth century, with one individual in particular attesting prominently as *dux* or *princeps* between 798 and *c.* 825: this last would appear to be the man who obtained a grant of privileges from King Coenwulf for an early minster at Pershore (S 786; for the authenticity of this text, see Kelly, *Abingdon*, pp. cvi–xi). Islington is mentioned in **25**, with a quota of two men, so it would appear that the land passed to the church of London at some point between 903 and *c.* 1000 (for the place-name, see *PN Middx*, p. 124). Æthelfrith's ten-hide estate had been broken up by 1066. The canons of St Paul's held four hides there, divided into two manors of two hides (GDB 128r; *DB Middx* 3:22–3); another five hides at Islington, later known as the manor of Barnsbury, were attached to the bishop's manor of Stepney (GDB 127r; *DB Middx*, 3:2: *VCH Middx*, viii. 51), and there were two further manors of half a hide each held TRE by individuals from Geoffrey de Mandeville and the king (GDB 129v, 130v; *DB Middx* 9:3, 23:1). On the history of these estates, see further Keynes 1993*a*, p. 316. William I's spurious 'Coronation Day' diploma for St Paul's refers to the restoration of eight or nine hides at Islington, among other estates supposedly taken unjustly from the church in the time of William's predecessors (Bates, *RRAN: Acta of William I*, no. 183; see above, pp. 102–3)

S 367 is the only one of the three texts to contain a full witness-list, with twenty-five subscriptions. S 371 has only two names, while **10** has twelve, all appearing in S 367 apart from the twelfth, Abbot Athelun (most probably a misreading of Abbot Æthelm, as in S 367; although see Keynes 1993*a*, p. 311 n. 46, noting subscriptions of an Abbot Æthelhun in S 218, 225). In S 367 the subscriptions of the king and his co-rulers are followed by those of Archbishop Plegmund and the bishops of Lichfield, Dorchester-on-Thames (a new Mercian see, transferred from Leicester), Worcester, Hereford, Selsey (?) and Rochester. The absence of West Saxon bishops seems to confirm the implication of the text that the meeting related primarily to Mercian affairs. In **10** the order of the episcopal subscriptions has become confused, possibly reflecting a misreading of columns in the original, and only the first four bishops are mentioned. S 367 (where the order of witnesses is also rather muddled) continues with the subscriptions of Ælfwyn (daughter and heir of Æthelred and Æthelflæd), four *comites* or ealdormen, two abbots (Ælfhelm and Cynhelm), five *ministri* or thegns and two unstyled individuals who are probably also thegns (see full discussion in Brooks and Kelly, *Christ Church*, no. 101).

10 has only four subscriptions after those of the bishops: the two individuals who were unstyled in S 367, one of the ealdormen (Ordlaf) and one abbot. For Ordlaf see S 1445 (Brooks and Kelly, *Christ Church*, no. 104).

Æthelfrith was evidently a Mercian ealdorman, in office by 883 (S 218); it has been argued he controlled the southern and eastern areas of English Mercia (Hart 1973, p. 116). He attested two other diplomas of Æthelred in 884 and 888 (S 219–20), two Worcester episcopal charters in 896 and 904 (S 1441, 1280) and a diploma of Æthelflæd in 915 (S 225). There is a suggestion that he may have been of West Saxon origin, since the inheritance of his son Æthelstan 'Half-King' lay in Devon, and since S 371 may indicate that he had interests in Somerset (Hart 1973, pp. 116–18; Keynes 1993a, p. 307).

Æthelfrith was given two options for replacing his hereditary landbooks. If the exact details of the lost document could be remembered (? by the ealdorman, or by the scribe who wrote the original), then it could simply be rewritten: one wonders whether similar provisions could account for some of the less satisfactory diplomas in the Anglo-Saxon corpus. Where memory failed, he could make use of 'this charter' to prove ownership. **10**, with S 367 and S 371, presumably represents the second option: a document recording the decision by Edward and the Mercian rulers, with the agreement of the Mercian witan, was adapted to include details of three separate estates. The resulting diplomas would have represented the new landbooks for each property. There is no way to tell whether these three diplomas (with many others) were drawn up at the meeting where Æthelfrith was given permission to replace his lost documentation, or whether he went away with the common text and witness-list and subsequently had the replacement texts drawn up in an independent scriptorium, perhaps some time later. One hint that the three surviving documents may not have been produced on the same occasion is the series of variant readings in **10**, distinguishing that text from S 367 and S 371, which tend to stand together (see apparatus above). The slightly confused order of the witness-lists in S 367 and in **10** perhaps reflects copying from a model or memorandum where the subscriptions were arranged in a mildly irregular way. It is not clear whether any inference should be drawn from the past tense used in all three documents in the reference to Æthelred and Æthelflæd, who 'then' ruled the Mercians. This could simply be a reflection of the narrative form of the document in this section. Alternatively, it could imply that all three diplomas were actually drawn up some time later, when the political situation in Mercia had changed (Æthelred died in 911, after which London and its territory passed under the control of King Edward (see above, pp. 28–9); Æthelflæd died in 918 and subsequently the whole of Mercia was annexed to Wessex).

These three documents form part of a wider group of 'replacement' diplomas issued in the early years of the tenth century (see Keynes 1993a, pp. 312–14; Kelly, *Abingdon*, pp. 82–3). Closely related is S 361 (A.D. 900, probably for 904), another narrative document relating a request for a new charter made to King Edward and the Mercian rulers, this time for an estate at Water Eaton, Oxon. As in **10**, the text of S 361 begins with an invocation of the *Regnante* type, followed by a dating clause; it was witnessed by three Mercian bishops and a selection of Mercian nobles, including Ealdorman Æthelfrith (beneficiary of **10**, S 367, 371), most of whom also appear in the witness-list of S 367. There are two corresponding diplomas from Wessex, in the name of Edward alone, both renewing lost charters of King Æthelwulf: S 368 (A.D. 903) and S 369 (A.D. 903; Kelly, *Abingdon*, no. 19), the latter replacing a diploma that had been dropped in water and was no longer legible. Also from Mercia comes a text in the name of Ealdorman Æthelred, a replacement for a charter that had been seized by the Vikings (S 222, A.D. 883 × 911; probably dating from Alfred's time). Finally, in 915 or 916, Æthelflæd issued a diploma in her own name, apparently covering an estate in Berkshire, to replace another charter that had been consumed in a fire (S 225; Kelly, *Abingdon*, no. 20). This concentration of 'replacement' diplomas, issued over a relatively short time, is unparalleled; and it seems reasonable to draw a connection with the fact that very few new royal landbooks appear to have been issued in that period. Relatively few charters in the name of King Alfred have survived, when compared with the issues of his father and brothers, and the decline in charter-production under Edward seems to have been even more pronounced. Setting aside the 'renewal' charters, the bulk of Edward's landbooks consist of direct grants the Old and New Minsters in Winchester, some of questionable authenticity. No surviving charter of Edward can be securely dated after *c.* 909. which raises suspicions that there may have been a complete or near-complete moratorium on the production of royal diplomas in the last decade and a half of Edward's reign. It is possible that the flurry of 'renewal' diplomas and King Edward's apparent reluctance to make extensive new land-grants are both manifestations of a chaotic tenurial situation, the result of decades of Viking wars and the new pressures of the West Saxon conquest of Danish-held areas. When regular charter-production resumed under Æthelstan, it had a very different character (see the commentary to **11**).

11

Part of a dating clause and witness-list from a
diploma of King Æthelstan. A.D. 935

H. Bodleian, James 23, p. 34: extract, s. xvii[1]
Ed.: Gibbs p. 5 (J10)
Listed: Sawyer 1792 (LonStP 9)

—Anno Domini .dccccxxxv.—in civitate a Romanis olim constructa quæ Cirnecester dicitur tota optimatum generalitate sub ulnis*a* regiæ dapsilitatis ovanti perscripta est—Ego Æthelstanus singularis privilegii ierarchia preditus rex. etc—Ego Constantinus subregulus. Ego Eugenius subregulus. Ego Hopel subregulus. Ego Vithual*b* subregulus. Ego Morcant subregulus. Ego Ælfwine episcopus.

a *For* alis (*compare S 425 etc.*)   *b* *For* Iuthal (*or a similar spelling*)

This is an extract by Richard James from a diploma on the lost St Paul's roll (see pp. 67–70); the punctuation is his. The ultimate source of the dating clause and partial witness-list was one of the last charters of the scribe/draftsman, generally known as 'Æthelstan A', who is thought to have been responsible for writing virtually all the diplomas in the name of King Æthelstan that were produced between 928 and *c.* 935 (see Keynes, *Diplomas*, pp. 42–4; *BAFacs.*, p. 9). Following on from the apparent hiatus in charter-production in the last decades of Edward the Elder's reign (see previous commentary), the products of 'Æthelstan A' represent a significant new departure, to be associated with the extension of West Saxon rule over the Danelaw through conquest and submission. Most significantly, the diplomas of 'Æthelstan A' are supra-regional, in contrast to the regional production of the ninth century: they are dated from widely-scattered places in the newly-united English kingdom, they grant lands in many different areas, and they are in favour of many different ecclesistical establishments as well as laymen. These are centralised products, perhaps the work of a scribe attached to the royal household (as argued by Keynes, *Diplomas*, pp. 43–4; *BAFacs.*, p. 9), although it has also been suggested that 'Æthelstan A' was a member of the episcopal scriptorium at Winchester, to which the king delegated production of royal diplomas during this period (Chaplais 1965, p. 61 (pp. 41–2); *idem* 1985, pp. 47–9). The attribution of the surviving royal diplomas from 928 × 935 to a single scribe/draftsman rests on two foundations: in the first place, both surviving originals from this period were written by the same scribe (S 416; S 425: Brooks and Kelly, *Christ Church*, no. 106); and, secondly, the formulation is highly distinctive and highly standardised. The language is literary, characterised by recondite vocabulary and heavily influenced by the work of Aldhelm of Malmesbury (d. 709). Other characteristic features are: a sanction on the theme of the Last Judgement; a complex dating clause with a range of erudite dating elements, including epacts and concurrents as well as a calendar date; reference to the place of issue; and an extraordinarily long witness-list (the two originals have respectively 103 and 92 subscriptions), which includes the subscriptions of various 'sub-kings' who had submitted to Æthelstan's authority.

Such is the standardised nature of 'Æthelstan A' diplomas that it is possible to reconstruct much of the formulation of the lost text from which this dating clause and witness-list ultimately derive. The date is a crucial factor, for the products of 'Æthelstan A' can be periodized. The diplomas which he drafted between 931 and 933 all have the same proem, beginning *Flebiliter fortiter detestanda* (see S 416, a surviving original from this group); a diploma of this type may have been imitated by the draftsman or forger of a diploma in the name of King Edgar from which **18** is an extract (see below, p. 179). In 934 a new standardised model was introduced, with a proem beginning *Fortuna fallentis seculi* (represented by S 425, an original from that year). There was a further change of fashion in 935, when the elaborate 'Æthelstan A' model was jettisoned in favour of a more practical and flexible type of formulation which dominated charter-production until *c.* 951 (see discussion of **14**); it seems likely that 'Æthelstan A' died or retired at around this time. There may have been a period of overlap between the two styles, although the evidence is not clear-cut. There are two acceptable 'Æthelstan A' diplomas from 934 (S 425, 426) and three others from the same year which pose more difficulties but which can be associated with precisely-dated documents of the type, the latest emanating from a meeting on 16 December (S 407, 427–8). In 935 some royal diplomas were being produced in the new style (see S 429–30), but it is possible that 'Æthelstan A' was still active. The extract represented by **11** has the incarnation year 935, but lacks the additional dating elements (such as an indiction) which would confirm that James was copying his source accurately. There is also no calendar date. However, this is some confirmatory evidence that at least one other 'Æthelstan A' diploma was drafted in 935. S 434 is a Malmesbury forgery which includes some elements of the 'Æthelstan A' model (S 435–6 are related forgeries, based on the same exemplar). It has a complex dating clause headed by the incarnation year 937, but with other elements that point to a date of 21 December 935 (see Kelly, *Malmesbury*, nos 22–4).

If **11** is correctly dated 935, then it is overwhelmingly likely that the lost diploma was formulated on the standardised *Fortuna fallentis seculi* model represented by S 425. All details of the conveyance have been lost, and there is no good reason to assume that the beneficiary was St Paul's or the London bishopric: in Anglo-Saxon England it was the usual practice for a diploma to function as a transferable title-deed, being passed on with the land to a new owner. The conveyance took place at Cirencester, described as 'a city once constructed by the Romans'. Most 'Æthelstan A' diplomas employ a form of words such as *in villa omnibus notissima* (S 416), *in civitate famosissima* (S 418a), *in civitate opinatissima* (S 425). The detail about Cirencester's Roman origins finds its closest parallel in a reference to London in an episcopal profession of 838/9: *in loco preclaro antiquorum Romanorum arte constructa* (Richter, *Professions*, no. 18). Cirencester was the Romano-British town of *Corinium* and apparently a significant ecclesiastical centre in the ninth century (see John Blair in *Blackwell*, p. 105). A diploma of 956 in favour of Worcester is dated from Cirencester (S 633). In documents from the reign of Æthelred the Unready it is described as a *villa regia* and the meeting-place of a synodal council (S 896, 937; Kelly, *Abingdon*, nos 128, 129). A 'great council' assembled there in 1020 (*ASC*). The manor was in the king's hands in 1066 (GDB162v; *DB Gloucs.* 1:7–8).

James has noted only seven of the subscriptions in what would have been a very long witness-list. Five are those of *subreguli*: Constantine of Scotland and Eogan of Stratchclyde had formally submitted to Æthelstan in 927 (*ASC*). In 934, presumably in response to some challenge from Constantine, Æthelstan attacked Scotland by land and sea (*ASC*; Stenton, *ASE*, p. 342). Constantine attests only two of Æthelstan's diplomas, both later than the 934 campaign: S 426 (dated from Buckingham, 13 September 934) and **11** (apparently 935). Eogan attests once in 931 (S 413, dated from Worthy in Hants.) and once in 935 (S 434). In 937 these two men allied with the Norse of Dublin to invade England, but were defeated at the battle of Brunanburh (see Stenton, *ASE*, pp. 342–3). The other three *subreguli* attesting **11** are the Welsh kings Hywel Dda of Dyfed, Idwal of Gwynedd and Morgan of Morgannwg. Ælfwine of Lichfield (also known as Ælla) is almost inevitably the first-ranked provincial bishop in 'Æthelstan A' diplomas; his high ranking may have some bearing on discussion of the circumstances in which 'Æthelstan A' diplomas were produced, since it was not justified by seniority.

12

King Æthelstan confirms for St Paul's minster ten hides (mansae) *at Sandon with Rothe* (? *Roe Green in St Peter's*) *and eight hides at Ardeley with Luffenhall, Hertfordshire: ten hides at Belchamp St Paul's with Wickham St Paul's, eight at Heybridge and twelve at Runwell, Essex; thirty hides at* Eduluesnæsa (*The Naze, Essex*); *ten hides at West Drayton, Middlesex; eight hides at Barnes, Surrey; and ten hides at Neasden with Willesden, Middlesex.* [A.D. 924 × 939]

C. GL 25504 (*Liber L*), 7v–8v: copy, s. xii[1]
  Rubric: Privilegium Adelstani regis 'anno gracie circiter .dccccxxx.' [*added by medieval annotator*]
D. St Paul's D. & C., *Liber B*, 20r: copy, s. xii[ex] (lost)
E. GL 25501 (*Liber A*), 56r (original foliation 38r): copy, s. xiii[med]

P. GL 25516 (*Liber I*), 136r: incomplete copy, s. xiv[1]
Ed.: a. Dugdale, *St Paul's*, pp. 184–5. from D (SP1)
      b. *Mon. Angl.*, iii. 301–2, from D (MA)
      c. Dugdale, *St Paul's* (2nd edn), App. p. 9, from D (SP2)
      d. Dugdale, *St Paul's* (3rd edn), p. 292
      e. Kemble 1127, from *Mon. Angl.*
      f. Birch 737, from C, E, *Mon. Angl.* and Kemble
Listed: Sawyer 453; Gelling, *ECTV*, no. 326
Edited from C, with variants from E and MA (*Mon. Angl.*)

In nomine Domini nostri Iesu Christi salvatoris. Ea quę secundum legem salubriter diffiniuntur, licet solus sermo sufficeret, tamen pro ęuitanda futuri temporis ambiguitate fidelissimis scripturis et documentis sunt commendanda. Quamobrem ego Adelstanus[a] rex Anglorum, pro ęternę retributionis spe et relaxatione peccaminum[b] meorum, ad laudem Domini nominis et ad honorem sancti Pauli apostoli et gentium doctoris, regali auctoritate renouaui atque restauraui libertatem ad monasterium ipsius statutum in Lundonia[c] ciuitate, ubi diu sanctus Erkenpaldus episcopatum tenuit, qui etiam propensius in monasterii studens proficuo, illud priuilegium, quod hactenus in pręfato habetur monasterio, in Romulea urbe petebat, aliaque quamplurima priuilegia quę nostri antecessores pro redemptione animarum suarum et pro cęlestis regni desiderio constituerunt in illo monasterio scripta continentur.

Hęc est interim illa libertas quam ut perpetualiter in sepedicto monasterio permaneat animo libenti constituo, id est .x.[d] mansas ad Sandonam [e]cum Roðe,[e] et .viii. ad Eardeleage[f] cum Luffenheðe,[g] et .x. ad Bylcham[h] cum Þicham, et .viii. ad Tidpolditun,[i] et .xii. ad Runpeolla,[j] et .xxx. ad Eadulfes næsa,[k] et .x. ad Drægtun,[l] et .viii. ad Berne, et .x. ad Neosdune[m] cum Þillesdune.[n]

Hanc ego[o] libertatem, pro petitione et admonitione uenerabilis episcopi Teodorici[p] qui tunc temporis eidem monasterio prefuit, placabili mentis deuotione dictare, scribere,[q] commendare procuraui. Si quis uero[r] quod non optamus huius decreti aduersitatem infringere temptauerit aut aliter quam a nobis statutum est[s] mutare pręsumpserit, sit a consortio Domini nostri Iesu Christi segregatus et cum lupis rapacibus ponatur, et eius ligaturis se constrictum sciat cui Christus claues cęlestis regni commendans ait, Tu es Petrus et super hanc petram edificabo[t] ęcclesiam meam et tibi dabo claues[u] regni cęlorum, et quodcunque ligaueris super terram erit ligatum et in cęlis,[v] et quodcunque solueris super terram erit solutum et in cęlis.[1] Denique adhuc pro ampliori firmitatis testamento omnimodo pręcipimus atque pręcipiendo obsecramus, ut maneat ista libertas insolubiliter ab omni seculari seruitio cum omnibus per circuitum ad se rite pertinentibus, campis, pratis, pascuis, siluis, riuulis, tribus exceptis, expeditione, pontis arcisque constructione, et exercitu.[w] Idcirco uero huius donationis munificentiam tam firmiter atque inmobiliter imperamus quia pro^x hoc a Domino cęlestem beatitudinem accipere speramus, illo annuente cui est honor et potestas et imperium per infinita secula seculorum.

Deinde huius decreti consentiens testis fuit Adelgarus^y archipręsul ⟨et⟩^{z} Oskytel^{a2} metropolitanus Eboracensis^{b2} ęcclesię, et Ælfstanus^{c2} Lundoniensis^{d2} episcopus, et Aðulf^{e2} Herefordensis basilice episcopus,^{f2} et Ælfere dux, et Brihtnoð^{g2} dux, et Ælfric abbas, et Ælfstan abbas, et alii multi.

^{a} Ethelstanus MA ^{b} peccatorum MA ^{c} Londonia MA ^{d} *Words substituted for numerals* E, MA $^{e...e}$ *Omitted* E; cum Rode MA ^{f} Erdelege E; Ardeleage MA (*with marginal note* modo Yeardley) ^{g} Luffenhale E; Luffenhaele MA ^{h} Bilcham E
^{i} Tidwolditone E; Tinwolditune MA (*with marginal note* nunc Heybridge) ^{j} Runewelle E; Runawella MA ^{k} Eduluesnasse E; de Eadulfesnesa MA ^{l} Nortone E; Draitune MA
^{m} Neasdone E ^{n} Willerdone E; Wellesdune MA ^{o} *sic* C, E; ergo MA (*perhaps correctly*) ^{p} Theodrici E; Theodorici MA; *for* Theodredi ^{q} *Word omitted* E
^{r} ergo E ^{s} *Word omitted* E, MA ^{t} edif[...]bo C (*MS damaged*) ^{u} da[.....]aues C (*MS damaged*) ^{v} MA *omits remainder of biblical quotation* ^{w} excercitu E, MA
^{x} per MA ^{y} *Name written in display capitals* C ^{z} C *is damaged here; word omitted* E
^{a2} Oskitel MA ^{b2} metropolit[......]racensis C (*MS damaged*); Ebur- MA ^{c2} Ælf[.....] C (*MS damaged*); Adelstanus E; Ælfstanus MA ^{d2} Londonigensis C ^{e2} Adulf MA
^{f2} E *concludes:* et aliis in carta. Sequitur carta regis eiusdem in Anglico sermone de verbo in verbum. ^{g2} Brithnoth MA

^{1} Matt. xvi: 18–19

12 is part of a dossier of mostly spurious charters which was copied into the main St Paul's cartularies (see above, pp. 60–1). As well as the extant texts in *Liber L* and *Liber A*, (MSS C, E) there was a copy in the lost *Liber B* (MS D), which was the source for Dugdale's printed editions in *St Paul's* and *Mon. Angl.* There is also a summary version of the charter, together with several scattered references, in a survey of individual St Paul's manors in a fourteenth-century register, *Liber I* (p. 54). This begins 'Ethelstanus rex, filius regis Edwardi, filius primi monarche Aluredi, renouauit et confirmauit monasterio S. Pauli...', and continues with the enumeration of estates (omitting the reference to *Rothe*, as does MS E), then a summary of the immunity clause (referring to freedom *ab omni generali seruicio*) and of the immunity clause. The concluding note in in MS E refers to the existence of an Old English version, supposedly verbatim (see note ^{f2}). If this is correct, the Old English would be a translation of the Latin, since the forger's exemplar was a Latin document (see next paragraph). However, there is some possibility that the cartularist mistook a separate vernacular diploma of Æthelstan (**13**) for a version of **12** (see p. 65). Dugdale indicates that both **12** and **13** were copied on the same folio in the lost *Liber B*, which may have been based on the same exemplar as this section of *Liber A*.

12 is closely related to **29**, in the name of Edward the Confessor, and to two Chertsey privileges dated 967 and 1062 (S 752 and 1035; Kelly, *Chertsey*, nos 8, 11). There was evidently collusion between St Paul's and Chertsey in the production of forged documents (see pp. 75–6). In this case it is clear that the Chertsey privileges had a prior existence, and were used as models by the St Paul's forgers: a suggestive detail is the reference in the sanction to St Peter (dedicatory saint of Chertsey), although the underlying intention may have been to invoke papal authority. S 752 and 1035 are relatively elaborate and sophisticated documents, noticeably well-produced. The common text was in part based on King Ine's grant of privileges to the West Saxon churches (S 245, A.D. 704; Kelly, *Malmesbury*, no. 8), but there are other elements which point to a date of composition in the later Anglo-Saxon period. S 752 is condemned by an internal reference to a non-contemporary abbot of Chertsey, but there is some possibility that S 1035 is based on a genuine diploma of the Confessor, or one written not long after its ostensible date of 1062. Both these documents include long lists of estates, with some circumstantial detail which shows that the draftsmen were drawing upon pre-Conquest documentation. They were almost certainly prepared under the supervision of Abbot Wulfwold (*c.* 1058–84), but may reflect an overhaul of the archive under a previous abbot, connected with an application to Pope Victor II (1055–7) which resulted in a papal privilege guaranteeing the abbey's lands (*Councils & Synods*, no. 75).

By contrast, **12** is of poor quality. It is considerably briefer than the Chertsey texts; there is no dating clause; the witness-list is quite impossible (see below). There is good reason to think that it has been rather clumsily adapted from S 752. The central part of the dispositive section of S 752 and 1035 comprises a historical passage mentioning Frithuwald and Eorcenwald and the latter's journey to Rome; this information is dependent upon earlier documentation in the abbey's archives (S 1165, 1247; and the genuine privilege of Pope Agatho, Jaffé no. 2115). St Paul's also had a connection with Eorcenwald, but this had to be phrased rather differently; this section in **12** reads very awkwardly and would seem to be an adaptation of the passage in the Chertsey texts. Another problematic passage appears after the list of estates. In S 752 the corresponding list of places is followed by a sentence in which the donor says that he grants the privilege to the abbot of Chertsey at the request of Bishop Æthelwold; in S 1035 a different abbot is mentioned, and the grant is said to have been made at the request of the king's *optimates*. Here the forger of **12** has adapted his model (evidently S 752) so that the grant is made at the request of the bishop of London (Theodoric, a mistake for Theodred); but the bishop was also the beneficiary, so the forger has had to change the sentence, which ends on the lame note that the king has caused this charter to be written, instead of the emphasis on the grant to the beneficiary. The adaptation of this passage in **29** is even less convincing, for the forger has simply mentioned St Eorcenwald. **12** was clearly the model for **29**.

In **12** the witnesses are listed, in a form which shows post-Conquest influence. S 752, by contrast, seems to have had a conventional witness-list, although the Chertsey cartularist has reduced this to only three subscriptions (King Edgar, Archbishop Osketel and Abbot Ælfric [of Malmesbury]). The first witness to **12** is Æthelgar of Canterbury (988–90), incompatible with the second, Osketel of York (956–971). There was a Bishop Ælfstan at London from 959 × 964 to 995/6; Athulf was bishop of Hereford from 971 or before until 1013 × 1016. Ælfhere was ealdorman of Mercia from 956 to 983; Brithnoth was ealdorman of Essex from 956 to 991. As in S 752 there is a subscription of an Abbot Ælfric, while Abbot Ælfstan is probably the man who attested Edgar's diplomas from 964 and who became bishop of Ramsbury in 970. With the exception of Archbishop Æthelgar, all these witnesses could have attested a charter from the later part of Edgar's reign. It seems almost certain that the forger of **12** not only modelled his charter on S 752 (A.D. 967), but also borrowed its witness-list. He probably found the need to substitute the name of a different archbishop because in 967 the incumbent was the celebrated Dunstan; the latter's career was too well-known for his subscription to have passed muster in a diploma attributed to King Æthelstan.

12 must have been forged after the production of S 1035 at Chertsey (in 1062 or shortly afterwards) and before the compilation of the exemplar of *Liber B* in the second quarter of the twelfth century. The most likely period would seem to have been during the time of Bishop Maurice (1085–1107) or of his successor Richard I de Belmeis (1108–27). Both these men were in conflict with the canons over the rights and revenues of the chapter, and both were accused of exploiting lands which rightly came under the control of the canons. This was also the time which saw the consolidation of the prebends (see above, pp. 46–9, 106). The list of estates in **12** is pertinent, since almost all the places mentioned here formed part of the common lands of the chapter, the *communa*, the revenues of which were allocated to the maintenance of the cathedral officers. The only exception to this observation is the final pair of estates on the list (Neasden and Willesden in Middlesex), which came to form part of the prebendal lands. The list of estates in **12** refers to all but three of the manors held TRE by St Paul's in Essex, Hertfordshire and Surrey. The likelihood is that **12** was forged in order to provide a firm title to certain estates of the *communa*, which were farmed out in return for a fixed quantity of supplies, later commuted to a money-rent.

The Estates

1. (Herts.) 10 hides **Sandon** with *Rothe* (*cf.* Roe Green and Roe Wood in Sandon: *PN Herts.*, p. 165; OE *roth*, 'clearing'). Sandon is mentioned in **25**, with a quota of one man. The canons had a manor of ten hides there TRE/TRW, with land for twenty ploughs (GDB 136r; *DB Herts.* 13:5); it had the same assessment in the 1181 inquisition (Hale, *St Paul's Domesday*, p. 141). The canons leased a half hide at Sandon to Æthelweard in the later eleventh century (*HMC 9th Report*, p. 65; see below, pp. 230–1). Together with *Rode* and Luffenhall (see next entry), Sandon supplied the chapter with farm or provisions for approximately ten months of the year (*VCH Herts.*, iii. 271).

2. (Herts.) 8 hides at **Ardeley** (also Ardleigh; *PN Herts.*, p. 151) with **Luffenhall**. In 1066 the canons held six hides at Ardeley and two hides at Luffenhall (GDB 136r; *DB Herts.* 13:3–4); in 1181 the Ardeley assessment was increased to seven, while the Luffenhall holding was still reckoned at two hides (Hale, *St Paul's Domesday*, pp. 140–1). The manor was allocated for the maintenance of the keeper of the brewhouse (*VCH Herts.*, iii. 194). Luffenhall parish lies partly in Clothall, partly in Ardeley; the St Paul's land there was taxed with Sandon (see above), but was regarded as part of Ardeley for spiritual purposes (see *VCH Herts.*, iii. 271). The place-name forms of Luffenhall generally indicate an original reading –*healh*, but the version in MS C and in the second Domesday reference may imply an alternative name in –*hæth*, perhaps based on a nearby heath (*PN Herts.*, p. 156).

3. (Essex) 10 hides at **Belchamp St Paul's** with **Wickham St Paul's** (see *PN Essex*, pp. 408–9, 467). In **25** Belchamp has a quota of one man. The *Wicun* mentioned in that document has been identified with Wickham, but probably incorrectly (see p. 196). One of the Essex Belchamps (presumably a different one) is mentioned in an eleventh-century will (S 1521). Belchamp was held by the canons TRE with an assessment of five hides, as was Wickham, assessed at 3 hides less one virgate (LDB 12v–13r; *DB Essex* 5:3–4). The manors had the same assessments in the 1181 inquisition (Hale, *St Paul's Domesday*, pp. 141–2).

4. (Essex) 8 hides at **Heybridge** (alias *Tidwoldi(ng)tune*: *cf. PN Essex*, pp. 303–4). In a will of the mid tenth century St Paul's was granted a food render from

Tidwoldingtone (S 1483), and in *c.* 1000 *Tidwoldingtune* was given to St Paul's by Ælfflæd for the use of the community (S 1486): see further discussion, pp. 94–5, 177. The canons held *Tidwoldingtuna* in 1066 and after, with an assessment of eight hides (LDB 13v; *DB Essex* 5:10); a half hide of this had been abstracted by Ralph Baynard (see p. 106). The manor had an assessment of seven-and-a-half hides in the 1181 inquisition (Hale, *St Paul's Domesday*, p. 142).

5. (Essex) 12 hides at **Runwell** (*cf. PN Essex*, pp. 265–6). The canons had eight hides here in 1066 and after (LDB 13v; *DB Essex* 5:9); it had the same assessment in the 1181 inquisition (Hale, *St Paul's Domesday*, p. 143).

6. (Essex) 30 hides at **The Naze** (*Edulesnæsa, Aedulvesnasa*). For the place-name, see *PN Essex*, pp. 354–5. The manor was held by the canons in 1066 and assessed at twenty-seven hides (LDB 13v; *DB Essex* 5:11); it had the same assessment in the 1181 inquisition (Hale, *St Paul's Domesday*, p. 142). Bishop Richard de Belmeis I appropriated the wood at *Aedulvesnasa* and included it in his park at Clacton on Sea; he restored it before his death (see Gibbs, no. 60 (pp. 43–4); Crosby, *Bishop and Chapter*, p. 32). For the history of the manor, see Faith 1996,

7. (Middx) 10 hides at **West Drayton**. A St Paul's estate here is mentioned in **25**, with a quota of one man. The manor was held by the canons in 1066 and after, with an assessment of ten hides (GDB 128r; *DB Middx* 3:30; for the identification, *cf.* Pinder 1991, p. 2, and *DB Middx*, notes). It had the same assessment in the 1181 inquisition (Hale, *St Paul's Domesday*, p. 145). In MS E there is a substituted reference to Norton (Mandeville) in Essex, a half-hide manor said to have been given to St Paul's after 1066 by Godgifu, the holder TRE; the Domesday reference mentions that the canons could not show a writ nor prove the king's agreement or the donation (LDB 13r; *DB Essex*, 5:6). The 1181 inquisition refers to forty acres at Norton (Hale, *St Paul's Domesday*, p. 143).

8. (Surrey) 8 hides at **Barnes**. This is mentioned in **25**, with a quota of one man (see further, pp. 197–8). The canons held a manor or eight hides there, which paid tax with the archbishop of Canterbury's manor of Mortlake and was accounted there (GDB 34r; *DB Surrey* 13:1). On the relationship of Barnes with Mortlake, see further *VCH Surrey*, iv. 3–8. The assessment in 1181 was four hides (Hale, *St Paul's Domesday*, p. 145).

9. (Middx) 10 hides at **Neasden** with **Willesden**. Neasden is not in DB, but appears in **25**, with a quota of four men. The canons had a fifteen hide manor at Willesden, which was for their household supplies (GDB 127v; *DB Middx*, 3:17); this would have included the Neasden holding (see further below, p. 196).

13

King Æthelstan confirms the privileges of St Paul's minster,
first granted in the time of King Sebbi. [A.D. 924 × 939]

D. London, St Paul's D. & C., *Liber B*, 20r: copy, s. xii^{ex} (lost)

Ed.: a. Dugdale, *St Paul's*, p. 185, from D (SP1)

    b. *Mon. Angl.*, iii. 302, from D (MA)

    c. Dugdale, *St Paul's* (2nd edn), App. pp. 9–10, from D (SP2)

    d. Dugdale, *St Paul's* (3rd edn), pp. 292–3, from D

    e. Kemble 1126, from *Mon. Angl.*

    f. Thorpe, *Diplomatarium*, pp. 176–7 (English, with translation), 177–8 (Latin), from *Mon. Angl.*

g. Birch 735 (English), 736 (Latin), from Kemble and *Mon. Angl.*
Listed: Sawyer 452; Gelling, *ECTV*, no. 214

(*a*) *Old English version*
Edited from SP2 (Dugdale, *St Paul's*, 2nd edn), with variants from SP1 (first edition) and MA (*Mon. Angl.*)

*a*On þam halgan naman ures halendes Cristes, se þe us gescop, þa þe sylfe næron, 7 us eft alysde mid his agenum life, þa þa fordone*b* pæron þurh þaes deofles lare, 7 mid ealle for-scylgode*c* into þam ecan susle, ac his myccle arfæstnesse us*d* alysde of ðam. Nu ic Aðelstan, cyning ofer Ængla þeode, cyþe minum þitum 7 on þisum geþrite mid þordum afæstnige, þ ic þille friðian*e* ealle þa lande are into S. Paules mynstre, 7 þæreto gesetan þysne priuilege,*f* þ is synderlic freols, S. Paul to lofe, þan halgan apostle þe þeos stop is halig,*g* minre saule to alysednesse 7 mine synnan to forgifenesse, be þam þe Sybba cyng hit ærest hit gefreode 7 se halga Erkenþold, 7 hig begen þæreto*h* gebugen mid ealle Gode geþeopode, 7 þa stope gegodeden, 7 se mære Biscop*i* S. Erkenwold þæne freols gefette on Romebirig, þe on þisse Cartan is aþriten, 7 manega oþre freolsas heron geþriten synd þe mine forgengan gesetten,*j* heora saule*k* to alysednesse.*l* Se þe þysne freols geeacnige, God his lief her on life 7 him heofona rices myrhþe*m* sylle, þonne he heonon faran sceole. Se þe þænne þa are þænce to þeofigenne, oððe*n* on oððre þison to aþadenne*o* on oðre hit her beforen aþriten is, sy his lif her gelittled, 7 þenne he heonon faran sceole, sig a his þunung on helle grund, buton he hit her ær his ænde þes tiþelicor gebete þið þæne æcan God þe ah ealra þinga geþeald. Forþi þe spa fæstlice þysne freols bebeodað, þ þe spa moten eft ealle æt gædere heofonan rices*p* myrhþe habban mid þam ecan Gode þe ah ealra þinge geþeald. Amen.

a Alia carta eiusdem Regis Adelstani Saxonice *rubric* SP1, MA, SP1   *b* rordone SP1, MA
c ? *For* forscyldoge   *d* ur SP1, MA   *e* friggen SP1, MA   *f* frivilege SP1, MA
g haling SP1, MA   *h* beggen þærto SP1, MA   *i* Biscof SP1   *j* gesettyn MA
k raule SP1, MA   *l* alysnesse SP1, MA   *m* myrcþe SP1, MA; *a spelling for* mirigþ
n oððre SP1, MA   *o* ? *For* awændenne   *p* riches SP1, MA

(*b*) *Latin version*
Printed from SP2 (Dugdale, *St Paul's*, 2nd edn), with variants from SP1 (first edition) and MA (*Mon. Angl.*)

*a*In Sancto nomine nostri Servatoris Christi, qui nos creavit, quando nosmet ipsi non eramus, & nos redemit cum sua propria vita, quando perditi fuimus ex Diabolici doctrina, & penitus damnati in æternum sulphur: sed ejus magna clementia nos liberavit ab eo. Nunc ego *Athelstanus* Rex super Anglicam gentem, notum facio meis sapientibus, & in hoc scripto verbis confirmo; quod liberabo omnem terram ad S. Pauli Monasterium (spectantem:) Et insuper constituam istud priuilegium; hoc est, singularem immunitatem, in laudem S. Pauli, illius Sancti Apostoli, cui hic locus est sacratus; in animæ meæ redemptionem, & peccatorum meorum remissionem, secundum quod *Sebba* Rex eundem (locum) primo liberavit, & S. *Erkenwaldus*; quorum ambo eo se contulerunt, omnino Deo inservierunt, & illum locum locupletarunt, magnusque ille Episcopus S. *Erkenwaldus*, illud Privilegium impetravit Romæ, quod in hac Charta scribitur: Et plura alia Privilegia hic inscribuntur, quæ mei prædecessores irrogarunt in animarum suarum redemptionem. Qui hoc Privilegium adauxerit, Deus ejus vitam in hoc mundo (conservet) & ei cœlorum regni gaudia concedat, quando hinc decesserit. Qui vero quid illinc abstulerit, sive in alium usum converterit, aliter (scilicet) quam hic suprascriptum est; sit ejus vita hic decurtata; et quando hinc decesserit, semper sit ejus habitatio in Inferni fundo, nisi id hic ante finem suum diligentius compenset apud æternum Deum, qui omnium rerum habet potestatem. Idcirco tam firmiter hoc privilegium (observari) præcipimus, ut ita nos omnes denuo possimus simul cœlorum regni gaudia assequi cum æterno Deo, qui omnium rerum habet potestatem. Amen.

a Eadem carta Latine *rubric* SP1, MA, SP2

The only sources for **13** are the printed texts in *Mon. Angl.* and *St Paul's* (note that the antiquarian copies cited in the first edition of Sawyer are for S 980, i.e. KCD 735). Dugdale's source was the lost *Liber B* (see above, pp. 62–4). The vernacular text in the first edition of *St Paul's* contains a series of errors which were corrected in the second edition; it is not clear whether these were printer's errors, linked to the use of an unfamiliar font, or whether they reflect existing corruption in the manuscript or a poor transcript. There is a strong possibility that the Latin version is Dugdale's own translation of the Old English text: he provided translations of the other vernacular documents which he prints (**22, 27, 28**). However, the Latin version of these other examples is preceded by the heading *Id est*, which is rather more explicit. Moreover, there is evidence that a number of the St Paul's charters did exist in bilingual versions (see **12, 21, 23, 31**; and above p. 65).

13 would appear to be a very loose vernacular version of the same Chertsey model used for the fabrication of **12** and **29** (i.e. S 752; see above, pp. 75–6, 162–3). It includes abbreviated versions of most of the principal clauses (with the substitution of a creed for the proem), with the emphasis on general freedom for the endowment, rather than on particular estates. The reference to King Sebbi is probably a replacement for the reference to 'king' Frithuwald in S 752. The *Miracula S. Erkenwaldi*, written by Arcoid in the 1140s (see pp. 111–12), refers to a tomb of King Sebbi which formed a prominent feature of the pre-Conquest basilica (Whatley, *Saint of London*, p. 120). The draftsman of **13** has imposed a notification clause (*ic...cythe minum witum*), which reflects post-Conquest priorities.

14

King Eadred grants twelve hides (mansae) *at Shopland,*
Essex, to Eawynn, a nun. A.D. 946

H. Bodleian, James 23, p. 34: extract, s. xvii[1]
Ed.: Gibbs, p. 6 (J12)
Listed: Sawyer 1793 (LonStP 10); Hart, *ECE*, no. 12

Quapropter ego Eadredus, rex Anglorum cæterarumque gentium in circuitu persistentium gubernator et rector, cuidam religiosæ sanctæ conversationis monialis fæminæ ⟨vocitatæ⟩*a* nomine Eapynne 12 mansas eternaliter tribuo in illo loco ubi ruricoli apellativo usu ludibundisque vocabulis nomen indiderunt Scopinglande, ut eandem*b* supra taxatam vitæ suæ cursu fæliciter possideat. Igitur, imminente dissolutionis suæ calle corporis et animæ successorum, sibi carorum cui sibi libuerit mente liberali largiatur, et ipsi.*c* Perpetue namque huius tramitibus mundi hoc quod concessi terræ prenotatum a cunctis laboribus vitæ mortalium permaneat abdicatum, preter id quod nobis omnibus communiter indigeri videtur, id est tria: exercitus aditum, pontis ædificium, munitionis castellique auxilium. Anno Domini .dccccxlvi.

a vocitatæ *altered to* vocitato   *b* sc. terram   *c* *For* ipse (*all versions of this model read* ipsi)

This is an extract by Richard James from a document on the lost medieval roll (see above, pp. 67–70). Eawynn was the beneficiary of a second royal diploma in 946, covering nineteen hides at Hockley in Essex and preserved in the Barking archive (S 517b). It has been suggested that she may have belonged to the revived foundation of Barking (Hart, *ECE*, no. 12). Eorcenwald founded the original double monastery there at some point before 664, with his sister Æthelburh acting as its first abbess; she was succeeded by Hildelith, who is said to have been abbess for many years and who was still alive in *c*. 716 (Bede, *HE*, iv. 6–10; Tangl, no. 10). Thereafter the house disappears from the record until the tenth century. It is unlikely that there was continuity of religious life at Barking during the Danish raids and invasions of the ninth century, but the preservation of a significant number of early Barking charters argues for corporate continuity of some kind; one possibility is that what remained of the community took refuge within the city of London, perhaps on the site of All Hallows Barking, which had a later association with the abbey (Brooke and Keir, *London*, p. 137; see above, pp. 8, 21). Religious life had been re-established at Barking by 950 at the lastest, for in that year the *familia* received a land-grant from King Eadred (S 552a), and at around the same time it was a beneficiary of the will of Ealdorman Ælfgar (S 1483, A.D. 946 × *c*. 951). See further, Foot, *Veiled Women*, ii. 27–33.

Of the two estates which Eadred granted to Eawynn in 946, one certainly descended to Barking: Hockley was in the nuns' possession in 1066 (LDB 18v; *DB Essex* 9:13). But this does not necessarily prove an association. The two charters in favour of Eawynn form part of a group of thirteen diplomas issued between 939 and 955, all in favour of women beneficiaries described as 'religious' or specifically as nuns (see also S 448–9, 464–5, 474, 482, 485, 493, 534, 535, 563; and discussion under Kelly, *Shaftesbury*, no. 13; *eadem*, *Abingdon*, nos 30, 35; Brooks and Kelly, *Christ Church*, no. 118). Only one of these women is explicitly linked with a minster community (Ælfgyth of S 563 and presumably also S 493 is described as a nun of Wilton). It has been suggested that most of these women may have been widows or vowesses, living on their own estates, perhaps in association with other women of the same condition who dispersed after the death of the patroness (see Foot, *Veiled Women*, vol. i, chapter 5). If Eawynn was in this situation, then her property could have been divided on her death between various religious and non-religious heirs, with estates passing separately to St Paul's and Barking. Shopland would appear to have belonged to the London bishopric before the end of the century, for it is mentioned in **25**, with a quota of one man, but the estate was subsequently lost or alienated. In 1086 it was listed among the lands of Count Eustace, with an assessment of five hides; it had been held by a freeman before the Conquest and then by Engelric (LDB 34v; *DB Essex* 20:80).

The statement of powers and immunity clause in this fragment align it with a distinctive group of charters from 940–3 (S 471, 486–7, 492). These have a proem beginning *Manifestum est cunctis* and a sanction beginning *Sic* (for *Si quis*) *demonice fermentationis*; the wording of the statement of powers and immunity clause are verbatim as in this fragment. Clearly all these charters were based on a single model (see discussion in Kelly, *Abingdon*, no. 33). James's confusion about the reading of *vocitate* (see note[b]) suggests that the draftsman may have failed to feminise the past participle *vocitato* in the model; the same error was made in S 487, another grant to a religious woman. There is a very good chance that the original of **14** was written by the charter-scribe known to modern scholars as 'Edmund C', who was responsible for five of the surviving originals from the period 944–9 (S 497, 510, 528, 535, 552): see Keynes, *Diplomas*, pp. 16, 26; *idem* 1985, pp. 149–50. It can be stated with some confidence that the Shopland diploma would have had an appearance and layout similar to that of the other mainstream diplomas produced between *c.* 935 and *c.* 951: a horizontal (long rectangle) format; significant words (name of donor, beneficiary, estate) emphasised by the use of capitals and punctuation; a smaller register script of script used for the vernacular bounds (compare, for example, S 510, 528). The formulation of centrally-produced diplomas in this period was noticeably different from the florid 'Athelstan A' type (see **11**). There was greater tolerance of variation, with some use of standardised models (such as the type reflected in **14**).

15

King Eadwig grants ten hides (cassati) *at Orsett, Essex, to Bishop Brihthelm.* [A.D. 957]

H. Bodleian, James 23, pp. 34–5: extract, s. xvii
Ed.: Gibbs, p. 6 (J13)
Listed: Sawyer 1794 (LonStP 11); Hart, *ECE*, no. 14

—Brithelemo episcopo .x. cassatos perpetualiter concedo in illo loco ubi ruri-colæ appellativo usu ludibundisque vocabulis nomen indiderunt æt Orseaþan. Anno Domini ⟨957⟩.[a] Ego Eadwig rex Anglorum prefatam donationem cum sigillo sanctæ crucis confirmavi. Ego Edgar eiusdem frater regis fieri celeriter consensi.

[a] 1457 H

15 is an extract made by Richard James from a diploma on the lost St Paul's roll (see pp. 67–70). The date in the excerpt is probably an error for 957 (*dcccclvii*): Eadwig became king in late 955 and died in 959. In the course of 957 Eadwig's brother Edgar took control of Mercia and the rest of the kingdom north of the Thames, leaving Eadwig king only of Wessex and the south-east. Essex seems to have fallen into Edgar's domain (see above, pp. 31–2). The St Paul's charter predates the division, for it is attested by Edgar as 'the king's brother'. The beneficiary is presumably the bishop of London, appointed 951 × 953 and in office until 957 × 959 (see above, pp. 118–19). The formula introducing the English place-name was used occasionally between 940 and 958 (S 468, 471, 476 etc.; also **14**).

Two places named Orsett are mentioned in the naval assessment list of *c.* 1000 (**25**), the second being distinguished as 'the western Orsett'; both have a quota of a single sailor. A brief extract in Selden's notes appears to refer to a place named *Horseda*, granted to a deacon named Werenberht between 971 and 992, perhaps in 982 (**19*b***). It seem likely that this is a version of the place-name Orsett, which is *Orseda(m)* and *Dorseda(m)* in Domesday, in which case either **15** or **19*b*** may refer to 'the western Orsett' of **25**. Before and after 1066 Orsett was an episcopal manor; its assessment was thirteen hides, of which one was held from the church by Engelric and later passed into the possession of Count Eustace (LDB 9v, 26v; *DB Essex*, 3:2, 20:4). It seems likely that the Domesday manor represents the amalgamation of the ten hides of **15** with the land later granted to Werenberht.

16

King Edgar grants fifteen hides (mansiones) *at Navestock, Essex, to St Paul's minster.* A.D. 867 [for 957 × 958]

C. GL 25504 (*Liber L*), 9r–10r: copy, s. xii[1]
    Rubric: De Nasingstoc 'anno gracie .dcccclxvii.' [*addition by later medieval hand*]
D. St Paul's D. & C., *Liber B*, 20r (?): copy, s. xii[ex] (lost)
E. GL 25501 (*Liber A*), 56r (old foliation 38r): copy, s. xiii[med]
    Marginal rubric: Karta Adgari regis.
H. Bodleian, James 23, p. 33: extract, s. xvii[1]
P. GL 25516, 73r: copy, s. xiv[1]
    Rubric: Carta Regis Eadgari de manerio de Nastoke
Ed.: a. Dugdale, *St Paul's*, pp. 186–7, from D (SP1)
    b. *Mon. Angl.*, iii. 302–3, from D (MA)
    c. Dugdale, *St Paul's* (2nd edn), App pp. 10–11, from D (SP2)
    d. Dugdale, *St Paul's* (3rd edn), pp. 293–4, from D
    e. Kemble 1259, from *Mon. Angl.*
    f. Birch 1210, from E, Kemble and *Mon. Angl.*
    g. Pierquin, *Recueil*, pt 5, no. 24, from Birch
    h. Gibbs, pp. 2–3 (from H) and n. 2 (from E)
Listed: Sawyer 337; Hart, *ECE*, no. 9
Edited from C, with variants from E, P and MA (*Mon. Angl.*)

In nomine Dei summi, ipsoque inperpetuum Domino nostro Iesu Christo regnante ac disponente ubique omnia sceptra quoque regalia temporaliter gubernanda distribuerit, accommodauerit cui uult. Unde ego Eadgærus*a* rex, rogatus quidem ab episcopo*b* meo Deorwulfo*c* et principe meo Ealdredo,*d* ut aliquam partem terrę *e*liberam darem*e* inperpetuum in monasterium sancti Pauli apostoli doctoris gentium, id est .xv. mansiones in loco qui uocitatur*f* Næsingstoc,*g* et michi collato*h* digno precio, id est .lx.*i* mancas*j* in auro puro,*k* et nunc*l* ego Eadgærus*m* rex, cum consilio atque consensu episcoporum meorum et sapientium meorum, pręcipio in Dei omnipotentis nomine ut hęc supradicta terra sit liberata ab omni tributo regali uectigali, siue notis siue ignotis,*n* maioris uel minoris, quamdiu christiana fides in terra seruatur. Si quis hanc benedictionem largitatis augere Deo uoluerit, sua bona in cęlesti regno augeantur et multiplicentur. Et qui hanc donationem meam temptauerit frangere aut diminuere, anathema sit marenatha*o* in die iudicii ante tribunal Christi, nisi ante cum satisfactione emendauerit. Actum est autem*p* anno ab incarnatione Domini nostri Iesu Christi .dccclxvii.*q* indictione*r* .xv.

⟨+⟩*s* Ego Eadgarus*t* rex hanc cartulam signo sanctę crucis Christi corroboraui et confirmaui, consentiens et subscripsi, et ceteros testes idoneos*u* ut idipsum*v* agerent adhibui quorum nomina infra scripta sunt.*w*

Ego Odo*x* archiepiscopus consensi et subscripsi.	[*Canterbury*]
Ego Þulfhære*y* dux.	
Beorhtuulf*z* dux.	
Drihtþald*a2* dux.	
Ego Ealhferd*b2* episcopus consensi et subscripsi.	[*Winchester*]
Ego Mucel dux.	
Eastmund*c2* dux.	
Ego Heahmund*d2* episcopus consensi et subscripsi.*e2*	[*Sherborne*]
Ego Æðeluulf*f2* dux.	
Ælfred dux.	
Ego Deoruulf episcopus consensi et subscripsi.*g2*	[*London*]
Ego Ealdred dux.*g2*	
Ælfstan dux.*h2*	
Garuulf minister.	
Ægbærht minister.	
Ægfreð minister.	
Æla minister.	
Æðelfred minister.	
Ealhheard abbas.	
Þulfhelm minister.	
Acca minister.	

Þynsige minister.

Æðelþard presbyter.

Æðelstan presbyter.

Þulfred dux.

Þærfred abbas.

   a Adgarus E; Eadgarius P; Eadgarus MA   *b* archiepiscopo E   *c* Doruulpho E; Deorulfo
P; Deorwlfo MA   *d* Ældredo E, MA   *e...e* liberabo P   *f* uocatur E, P, MA
   g Nasingestok E; Nastoke P; Nasinstock MA   *h* conlato P; cum lato MA   *i* sexaginta E
j mancas C, MA; marcas E; marcos P (*probably for* mancusas)   *k* purissimo MA
l P *omits* nunc *here and inserts it after the king's name*   *m* Ædgarus E; Eadgarus MA
n innotis C; sine uotis sine innotis P   *o* mane natha C; maranatha P; marenata MA;
for marenatha   *p* h' E; hoc MA (*from misreading of the Insular abbreviation for* autem)
q .dccclxvii. *altered to* .dcccclxvii *by a later hand* C; .dccclxvii. E, MA   *r* indictiones C
s Cross *supplied only in* P *and* MA   *t* Ædgarus E; Eadger P; Eadgarus MA   *u* ydoneos P
v ad ipsum MA   *w* E *concludes:* Ipsa nomina sunt in carta.   *x* Name in display capitals C
y Þulfere P; Wulfhere MA   *z* Ego Borryulf P   *a2* Ego Drathiald P; Brihtwald MA
b2 Calehperd P   *c2* Easmund P; MA *supplies* Ego   *d2* Eg⟨o⟩ Headmund P; Eadmund MA
e2 P *ends here*   *f2* Adelwulf MA   *g2* These two subscriptions omitted MA
h2 The remainder of the witness-list in MA *runs as follows:* Wulfred dux, Werfred dux [*recte*
abbas], Garwlf minister, Ealheard abbas, Æthelward pr[esbyter], Æcbert minister, Wulfhelm
minister, Ædelstan pr[esbyter], Acca minister, Æla minister, Wynsie minister, Ælfred minister.

16 was part of the dossier of mostly forged charters which was copied into the main
St Paul's cartularies (see MSS C, D, E). Ralph Diceto's 'greater register' (MS D, *Liber
B*), now lost, was the source of Dugdale's edition in *St Paul's* and *Mon. Angl.* (see
pp. 62–4). A copy of **16** also appears in a collection of Navestock records in a fourteenth-
century survey of St Paul's manors (MS P; *Liber I*), and copies may have existed in two
other lost cartularies, Diceto's 'lesser register', known as *Liber C*, and another
compilation with some pre-Conquest material, *Liber G* (see above, pp. 52–3, 55).
Richard James made an extract from a version of the document on a lost medieval roll
(MS H; see pp. 67–70). The reference to this charter in Henry Wharton's *De episcopis
et decanis Londoniensibus* (*cf.* Gibbs, p. ix) probably derives from study of one of
the cartulary copies, rather than the text on the lost roll. The unusually large number of
copies may reflect the survival of a single-sheet version into the later medieval period
(see pp. 54–5; and note the concluding comment in MS E, see *w*). The order of
subscriptions in the extant manuscripts and in Dugdale's edition is confused, presumably
due to the misreading at some stage of subscriptions arranged in columns.

   16 is a forgery apparently modelled on a charter of King Æthelred of Wessex dated
867 (see further below). The names of the king and archbishop of Canterbury have been
changed, and there can be little doubt that the details of the beneficiary have also been
altered. The model may have been an earlier title-deed for Navestock, which came into
the community's possession with the estate and which was subsequently emended to
create a direct grant. It is entirely unsafe to use **16** as evidence that St Paul's first acquired
Navestock as early as 867: if the forger's model already named St Paul's, there would
have been no need to produce a forgery. The original beneficiary could have been a
layman or a named ecclesiastic, or even another religious house whose lands were later

absorbed into the episcopal estate. Navestock is mentioned in the naval assessment list (25) with a quota of four men, so it would appear to have formed part of the endowment of the London diocese by *c.* 1000 (which may indicate that it was indeed acquired from Edgar or in Edgar's reign). In 1086 several Navestock manors were noted among the lands of the canons, with background details which imply that the St Paul's holdings there were the subject of considerable dispute around the time of the Conquest; it seems possible that the property had been lost to the community in the first half of the eleventh century, and that advantage was taken of the disturbances of the Conquest to to regain possession. A total of five hides less twenty acres at Navestock was held as two manors by two freemen, Howard and Wulfsige in 1066; the canons claimed to have acquired this land through King William's gift. Another manor consisting of a hide plus forty acres had been held by Thurstan the Red in 1066 but was seized (*invasit*) by St Paul's; in the same village the canons also had two hides, which had been held by seven free men before the Conquest, and the Hundred testified that another hide and twenty acres held by a priest also belonged to St Paul's (LDB 13rv; *DB Essex* 5:8). This entry concludes with the statement *modo est in manu regis*. A further Navestock manor, held TRE by Gotild and TRW by Ralph de Marcy from Hamo the Steward, was part of a claim made by St Paul's after 1086, settled by a compromise in 1120 (LDB 56r; *DB Essex* 28:14; cf. *VCH Essex*, iv. 143; *HMC 9th Report*, p. 316 and p. 66a; Round 1891). The spurious 'Coronation Day' diploma in the name of King William mentions fifteen hides at Navestock among the estates supposedly restored to St Paul's on that occasion, after being seized 'by certain men' during previous reigns (Bates, *RRAN: Acta of William I* no. 183: see pp. 102–3). **16** was in existence by the time of the production of *Liber L* in the second quarter of the twelfth century, and was probably produced after the Conquest to strengthen the canons' claims to the estate. Navestock remained a St Paul's manor until 1540, when it was ceded to Henry VIII along with other manors in exchange for property elsewhere (*L. & P. Hen. VIII*, xix.1, p. 495).

The formulation and the witness-list, together with the 867 date, show conclusively that the forger of **16** was drawing upon a ninth-century diploma in the name of a West Saxon king: presumably Æthelred (865–71). The East Saxons had acknowledged the overlordship of Æthelred's grandfather Ecgberht in *c.* 826 (*ASC s.a.* 825) and Essex thereafter seems to have remained part of the West Saxon realm (see above, pp. 19–20). **16** provides the only evidence that West Saxon kings granted bookland in Essex: but this can be explained by the almost complete destruction of the pre-tenth-century documentation for this region (only the fragmentary archives of St Paul's and Barking include earlier records covering land in Essex). The year 867 was a difficult time for East Anglia and the neighbouring provinces. The 'Great Army' of the Danes had landed in East Anglia in late 865, had wintered there and made a peace agreement, before seizing Northumbria in 866–7; by late 867 the threat had turned to Mercia. Æthelred of Wessex may well have been anxious to consolidate the support of the East Saxon magnates and churches. The conveyance of Navestock, to an unknown beneficiary, was made at the request of Deorwulf, bishop of London (for his dates and career, see pp. 115–16) and of Ealdorman Ealdred, who is likely to have been the ealdorman of Essex (he otherwise attests S 327, dealing with land in Rochester, and S 335, dated from Micheldever, Hampshire). The 867 diploma was also attested by Bishops Ealhferth of Winchester and Heahmund of Sherborne, the latter appointed in that year after the death of his predecessor. The subscription of Oda, archbishop of Canterbury from 941 until 957/8, reflects interference by the later forger: Oda's name may have been substituted for that of Ceolnoth (833–70). The association of Oda and King Edgar provides ostensible dating limits of 957 × 958 for the spurious diploma, since Edgar was elected king of the Mercians in 957 and Oda's death can most probably be placed in June 958 (see Kelly, *Abingdon*, pp. xcv–vi). It seems probable that the later forger borrowed these names from a diploma or other document issued during Edgar's two-year reign as king of the Mercians, during which he controlled Essex (see S 676, and above, p. 31). The ten ealdormen who attest **16** were all West Saxons active in the 860s; their subscriptions can be found in other charters of Æthelred and his brothers (note especially Eastmund, all of whose subscriptions are concentrated around the year 867: *cf.* also S 1204, 338). The subscribing thegns were likewise ninth-century West Saxons (for example, the distinctively-named Garulf attests 863 × 867). The witness-list also includes the names of two abbots (Ealhheard, who also attests S 335–6, 338, ?1201; and Werferth, witness to S 308, 315, ?317, 327) and two priests (neither of whom occurs elsewhere).

The protocol consists of a verbal invocation of the *In nomine* type with an awkward ablative extension. A very close parallel for this appears in a Rochester charter of 788 (S 129; Campbell, *Rochester*, no. 12): *In nomine Dei summi et saluatoris nostri Iesu Christi ipsoque inperpetuo regnante disponenteque suauiter omnia terrena quoque sceptra et regalia iura temporaliter distribuerit.* It seems likely that the St Paul's version is a botched adaptation of this formula or one very like it. Although the inspiration for this protocol is clearly an earlier text, it would not seem out of place in a charter of 867; at this period extended invocations voicing similar sentiments are fairly common (compare S 332, 339, and see *In nomine Dei summi regis eterni* in S 338, also dated 867). The rogation clause probably has a genuine basis: references to Deorwulf and Ealdred are entirely consistent with the 867 date. The construction of the dispositive section is confused, presumably as the result of poor adaptation of the model. The unit of land-assessment is the *mansio*, common in the tenth century but not in the ninth (*cf.* also S 286, 301, 306, all late copies and the latter two spurious). The immunity clause has been adapted from a genuine formula of 867: the phrase *quamdiu christiana fides in terra servatur* also occurs in S 339 from the following year (and see the corresponding pairs of adjectives in S 338: *intus et foras magnis ac modicis*). The sanction and dating clause were also taken from the 867 model.

17

King Edgar grants forty hides (cassati) *at* [*Hadham, Hertfordshire*]
to Æthelflæd, widow and nun. A.D. 969

H. Bodleian, James 23, p. 32: paraphrase/extract, s. xvii[1]
I. London, Lincoln's Inn, Hale 84, 93r: extract, s. xvii[1]
Ed.: Gibbs, p. 1 (J1), from H
Listed: Sawyer 1795 (LonStP 12); Gelling, *ECTV*, no. 169

(*a*)
Edited from I

Hinc ego Eadgar Anglorum basileus, per omnipatrantis inexpugnabile dexteram uniuerse Britannie regni subthronizatus solio, quandam telluris portionem, .xl.

uidelicet cassatos, scilicet in loco qui a ruricolis huiusque prosapie noto nuncupatur uocabulo ⟨Hadham⟩,[a] cuidam uidue que sanctimonialis ob amorem eterni caelestique sponsi[b] dicata [......][c] uelamine, olim patri meo videlicet regi Eadmundo legitimo usque ad uite finem copulata conubio, et ab ineunte etate Æþelflæt nobili appellatur vocabulo, ob eterne vite brauium supernorumque ciuium contubernium perpetua largitus sum hæreditate, quatenus ipsa uita comite cum omnibus utensilibus suis summa[d] moderatoris clementia in ipsa telluris edidit superficie uoti compos perfruatur et post uitæ transitum sue quibuscunque uoluerit successionis cleronomis perpetualiter contradendo derelinquat. ⟨This she had granted to the church of Paules.⟩[e] Sit igitur ⟨saith the king⟩[e] prefatum rus omni terrene seruitutis iugo liberum fiscalique tributo solutum, tribus his exceptis, rata uidelicet expeditione, pontis arcisue restauratione.

⟨Hadham is the land granted and then it is bounded in Saxon. Anno 969, indictione 4. Diuers duces.⟩[f]

[a] *Place-name omitted here but supplied in concluding note (reason for omission unclear, but perhaps simple error)*   [b] *For* sposi   [c] *Reading unclear, perhaps* uidelicet   [d] *Probably for* summi (*sc.* moderatoris)   [e] *Selden's interpolated comments*   [f] *Selden's concluding note*

(b)
Edited from H

Viduæ uxori patris sui Eadmundi, quæ ab ineunte ætate Æþelflæt nobili appellabatur vocabulo, permittit rex Eadgar ut post mortem suam donet Hædham villam, cum omnibus suis supellectilibus Deo agioque predicatori gentium Paulo[a]—Et sit igitur inquit[b] prefatum rus omni terrenæ servitutis iugo liberum, fiscalique tributo solutum, tribus hiis exceptis, rata videlicet expeditione, pontis arcisve restauratione.

[a] *This sentence seems to be a paraphrase of the content of the document*   [b] *James has inserted this word into the formula*

It can be assumed with some confidence that Selden's substantial extracts (*a*) and the notes by James (*b*) derive from the same document on the lost medieval roll, a diploma of King Edgar granting land to his stepmother, Æthelflæd (for the manuscript sources, see above, pp. 67–70). According to Selden, the diploma was dated to the year 969 and the fourth indiction (969 was actually the twelfth indiction, which suggests either a misreading of *iiii* for *xii*, or a miscopying of the incarnation year). The formulation in these antiquarian notes seems broadly compatible with the date. Selden's extract (*a*) begins with the exposition. The king's royal style is an adaptation of one devised for Æthelstan by the scribe/draftsman 'Æthelstan A' in 931 (see **11**) and used in the majority of royal diplomas until 933 and occasionally thereafter; other adapted examples in Edgar's diplomas occur in S 692, 740, 777, 781, 822. The influence of the distinctive formulation of 'Æthelstan A' diplomas from 931 × 933 can also be seen in **18**, another fragment of a diploma in Edgar's name. The elements of the dispositive section seem entirely acceptable. The statement of powers is a slightly adapted version of a formula used first in 961; the immunity clause was also devised in the same year. Both formulas are constituents of the standard model for Edgar's diplomas, associated with a scribe known as 'Edgar A' (see Keynes, *Diplomas*, pp. 70–9). There are grounds for associating the 'Edgar A' model with Æthelwold, abbot of Abingdon and later bishop of Winchester (Kelly, *Abingdon*, pp. cxv–xix), and the vocabulary of **17** tends to reinforce this hypothesis. The adjective *inexpugnabilis* inserted into the royal style and the phrase *vitae bravium* later in the text both appear in the same chapter of the foundation charter of New Minster, Winchester, which was drawn up by Æthelwold in 966 (S 745, cap. xvi; Miller, *New Minster*, no. 23). The appearance of the word *prosapia* in the introduction to the place-name (with the meaning 'race, nation') is paralleled in King Eadwig's great 959 privilege for Abingdon, which seems to be Æthelwold's work (S 658; Kelly, *Abingdon*, no. 83), in the similar privilege for Romsey (S 812) and in a related document in favour of Queen Eadgifu (S 811, probably 959 × 961); it is also found in S 680, which seems to be an early product of 'Edgar A'. Part of the formulation of the immunity clause recurs in **18**, an extract from a spurious diploma of Edgar in favour of St Paul's (*fiscalique tributo*; see also S 535). The reversion rider in extract (*b*) has the same wording as the reference to the beneficiary in **18** (*agio prædicatori gentium Paulo*), which may mean that **17** was the model for **18**, or that the reversion rider was added to the former document at around the same time that **18** was forged (see below). According to Selden, the copy of the Hadham diploma on the lost roll included a set of vernacular bounds.

Æthelflæd was the daughter of Ælfgar, ealdorman of Essex, who became the second wife of King Eadmund at some stage between 944 and 946. She seems to have been known as Æthelflæd 'of Damerham', after an estate which she acquired from Eadmund before his death and subsequently passed on to Glastonbury (*ASC D*, s.a. 946; S 513). The *Liber Eliensis* refers to her (perhaps erroneously) as the wife of Ealdorman Æthelstan (Blake, *Liber Eliensis*, p. 136), so she may have subsequently remarried (see discussion in Whitelock, *Wills*, pp. 141–2): but in **17** she is explicitly referred to as a nun (*sanctimonialis*). It seems probable that she was living a devout life as a consecrated widow, perhaps on her own estates, or perhaps in a religious house on an independent footing (for this class of 'nun', and for discussion of the terminology, see Foot, *Veiled Women*, chapter 5; and **14** above). Æthelflæd's will, together with those of her father Ælfgar and her sister Ælfflæd, wife of Ealdorman Brihtnoth of Essex, have been preserved in the archive of Bury St Edmunds (S 1494, 1483, 1486).

Edgar's grant to Æthelflæd apparently consisted of forty hides at Hadham. In the copy seen by the antiquaries, the diploma seems to have included a section (appearing before the immunity clause) concerning the reversion of the estate to St Paul's after the beneficiary's death. James's extract (*b*) implies that this last provision was the principal function of the charter, but the longer version in (*a*) shows that the form of the document was that of a normal royal land-grant, the reference to the reversion being supplementary and presumably an addition (since later in the text Æthelflæd is given the right to bequeath the estate freely to her chosen heirs). A similar reference to reversion to a religious house, this time to Glastonbury, is to be found in King Eadmund's diploma granting to Æthelflæd the estate at Damerham (S 513). The Damerham bequest is mentioned in Æthelflæd's will (S 1494, A.D. 962 × 991, probably after 975): she leaves it to Glastonbury on behalf of the souls of King Eadmund, King Edgar and herself. The case of Hadham is more complicated. The bequest to St Paul's is mentioned in the will, but it is deferred: the estate was first to pass to Æthelflæd's sister Ælfflæd and Ælfflæd's husband, Ealdorman Brihtnoth, for their lifetimes, with reversion to the London bishopric. The last survivor of the three, Ælfflæd, appears to have completed the bequest, finally transferring the estate in her own will (S 1486). It had been a long wait, for Ælfflæd may have survived into the new millenium—her will was drawn up after the death of her husband in the Battle of Maldon in 991, and before the demise of Queen Ælfthryth, which probably took place in November 1000 or 1001, although one source gives 1002 (see Keynes, *Diplomas*, p. 210 n. 203, p. 259); but it is not impossible that Ælfflæd herself lived longer. The terminology of the bequests in the two wills is important: Hadham is to become part of the episcopal estate (*to bisceophame* see Whitelock, *Wills*, p. 140; *ToOED*), while Ælfflæd grants Heybridge to St Paul's for the use of the community (see above, pp. 94–5).

It could be significant that the texts of both S 513 and **17** appear to have included references to reversion; perhaps in both instances Æthelflæd promised the estate to the church and had a section added to the original diploma expressing her intentions (to guarantee the church's rights). In the case of Hadham, the intention to delay the reversion over more than one lifetime would provide a very strong reason for adding a rider to the original diploma. If, as both extracts suggest, this rider was to be found in the body of the text, before the immunity clause, this would imply that a revised copy of the original diploma was produced at some stage (in S 513 the rider is actually part of the statement of powers). However, there are grounds for doubting whether the Hadham rider was contemporary. James's extract indicates that the grant (of reversion) was made 'to God and to Paul, teacher of the Gentiles'. Very similar wording appears in **18**, which may have been forged on the basis of **17**. This is not the usual language of Anglo-Saxon documents—it would be far more satisfactory if the grant had been made to the community or church, or to the bishop on its behalf.

Moreover, the subsequent history of Hadham is complicated, which may suggest that Æthelflæd and her heirs did not simply pass on the forty hides of Edgar's grant to St Paul's. In 1068 the bishop of London held four manors in Much and Little Hadham (GDB 133v–134r). The largest parcel was a manor of seven and a half hides at Much Hadham, a beneficial assessment, since there was land for 22.5 ploughs (*DB Herts.* 4:2): this had belonged to the bishopric in 1066. There were also smaller properties reckoned at two hides, a half hide and one hide (*DB Herts.* 4:6–7, 9); in 1066 all this land had been held by various freemen, with rights of alienation. But there is an additional detail which is relevant to the diploma represented by **17**. Domesday Book lists the Hadham manors among other holdings by the bishopric in the same hundred (Edwinstree), at Throcking, Pelham and elsewhere, almost all in different hands TRE (*DB Herts.* 4:1–20). These entries are followed by a note: *Has xxxvi hidas tenet episcopus London' et sui milites et cum his reclamat .iiii. hidas quas tenet abbas de Ely in Hadam* ('These 36 hides are held by the bishop of London and his men-at-arms, and with them he lays claim to four hides which the abbot of Ely holds in Hadham'). There is a separate entry for the four hides among the Ely holdings, with a note that they had belonged to the abbey in 1066 'as the whole shire testifies' (GDB 135r; *DB Herts.* 8:3). The *Liber Eliensis* claims that Hadham was one of three estates granted by Æthelflæd to Ely (the others being Fen Ditton in Cambs. and Kelshall in Herts.) and that she confirmed these bequests in her will (Blake, *Liber Eliensis*, pp. 137, 423). But Æthelflæd's will (S 1494) mentions only the (deferred) bequest of Ditton.

Reconciling the evidence from St Paul's, Ely and Domesday Book proves difficult. In a brief note Keynes argues that the forty hides granted to Æthelflæd in 969 may have been divided between St Paul's, Ely and perhaps other parties as well, with the charter descending to St Paul's; he suggests (on the basis of the Domesday evidence) that the bishops of London essentially owned only their 7.5-hide Hadham manor in 1066 and did not build up their accumulated 36-hide holding in Edwinstree Hundred until King William's reign (Keynes 1993a, p. 306 n. 26). An alternative interpretation is suggested by a detail in Æthelflæd's will (S 1494). As well as granting 'the land at Hadham' to Ælfflæd and Brihtnoth, with reversion to St Paul's, Æthelflæd made a separate bequest of land at Hadham to her reeve Ecgwine, 'as it had been arranged in former times' (*swa hit on ealddagum gestod*). The manuscripts of the will give conflicting testimony of the number of hides involved: either four (*iiii*) or seven (*vii*); Whitelock preferred the reading 'four' (*Wills*, p. 36). There seems to be a good chance that the four hides bequeathed to Ecgwine represent the land which later came into the possession of Ely, in which case the account in the *Liber Eliensis* of a direct bequest by Æthelflæd may be a fiction. If Edgar's initial grant to Æthelflæd did indeed involve forty hides at Hadham (it is possible that the figure was supplied at St Paul's at a later date), then it seems likely that she reserved the bulk of the estate for reversion to St Paul's, but detached a portion for her reeve. The original landbook, covering the whole forty hides as described in a boundary clause, descended to St Paul's, and may have provided the foundation for the church's claim to the four hides that passed to Ely. On this scenario, St Paul's would seem to have lost control of most of the thirty-six hides at 'Hadham' (i.e. in Edwinstree Hundred) at some stage between the reversion after Ælfflæd's death (*c.* 991 × 1002, or a little later) and 1066. Much of this territory was held by free men TRE, but was gained or regained by Bishop William after the Conquest (see above, pp. 104–5).

18

King Edgar grants seventy hides (cassati) *to St Paul.* [A.D. 957 × 975]

M. BL Lansdowne 364, 134r: extract, s. xvii^med
Listed: LonStP 18

Ego Edgarus infima terrenarum lucra quasi ⟨peripsema⟩^a quisquiliarum detestans, do 70 cassatos agio prædicatori gentium Paulo, omni ⟨terrene⟩^a seruitutis ⟨iugo⟩^a liberos fiscalique tributo liberos, exceptis expeditionis,^b pontis arcis⟨ve⟩^a restauratione. Si quis nostræ dapsilitatis munificentiam infringere vel elidere tentaverit, noscat se cum Juda proditore Christi æterna confusione edacibus flammis periturum.

> ^a *These words are not found in the MS, but have been supplied from similar formulas in other diplomas*   ^b *For* expeditione

The scholar who made this extract was primarily interested in the formulas of Anglo-Saxon charters; he may have been using the same lost medieval roll as James and Selden (see above, pp. 58–9). He gives us enough of this lost charter of Edgar to show that the draftsman was heavily influenced by a diploma of King Æthelstan, one of the group of 'Æthelstan A' charters with a proem beginning *Flebilia fortiter detestanda* which were issued between 931 and 933 (for 'Æthelstan A' see the commentary to **11**; for an example of this model, see S 416). The clause following the king's name in the fragment is ultimately derived from the distinctive and elaborate exposition of the Æthelstan diplomas, and several elements of the anathema show the influence of the characteristic sanction of the model. The draftsmen of other diplomas of Edgar used Æthelstan's diplomas as a model (see **17**); in these cases the borrowed formulas are usually unmodified, but in the St Paul's fragment there has been far more adaptation. The immunity clause may have been adapted from the formula in **17**. The reference to the beneficiary has same wording as the reversion 'rider' in **17**, which may itself be suspicious (see p. 176). There is no internal evidence which would help fix the date. Edgar was elected king of the Mercians in 957, succeeded to the whole English kingdom in 959 and died in 975. He controlled Essex during the period 957–9 (see S 676 and p. 31): a forgery dealing with a St Paul's estate in Essex can be ostensibly dated to 957 or 958 (see **16**). It is possible that **18** is an extract from a genuine charter of Edgar with formulation based partly on a diploma of Æthelstan, but it seems more likely that the source of the fragment was a fabrication, perhaps one modelled on **17**.

There is a chance that the seventy hides of Edgar's charter are to be connected with the seventy hides in the Dengie area granted by King Swæfred to Bishop Ingwald in the early eighth century (**6**). By the eleventh century the bishop's great estate in this area was known as Southminster (see p. 147). It may have been thought desirable to replace the ancient charter with one in the name of a more celebrated king which perhaps included the contemporary name of the estate and more specific details about its extent and its immunity. There could be a link between the forgery of such a text and the seizure of the Southminster estate by Cnut; the manor was not regained until 1066 × 1075 (LDB 10r; *DB Essex* 3:9; see above, p. 39).

19

(a) *Extract from a diploma of King Æthelred.* A.D. 982

M. BL Lansdowne 364, 134r: extract, s. xvii[med]
Listed: LonStP 14

Ego Elthredi do 10 mansas terræ … exceptis expeditionis obsequio pontis arcisque ædificatione: quisquis diabolica inflammatus invidia istam terram diminuet, vita ipsius in præsenti annorum curriculo in omni miseria luctu et mærore permaneat, et post labilis vitæ defectum eum Acherontis tenebraris[a] custodibus, inter flammivomas hydrarum legiones cum his qui dixerunt, Domine recede a nobis.[1] Anno 982

---

[a] *For* tenebrariis   [1] *cf.* Ex. 14: 12

(b) *Extract from a diploma* [? *of King Æthelred*] *in favour of Werenberht,*
deacon, probably concerning land at Orsett, Essex. [A.D. 971 × 992, ?982]

I. London, Lincoln's Inn, Hale 84, 93r: extract, s. xvii[1]
Listed: LonStP 17

De Horseda ⟨gives to⟩[a] fideli meo diacono Werenberhto ... tribus istis ad regalem
necessitatem, exceptis expeditionis obsequio, pontis arcisque coedificatione.
+ Ego Oswold Eborace ciuitatis archispeculator sub sigillo sancte crucis
subscripsi.

   [a] *Selden's insertion*   [b] *Reading unclear*

The first of these two extracts (*a*) is found in a seventeenth-century notebook in a
collection of formulas taken from early St Paul's muniments, while the second (*b*) is a
brief note made by Selden from a document on the lost St Paul's roll (see pp. 68–70,
71–2, for the MS sources). The two fragments include very similar reservation clauses,
which raises the possibility that they were both extracted from the same diploma,
although the overlap is not sufficiently substantial to be conclusive.

The note-taker responsible for (*a*) was essentially interested in the formulation of early
documents, and gives little information about their content. From the date it would
appear that his source was a diploma of King Æthelred 'the Unready' (978–1016), son of
King Edgar. There were significant developments in charter-production during Æthelred's
long reign. During the period between the demise of the 'Æthelstan A' model in 935 (see
11) and the death of Edgar in 975, the majority of royal diplomas had been drawn up on a
fundamentally similar pattern (see the commentary to **14**). New formulas were generated
throughout the period, but there was a basic underlying tendency to reuse existing
formulation, sometimes combining it in new variations, sometimes following a more
rigid and standardised formulaic model: thus in Edgar's reign the standard type was the
fairly homogeneous 'Edgar A' model (see the commentary to **17**). In the early years of
Æthelred's reign, charters were still being produced with 'Edgar A' formulas, but the
draftsmen of royal diplomas seem to have become increasingly less inclined to reproduce
standardised wording and much readier to devise new formulas of their own or to rewrite
and elaborate existing formulas. This tendency makes it more difficult to demonstrate
continuity in charter-production, and there is an ongoing debate about whether the central
agency of the middle decades of the tenth century continued to operate through
Æthelred's reign and into the eleventh century (see Keynes, *Diplomas*, which is an
exhaustive study of charter-production in Æthelred's reign). At least occasionally royal
diplomas were drawn up in other circumstances: see, for instance, S 931b in which
Bishop Ælfhun of London claims some responsibility for the writing of that diploma and
of two others, one evidently S 931a. This trend increases the difficulty of analysing
formulation in its contemporary context, since many elaborate formulas seem to have
been used once and never revived, while in other cases ancient models were resurrected.

The extract (*a*) essentially consists of a reservation clause (very close to the
corresponding clause in the second extract) and a rather literary anathema. In the former
the phrase *expeditionis obsequio* is unusual. It occurs in several 'alliterative' diplomas of
the 950s (S 544, 549, 552a, 556–7, 569) and in a clutch of Evesham forgeries (S 115,

1174–5). The ambitious anathema is probably acceptable in a charter of 982 (compare S 839–40 and especially S 845, although none is really of the same type as that of the fragment); several diplomas from the reign of Edgar, including the New Minster foundation charter (S 745), have a reference to *Acheron* in their sanctions (see also S 712, 736, 821).

Selden's much shorter note (*b*) was taken from a diploma in favour of a deacon named Werenberht, and apparently concerned an estate at *Horseda*. There seems to be a good chance that this is Orsett, Essex, which appears in Domesday as *Orseda(m)* and *Dorseda(m)*: see LDB 9v, 26v; *DB Essex*, 3:2, 20:4; the place-name means '(at the) pits where bog-ore was obtained' (*æt Orseathum*; see *DEPN*, p. 351; Gelling, *Signposts*, pp. 122, 123). Ten hides at Orsett were granted to Bishop Brihthelm in 957 (see **15**). By the end of the century, the lands of the London diocese included an estate at 'Orsett' and another at 'western Orsett' (see **25**). In 1086 the bishop's manor there was reckoned at thirteen hides, which may have been a low assessment, since there were thirty-six ploughs on the manor TRE (LDB 9v; *DB Essex*, 3:2). It seems possible that the estates granted to Bishop Brihthelm and to Werenberht represent the two 'Orsett' estates of **25**, and that these were later combined to form the Domesday manor. If (*a*) and (*b*) were indeed taken from the same diploma, then Werenberht's estate was also reckoned at ten hides. Selden's notes continue with a heading *De nemore eius de Crundelun*, referring to a diploma of 986 which would seem to have been linked with the Orsett diploma in favour of Werenberht (see **20c**). This possibly refers to Crondon in Orsett.

Werenberht is otherwise unknown. It seems likely that he was attached to the St Paul's community or to the bishop's household, although there is no proof of this. If his 'Orsett' property was one of the two estates mentioned in **25**, then it would have passed into the possession of the London Church by *c.* 1000. Apart from the reservation clause, essentially the same as the formula in (*a*), Selden provides only the subscription of Archbishop Oswald, who was appointed to York in 971 and died in 992. He could have subscribed as archbishop a late diploma of Edgar or a charter of Edward the Martyr (975–8), but it is more likely that the source of the extract was a diploma of Æthelred, possibly the 982 document seen by the scholar who excerpted (*a*). Selden's notes continue with a reference to a related diploma dated 986, which strongly suggests that Werenberht's diploma was earlier than that date. There is interest in Oswald's erudite style *archispeculator*, seen also the extracts from the 986 diploma (**20b/c**), where it is applied to Archbishop Dunstan. This style does not seem to have been used in any other diplomas, although it is clearly related to the episcopal styles *superspeculator* and *subspeculator* in three charters from the 980s (in S 859 the bishop of London attests as *superspeculator*; in S 870 the bishop of Selsey is *superspeculator* and in S 871 he is *subspeculator*). Such recondite styles are exceptional in tenth- and eleventh-century diplomas. Usually bishops are styled *episcopus* or, more rarely, *presul* (with the archbishops as *archiepiscopus* or *archipresul*); occasional variants are *pontifex* and *antistes* (variously prefixed to refer to archbishops). Some diplomatic models included variant episcopal styles as a stylistic feature: for instance, the 'alliterative' diplomas of the 940s and 950s (see, for example, S 544, 566, 569, and discussion in Sawyer, *Burton*, pp. xlvii–ix; the most literary style in these texts is *didasculus*); and the '*Orthodoxorum*' diplomas associated with Abingdon (see S 673, 786, 811, and the related S 690; and discussion in Kelly, *Abingdon*, pp. c–ci), which use the erudite styles *catascopus* and *speculator*. In some circumstances unusual styles are attached to specific individuals, conceivably reflecting their own preferences or chosen to mark them out in some way: Wulfstan I of York is consistently styled *archons* (in a subscription of a standardized type in a number of diplomas from the 940s: see S 519, 523, 525–6, 528 etc.); Ælfsige of Winchester is regularly *presul* in 956–8. Overall, the use of unusual styles is rare and is of especial interest where only a single bishop is distinguished in this way (as is in the case in the 980s diplomas with variants on *speculator*). The influential Ælfheah of Winchester is *previsor* in S 430, *hierarchus* in S 429, *speculator* in S 522. Ælfheah's successor Ælfsige is *speculator* in three diplomas of 956 (S 583, 595, 622). (Other styles to note: the bishop of Crediton is *archimandrita* in S 870; the style *catascopus* is applied to Ordbriht of Selsey in S 880 and Wulfsige of Sherborne in S 892.)

It is of particular interest that *archispeculator* appears only in **19***b* and in the related 986 diploma (**20***b/c*), which may deal with a grant of additional property in the same area. In such circumstances Werenberht may have offered his 982 landbook for scrutiny while the second diploma was being drawn up, thus providing a context for the repetition of the unusual archiepiscopal style.

20

Extracts from a diploma or diplomas of King Æthelred. A.D. 986

(*a*) *Anathema from a charter dated A.D. 986.*

M. BL Lansdowne 364, 134r: extract, s. xvii[med]
Listed: LonStP 16

Si dæmonica inflatus contumacia invidus huius donationis eversor existere temptet, sciat se in tremendi examine die cum malignorum spirituum comitibus a Domini facie inextinguibili infernalium ignium paludem discessurum. Anno 986.

(*b*) *Dating clause and part of a witness-list from a charter of King Æthelred dated A.D. 986.*

H. Bodleian, James 23, p. 32: extract, s.xvii[1]
Ed.: Gibbs p. 1 (J2)
Listed: Sawyer 1796 (LonStP 15)

Acta est autem hæc prefata donatio anno dominicæ incarnationis .dcccclxxxvi., indictione .xiiii., regni autem ei⟨us⟩ .viii., in urbe nobilium heroum scilicet Londonia.[a]
+ Ego Æthelredus totius Angliæ rex trabeatus hanc meam donationem taumate[b] sanctæ crucis corroboraui.
+ Ego Dunstan Dorobernensis ecclesiæ archispeculator prefatum regis donum victriagiæ crucis triumpho stabiliui.
+ Ego Oswold Eboracæ civitatis archipresul pretitulatam senioris mei dationem tripudiantis virgulæ vexillo consolidavi. etc.

[a] *The subscriptions are written as text, not arranged in a column*   [b] caumate H

(c) Rubric and one incomplete subscription from a charter dated A.D. 986.

I. London, Lincoln's Inn, Hale 84, 93r: extract, s. xvii[1]
Listed: LonStP 15

De nemore ipsius de ⟨Crundelun⟩[a]
+ Ego Dunstanus 'Dorobernensis' archispeculator
(Marginal note) 986, indictione .xiii., regni autem ⟨....⟩[b] (Æthel) .viii. in urbe
nobilium heroum

[a] *Reading not certain*   [b] *An interlineated word (? eius) followed by two erasures*

These three extracts appear among the notes of the anonymous scholar of BL
Lansdowne 364 (*a*), of James (*b*) and of Selden (*c*). There is an overwhelming likelihood
that James and Selden were both studying the same diploma on the lost St Paul's roll
(see pp. 67–70); both quote the same arcane style for Archbishop Dunstan, and refer to
the same dating clause. There is no overlap with the first extract, but there is a good
chance that it comes from the same diploma.

This would appear to have been a charter in the name of King Æthelred, dated 986 and
referring to a transaction which took place in London, dubbed here 'the city of noble
heroes' (on this, see below). The word *ipsius* in the rubric quoted by Selden links this
extract with the previous reference in his notes, to a diploma in favour of a deacon named
Werenberht, apparently dealing with land at Orsett in Essex, possibly dated 982 (**19***b*).
Both diplomas included the style *archispeculator* for 'archbishop', applied to Oswald of
York in **19***b* and Dunstan of Canterbury in **20***b/c*; there is no other instance of this usage,
and the likelihood is that the scribe of the later charter read, and was influenced by, the
earlier diploma (see commentary to **19**). The transaction of 986 apparently concerned an
area of woodland, linked either to Orsett or to Werenberht himself. The place-name looks
to be the dative plural form of OE *crundel*, 'chalk-pit, quarry, hollow'. It is tempting to
suggest a connection with Crondon, a detached part of Orsett which was later one of the
bishop's parks (Pamela Taylor, personal comment).

The anathema noticed in (*a*) is not particularly remarkable and seems perfectly
acceptable in a diploma of the given date; the sanctions of a number of other charters
issued at this time include a future participle in the accusative and several use the
imagery of eternal fire (see S 859, 862, 871). The incarnation year and indiction given in
(*b*) are compatible; Keynes comments that if the regnal year was calculated from the
king's accession the diploma was issued before 18 March 986, if from his coronation
then after 3 May (*Diplomas*, p. 245). The second extract continues with some very
distinctive features which suggest that the diploma had considerable literary pretensions.
It is dated from London, which is described as 'city of noble heroes' (*urbs nobilium
heroum*). Very few of Æthelred's diplomas mention a place of issue, and the other
references are all later than 986 (see Keynes, *Diplomas*, pp. 127–8). Three of these are
complex documents concerning restoration and confirmation of the lands and privileges
of religious houses (S 876, 891, 909). The fourth is a grant to the king's 'faithful man',
issued *in civitate Dorobernensis que est metropolis Cantuariorum* (S 905). This definition

of Canterbury is the only near parallel to the reference to London in **20b**, and it does not nearly match its mythic quality. The vocabulary of the subscriptions also indicates that the draftsman was aiming high. The king is *trabeatus*, i.e. wearing the *trabea* or robe of office. Dunstan, *archispeculator* of the church of Canterbury (see above), confirms the king's grant with the triumph of the *victriagia* cross (a difficult word, perhaps a neologism from *victoria*, 'victory', and *agere*, 'to bring'; perhaps a corruption of *victorialia*), while Oswald of York strengthens the gift of his senior (presumably meaning 'lord', i.e. the king) with 'the banner of the rejoicing rod' (i.e. with the sign of the cross).

21

King Æthelred confirms the lands of St Paul's minster. [A.D. 978 × 995/6]

C. GL 25504 (*Liber L*), 11v–12r: copy, s. xii[1]
  Rubric: Priuilegium Æþelredi insignis Anglorum regis.
D. St Paul's D. & C., *Liber B*, 21r (?): copy, s. xii[ex] (lost)
E. GL 25501 (*Liber A*), 39r: copy, s. xiii[med]
  Marginal rubric: Carta Aluredi regis.
Ed.: a. Dugdale, *St Paul's*, p. 188, from D (SP1)
   b. *Mon. Angl.*, iii. 303, from D (MA)
   c. Dugdale, *St Paul's* (2nd edn), App. p. 12, from D (SP2)
   d. Dugdale, *St Paul's* (3rd edn), p. 295, from D
   e. Kemble 1311, from *Mon. Angl.*
Listed: Sawyer 941; Gelling, *ECTV*, no. 230
Edited from C, with variants from E and MA (*Mon. Angl.*)

[a]Ego Æþelredus[b] rex, una cum Ymma[c] regina et cum principibus meis, coram conuentu Dei sacerdotum, reuerentissimo[d] scilicet antistiti Ælfstano,[e] terras monasterii beati Pauli apostoli quas a prędecessoribus meis siue a me donatas, seu a regibus gentium exterarum seu a principibus seu a quibuslibet hominibus, sub confirmationis testimonio omnes perpetualiter possidendas contuli, quatinus michi criminum meorum flagitia a Domino uenia relaxetur et confusiones scandalorum scismata[f] simultatumque[g] dehinc aboletur et, ut firmius hec donationis cartula roboretur, etiam presentibus ducibus, comitibus omnique ordine sacerdotali, uexillum sanctę crucis manu propria infixi, et testes idoneos ad subscribendum[h] eadem signi impressione dignum curaui, quorum numerus et nomina subter adnexis[i] figuris agnoscuntur. Si quis uero quod absit, tirannica[j] potestate fretus aut fastu superbię tumidus, contra hoc decretum a me confirmatum in magno seu in modico nocere aut irrita facere temptauerit, nouerit se iudicante Domino uiuos ac mortuos gehennę suppliciis missus perpetuasque luere penas.[k] VALETE

---

[a] Alia confirmationis carta præfati Regis Æthelredi, de terris a se, vel a prædecessoribus suis, collatis *rubric* MA	[b] Aluredus E; Æthelredus MA	[c] Emma MA	[d] reverendissimo MA	[e] Adelstano E	[f] scisimata E	[g] *Probably for* scismataque simultatium	[h] scribendum MA	[i] anexis E	[j] tyrrannica C	[k] E *ends here, omitting valediction*

21 is part of the dossier of mostly forged pre-Conquest documents which were copied into the main St Paul's cartularies (MSS C, D, E). In *Liber A* (MS E) the text of **21** is followed by that of Cnut's charter on the same theme (**26**), and then by a note 'Sequitur carta predicti Aluredi regis in Anglico sermone, de uerbo ad uerbum sicut prescriptum est'. This could refer to a vernacular version of **21**, although it is also possible that the cartularist could not read Old English, and was mistakenly referring to **24**. Dugdale's edition of **21** in *Mon. Angl.* and *St Paul's* was probably based on the version in the lost *Liber B* (MS D), although there is no explicit attribution (see further above, pp. 62–4). Dugdale's text is as usual partly normalised, with **v** for consonantal **u** and **ae** for **e**, and he may also have substituted the conventional spelling of the queen's name (note ᶜ). Kemble's text is taken from *Mon. Angl.* although he cites 'Reg. B' at St Paul's as his source (see KCD, vol. vi, pp. xxiii, xxv). A copy of the anathema appears in a collection of Anglo-Saxon formulas extracted by a seventeenth-century scholar from various St Paul's muniments (BL Lansdowne 364, fol. 134r; see pp. 71–3).

Æthelred's charter is clearly spurious. Queen Emma, who married King Æthelred in 1002, could not be co-donor in a charter in favour of Bishop Ælfstan of London, who died in 995 or 996 (moreover, in genuine charters she is always referred to by her English name Ælfgifu). The document is undated; its ostensible dating limits are either 978 × 995/6 (based on the reference to Ælfstan) or 1002 × 16 (privileging the reference to Emma). **21** should be considered alongside **26**, a diploma in the name of Cnut which was also intended to provide a blanket confirmation of the landed endowment of St Paul's, and which concludes with the word AMEN as **21** concludes with a valediction (VALETE). The first part of **21**, as far as *terras monasterii … apostoli*, is closely related to the spurious 'Coronation Day' charter in the name of William I, purportedly restoring several lost estates (Bates, *RRAN: Acta of William I*, no. 183; see pp. 102–3). A comparison of the two texts explains an odd feature of **21**, the reference to the bishop of London in the form *reuerentissimo scilicet antistiti Ælfstano*, where the word *scilicet* apparently connects with the previous phrase *coram conuentu Dei sacerdotum*. William's charter has the same phrase, followed by an elucidation *reverendis scilicet archiepiscopis Aldredo et Stigando ceterisque episcopis et abbatibus huius patrie*. From this it may well follow that **21** was forged after William's charter, and partly modelled on it. The beginning of the text is particularly unconvincing: a pre-Conquest royal diploma would require some protocol, in the form of a proem and exposition (perhaps preceded by a verbal invocation), and would not have involved a blanket confirmation of this type. The royal style is the fail-safe *rex*, as in other dubious St Paul's texts (see **1**, **16**). The reference to grants by foreign kings seems odd in a late Anglo-Saxon context, while the phrase *a quibuslibet hominibus* may have been borrowed from William's charter.

26 is partly based on a seventh-century model, and the forger of **21** may also have been influenced by the formulation on an early text (most probably a land-grant, to judge from the phrase *donationis cartula*). The lengthy rogation clause, with the reference to 'suitable witnesses' whose names appear below and to signing *manu propria*, has some details in common with the simpler formulation of some very early diplomas (S 8, 13, 19, 259, 1165, 1167, 1248 etc.). The anathema includes some phrases which recall typical formulas of the West/East Saxon diplomatic tradition (see pp. 77–9): *tirannica potestate fretus* (compare S 71, 73, 236, 1248 etc.), and the reference to 'the living and the dead' (S 231, 241, 264, 1248); while the lack of an 'escape clause', giving the transgressor the opportunity to repent and make restitution, could be an early feature.

But other elements of the wording look later—as *fastu superbie tumidus* (compare S 177, 343) and *gehenne suppliciis* (compare S 840, 845, 865)—and it seems likely that any early source has been recast, either by the forger or by the draftsman of an intermediate text. The use of the term *luere penas* has a close counterpart in the spurious diploma of Edward the Confessor (**29**), in a section where the forger has departed from the original formulation seen in **12** and its Chertsey models; it also appears in another unreliable diploma attributed to King Æthelred (**23**) and in a brief memorandum which is probably an abbreviated translation of a lost Old English document (**31**). It seems likely that all four texts were drawn up in the same climate and possibly by the same agency, perhaps in order to remedy the loss of the pre-Conquest title-deeds to the lands of the canons (see pp. 75–7).

22

Æthelflæd bequeaths four hides at Laver, Essex, and two at Cockhampstead, Hertfordshire, to St Paul's minster. [*c.* A.D. 1000]

D. St Paul's, D. & C., *Liber B*, 20v (?): copy, s. xii^{ex} (lost)
Ed.: a. Dugdale, *St Paul's*, p. 187, from D (SP1)
    b. *Mon. Angl.*, iii. 303, from D (MA)
    c. Dugdale, *St Paul's* (2nd edn), App. p. 11, from D (SP1)
    d. Dugdale, *St Paul's* (3rd edn), p. 294, from D
    e. Kemble 972, from *Mon. Angl.*
    f. Thorpe, *Diplomatarium*, pp. 542–3, from Kemble and *Mon. Angl.*, with translation
    g. Whitelock, *Wills*, p. 66 (no. 22), from Kemble and Thorpe, with translation
Listed: Sawyer 1495; Hart, *ECE*, no. 37
Edited from SP1 (Dugdale, *St Paul's*), with superior readings from SP2 (2nd edn) and MA (*Mon. Angl.*)

^{a}Her sputelað on ðam cpide ðe Egelfled gecpeden hæfð, God to lofe 7 hire saule to ðerfe 7 hire hlafordes, þ is þonne ða feoper hida landes æt Lagefare 7 tpa hida æt Cochæmstede,^{b} þe hy gean for hire saule 7 for hire hlafordes^c into S. Paules mynstre on Lundene, ðan gebroðran to bigleofan, ðam þe ⟨ðær⟩^{d} dæghamlice God ðeniað, be ðes cynges fulle geleuen Æðelredes, on ðera manna gewitnesse ðe heora naman her standað, þ is ðonne Egelnoð arcebiscop^e 7 Þulfstan^f arcebiscop 7 Ælfun biscop on Lundene 7 Ælfric abbot 7 Þigard^g abbot 7 Ælsi abbot on Coppaforde^h 7 Ælfere ealdorman^i 7 Brithnoð ealdorman 7 Ædric ældorman 7 Ælfsige cynges þegn 7 Ufegeat scireman 7 Frena cynges þegn, 7 spa hpilc man spa ðisne cpide apende, sy he Judas gefere ðe urne Drihten belepde en helle pite.^{j}

    ^{a} Carta Regina Egelfledæ, uxoris Edgari Regis, de quatuor hidis terræ apud Lagefare, et duabus apud Cochamstede *rubric* SP1, MA, SP2 ^{b} Cochamstede MA ^{c} hlapordes SP1 ^{d} þæs SP1, MA, SP2 ^{e} arbiscop SP2 ^{f} Wulfstan MA ^{g} Wigard MA ^{h} *sic* SP1, MA, SP2 (? *for* Coppanforde) ^{i} ealdodman SP1 ^{j} pide MA

Here it is declared in this document what Æthelflæd has bequeathed for the praise of God and for the benefit of her soul and her lord's soul: that is the four hides of land at Laver and the two hides at Cockhampstead which she grants for her soul and for her lord's soul to St Paul's minster in London for the sustenance of the brethren who daily serve God there; with the full permission of King Æthelred, in the presence of the men whose names are written here: that is, Archbishop Æthelnoth and Archbishop Wulfstan and Ælfhun bishop of London and Abbot Ælfric and Abbot Wigheard and Abbot Ælfsige of *Cowwaford* and Ealdorman Ælfhere and Ealdorman Brihtnoth and Ealdorman Eadric and Ælfsige the king's thegn and Wulfgeat the sheriff and Frena the king's thegn; and whatsoever man alter this bequest may he be a companion of Judas who betrayed our Lord in the torment of Hell.

22 survives only in Dugdale's printed versions in *Mon. Angl.* and *St Paul's*. There is no specific manuscript attribution, but the source was almost certainly the lost *Liber B*, from which Dugdale drew the preceding and following documents (**16, 23**). The differences between the various editions may be in part due to subsequent correction of printers' errors in the first edition, but it is also possible that the text was sometimes deliberately 'improved' (see above, pp. 62–4). In all three editions, the vernacular text is followed by what appears to be Dugdale's own Latin translation, headed *Id est*. Kemble cites as his source 'Reg. B' at St Paul's, as does Thorpe (with the error fol. 206 for fol. 20*b*): in both cases they used *Mon. Angl.*, which was the origin of the *Liber B* reference (see p. 185).

For commentary on **22**, see that on **23** (pp. 188–91).

23

King Æthelred confirms Æthelflæd's bequest to St Paul's minster of four hides (mansae) *at Laver, Essex, and two at Cockhampstead, Hertfordshire.* [c. A.D. 1000]

C. GL 25504 (*Liber L*), 10rv: copy, s. xii[1]
    Rubric: Priuilegium Ædelredi Regis Anglorum.
D. St Paul's D. & C., *Liber B*, 21r: copy, s. xii[ex] (lost)
E. GL 25501 (*Liber A*), 56r (original foliation 38r): copy, s. xiii[med]
    Marginal rubric: Karta Ædredi regis.
H. Bodleian, James 23, p. 33: extract, s. xvii[1] (witnesses only)
Ed.: a. Dugdale, *St Paul's*, pp. 187–8, from D (SP1)
    b. *Mon. Angl.*, iii. 303, from D (MA)
    c. Dugdale, *St Paul's* (2nd edn), App. p. 12, from D (SP2)
    d. Dugdale, *St Paul's* (3rd edn), pp. 294–5, from D
    e. Kemble 1300, from Mon. *Angl.*
    f. Gibbs, p. 3 (J5), from H
Listed: Sawyer 908; Hart, *ECE*, no. 38
Edited from C, with variants from E and MA (*Mon. Angl.*)

[a]In nomine Domini et saluatoris nostri Iesu Christi. Ego Æðelredus,[b] Dei gratia Anglorum basileus,[c] notifico uobis fidelibus et amicis meis[d] quod Ægelflæd[e]

meo concessu duas de possessione sua terras, Deo ad laudem sibique post discessum^f ad salutem, beatissimo atque doctori gentium Paulo eiusque ęcclesię fratribus, die noctuque^g famulantibus, cum summa deuotione obtulit,^{h} quarum hęc sunt nomina: Lagefare cum quattuor mansis et Cochamstede^i cum duabus mansis. Hanc uero donationem perpetuam esse concessimus, et si aliquis eam in aliud quam constituimus transferre uoluerit, cum Iuda qui Dominum tradidit pęnas luat herebi^j et inde nequaquam possit eximi, nisi ad satisfactionem uenerit. Huius autem^k donationis isti sunt testes^l idonei. Ægelnoðus^m archiepiscopus Cantuarię,^{n} Þulfstanus^o Eboracensis archiepiscopus,^{p} Ælfunus Lundoniensis^q episcopus, et Ælfricus abbas, ^{r}et Þigerdus abbas, et Ælfþius abbas,^{r} et Ælfredus dux, et Brihtnoðus^s dux, et Eadricus^t dux, et Ælfsius satrapa regis, ^{u}et Ufegeat satrapa regis,^{u} et Fræna satrapa regis, et Hargodus presbyter, et Ælfricus diaconus, et Þulfricus^v presbiter.^{w}

---

^{a} Carta Regis Æthelredi, patris sancti Regis Edwardi, donationem Ægelfledæ confirmans *rubric* MA ^{b} Ædeldredus E; Edelredus MA ^{c} basilicus E ^{d} meisque amicis MA ^{e} Ægelfled C; Egelfled MA ^{f} decessum E ^{g} *The word* Deo *may have fallen out here* ^{h} optulit E ^{i} Cohamstede (*partly written on erasure*) E ^{j} *Word omitted* MA ^{k} *Word omitted* E ^{l} sunt isti testes E; sunt testes isti MA ^{m} Egelnoldus E; Ægelnothus MA ^{n} Cantuarie archiepiscopus E, MA ^{o} Wulstanus E; Wolfstanus MA ^{p} E *concludes:* et alii in carta. Hæc eadem carta est in anglico sermone de verbo ad verbum ^{q} Lond- MA $^{r...r}$ MA *omits these two subscriptions* ^{s} Brithnodus MA ^{t} Ædricus MA $^{u...u}$ MA *omits this subscription* ^{v} Wuluricus MA ^{w} H *reads* In charta regis Athelredi pro testibus subscribuntur. Ægelnothus Cant' Archiepiscopus, Wlstanus Ebor' Archiepiscopus, Ælfricus Abbas, Ælfredus dux, Brichtnothus dux, Eadricus dux, Ælfsie satrapa Regis, et Ufegeat satrapa regis, et Fræna satrapa Regis ... Dein⟨d⟩e scribitur denuo Brithnoth nomine ealdormanni, similiter et Eadric, et Ælfsie kinges steing, et Þfegeat scireman.

---

23 is one of a small group of mostly forged diplomas which were copied into the main St Paul's cartularies (MSS C, D, E). The text in the lost *Liber B* was the source of the editions by Dugdale in *St Paul's* and *Mon. Angl.* Kemble's text is from *Mon. Angl.*, although he cites 'Reg. B' as his source (see KCD vol. vi, pp. xxiii, xxv). There may have been versions of this charter in two further lost cartularies, *Libri C* and *G* (see pp. 52–3, 55). Richard James extracted a partial witness-list from a text of **23** on the lost medieval roll (MS H; for the roll, see pp. 67–70), and also cites some names from an Old English document, evidently **22** (see note ^{w}). In both sections he reproduces some Anglo-Saxon letter-forms (**f, g, r, s**), which suggests that the source-document in the lost roll had been copied from a fairly early original.

    22 is a vernacular document concerning a bequest by a woman named Æthelflæd to St Paul's, **23** a Latin charter purporting to be King Æthelred's confirmation of that bequest. Both texts are equipped with nearly identical witness-lists which are chronologically inconsistent. In their present form both documents must be considered spurious, but it seems probable that **22** at least is based on authentic documentation. In the lost *Liber B*, **22** and **23** seem to have been copied consecutively. The extant cartularies *Liber L* and *Liber A* have copies of Æthelred's charter only. The scribe of *Liber A* noted that there was also a verbatim version of **23** in the vernacular (see note [p]); it is possible that this is an erroneous reference to **22**.

Apart from the impossible witness-list, **22** would seem generally acceptable; the language is recognisably pre-Conquest, and much of the formulation can be paralleled in other wills and vernacular documents. The introductory phrase is of a very common type: see for example S 939, 1485–6, 1524, and for *cwide*, see S 1494, 1511 etc. (the introduction to **31** may be a Latin translation of a similar formula). While Anglo-Saxon wills do not usually include a witness-list, there are other examples (as in S 1530 and the vernacular versions of S 1228, 1425). The anathema is probably also acceptable (see S 1487–8, 1521, 1537 etc.). Whitelock has suggested that **22** is essentially genuine, and that the incompatible witnesses may have been added by a later scribe to replace text lost when the original was damaged (*Wills*, p. 175). This is not really convincing, given the fact that **23** shares the same witness-list; and the background of disputed tenure (see below). It seems safer to assume that both **22** and **23** were revised and 'improved' as part of a later territorial claim. If as is suggested above (pp. 75–7), the pre-Conquest title-deeds to the canons' lands were no longer available in the later eleventh century, it is possible that both these documents were actually concocted from other sources. The impossible witness-lists may support this view (see below).

Dugdale identified Æthelflæd with the widow of King Eadmund who bequeathed Hadham to St Paul's (**22** note [a]; see **17**). Laver, Cockhampstead and Hadham are very close to each other, lying within a ten-mile radius. Whitelock rejected the identification between the Æthelflæd of **22** and the royal widow, because the latter's will mentions neither Laver nor Cockhampstead (S 1494; see *Wills*, p. 176). This is not an insuperable problem, since we cannot be certain that a will would necessarily cover all the testator's property; some lands may have been dealt with by separate arrangements, or could have been acquired after the will was drawn up, and disposed of separately. A source available to a seventeenth-century scholar dated Æthelflæd's grant to 980 (BL Lansdowne 364, 8r), which would be compatible with the identification with the former queen, who appears to have died between 975 and 991 (Whitelock, *Wills*, p. 138). On the other hand, Whitelock's alternative identification is appealing. A diploma of 1012 (S 926; Campbell, *Rochester*, no. 33) concerns land in Huntingdonshire forfeited by a certain Æthelflæd for helping her brother Leofsige, the ealdorman of Essex who was exiled for murder in 1002 (*ASC*; S. Keynes, 'Crime and Punishment in the Reign of Æthelred the Unready', in *People and Places in Northern Europe 500–1600: Essays in Honour of Peter Hayes Sawyer*, ed. I. Wood and N. Lund (Woodbridge, 1991), pp. 67–81 at 79–80). The confiscation of Æthelflæd's lands could have thwarted the bequest to St Paul's and would provide a context for the community to have sought the king's agreement for the bequest to go ahead. There would be a close parallel in the case of Æthelric of Bocking, who had bequeathed land at Rayne in Essex to St Paul's and an estate at Copford to Bishop Ælfstan. When Æthelric died in *c.* 995 × 999, old accusations of treachery were renewed and there was an attempt to have his property seized; but Archbishop Ælfric persuaded King Æthelred to confirm the will (S 1501, 939; Brooks and Kelly, *Christ Church*, nos 136–7; see above, p. 95).

It is a problem that King Æthelred's supposed confirmation of Æthelflæd's bequest is far less convincing than **22**. In form it falls between a writ and a royal diploma. There is a verbal invocation, followed by a notification clause, a brief dispositive phrase, a sanction and a witness-list in the form of a list, instead of separate subscriptions. Several of

Æthelred's diplomas do contain a general notification clause of some kind (Keynes, *Diplomas*, pp. 111–12), but the wording here does not seem acceptable (although *cf.* S 912 for the use of the second person rather than the third). The anodyne verbal invocation might well be used in a pre-Conquest diploma (see S 220; Crick, *St Albans*, no. 6), and there is no concrete objection to the royal style *Anglorum basileus* (compare S 892–3, 918), although this is usually qualified by a more ambitious humility formula than the hackneyed *Dei gratia*. Æthelred's diplomas are usually more elaborate and literary confections (compare, for instance, S 906, Æthelred's confirmation of the the will of Wulfric Spott and the endowment of Burton Abbey; Sawyer, *Burton*, no. 28). The wording of the dispositive section is awkward, especially the reference to the estates, and the witness-list is in the form associated in the pre-Conquest period with vernacular documents rather than Latin diplomas (this was also the form used in post-Conquest Latin writs). One reason for suspicion is the use of the phrase *penas luere* in the sanction; this also appears in two spurious diplomas (**21, 29**) and in **31**, which appears to be a post-Conquest Latin translation of an Old English memorandum. It could be suggested that **23** is a poor translation of a lost vernacular document (perhaps the text referred to by the compiler of *Liber A*; see note *P*): King Æthelred's confirmation of the will of Æthelric of Bocking is in Old English (S 939). But it is more likely that **23** is a later confection, produced at St Paul's to bolster its claims to the two estates.

The impossible witness-list shared by **22** and **23** underlines the probability that any records of Æthelflæd's bequest had been tampered with or fabricated. Both documents have three episcopal subscriptions: Æthelnoth of Canterbury (1020–38), Wulfstan of York (1002–23), and Ælfhun of London (appointed 1002 × 1004, died *c.* 1014); only the latter two could have witnessed a diploma of Æthelred. Also attesting are three or four abbots: Ælfric (a common name: in Æthelred's reign there were men so-called at several houses); Wigheard (attested *c.* 1002: *cf.* S 905, 914); and Ælfsige (**22**) or Ælfwig (**23**). The last-attesting abbot in **22** is linked with *Cowwa[n]forde*, which may be an error for *Coppanforde*, i.e Copford in Essex (*PN Essex*, p. 385), where Bishop Ælfstan had been left an estate by Æthelric of Bocking (S 1501; see above, p. 95). If the Abbot Ælfwig of **23** is a different man, then he may have been the abbot of Westminster *c.* 997 × *c.* 1020. There are three attesting ealdormen: Ælfhere of Mercia (died 983; the reading Ælfred in **23** is a probable error); Brihtnoth of Essex (died 991); and Eadric, presumably Eadric Streona, ealdorman of Mercia 1007–17. **22** has only three more witnesses: Ælfsige, the king's thegn (possibly the thegn of that name who attested prominently *c.* 980–995; see Keynes, *Diplomas*, p. 183); *Ufegeat*, described as *scireman* or sheriff, who is perhaps the thegn Wulfgeat who attested from *c.* 986 and suffered forfeiture in 1006 (*ibid.*, pp. 210–11); and Fræna, king's thegn (evidently the man mentioned *ASC* s.a. 993, who attested occasionally between *c.* 980 and 1004: *ibid.*, pp. 205–6). In **23** these men are all *satrapes regis*. **23** adds to the list three minor ecclesiastics: Hargod, priest; Ælfric, deacon; and Wulfric, priest. The latter is just possibly the same man who was granted land near Christ Church in Dorset in 985 (S 859).

This combination of incompatible witnesses must represent an invented list. These men flourished at different times in Æthelred's reign and beyond (in the case of Archbishop Æthelnoth). Their names cannot have been borrowed from a single witness-list in a contemporary diploma, or from two separate lists (for example, separate lists attached to **22** and to **23**). It is possible that the compiler of this list collected names from a series of documents associated with these estates (or with others), such as an initial royal diploma and subsequent records of transfer of tenure and litigation. Alternatively, the source of the names and styles may have been a confraternity book or *Liber Vitae*, which listed the names of those who had entered into an association with the St Paul's community and who were given liturgical commemoration.

St Paul's did not hold land at Laver or Cockhampstead in 1066 or subsequently, but the canons certainly claimed territory there: King William's spurious 'Coronation Day' charter, supposedly restoring lands unjustly seized in the days of his predecessors, mentions four hides at Laver and three at Cockhampstead (Bates, *RRAN: Acta of William I*, no. 183; see discussion above, pp. 102–3). It is to be assumed that **22** and **23** were pertinent to this claim. By 1086 the four hides at Laver had been split up. Under the lands of Count Eustace were two small manors each assessed at one hide and forty acres, held by Leofwine and Alwin TRE and subsequently seized by Engelric before being passed on to the Count (LDB 30v; *DB Essex* 20:45); this was probably High Laver (*VCH Essex*, iv. 88). Another manor, assessed at only forty acres, had been held by Brictmær in 1066, and was now in the hands of one of the Count's tenants (LDB 31r; *DB Essex* 20:47); this may have been Little Laver (*VCH Essex*, iv. 98). Finally, there was a manor assessed at a single hide held by Saxi, and then by Ralph of Tosny (LDB 91r; *DB Essex* 51:2), probably to be identified with Magdalen Laver (*VCH Essex*, iv. 105). Some land at Laver was also claimed by Christ Church, Canterbury (S 1047, Latin version; see Brooks and Kelly, *Christ Church*, no. 181A). Cockhampstead had an assessment of two hides, and was held by a thegn of Earl Harold with alienation rights TRE; by 1086 it was also in the possession of Count Eustace (GDB 137v; *DB Herts.* 17:13).

24

King Æthelred grants judicial privileges to the priests
of St Paul's minster. [A.D. 978 × 1016]

H. Bodleian, James 23, p. 32: copy, s. xvii
Ed.: a. Gibbs p. 2 (J3)
    b. Harmer, *Writs*, no. 52, with translation
Listed: Sawyer 945; Gelling, *ECTV*, no. 234

Æþelred kinc grete mine ⟨biscopes⟩*[a]*. 7 mine eorles . 7 ealla mine þeinas of þam sciram*[b]* þær mine preostas on Pales mynstre habbað land inne freondlice. 7 ic cyþe eop þ ic pille, þ hig beon heora saca, 7 heora socna þeorða æiþer gebinnan burh 7 butan. 7 spa godera laga þyrþe. nu spa ful 7 spa forð*[c]* spa hig betste pæron on æniges kinges dæge. oþþe on æniges ⟨biscopes⟩*[d]* on eallum þingan.*[e]*

    [a] H *omits a word here, but supplies* Beres (*apparently a mistaken expansion of* b'es) *in the margin*   *[b]* *For* sciran   *[c]* ford H   *[d]* beres H   *[e]* Similiter in privilegio Cnuti et Edwardi. Quære ergo quis sit Beres *concluding note* H

[I] King Æthelred send friendly greetings to my bishops and my earls and all my thegns in the shires where my priests in St Paul's minster hold land. And I inform you that it is my will that they be entitled to their sake and soke both within the burh and outside and entitled now to as good laws in all things, as fully and completely, as they ever were in the days of any king or any bishop.

24 was transcribed by Richard James from the lost medieval roll (see pp. 67–70); the punctuation is his. It is an interesting detail that James has made an attempt to imitate Anglo-Saxon script. It appears from his comment at the end of the text that the roll also contained the writs of Cnut and Edward (**27, 28**; both with the word *beres*, presumably a misreading of *b'es, biscopes*), and this is partly confirmed by the Lincoln's Inn manuscript, which has an extract from **28** that would have been taken from the lost roll (see p. 69).

  24 is very close indeed to the corresponding writ in the name of the Confessor (**28**), with the same redundant phrase (*swa full and swa forth*) which Harmer considered a possible interpolation in Edward's writ. **24** is slightly shorter, lacking the veto on unwelcome new recruits which made **28** so popular with later generations of canons, and also the brief anathema. It is possible that James did not copy the complete text, although it is necessary to bear in mind that the veto clause in **28** was perhaps a later addition (see below, pp. 209–10). There are also close links with the corresponding writ in the name of Cnut (**27**). On the whole, **24** is unlikely to be genuine. It is one of only two surviving writs in the name of King Æthelred, the other being S 946, also of uncertain authenticity. A case can be made that documents in writ-form were being produced as early as the time of Alfred, although it is possible that they were not sealed until the Confessor's reign (see the commentary to **27**). However, given the lack of surviving early examples, it is difficult not to be suspicious of **24**. Harmer suggested that it could represent a version of **28** in which the king's name has been changed (*Writs*, pp. 236–7).

25

List of the contibutions required from St Paul's estates for the manning of a ship. [*c.* A.D. 1000]

B. CCCC 383, 107r: copy, s. xii
Ed.: a. Liebermann 1900, pp. 23–4
    b. Robertson, *Charters*, no. 72 (p. 144), with translation, p. 145
    c. Taylor 1992, pp. 293–4

[S]cipmen. Of Ticc[a] .iiii. Of Tillingaham .ii. Of Dunmæwan. 7 of Tollesfuntan .i. Of Næsingstoce. 7 of Neosdune .iiii. Of Hinawicun. 7 of Tollandune .ii. Of Gnutungadene. 7 of Bræmbelege .i. Of þottanheale .i. Of Clopham .ii. Of Bærnun. 7 of Ceswican. i. Of Drægtune .i. Of Caddandune .i. Of Sandune .i. Of Ceaddingtune .i. Of Fullanhamme .v. Of Forþtune .iii. Of Stybbanhyþe. 7 of Gislandune .ii. Of Orseaþun .i. Of Ligeandune .i. Of Seopinglande[b]. 7 of þam westrum Orseaþum .i. Of Bylcham .i. Of Coppanforda 7 Holande .i. Of Suðmynster .v. Of Claccingtune .ii. Of Hæþlege. 7 of Codanham .i.

---

  [a] *For* Cicc   [b] *For* Scopinglande

Translation (with inserted numbers linking text to commentary)
Seamen: from (1) St Osyth four; from (2) Tillingham two; from (3) Dunmow and from (4) Tolleshunt one; from (5) Navestock and from (6) Neasden four; from (7) *Hinawicun* and from (8) Tollington two; from (9) *Gnutungadene* and from (10) Bromley one; from (11) Tottenham [Court] one; from (12) Clapham two; from (13) Barnes and from (14) Chiswick one; from (15) West Drayton one; from (16) Caddington one; from (17) Sandon one; from (18) *Ceaddingtune* one; from (19) Fulham five; from (20) *Forthtune* three; from (21) Stepney and from (22) Islington two; from (23) Orsett one; from (24) Laindon one; from (25) Shopland and from (26) 'western Orsett' one; from (27) Belchamp [St Paul's] one; from (28) Copford and (29) Holland one; from (30) Southminster five; from (31) Clacton two; from (32) Hadleigh and from (33) *Codanham* one.

CCCC 383 is a collection of Anglo-Saxon legal material, compiled *c.* 1125–30 (Ker, *Catalogue*, no. 65; Wormald, *Law I*, pp. 228–36). The document edited here as **25** represents an early addition to the manuscript, written in what appears to be a contemporary hand (see Plate 1). Its inclusion indicates that CCCC 383 was of St Paul's provenance, and may indicate that the manuscript was actually written there (Wormald, *Law I*, p. 230 n. 268). **25** is a very bare text, comprising a list of names linked with numbers which are evidently those of the *scipmen* or sailors to be provided (or funded) from these places. It is edited here for reasons of completeness and convenience, although it is not technically a charter. There have been many previous discussions of its content: see, in particular, Liebermann 1900; Robertson, *Charters*, pp. 389–92; Hart, *Danelaw*, pp. 205–20; Taylor 1992, especially pp. 293–303.

It is generally agreed that this document relates to the manning of a warship for the English fleet. The named estates would have been expected to pay for the provision of a fixed number of sailors; the levy would have been in the nature of a naval tax or geld, rather than a draft of men (for the operation of such gelds, see Lawson 1984). The majority of the places in the list can be connected with the endowment of the London bishopric, which makes it probable that the document is to be connected with the obligations laid upon the episcopal estate in this respect. Liebermann suggested a date of *c.* 1000, which has not seriously been challenged. The *terminus post quem* is provided by the reference to Holland in Essex, which was acquired between 971 and 984 (see pp. 96–7). Also possibly relevant is the reference to two different estates at Orsett in Essex (23, 26). The archive contained two separate diplomas for estates here, the second probably dated 982 and in favour of an individual deacon (**19b**; see p. 181), which may mean that the land in question did not become a possession of the church until afterwards. On the other hand, there is no mention of Hadham and Heybridge, which were inherited respectively by the bishop and the canons on the death of Ælfflæd, which probably took place between 991 × *c.* 1000 (S 1486; see pp. 176–7). Hart has suggested a closer dating for **25** of *c.* 995 × 998 (*ECE*, no. 28), because the list includes Copford, given by Æthelric of Bocking in around 995 (S 1501, 939), and omits Barling, given in 998 (S 1522). But there are problems here. Æthelric's bequest appears to relate to appurtenances to an estate at Copford which the bishop already owned (see p. 95); moreover, the ratification of the will took place in 995 × 999 and may not have been implemented until an even later date. So the reference to Copford is not relevant to the date. Furthermore, the bequest of Barling in the will dated 998 was to Bishop Wulfstan as his personal property; it may have been some time before the estate was reckoned as part of the endowment of the London Church (in addition, the fact that the will is dated 998 does not necessarily mean that the testator died and that his bequests were honoured in that year). A final point to bear in mind is that there may have been a time-lag between the acquisition of new estates by St Paul's and their inclusion in the naval assessment. Liebermann's general estimate of *c.* 1000 still seems preferable.

The St Paul's document can be associated with an entry in the Chronicle *s.a.* 1008, to the effect that King Æthelred had ordered the energetic building of ships throughout the kingdom, namely a warship from every 310 hides (this is an unexpected figure, and it has been suggested that the text originally referred to a warship from every 300 hides and some other piece of naval equipment from every ten hides: see Whitelock, *EHD*, p. 241 n. 3; Abels, *Lordship*, p. 246 n. 77). Also highly relevant is a letter of Æthelric, bishop of Sherborne, datable to 1002 × 1014 (S 1383; O'Donovan, *Sherborne*, no. 13), concerning the liability of his diocese to 'ship-scot'. He complains that he is thirty-three hides short of the 300 hides which other bishops had in their diocese for this purpose and on which his predecessors could reckon. It seems probable that, whatever the effect of the new initiative of 1008, there was an existing arrangement tying the provision of funds/men for these purposes to units of 300 hides (for the background, see Hollister, *Anglo-Saxon Military Institutions*, pp. 108–15). There is an instructive parallel in a document relating to the levies for the maintenance of Rochester Bridge, which was co-ordinated through groups of estates belonging to various lords; the provisions point to a date in the early eleventh century, but may well build on earlier arrangements (Robertson, *Charters*, no. 52; see Brooks 1992*b*).

The numbers in the text produce a total of forty-five men, which may be a difficulty: other texts would seem to indicate that an Anglo-Saxon longship in the reign of Æthelred had sixty oars or more (Keynes, *Diplomas*, p. 225; and *cf.* Lawson 1984, pp. 721–2, 737–8, for eighty-oar ships in Harthacnut's reign). Abels accepts the ostensible lower total and suggests a connection with the 'twenty-benchers' that were the standard levy in eleventh-century Scandinavia; he goes on to argue that there may have been no typical ship-levy in late Anglo-Saxon England (*Lordship*, pp. 108–10). But an alternative reading of **25** produces a higher total. Several of the estates in the list seem to be paired: for instance, 'from Navestock and Neasden four' (see the map in Hill, *Atlas*, p. 93). Some of these links make some kind of administrative sense (for example between Barnes and Chiswick, which face each other across the Thames); while others are between distant estates which seem to have no relation. These pairings might represent some unexpected quirk of management of the St Paul's endowment, or it could be that they are a simple textual illusion: it has been suggested that the original compiler of the list or a later copyist simplified his task by pairing up otherwise unconnected places which had the same liability (Taylor 1992, pp. 298–9). Reinterpretation on these lines produces a total of fifty-nine *scipmen*. That is still one short of an assumed normal levy of sixty, but it could be explained fairly easily by the loss of a single minim during copying.

The history of the individual estates is analysed below. The geographical spread is discussed in the Introduction (pp. 97–100, and see Map 2), where it is suggested that the list falls into two circuits, with items 1–18 (i.e. St Osyth to *Ceaddingtune*) representing lands primarily exploited for the support of the canons, and items 19–33 (Fulham to

Codanham) representing the estates allocated to the bishop for the needs of his household and the diocese.

The Estates

1. **St Osyth** (*Cicc*) (Essex) had been bequeathed by Bishop Theodred to St Paul's in *c.* 950 as *beodland*, i.e. to provide for the sustenance of the community (see above, pp. 90–4). For the place-name 'Chich', see *PN Essex*, pp. 347–8; *DEPN*, p. 102. This may have been the site of an early minster, connected with the cult of St Osyth (discussion in Foot, *Veiled Women*, ii. 158–62). The manor was listed among the bishop's lands in Domesday, with an assessment of seven hides (LDB 11r; *DB Essex* 3:14). Hart has argued that *Cicc* was originally a district-name; that at the time of Theodred it referred to the whole area between the river Colne and Horsey Island, including the later manors of St Osyth, Clacton and The Naze; and that in **25** (where Clacton is covered separately), the substantial assessment of four *scipmen* from *Cicc* indicates that the name still covered The Naze as well as St Osyth (Hart, *Danelaw*, pp. 209–11). The difficulty here is that we cannot be sure that there was a precise correlation between the size of the holding and the naval obligation (see Abels, *Lordship*, pp. 158–9: although the Domesday figures cited there are not properly applicable). It would also appear that the Domesday reckoning for Chich/St Osyth was a beneficial assessment; there was land for twelve ploughs TRE and the value was given as £18. *Cicc* is not an obvious candidate for a district-name (the reference is probably to the creek on the River Colne where the estate-centre is located), and it seems topographically unlikely that in **25** it refers to St Osyth and The Naze, but not the intervening Clacton. The most likely option is that *Cicc* here and in S 1526 refers essentially to St Osyth, possibly representing the endowment of a dissolved minster. For the history of St Paul's estates in this area, see Faith 1996. There were other Domesday holdings at *Cicc*, a manor of three hides and forty acres held by Edward TRE and later by Engelric and then Count Eustace and a property of two-and-a-half hides held by Siward TRE and later by Ranulf Peverel (LDB 32v, 75v; *DB Essex*, 20:63, 34:33); these were the later manors of Earls Hall and St Clere's Hall in St Osyth (*VCH Essex I*, p. 469 n. 5, p. 531 n. 8). The former estate is probably the 'Little Chich' mentioned in the will of Leofgifu (S 1521), which may represent the land at 'Chich' claimed by Christ Church, Canterbury (S 1645; Brooks and Kelly, *Christ Church*, no. 177; see Hart, *ECE*, no. 53).

2. **Tillingham** (Essex) had been also bequeathed by Bishop Theodred to St Paul's in *c.* 950, this time as *are*, i.e. its own property. It was one of the canons' manors in Domesday, with an assessment of twenty hides (LDB 13r; *DB Essex* 5:5). The manor was later to be claimed as part of the early endowment (see **1**).

3. **Dunmow** (Essex) was another estate bequeathed by Bishop Theodred to St Paul's in *c.* 950, 'for the brethren'. At the time of the Domesday survey there were a number of manors in lay hands at Great and Little Dunmow, with no sign of any interest by the bishop or canons in 1066 or after.

4. **Tolleshunt** (Essex). This reference in the 'Ship List' is the only evidence for a connection between the London episcopal estate and Tolleshunt (although in the later thirteenth century a bishop purchased land there as his private property: see Taylor 1992, p. 296 n. 44, commenting on Liebermann 1900, p. 22). A four-hide estate at Tolleshunt was granted to a 'religious woman' named Æthelgifu by King Eadred in 946 (S 517a, preserved

in the Barking archive). In 1086 Tolleshunt was divided into several manors, all in lay hands, none with any St Paul's connection. There is possibly some interest in the detail that the first element of the place-name is the personal name Tolla, also found in Tollington in Islington (see below) and in Tollesbury, Essex, a Barking manor (*PN Essex*, p. 306).

5. **Navestock** (Essex) was supposedly granted to St Paul's by King Edgar (see **16**, which is spurious). The ownership of Navestock was disputed in 1066 and it would appear that the canons had taken advantage of the Norman invasion to attempt to reoccupy lands which had slipped from their control at some point between the compilation of **25** and the Conquest (see p. 173).

6. **Neasden** (Middlesex). At the time of the Domesday survey, Neasden would appear to have been reckoned under the canons' manors of Willesden and Harlesden (GDB 127v; *DB Middx*, 3:17, 18). It is mentioned in **12**, in a context which suggests that it still formed part of the *communa* of the chapter when that charter was forged (see pp. 164–5). Subsequently the chapter's holdings at Willesden, Harlesden and Twyford were divided into eight prebends, including the prebend of Neasden (*VCH Essex*, vii. 208); the first prebendary would appear to have been appointed in the early twelfth century (Le Neve, *Fasti 1066–1300*, p. 63).

7. *Hinawicun*. The place-name means '[at the] dairy-farms of the religious community' (*hiwan*, gen. *higna*; *wic*). For *wic* as a place-name element, and the common meaning 'farm', especially 'dairy-farm', see *DEPN*, pp. 515–16. Most commentators have decided for an identification with Wickham St Paul's, held by the chapter TRE and assessed at three hides less one virgate (LDB 13r; *DB Essex* 5:4), the prefix distinguishing it from the episcopal manor at Wickham Bishops (LDB 10v–11r; *DB Essex* 3:13): see, for example, Hart, *ECE*, no. 28; Taylor 1992, p. 293; and the sceptical notes in Gelling, *Signposts*, pp. 68, 72. The spurious pancarta of Æthelstan (**12**) certainly contains a reference to Wickham St Paul's, but there the place-name form is *Wicham*, which is the same spelling as in the two Domesday references and which points to an original *wic-ham*, 'dwelling-house, manor'. No other references to Wickham St Paul's include the prefix. The identification with *Hinawicun* must be regarded as conjectural, and is effectively based on the circular argument that **25** refers to St Paul's estates, and that Wickham is a similar name to *Hinawicun*. There is no evidence as to the date when the Wickham manors became part of the episcopal endowment; they may have been acquired later than *c.* 1000. It is argued above that this section of the list of estates in **25** forms a rough circuit around London (see pp. 97–100). On this basis, *Hinawicun* would be most naturally placed in Middlesex, between Neasden and Islington. This was the approximate location of the twenty-four hides traditionally claimed by the canons as a donation of Æthelberht of Kent (see above, pp. 83–4). It is possible that *c.* 1000 part of this territory was devoted to a series of farms providing essential supplies for the chapter. The prefix *higna* might then recognise the long-standing link between this area and the St Paul's community.

8. **Tollington** in Islington (Middlesex) was no longer part of the episcopal estate in 1066. The Domesday manor was held TRE by Eadwine, the man of King Edward, with the right to sell; after the Conquest it was held from the king by Ranulf, brother of Ilger, with an assessment of two hides (GDB 130v; *DB Middx* 22:1). The place-name means 'Tolla's hill' or perhaps more narrowly 'Tolla's hill-pasture' (*PN Middx*, p. 126); the first element is same personal name as Tolleshunt (see 4 above).

9. *Gnutungadene* remains unidentified. There is no etymological basis for the suggested link with Hungerdown in Hackney, Middlesex (as K. McDonnell, *Medieval*

London Suburbs (London and Chichester, 1978), pp. 19–20; cited in Taylor 1992, p. 296); the second element is *denu*, '(main) valley', which is unlikely to evolve into '-down' (*cf.* Gelling and Cole, *Landscape of Place-names*, pp. 113–22). It has also been suggested that there may be a connection with Notting Hill (Hart, *Danelaw*, p. 205 n., p. 207), but this should also be rejected. The earliest references to Notting Hill are late medieval and seem to point to an element *Cnotting*, from the personal name Cnotta (*PN Middx*, pp. 129–30), but it has been pointed out that in this case Notting is probably a family name, originally from Knotting, Bedfordshire (*DEPN*, p. 345). The place-name in **25** would anyway require considerable modification to fit such an identification. Its position in the list would be best compatible with a location in Middlesex, probably between Islington and Bromley.

10. **Brœmbeleage**, probably **Bromley by Bow** (Middlesex), which was at a later date part of the bishop's manor of Stepney (*PN Middx*, p. 135). This may correspond to the part of the manor which was held by canons for their supplies: see 21 below. Hill (*Atlas*, p. 92) maps this as a reference to Bromley in Kent, but there is no support for the identification; the estate there was associated with Rochester in this period (see S 893).

11. **Tottenham Court** (Middlesex) was a Domesday manor of the canons, with an assessment of five hides (GDB 128r; *DB Middx* 3:20). The original name was in *-healh*, but would seem to have been altered through the influence of the better-known Tottenham (*PN Middx*, p. 143).

12. **Clapham** (Surrey) was Liebermann's suggestion for *Clopham*, which is etymologically acceptable and perhaps compatible with the following reference to another Surrey estate. A thirty-hide estate at Clapham is mentioned in the ninth-century will of Ealdorman Ælfred (S 1508; Brooks and Kelly, *Christ Church*, no. 96; A.D. 871 × 888). It was left to Ælfred's wife and daughter, and to his daughter's children if she had them; otherwise it was to be brought back within the male line of Ælfred's kin. The holder of Clapham was to pay an annual render of 200 pence to the minster at Chertsey. Taylor considers it highly unlikely that St Paul's would have held a substantial estate in Surrey *c.* 1000, arguing that it was by then the practice to dispose of extra-diocesan estates; she suggests that the place-name may be an error for *Clopton*, and proposes an identification with Clapton in Stepney (Taylor 1992, p. 297; *cf. PN Middx*, p. 105). The emendation seems unjustifiable, given that Clapham in Surrey is a perfectly good fit. Both Clapham and Clapton, together with a slew of similar names, have the first element *clop*, meaning 'lump, hillock, hill' (*DEPN*, pp. 108–9). There is really no problem in St Paul's holding a large estate in Surrey at this period. The episcopal estate included land at Wimbledon and Sheen fifty years before, according to Theodred's will (see pp. 92–3). Even if there was a policy by *c.* 1000 not to seek property outside the diocese (a debatable point), land at Clapham could have been obtained fairly recently, for example through a bequest or an inheritance, and then subsequently disposed of. The Surrey manor was held TRE by Thurbern from the king, and later by Geoffrey de Mandeville on the spurious grounds that it had previously belonged to Asgar the Constable (GDB 36r; *DB Surrey*, 25:1).

13. **Barnes** (Surrey) is mentioned in the spurious pancarta of Æthelstan (**12**). The manor there was the only St Paul's holding in Surrey at the time of the Domesday survey. It was a manor of the canons, assessed at eight hides, which was accounted with the archbishop of Canterbury's manor of Mortlake (GDB 34r; *DB Surrey* 13:1: *cf.* GDB 30v–31r; *DB Surrey* 2:3). In the list of estates, Barnes is linked (perhaps fortuitously)

with Chiswick, which lies directly across the Thames. The place-name means 'the barns' (*PN Middx*, pp. 11–12), which is perhaps to be connected with storage of produce from the estates at Wimbledon and East Sheen which had belonged to the bishopric earlier in the century.

14. **Chiswick** (Middlesex) can be identified with the five hides which the canons held in the bishop's manor of Fulham, for their supplies; it was later constituted as the prebends of Chiswick and Sutton (GDB 127v; *DB Middx* 3:14; *cf.* Gibbs, p. xxiii; *VCH Middx*, vii. 71). The name means 'cheese *wic*', that is, it was a dairy-farm specialising in cheese (*PN Middx*, pp. 88–9).

15. **West Drayton** (Middlesex) was a Domesday manor of the canons, assessed at ten hides (GDB 128r; *DB Middx*, 3:30; see p. 165). It is mentioned in the spurious pancarta of Æthelstan (**12**).

16. **Caddington** (Hertfordshire/Bedfordshire). At the time of the Domesday survey Caddington straddled the county boundary, but was entirely transferred to Bedfordshire in 1897. An estate here was held by Eadwine 'of Caddington' in *c.* 1050, and was bequeathed by him to his son Leofwine (S 1517; Crick, *St Albans*, no. 14). Leofwine was the holder of 'Caddington' estates in both Beds. and Herts. in 1066; both properties had passed into the hands of the canons by 1086 (GDB 136r, 211r; *DB Herts.*, 13:2; *DB Beds.*, 12:1). The entry for the Bedfordshire Caddington mentions that the canons had a royal writ to the effect that Leofwine had given them the land. The reference in **25** would seem to show that St Paul's had an earlier interest in Caddington. It may be significant that Eadwine left to the minster at Abingdon the reversion of an estate at *Pyrian*, which he had purchased from that community earlier in the century (see discussion in Kelly, *Abingdon*, pp. cxlviii, 502, 507). It is conceivable that St Paul's had similarly sold Caddington to Eadwine or his family in the same period (in line with the practice of disposing of distant properties), and that this was recognised by a subsequent promise of reversion.

17. **Sandon** (Hertfordshire) is mentioned in the spurious pancarta of Æthelstan (**12**). The canons' manor there was assessed at ten hides TRE/TRW (GDB 136r: *DB Herts.* 13:5). A half hide there was leased by the canons to Æthelweard in the later eleventh century (see pp. 230–1).

18. ***Ceaddingtune*** is unidentified. The name is etymologically the same as Cheddington in Dorset (*DEPN*). There is a Buckinghamshire Cheddington, conveniently close to Caddington, but this has a different origin (*Cetendune*, probably 'Ceatta's down'; *cf. DEPN*; Gelling and Cole, *Landscape of Place-Names*, p. 168). It is argued above (pp. 98–100) that *Ceaddingtune* was the last place in the first half of the list of estates in **25**, covering the lands which were particularly associated with the canons. The topographical arrangement of this part of the list would seem to run from the Essex holdings, to a circuit round London, to Hertfordshire: on this basis, *Ceaddingtune* would probably have been located in Hertfordshire or perhaps even further afield. There are no grounds for Hart's speculation that the name is a mistake for Beddington in Surrey (*Danelaw*, p. 207).

19. **Fulham** (Middlesex). Bishop Wealdhere acquired fifty hides here in the early eighth century (**3**); for discussion of the history of the estate, see pp. 140–1. The episcopal holdings totalled fifty hides TRE, with forty hides in the hands of the bishop himself, five held by two of his freemen with no rights of alienation, and five held by the canons of St Paul's for their supplies (GDB 127v; *DB Middx*, 3: 12–14). The land allocated to St Paul's became the prebend of Chiswick (see 14 above).

20. *Forthtune*. An identification has been proposed with Fortune (*cf.* Fortune Gate Road) in Willesden/Harlesden, which has the form *Forton(e)feild* in a reference *c.* 1300 (Taylor 1992, p. 296;*VCH Middx*, vii. 208; *cf. PN Middx*, p. 161). Gover *et al.* suggested that the modern name developed from *foran-tun*, 'in front of the *tun*' (i.e. Harlesden). This would be incompatible with the form in **25**, where the second element is certainly *tun*, 'settlement, farm', while the first is perhaps a corruption of *ford*, 'ford', with an original *d* mutating to *eth* and then to *thorn* (which would be expected to produce a later form *Forton*; *cf.* Gelling and Cole, *Landscape of Place-Names*, p. 168). There are other places called 'Fortune' in the London area, including Fortune Gate in Hampstead, Temple Fortune in Hendon and The Fortune in Edgeware (*PN Middx*, pp. 113, 59, 51). There is a good chance that at least some of these names arise simply from the word 'fortune' and its pleasant connotations (Margaret Gelling, pers. comm.). Whatever the case, the estate mentioned in **25** probably lay between Fulham and Stepney, either in Middlesex or on the Surrey side.

21. **Stepney** (Middlesex) was an episcopal manor in 1066, with thirty-two hides held by the bishop himself (GDB 127r; *DB Middx*, 3:1). The Domesday entry is followed by details of other estates associated with Stepney and held by a variety of tenants from the bishop (GDB 127rv; *DB Middx*, 3:2–11). Firstly there were five hides of which half had been held TRE by Sired the canon and half by the canons of St Paul's for their supplies. Another five holdings totalling ten hides had been in the bishop's lordship TRE; six of these ten hides are explicitly linked with the manor of Stepney. There is also a reference to one hide and one virgate held by the canon Engelric from the bishop TRE/TRW. It has been suggested that Stepney was an early possession of the London Church (see p. 87).

22. **Islington** (Middlesex). A ten-hide estate at Islington was granted by King Coenwulf of Mercia (796–821) to his *comes* Beornnoth, and was in the possession of Ealdorman Æthelferth in 903 (**10**). Islington is listed as a Domesday manor of the canons, with two separate holdings of two hides (GDB 128r; *DB Middx*, 3:22–3). But there was also an episcopal holding in Islington, later known as Barnsbury, which was reckoned as part of the bishop's manor at Stepney (see *VCH Middx*, viii. 51). This can be identified with the five hides held by Hugh de Bernières in 1086; before the Conquest half of this manor was held by Canon Sired in his own right, while the other half was held by the canons for their supplies (GDB 127r; *DB Middx*, 3:2). There were also two small manors, each assessed at half a hide, which were held TRE by men of King Edward, with full alienation rights (GDB 129v, 130v; *DB Middx*, 9:3, 23:1).

23. **Orsett** (Essex). Bishop Brihthelm received ten hides at Orsett from King Edgar in 957 (**15**), and there seems to be a good chance that a separate property there was granted to a deacon named Werenberht in 971 × 992 (**19***b*). The episcopal manor at Orsett was assessed at thirteen hides TRE, of which one was held from the bishop by Engelric and later acquired by Count Eustace (LDB 9v, 26v; *DB Essex*, 3:2 and 20:4). The place-name means 'ore-springs', 'pits where bog-ore was obtained' or 'chalybeate springs' (*DEPN*, p. 351; Gelling, *Signposts*, p. 123). **25** contains a later reference to 'western Orsett' (see **26** below), which may be a distinct reference to the portion of the later manor which had earlier belonged to Werenberht.

24. **Laindon** (Essex). The Domesday entry for Laindon lists the nine-hide manor there under the episcopal holdings in Essex, but states that it was held by Ælfthryth TRE (LDB 9v; *DB Essex* 3:1); conceivably this was a leasehold tenancy. A separate half-hide manor is mentioned under the details of the bishop's 'fee' (see pp. 104–5); this had been held

TRE by Wulfmær (LDB 12r; *DB Essex* 4:13). An earlier identification with Leyton (Robertson, *Charters*, p. 391) has no etymological support (*cf. PN Essex*, pp. 101, 161).

25. **Shopland** (Essex). Twelve hides here were granted by King Eadred to a nun in 946 (**14**), and presumably passed to the London Church before **25** was compiled. The estate seems later to have been broken up and lost or alienated; it was held by a free man TRE, then by Engelric, before passing to Count Eustace; the manor was reckoned at five hides (LDB 34v; *DB Essex* 20:80).

26. **'Western Orsett'.** See **23** above.

27. **Belchamp St Paul's** (Essex). The canons held the manor at the time of the Domesday survey, with an assessment of five hides (LDB 12v-13r; *DB Essex* 5:3). The estate formed part of the *communa* of the chapter (see **12**).

28. **Copford** (Essex). The will of Æthelric of Bocking mentions the bequest to Bishop Ælfstan of woodland and fields, apparently to be attached to an estate he already held at Copford (S 1501; Brooks and Kelly, *Christ Church*, no. 136; see above, p. 95). There was a challenge to the will after Æthelric's death, but its provisions were confirmed by King Æthelred between 995 and 999 (S 939; Brooks and Kelly, *Christ Church*, no. 137). The manor at Copford was held TRE/TRW by the bishop, with an evidently beneficial assessment of 1.5 hides (LDB 10v; *DB Essex* 3:10).

29. **Holland** (Essex). Land here was acquired as a part of an exchange with Ely Abbey between 971 and 984; for the circumstances, see above, pp. 96–7. This property had been lost or alienated before 1066. Manors at Great and Little Holland were held by Leofstan TRE; in 1086 he still held Great Holland, now as a tenant of Walter of Douai, but the second estate had passed to Engelric and later to Count Eustace (LDB 33r, 91rv; *DB Essex* 20:68; 52:3).

30. **Southminster** (Essex). The bishop held a substantial manor here in 1086, with an assessment of thirty hides; the Domesday entry notes that the estate had been seized by King Cnut but recovered by Bishop William after the Conquest (LDB 10rv; *DB Essex* 3:9). It seems very likely indeed that the Southminster manor represents part of the seventy hides at 'Dengie' granted by an East Saxon king to Bishop Ingwald in the early eighth century (**6**; see also **18**).

31. **Clacton** (Essex). The Domesday manor here was held by the bishop, with an assessment of twenty hides (LDB 11r; *DB Essex*, 3:15). There is no pre-Conquest documentation.

32. *Hæthlege*, 'heath-covered clearing' and (**33**) *Codanham*, 'Coda's farm'. Because these two entries are paired Liebermann suggested identifications with Hadleigh and Coddenham in Boxford, which are neighbouring places in southern Suffolk, near the Essex border. There is no later tenurial link with St Paul's. In 1066 Hadleigh belonged to the monks of Christ Church, Canterbury, who claimed to have been granted it by Brihtnoth of Essex (died 991) and/or his wife Ælfflæd (S 1637, 1639; Brooks and Kelly, *Christ Church*, nos 132, 138). The estate would certainly seem to have been held by Christ Church by the second quarter of the eleventh century, for it is mentioned in S 914, which was copied into a gospel-book at around that time and may have been produced not long after its ostensible date of 1006 (Brooks and Kelly, *ibid.*, no. 140). Ælfflæd was a benefactor of St Paul's (see pp. 94–5). Her will (S 1486) mentions Hadleigh, but only in the context of a boundary clause. However, the will of her sister Æthelflæd does refer to Hadleigh, in terms which suggest that there was an independent minster there (S 1494). Hadleigh was the site of an early royal vill, where the Danish king of East Anglia

was buried in 890 (Stevenson, *Asser*, p. 140; *cf.* Campbell, *Essays*, pp. 153–4). Conceivably there was an important royal church here under the East Anglian kings. It may have been the case that Christ Church assumed control over this minster and its property at some point in the first half of the eleventh century. Coddenham in Boxford was an outlier of the manor of Cavendish, which was held TRE by Norman (LDB 427v; *DB Suffolk*, 43:1).

Later commentators have been unhappy with a Suffolk location for these last two estates in **25**. An alternative proposal, which involves downplaying the pairing in the document, is for identifications with Hadleigh in Essex and Codham Hall in Great Warley, another Essex property (Hart, *Danelaw*, pp. 214–15; Taylor 1992, pp. 294–5). There is no Domesday entry for this Hadleigh and no early documentation, but it has been suggested that land here was reckoned under nearby Barling or Shopland. Codham is also invisible in Domesday Book and in early documents, but there is a Domesday entry for Warley; the manor there was held by Gyrth TRE, but there is a note that King William gave it to Bishop William because it had formerly belonged to St Paul's (LDB 10v; *DB Essex*, 3:11). There is a slight hitch in that the episcopal holding was in Little Warley and Codham lies in Great Warley; it has been argued that the boundaries were adjusted.

This evidence is not really conclusive. If the Essex identifications are correct, then it is odd that both places go unmentioned in Domesday and the early documentation. It might be useful to re-examine the prejudice against the Suffolk identifications. It is an unfounded assumption that all the estates in **25** would have had to lie within the diocesan boundaries; the list includes two Surrey properties and an extradiocesan estate at Caddington. There is also nothing to rule out the possibility that St Paul's or the London bishopric acquired an interest in a formerly independent minster in the Hadleigh area. Christ Church, Canterbury, had gained control there by the second quarter of the eleventh century, if not before; it is conceivable that there was an earlier period of London influence at Hadleigh. It should be borne in mind that, fifty years before, Theodred had been bishop of southern East Anglia as well as London, and that he was a major landowner in Suffolk (see above, pp. 91–4). Either he or his family, or some other Suffolk magnate, could have granted the London bishopric some rights in a minster at Hadleigh. Alternatively, the minster could have been a daughter-house of St Paul's, founded when the London Church was a key player in the re-establishment of ecclesiastical life in East Anglia. Liebermann's Suffolk identifications should not be rejected out of hand.

26

*King Cnut confirms the lands given by himself and his predecessors
to St Paul's minster in London.* [A.D. 1016 × 1035]

C. GL 25504 (*Liber L*), 12rv: copy, s. xii[1]
    Rubric: Privilegium Cnudi regis.
D. St Paul's D. & C., *Liber B*, 20v: copy, s. xii[ex] (lost)
E. GL 25501 (*Liber A*), 57r (original foliation 39r): copy, s. xii[med]
    Marginal rubric: Carta Cnudi regis.

Ed.: a. Dugdale, *St Paul's*, p. 188, from D (SP1)

　　b. *Mon. Angl.*, iii. 303–4, from D (MA)

　　c. Dugdale, *St Paul's* (2nd edn), App. pp. 12–13, from D (SP2)

　　d. Dugdale, *St Paul's* (3rd edn), p. 295, from D

　　e. Kemble 1320, from *Mon. Angl.*

Listed: Sawyer 978; Gelling, *ECTV*, no. 235

Edited from C, E and MA (*Mon. Angl.*)

*a*In nomine Domini Dei saluatoris nostri Iesu Christi. Ego Cnudus Anglorum rex concedo tibi Ælfþio*b* episcopo pro meę animę remedio, sciens michi in futuro prodesse seculo quicquid in pręsenti uita largitus fuero, omnes terras iuris mei uel antecessorum meorum ⟨datas⟩*c* ad augmentum monasterii*d* beati Pauli apostoli gentium doctoris, quod positum est in ciuitate Lundonie, omnes has terras consentiens confirmaui, testantibus episcopis et comitibus et istius terrę principibus. Si quis uero harum terrarum condonationem contradicere pręsumpserit, a paradisiaco*e* consortio exul existat.*f* AMEN.

　　a Carta Cnudi Regis Danorum et Anglorum, donationes Ecclesiæ sancti Pauli confirmans *rubric*
MA　　*b* Ælipio E; Ælfwino MA　　*c* *Supplied for sense*　　*d* monasterium E
　　e paradysiaco C　　*f* E *ends here*

26 was one of the small group of mostly forged charters which were copied into the main St Paul's cartularies (MSS C, D, E). It seems that there was a copy in the lost *Liber G* (see p. 55), while the lost *Liber B* was the source for the editions by Dugdale in *St Paul's* and *Mon. Angl.* Kemble took his text from *Mon. Angl.*, which was the source for his reference to 'Reg. B' (KCD vol. vi, pp. xxiii, xxv). A near-verbatim version of the section from *pro mee anime* to *largitus fuero* appears in a list of formulae compiled by the anonymous seventeenth-century scholar responsible for BL Lansdowne 364 (fol. 134r; see above, p. 72). It is conceivable that this was taken from a model used by the forger of **26**, rather than from **26** itself.

　　This is a clumsy fabrication. The forger apparently intended that **26** should be a confirmation by Cnut of lands given to the community by himself and his predecessors, but has failed to make this explicit in the confused dispositive section (where Cnut actually confirms to St Paul's 'all the lands under my lordship and under the lordship of my predecessors', which would indeed have been a bonanza for the community). **26** should be considered together with **21**, supposedly a general confirmation of St Paul's lands by King Æthelred. Both documents refer to witnesses, without giving details, and the concluding AMEN here corresponds to VALETE in **21**. The forger of **26** may have based his text in part upon a seventh-century model, for the passage beginning *sciens michi in futuro* seems to be a development of a formula seen in two early diplomas (S 45 from A.D. 692; and S 56, a conservative charter from 759). There is related wording in the proems of S 1165 (A.D. *c.* 670 × 675) and S 235 (A.D. *c.* 686 × 688), and the ultimate source may have been an Italian private deed (Chaplais 1968, p. 328 (pp. 78–9); Kelly, *Selsey*, pp. 16–17). The forger's model may also have supplied the verbal invocation (a standard formula, but of the type commonly seen in seventh-century documents) and the brief motivation clause (*pro anime mee remedio*; compare S 45, 235 etc.); it probably also suggested the use of the second person in the reference to the beneficiary, which is a very early feature (compare S 9, 1165, 1171 etc.). The phrase *ad augmentum monasterii* could be derived from this model (compare **2**; *ad augmentum monasterialis vitae*), and it may also be the source for (or an influence on) the wording of the anathema; there are no precise parallels for this, but the lack of an 'escape clause' (giving the transgressor the option of repentance and restitution) would be consistent with a relatively early date. Seventh-century anathemas in the West/East Saxon tradition (see pp. 77–9) could be adventurous (see, for example, S 1164, 1248). If the forger was using an early model, it would explain why he was unable to supply any plausible witnesses for a supposed charter of Cnut. It could be suggested, as a simple possibility, that the seventh-century source was the same document which supplied the witness-list attached to the forged diploma for Tillingham (**1**). **21** may also be based in part on a diploma of around this date.

In both **21** and **26** the bishop is named as the primary beneficiary of the confirmation of St Paul's lands, which seems a little odd in documents which must be post-Conquest forgeries. The explanation may be that in both cases the forgers were drawing on royal charters which did actually mention the bishop. In the case of **26**, the forger may have been partly influenced by a charter or writ of Cnut in favour of Bishop Ælfwig. There is a post-Conquest writ, either of William I or William II, which confirms to Bishop Maurice all the lands, men and customs which belonged to his bishopric, and which had been been enjoyed by his predecessors Bishops Ælfwig and William (Gibbs, no. 18; Bates, *RRAN: Acta of William I*, no. 191). This reference certainly implies the existence of some kind of document mentioning Ælfwig, perhaps comparable to Cnut's writs for Archbishop Æthelnoth (S 986–7) and various writs of Edward the Confessor issued in connection with episcopal appointments (S 1111–13, 1151, 1156, 1159–60; cf. Keynes 1988, p. 216). The forger's starting-point may have been a writ of Cnut confirming Ælfwig in the lands and rights of his bishopric; this was transformed into a diploma confirming the St Paul's estates, with some general formulation borrowed from an early diploma.

27

King Cnut grants judicial and financial privileges to
St Paul's minster. [A.D. 1033 × 1035]

D. St Paul's D. & C., *Liber B*, 20v (?): copy, s. xii^ex (lost)
Ed.: a. Dugdale, *St Paul's*, pp. 188–9, from D (SP1)
    b. *Mon. Angl.*, iii. 304, from D (MA)
    c. Dugdale, *St Paul's* (2nd edn), App. p. 13, from D (SP2)
    d. Dugdale, *St Paul's* (3rd edn), p. 296, from D
    e. Kemble 1319, from *Mon. Angl.*
    f. Thorpe, *Diplomatarium*, p. 319, from *Mon. Angl.*
    g. Harmer, *Writs*, no. 53 (p. 241), from Dugdale, *St Paul's* (2nd edn), with translation, p. 242
Listed: Sawyer 992; Gelling, *ECTV*, no. 236
Printed from SP1 (Dugdale, *St Paul's*, 1st edn), with variants from SP2 (2nd edition) and MA (*Mon. Angl.*)

^a Ic Cnud cyng grete mine biscopes^b 7 mine eorles 7 ealle mine þegenas on ðan sciran ðær mine preostas on S. Paules mynstre habbað land inne freondlice, 7 ic ciþe eoþ þ ic þylle þ hig beon heora sace*c* here 7 socna*d* þeorðe, tolles 7 teames, binnan tid 7 buton tid, 7*e* spa full 7 spa forþ spa hig hæfdon on æniges cynges deage fyrmest on ællan ðingan, binnan burh 7 butan, 7 ic nelle geþafian þ nan man æt ænigum þingan heom misbeode, 7 þyses is to gepitnesse: Ægelnoð arcebiscop 7 Ælfric arcebiscop 7 Ælpi biscop 7 Ælfþine biscop 7 Duduce biscop 7 Godþine eorl 7 Leofric eorl 7 Osgod ⟨Clape⟩*f* 7 Thored 7 oþre genoge. God hine apeorge þe þis apænde.

a Alia carta eiusdem regis Canuti de quibusdam immunitatibus eidem ecclesiæ per ipsum concessis, Saxonice *rubric* SP1, SP2, MA   *b* biscofes SP1, SP2   *c* saca MA   *d* *For* heora sace 7 here socna   *e* *Not needed for sense and perhaps intrusive*   *f* Clape SP1, MA, SP2

I, King Cnut, send friendly greetings to my bishops and my earls and all my thegns in the shires where my priests in St Paul's minster have land, and I inform you that it is my will that they be entitled to their sake and their soke, and to toll and team, in ⟨festive season⟩ and outside it, (and) as fully and completely as they had in the days of any king, in all things, within the burh and without, and I forbid any man to do then wrong in any thing. These are the witnesses: Archbishop Æthelnoth and Archbishop Ælfric and Bishop Ælfwig and Bishop Ælfwine and Bishop Duduc and Earl Godwine and Earl Leofric and Osgod Clapa and Thored and many others. May God curse he who shall alter this.

The manuscript source for Dugdale's editions of **27** in *St Paul's* and *Mon. Angl.* was probably the lost *Liber B* (see pp. 62–4). The texts of Kemble and Thorpe were taken from *Mon. Angl.* which was the source for their references to 'Reg. B.' (*cf.* KCD vol. vi, pp. xxiii, xxv). It appears that there was also a copy in the similarly mislaid medieval roll studied by James and Selden (see the commentary to **24**).

27 is similar to but distinct from the Confessor's writ on the same theme (**28**), which is closer to the suspicious writ of Æthelred (**24**). It has some points of contact with S 986, addressed to Archbishop Æthelnoth, which survives as a contemporary copy in a Christ Church gospel-book (S 986 is traditionally dated to 1020, but may belong instead to *c.* 1035: see Brooks and Kelly, *Christ Church*, no. 158). These are the only two writs in Cnut's name which concern grants of judicial and financial rights. Finally, **27** is nearly identical to a writ of William I, probably datable to 1066 × 1070 (Bates, *Acta of William I*, no. 184; Gibbs no. 3): if Cnut's writ is authentic, then William's could be understood as a confirmation. The latter lacks the witness-list which is such an unusual feature in **27**. Provision of witnesses is very untypical of pre-Conquest writs (see also S 985, 1110, 1116, 1123, generally including far fewer names than here; and discussion in Harmer, *Writs*, p. 73); this may be an indication of a developing form. The witnesses are chronologically consistent and provide dating limits for **27** of between 11 June 1033 (the appointment of Duduc to Wells) and 12 November 1035 (the death of Cnut). Both archbishops appear as witnesses: Æthelnoth of Canterbury (1020–38) and Ælfric Puttoc of York (1023–51). The first of the bishops is Ælfwig of London (1014–35). Ælfwine was bishop of either Winchester (1032–47) or Elmham ((? × 1019) × (1023 × 1038)), almost certainly the former; and Duduc was the contemporary bishop of Wells (1033–60). Godwine and Leofric were respectively earls of Wessex and Mercia. Osgod Clapa was a prominent thegn in Cnut's reign and a staller under King Edward; he was outlawed in 1046, organised some kind of sea-borne invasion from Flanders in 1049, which involved devastation of The Naze (a St Paul's estate), and died in 1054 (*ASC* C, D): see Harmer, *Writs*, p. 569; Nightingale 1987, pp. 564–5; and above, pp. 41–2. Thored may be the staller who appears in in the witness-list of S 981 (Brooks and Kelly, *Christ Church*, no. 154), together with Osgod Clapa.

Harmer notices two other unusual details of **27** which may reflect on its authenticity (*Writs*, pp. 239–40). Firstly, no other pre-Conquest writ is prefaced by the pronoun *Ic*, although there are parallels in epistolary documents. Harmer concludes that this form of greeting cannot be condemned outright as spurious; again it would be possible to argue that the form had not yet been completely standardised. Harmer is also suspicious of the inclusion of the formula *toll and team*, absent from **28** but seen again in post-Conquest St Paul's writs (Bates, *RRAN: Acta of William I*, nos 184, 185; cf. also Gibbs, nos 2, 6). She suggests that this may have been included by a later copyist, pointing to some small errors in the text which could suggest some reworking (see notes [d, e]). At the final count, it is the slight differences between **27** and **28** which suggest that the former was an independent document, not a fake based on Edward's writ.

If **27** is indeed (fundamentally) authentic, then it is surprising that St Paul's did not make greater use of it in the later middle ages. **28** was much copied and regularly enrolled, while **27** had a much more limited manuscript tradition. One reason for this was the additional clause in **28** which gave the canons a veto over new recruits, an issue of huge interest to later generations. Also potentially important was the fact that **28** would appear to have been extant as a sealed original (or pseudo-original), while there is a possibility that **27** was not issued in this precise form. Only a tiny number of writs in Cnut's name have been preserved (S 985–92), with the four examples from Christ Church, Canterbury, having the best claim to authenticity (S 985–8; Brooks and Kelly, *Christ Church*, nos 145, 156–8). All these Canterbury writs are preserved in the form of contemporary copies in gospel-books (see Ker, *Catalogue*, nos 247, 284), a detail which has figured largely in the debate on the production of pre-Conquest writs. It has been argued that these early examples of the writ-form are essentially informal records of oral notifications made to the shire-courts, noted down by the beneficiaries in sacred books as an added guarantee, but not at this stage issued as official sealed documents (see Chaplais 1966 pp. 174–5 (pp. 59–61)). Against this, there is evidence going back to the time of King Alfred for the standard use for royal business of written instruments associated with seals (Harmer, *Writs*, pp. 10–13; Keynes, *Diplomas*, pp. 137–41; *ibid.* 1988, pp. 214–17). It is possible that in the first instance the seal-impressions were carried loose as a badge of credence, and that it was not a relatively late date, perhaps as late as the Confessor's reign, that they were physically attached to the documents (Chaplais 1966, pp. 167–9 (pp. 51–3)). Before this innovation took hold, the accompanying written letters may have had a fairly ephemeral existence (as compared with royal diplomas), surviving only when the beneficiaries made a positive effort to preserve them,—for instance, by making copies in gospel books, as did the monks at Christ Church. After the Conquest, a sealed writ had evidentiary value, but it is unlikely that an earlier unsealed version would have had the same effect. If **27** represents a document which was originally produced as an unsealed writ, authenticated only by a separate seal-impression, this may explain why it was relatively uncelebrated by later generations of canons. There may be a connection here with the provision of witnesses, rare in the writ-form (see above); the lack of an attached seal perhaps made an extra guarantee advisable in a document with a wide significance.

Cnut's writ is potentially important for showing that the canons' assets were already separated from those of the bishop (see above, pp. 93–4, 100, 103). If it is genuine, then its existence conflicts with the general observation that the authentic diplomas in the archive would appear to deal with the estates of the bishops, rather than those of the canons—which could reflect the loss or destruction of the canons' muniments in the mid eleventh century (see pp. 76–7). One possibility is that the text survived because it was recorded in a gospel-book and thus kept apart from the primary title-deeds of the chapter.

28

King Edward grants judicial and financial privileges to the priests of St Paul's minster. [A.D. 1042 × 1066]

D. St Paul's D. & C., *Liber B*, 21v: copy, s. xii^{ex} (lost)
E. GL 25501 (*Liber A*), 1r: copy, s. xiii^{med}
F. GL 25272: copy, s. xiii^{ex} [roll]
G. PRO Ch.R. 12 Edw. III, m. 8: copy, s. xiv [Inspeximus, A.D. 1316]
I. London, Lincoln's Inn, Hale 84, 93r: extract, s. xvii^{med}
J. PRO DL 42/149, 113r: copy, s. xvii[1] [facsimile, with seal (Plate 2)]
K. Oxford, The Queen's College, 88, 186v: copy, s. xvi/xvii [partial facsimile, with seal]
L. BL Cotton Jul. C. vii, 198v: copy, s. xvii^{in} [partial facsimile, with seal]
O. BL Stowe 666, 67v: copy, s. xviii^{in} [facsimile, with seal]
Ed.: a. Dugdale, *St Paul's*, p. 190, from D (SP1)
    b. *Mon. Angl.*, iii. 304, from D (MA)
    c. Dugdale, *St Paul's* (2nd edn), App. p. 14, from D (SP2)
    d. Dugdale, *St Paul's* (3rd edn), p. 297, from D
    e. Kemble 887, from *Mon. Angl.*
    f. Thorpe, *Diplomatarium*, p. 416, from *Mon. Angl.* and BL Lansdowne 446, 91r [copy of 1338 Inspeximus, *cf.* G]
    g. Simpson, *Registrum statutorum*, p. 112 [from copy of 1338 Inspeximus, *cf.* G]
    h. Gibbs, p. 9, from E
    i. Harmer, *Writs*, no. 54, from SP2 (Dugdale, *St Paul's*, 2nd edn), with translation
Listed: Sawyer 1104; Gelling, *ECTV*, no. 253
Edited from J, with variants from E, G and MA (*Mon. Angl.*)

+^{a} Eadþeard^b cyngc^c gret mine b[iscop]es^d. 7 mine eorlas^e 7 ealle mine þegenas^f on þam^g sciran^h þær^i mine preostas^j on Paulus^k mynstre habbað^l land inne . freondlice^m : 7 ic cyðe eop^n þ ic þylle þ hig^o beon heora saca 7 heora socna^P þurðe^q ægðer gebinnan^r burh 7 butan^s . 7 spa godera lagana þurðe^t : nu ^{u}spa full 7 spa forð^u spa hig^o betste þæran^v on æniges cyngces^w dage^x . oððe^y on æniges^z b[iscop]es^{a2} on eallan þingan^{b2} . 7 ic nelle þ hig^o underfon ani ma^{c2} preosta^{d2} in to heora^{e2} mynstre^{f2} þonne heora^{g2} lande are^{h2} aberan^{i2} mage . 7 hig sylfe þillan^{j2} . 7 ic^{k2} nelle geþafian þ^{l2} heom ænig man æt anigan þingan^{m2} misbeode.^{n2}

^a *Pictorial invocation omitted* E, MA; Inspeximus cartam quam bone memorie dominus
Edwardus quondam rex Angl' progenitor noster fecit capelo ecclesie sancti Pauli London' in hec
verba + G   ^b Edwardus G; Eaoþeard J (*misreading of round-backed* **d** *with short ascender*);
Eadþard MA   ^c kynge G; cynge J; cyng MA   ^d b'es *in all MSS*   ^e eorles G
^f þegenes G, MA   ^g þan G, MA   ^h shiren G   ⁱ þear E; þer G; þar MA   ^j preaster
E; preostes G   ^k *sic* G, J; Paules E, MA   ^l mynistre habbad G   ^m freondliche G, MA
ⁿ kide eou G   ^o heo G   ^p heore sake 7 heore sokne G; heore socne MA   ^q pyrðe E;
weorþe G   ^r gebynnan E; eiþer bynnem G   ^s burgh 7 buten G; buton MA   ^t laghene
weorþe G   ^{u...u} *Possibly an intrusion* (*see commentary*)   ^v best weþen G; best þæron
MA   ^w on eni kynges G; cyngtes J; cynges MA   ^x dæge E, MA; daghen G; dagt J
(*misreading of Insular* **e**)   ^y oþer G; oððre MA   ^z æniger E; on eni G   ^{a2} b'er E
^{b2} alle þingen G   ^{c2} amina J   ^{d2} preosta (a *written on erasure*) G; preostas MA
^{e2} here E   ^{f2} minstre G; mynstra MA   ^{g2} heore G   ^{h2} are' J   ⁱ² abeoran G
^{j2} heo silfen willen G   ^{k2} hic E   ^{l2} þer E   ^{m2} hem eni man at eny þinge G
ⁿ² misbeode G, MA; misbedde E, J *and other MSS* (*see commentary*)

King Edward sends friendly greetings to my bishops and my earls and all my
thegns in the shires in which my priests in Paul's minster have land, and I
inform you that it is my will that they be entitled to their sake and their soke,
both within burh and without, and to as good laws now as fully and completely
as in the days of any king or of any bishop, and I forbid them to take into their
minster any more priests than their estates can bear and they themselves wish,
and I will not permit any man to do them wrong in anything.

28 was evidently regarded as the most important pre-Conquest document in the archive;
it was frequently copied, was submitted for enrolment on numerous occasions from the
fourteenth century onwards, and the original (or pseudo-original) was preserved into the
early modern period. It was omitted from the earliest St Paul's cartulary (*Liber L*),
possibly because it was in Old English (although other vernacular documents were
included in that collection). There may have been a copy in Ralph Diceto's 'greater
register' (*Liber B*, now lost; MS D), from which Dugdale printed a number of texts in his
Mon. Angl. and *St Paul's*. However Dugdale does not refer explicitly to *Liber B* as his
source for **28**, and his text has some details in common with the Inspeximus version
(MS G); he may have been been collating texts from more than one manuscript (see
further discussion above, pp. 62–4). **28** stands at the beginning of *Liber A*, the great
thirteenth-century cartulary (MS E); it was the only pre-Conquest document included in
the original compilation. This was the source of the transcript by Richard James in
Bodleian, James 25, p. 155 (see above, pp. 65–6). Toward the end of the thirteenth
century **28** was copied onto a roll with other significant royal writs (MS F); the language
here has been modernised, and the text has been partly rubbed away. It would appear that
there was a copy on another roll, perhaps of the same date, which was studied by Selden
in the early seventeenth century (MS I; see pp. 68–70). **28** was submitted with other
St Paul's documents for confirmation by Edward II in 1316; the original Inspeximus has
not survived, but there is a copy on the Charter Rolls (MS G). Edward II's Inspeximus
was confirmed by Edward III and on numerous occasions thereafter: for the details,
see above, p. 67. Edward III's Inspeximus was incorporated into the statutes of St Paul's,
and is thus contained in GL 25520 and in Cambridge, University Library, Ee. v. 21.

There was a copy of Henry IV's Inspeximus of 1400 on BL Harl. Roll. I. 1 (Davis, *Cartularies*, no. 606; now missing).

28 is the only pre-Conquest document mentioned in the section of the 1447 inventory which deals with loose documents (see pp. 54–5). It would appear that the original sealed writ was still available for study in the early modern period. Four antiquarian manuscript works include facsimile versions. The copies associated with Robert Glover, who died in 1588 (MS K), and Nicholas Charles, who died in 1613 (MS L), share a textual error (*mine eorlas and mine biscopes*, inverting the proper order) and have the same heading ('A Saxon Charter of King Edward the Confessor') and concluding note ('with this very seale broken just in this manner'). They appear to be independent copies of a lost intermediate exemplar, probably an earlier facsimile made by a sixteenth-century antiquary. The facsimile in a notebook associated with Robert Guillim (died 1620) is far superior and provides the basis for this edition (MS J; Plate 2). An almost identical facsimile appears in a manuscript work by John Anstis, who died in 1744 (MS O); this has more errors of transcription, but a very impressive appearance—the facsimile is more realistic, showing the complete document, and is lightly tinted. It is impossible to tell whether Guillim and Anstis both had access to the sealed original, or whether they were using an existing facsimile copy (conceivably that same copy from which the versions by Glover and Charles ultimately descended). If there was an intermediate exemplar, then it may well have been associated with the College of Arms, of which Guillim, Charles and Anstis were all members. For a more detailed discussion of these antiquarian notebooks, see above, pp. 70–1, 73–4.

The sealed writ reproduced by Guillim and Anstis could conceivably have been a genuine original document. The script is entirely persuasive, bearing a particularly close resemblance to that of an original writ from Christ Church, Canterbury (S 1088; Brooks and Kelly, *Christ Church*, no. 179; first three lines only, since the remainder was erased and rewritten in the twelfth century). The wording is nearly identical, which makes the similarity of the letter-forms and the punctuation even more striking. There is the same abbreviation for *biscopes* which so puzzled Richard James (see pp. 191–2). The initial E of the king's name has the same shape, and the **d** has the vestigial ascender which contributed to its misreading by Guillim as **o** (see note [b]). The confusion between **d** and **o** presumably also accounts for the reading *misbedde* for *misbeode* (note [n2]) in all the antiquarian versions and also in the medieval MS E; the scribe of the Inspeximus text (MS G) was more discerning. In the facsimiles, as in S 1088, internal **e** is hooked and final **e** has the extended tongue which produced Guillim's misreading **t** in *dagt* (see note[r]). Of even greater interest is the reproduction in the facsimiles of the seal impression and its attachment to the parchment. It was the normal practice to cut the long lower edge of Anglo-Saxon writs into two strips that remained attached at the left-hand corner; the upper was used for the seal impression and the lower as a wrapping tie (Bishop and Chaplais, pp. x–xi). One or both of these strips might be torn off, leaving a step. The facsimiles of **28** at first seem to indicate that the strip bearing the seal was still attached, but closer inspection suggests that this is an illusion; there is a clear step on the left-hand edge, and the seal-bearing strip appears to have been arranged behind it, to give an impression of the original attachment. The strip is half the width of the step; the wrapping-tie is missing. It certainly looks as if the document reproduced in these facsimiles was sealed in the usual Anglo-Saxon way. The two sides of the seal impression are copied separately, which was the normal convention of the antiquarian scholars; it does not mean that the two sides of the exemplar had actually been separated. The impression was clearly broken and worn, and some of the detail may be fanciful; it is impossible to tell from what remains whether or not this was indeed a genuine seal of the Confessor (see Harmer, *Writs*, pp. 105, 469–70).

As always, it is difficult to come to a firm conclusion about the absolute authenticity of a writ that survives only as a later copy. The physical similarity with S 1088 shows that a genuine writ of the Confessor certainly underlies the document reproduced in facsimile. But this could still be an early imitative fake, or a genuine writ that has been altered or interpolated—S 1088 is a useful warning here, for it is an original that was partly erased and rewritten. Harmer pointed out that there are particularly close formulaic links between **28** and the London *Cnihtengild* writ (**32**), which belongs to the first couple of years of Edward's reign. Textual parallels between the two London writs are not necessarily a positive sign, since there is now a general consensus that royal writs in the Confessor's reign were drawn up by scribes in a central agency attached to the king's court (on this issue, see Harmer, *Writs*, p. 243; Keynes 1988, pp. 215–16; and, for a dissenting view attributing production to the beneficiaries, Chaplais 1966). There were close links between the personnel of the *Cnihtengild* and the canons of St Paul's (see p. 217), and it is a possibility that one writ is an early fake based on the other.

There are two reasons to suspect that **28** is not entirely trustworthy. The first is a possible textual crux, which Harmer explains by reference to a similar passage in the *Cnihtengild* writ (see *Writs*, pp. 237–8). In **32** the beneficiaries are to be 'worthy of as good laws as they were [worthy of] in the days of King Edgar'. In **28** the phrasing is 'worthy of as good laws now *as fully and completely* as they were worthy of in the highest degree in the days of any king', which reads rather awkwardly. Harmer suggests that the italicised phrase (*swa full and swa forth*: see note ") may be an addition to the formula seen in **32** and suggests that its inclusion here could reflect later tampering with Edward's writ. But this is not conclusive: the phrase is a common writ-formula (compare **27**), and it is possible that the original draftsman was responsible for the infelicitous phrasing.

The second source of doubt is the detail in **28** which accounts for the deep and lasting veneration in which it was held by the later canons of St Paul's. The king forbids the expansion of the minster community beyond the resources of its endowment, and gives the priests a veto over new recruits. Control over recruitment was a burning issue between bishop and chapter in the time of Bishop Maurice (1085–1107) and indeed throughout the twelfth century and later (see above, pp. 48–9). The canons would certainly have cherished a royal charter which reinforced their autonomy and supported their claim to be able to reject the bishop's nominees. Some commentators are prepared to make a case that such a clause would have been appropriate in a writ of the Confessor's time. Gibbs (p. xxi) makes a connection with the successive appointment of two Normans (Robert of Jumièges and William) to the see of London in Edward's reign; perhaps these men wished to introduce foreign priests into the chapter (see also Harmer, *Writs*, p. 238). But it has been pointed out that both bishops were personal appointees of the king, and that he would have been unlikely to have damaged their interests by supporting the priests of St Paul's (Crosby, *Bishop and Chapter*, p. 314). The similarity between **28** and **32** might perhaps suggest that the former also belongs to the period 1042 × 1044, in which case it could be a reaction to conditions under Robert's predecessor, Bishop Ælfweard, who had a poor reputation and who would seem to have preferred the interests of Evesham Abbey over those of St Paul's (see pp. 121–2).

In the last resort, it is impossible to be sure whether this clause is genuine, or whether it is an interpolation into a genuine charter (or, indeed, whether the writ itself is a very good later fake). It may or may not be significant that such an important document did not find a place in *Liber L*, compiled in the second quarter of the twelfth century, that it may not have been copied in *Liber B* in the later twelfth century (see above), and that it was not among the St Paul's charters submitted for confirmation on the Cartae Antiquae Rolls in the reign of King John, which included several writs of William I (*The Cartae Antiquae Rolls 1–10*, ed. L. Landon, Pipe Roll Society (London, 1939), pp. 1–5, 12–13) . The first undoubted copy appears in *Liber A* in the middle of the thirteenth century, when **28** is suddenly given a pre-eminent position.

It has been argued that all three writs in favour of the St Paul's priests were probably produced during vacancies at London, and that the judicial privileges would have reverted back to the bishop when one was appointed (Crosby, *Bishop and Chapter*, p. 280). The context for this argument is a perceived parallel with Hereford, where a writ granting sake and soke to the priests of St Æthelberht's appears to belong to a period when there was no bishop in place at Hereford (S 1101, A.D. 1057 × 1060), and to have been nullified when Bishop Walter was appointed in 1061 and was granted the judicial privileges enjoyed by his predecessors (S 1102). A flaw in this argument is the detail that Cnut's writ for St Paul's (**27**) is actually witnessed by the incumbent Bishop Ælfwig (while the writ in Æthelred's name (**24**) is a probable forgery, modelled on **28**).

29

King Edward renews the liberties of St Paul's minster, with particular reference to eight hides (mansae) *at Barling and five at Chingford, Essex.*
[A.D. 1042 × 1066, or ? 908]

C. GL 25504 (*Liber L*), 12v–13v: copy, s. xii[1]
    Rubric: Priuilegium Eadpardi regis 'filii regis Aluredi anno gracie circiter dccccviii' [*added by medieval annotator*]
D. St Paul's D. & C., *Liber B*, 21v: copy, s. xii[ex] (lost)
E. GL 25501 (*Liber L*), 39r: copy, s. xiii[med]
Ed.: a. Dugdale, *St Paul's*, p. 189, from D (SP1)
    b. *Mon. Angl.*, iii. 304, from D (MA)
    c. Dugdale, *St Paul's* (2nd edn), App. pp. 13–14, from D (SP2)
    d. Dugdale, *St Paul's* (3rd edn), p. 296, from D
    e. Kemble 913, from *Mon. Angl.*
    f. Pierquin, *Recueil*, part 6, no 66, from Kemble
Listed: Sawyer 1056; Hart, *ECE*, no. 56
Edited from C, with variants from E and MA (*Mon. Angl.*)

[a]In nomine Domini nostri Iesu Christi saluatoris. Ea quę legaliter salubriterque determinantur, licet solus sufficeret sermo, ad euitandam tamen temporis futuri ambiguitatem fidelissimis scripturis et documentis sacris sunt commendanda. Quam ob rem ego Eadpardus[b] rex Anglorum, pro ęternę retributionis spe et relaxatione peccaminum meorum, ad laudem Regis ęterni et ad honorem sancti Pauli apostoli gentium doctoris, regali auctoritate[c] renouaui atque restauraui

libertatem ad monasterium ipsius statutum in Lundonia ciuitate, ubi diu sanctus Erkenpaldus episcopatum tenuit, hęc est enim illa libertas*d* quam ut ęternaliter in supradicto monasterio permaneat animo libenti constituo, id est octo mansas ad Bærlinga*e* et quinque ad Cingelforde*f*. Hanc ego libertatem, pro petitione et admonitione uenerabilis episcopi Erkenpaldi qui tunc temporis eidem monasterio prefuit, placabili mentis deuotione dictare, scribere, commendare procuraui. Denique adhuc pro ampliori firmitatis testamento omnimodo pręcipimus atque precipiendo obsecramus, ut maneat ista libertas, quam pręfatus Erkenpaldus episcopus in Romulea urbe a uenerabili papa Agatho petebat, insolubiliter ab omni humanę seruitutis iugo, cum omnibus per circuitum ad illud monasterium rite pertinentibus, tribus solummodo exceptis, expeditione, pontis arcisque constructione et exercitu.*g* Si quis uero, quod non optamus, huius decreti aduersitatem*h* infringere temptauerit aut aliter quam a nobis statutum est mutare presumpserit, sit a consortio Domini nostri Iesu Christi segregatus et cum lupis*i* rapacibus ponatur et cum nefandissimo Iuda, qui Christum tradidit, infernales inperpetuum luat pęnas, si ad satisfactionem et emendationem non uenerit.

a Carta Regis Edwardi Confessoris, de octo mansas apud Berlings, et quinque apud Cingeford *rubric* MA   *b* Edwardus E   *c* authoritate MA   *d* libertas illa MA   *e* Berling' E; Berlings MA   *f* Chingelforde E; Cingeford MA   *g* excercitu E   *h* aminadaversitatem MA   *i* *Word omitted* MA

29 is based on **12**, a forgery in the name of Æthelstan which is itself modelled on S 752, a Chertsey fabrication (see pp. 75–6, 162–3). **29** is clearly the latest in the chain, and reflects an adaptation of the general confirmation of lands represented by **12**, S 752 and by S 1035, which is probably the ultimate model for all these diplomas. Here the forger's intention seems to have been to produce a text that was closer to a straightforward grant of land, specifically of estates at Barling and Chingford. The adaptation is noticeably clumsy, most particularly in the passage following the disposition, where the model required a reference to the bishop at whose request the privilege had been granted; clearly at a loss, the forger of **29** named Eorcenwald (at least the forger of **12** made an attempt at the name of the contemporary bishop). The positions of the corroboration and anathema have been reversed, and both have been abbreviated and slightly rewritten. The sanction includes the phrase *penas luere*, also seen in two spurious diplomas of King Æthelred in favour of St Paul's (**21, 24**) and in a Latin memorandum based on a lost Old English document (**31**). There is no witness-list or dating clause in the extant text. The medieval addition to the rubric in *Liber L* (MS C) indicates that at some stage the donor was believed to have been Edward the Elder and the date 908. There are several references to the charter in the survey of manors in the fourteenth-century *Liber I*, also identifying the donor as Edward the Elder and providing a date 904 (fos 63r, 83v, 166r). The seventeenth-century scholar whose notebook is partly preserved as BL Lansdowne 364 also connected the grant with Edward the Elder ('King Edward the third before the Conquest [*sic*] grants to the monastery 8 mansas ad Berling et 5 ad Cyngford ... (fol 4v)). But when *Liber L* was originally compiled, it would appear that **29** was clearly ascribed to Edward the Confessor,

for it was copied last in a sequence of royal diplomas in roughly chronological order
(see pp. 61–2). It is also the last text in the sequence in the later *Liber A* (MS E), and was
in a similar position in the lost *Liber B* (see pp. 63–4).

The creation of a privilege of this type in the name of the Confessor might suggest that
the St Paul's forgers were aware that the Chertsey archive contained a similar diploma of
Edward (S 1035), although it seems to have been the Chertsey privilege of Edgar (S 752)
which was used as a model for **12**. But this may be a simple coincidence; in the post-
Conquest period it was particularly useful to be able to claim possession in the time of the
Confessor. It seems probable that **29** is supplementary to **12**, covering two estates for which
the canons' documentation was poor, and which could not be associated with Æthelstan's
privilege because they were known to have been later acquisitions. Both documents were in
existence by the second quarter of the twelfth century (see further, p. 164).

An estate at Barling was bequeathed to Wulfstan, bishop of London, in the will of
Leofwine, dated 998 (S 1522). It does not figure on the naval assessment list of *c.* 1000
(**25**), possibly because it was a personal bequest to the bishop, perhaps because the list
was drawn up before Leofwine actually died (see pp. 193–4). The canons had an manor
assessed at two and a half hides less fifteen acres at Barling in 1066 and later; there was
also an area of half a hide and ten acres, held by a freeman TRE, which the canons
appropriated after the Conquest (LDB 13v–14r; *DB Essex* 5:12). The manor at Chingford
belonged to the canons in 1066, with an assessment of six hides; subsequently Peter of
Valognes seized a hide and ten acres of meadow, and Geoffrey de Mandeville another ten
acres of meadow (LDB 12v; *DB Essex* 5:2). The document in *Liber L* which lists
invasiones of the canons' land (GL 25504, 47rv; *HMC 9th Report*, i. 65b; see Round
1891; and above, pp. 105–6), drafted *c.* 1100, mentions the usurpation by Peter de
Valognes and indicates that the hide had not yet been restored; the canons complain that
they still have to pay geld on it ('Petrus Valoniis aufert canonicis i hydam terræ et pratum
cum nemore quæ exauctores terræ eis iuraverunt in descriptione Angliæ pro qua scotum
et consuetudinem regi reddunt'). A spurious writ of Bishop H (? Herbert Losinga of
Norwich) to Ralph de Valognes, Peter's son, mentions his father's deathbed repentence
and restoration of the Chingford hide (Gibbs, no. 56 (pp. 40–1); see *VCH Essex*, v. 103).
It would appear that the disputed property was not actually restored, for in the 1181
survey of the St Paul's manors, Chingford is given an assessment of only five hides both
then and in the time of Henry I (Hale, *St Paul's Domesday*, p. 144). Round argues that the
canons had obtained a reassessment of the Chingford manor, so that they no longer had to
pay scot and geld on the missing hide. **29** was clearly forged at a time when the canons
had given up hope of regaining the hide and were thinking of Chingford as a five-hide
manor (unless the numeral was later altered).

30

King Edward grants one hide (mansa) *at* Sciredesforde
to Frǣwine, minister. [A.D. 1042 × 1066]

H. Bodleian, James 23, p. 32: extract, s. xvii[1]
Ed.: Gibbs, p. 1 n.
Listed: LonStP 18

Ita et rex Eadwardus confessor*a* cuidam suo fideli ministro vocitato Frepine unam mansam apud Sciredesforde in communi tellure concessit in propriam hæreditatem, et post se cuicunque sibi placuerit hæredi vel amico in genealogia vel extra. Et sit <inquit>*b* predictum rus liberum ab omni mundiali obsequio exceptis tribus causis etc.*c*

---

a Eadw. confes. H   *b* *James's addition to the formula*   *c* Postea dicitur ille Frepine preoste *concluding note* H

Richard James jotted this extract from a lost charter of King Edward into the margin of his notes from the lost St Paul's roll, next to his paraphrase of **17** (MS H). In the Lincoln's Inn manuscript, the heading *De Sciredesforde id est de* (M?)*ilanda* probably refers to the same diploma (fol 93r); for its position on the roll, see pp. 69–70. A thegn named Frewine attests a spurious Coventry diploma in the name of King Edward, dated 1043 (S 1000); the witness-list seems fundamentally acceptable, although the forger has added a few famous names to its higher reaches (see Keynes 1988, p. 198 and n. 73). The Essex Domesday has a Frewin as the pre-Conquest holder of Tendring, which later came into the possession of Count Eustace (LDB 32v; *DB Essex* 20:64). Tendring is immediately adjacent to Weeley, supposedly granted to St Paul's in the Confessor's reign (**31**). The name (OE Freawine or Freowine) is fairly rare, although there were two contemporary Worcester clerics so-called (see von Feilitzen, *Personal Names*, pp. 252–3). James's extract concludes with a note that Frewine is later called priest: this may be information derived from a separate document or note on the roll (not necessarily authentic), or perhaps a misreading by James of an abbreviated form such as *pr'* (? *prefectus*).

The formulation of James's note seems generally consistent with a pre-Conquest source, although the king's style (*confessor*) would not be contemporary; conceivably it was his own gloss. If so, then there is an outside chance that the donor was King Edward the Martyr (975–8). The dispositive phrase *cuidam* <*meo*> *fideli ministri vocitato* was first used *c*. 935 (compare **14**), while the immunity clause is a variant on a standard formula first devised *c*.939 (see S 447, 449 etc.). The hide granted is said to have been located 'in the common land', and would have consisted of scattered strips in fields farmed communally (for such references, see Kelly, *Shaftesbury*, p. 102). The statement of powers allows the beneficiary to leave the estate to an heir or friend within his kindred or outside. References to the kindred in this context are rare and usually restrictive in intention: thus in S 459 inheritance is limited to the beneficiary's *geneologia* (see Kelly, *Shaftesbury*, pp. 45–6, 51, and references cited there; also **9**). The draftsman of the diploma from which **30** is extracted may have modelled his text on an earlier document, experimenting slightly with the statement of powers.

The estate has not been identified. The first element *Scired* is likely to be a personal name; although there seem to be no other instances, it shares a first element with the relatively common name Scirweald (von Feilitzen, *Personal Names*, p. 356). Possible locations would be in the area of Tendring, which was held by a man called Fræwine in 1066 (see above), or else around Hadham in Hertfordshire, since James appears to associate the text with **17**. It is unfortunate that it is impossible to be sure of the first letter of the alternative name provided by Selden (? *Milanda* or *Nilanda*). Perhaps there could be a connection with the great lordship of 'Nayland' held TRE by Sweyn of Essex, which straddled the boundary of Suffolk with Essex across the river Stour; this is *Eiland* in Domesday Book (LDB 47r, 401rv; *VCH Essex*, i. 408). There is also Mayland (Hall), which was treated as part of Southminster (see *VCH Essex*, i. 395; *PN Essex*, p. 219).

31

Eadgifu and her husband grant land at Weeley, Essex, to the brethren of St Paul's church, with the permission of King Edward. [A.D. 1042 × 1066]

C. GL 25504 (*Liber L*), 13v–14r: copy, s. xii[1]
   Marginal rubric: De Wilgelea.
E. GL 25501 (*Liber A*), 56v (original foliation 38v): copy, s. xiii[med]
Ed.: Gibbs, p. 280, from C and E
Listed: Sawyer 1243a; Hart, *ECE*, no. 58
Edited from C, with variants from E

Literarum hic notificatione terrę quę est apud Wilgelea[a] demonstratur donatio, quam fidelis quędam nomine Eadgyua,[b] cum uiro suo necnon licentia et consensu Eadwardi basilei,[c] fratribus sancti Pauli ęcclesię ad laudem Dei et eiusdem doctoris gentium dedit et pro suorum relaxatione peccaminum inperpetuum concessit. Si autem aliquis hoc auertere pręsumpserit, eternales Iude traditori pęnas associatus luat, nisi citius satis dignam penitentiam egerit.[e]

   [a] Wigleya E   [b] Eadgiua E   [c] Edwardi basilici E   [d] Sequitur carta eiusdem Edgive in Anglico sermone de verbo ad verbum 'quam inuenies in quodam rotulo bullato [?] positam in quod [poi'ta' i' q°d]' E (*addition by a different but probably coeval scribe*)

This Latin memorandum is the last text in the brief collection of early texts found both at the beginning of *Liber L* and in the first continuation of *Liber A*. After the copy in *Liber A* comes a note to the effect that it was followed in the scribe's source by an English version (see note[d]). To this a slightly later scribe has appended the remark that 'you will find it [*presumably the English version*] in a certain sealed roll', perhaps a reference to the lost roll from which James and Selden made extracts (see above, pp. 67–70), although neither refers to this document.

   Dugdale would appear to have seen a copy of a grant by 'Edgiva (a noble woman)' of land at 'Wiggelie', supposedly in the lost *Liber C* (fol. 65v), according to a note in *St Paul's* (p. 5): for this manuscript, see above, pp. 52–3. The seventeenth-century compiler of a notebook, now partly preserved as BL Lansdowne 364, mentions the grant of Weeley in a brief narrative history of the church, after a reference to **29**: 'King Edward the third before the Conquest [*sic*] grants to the monastery 8 mansas ad Berling et 5 ad Cyngford and also confirms the gift of Ediva and her husband of Wygalsy (now Westbe. … [*page cropped*] fratribus sancti Pauli' (fol. 4v). He was probably dependent on either *Liber L* or *Liber A* for this reference.

   31 is anomalous in form for a Latin document and would be more satisfactory as a Latin memorandum based on a lost Old English exemplar (beginning *Her cwithe/swutelath*

on thisum gewrite, as S 1220, 1377, 1454 etc., or *Her swutelath on than cwide*, as in **22**),
as suggested by the rubric in MS E. The draftsman of the memorandum would appear to
have been influenced by **29**, the spurious privilege of Edward the Confessor for St Paul's;
this was evidently the source for the brief motivation clause (*pro suorum relaxatione
peccaminum*) and for the details of the anathema. There is also some reminiscent wording in
the dispositive section of **23**, another difficult text which may be a revised translation of a
genuine vernacular charter. All three documents were probably produced in the same
climate, during the later eleventh or early twelfth century.

31 concerns the grant of an estate at Weeley in Essex. The place-name means 'willow
wood' (see *DEPN*, s.v.; Gelling and Cole, *Landscape of Place-Names*, p. 240), with the
first element being *welig*, rather than *wih, weoh*, 'temple', as previously suggested (as *PN
Essex*, pp. 355–6). The main Domesday manor there is listed among the lands of Eudo
the Steward: there were three hides and thirty-eight acres held by Godwin TRE, and an
apparently separate area of two hides and forty-five acres which used to be attached to
the manor (? as sokeland) and which was held by two freemen before the Conquest (LDB
51v; *DB Essex* 25:22). Eudo later donated his Weeley manor to St John's Abbey in
Colchester (Hart, *ECE*, no. 119). Yet St Paul's did have a small holding in Weeley (see
Hale, *St Paul's Domesday*, pp. cx–cxi, 146), with rights of patronage over the church
there (Gibbs, nos 98–101). Hart (*ECE*, no. 58) suggests that the St Paul's holding was
invisible in Domesday because it was reckoned under the canon's great manor of The
Naze (*Ælduvesnasa*; LDB 13v; *DB Essex*, 5:11). For the history of St Paul's holdings in
this area, see Faith 1996.

The fact that Eadgifu's husband is not named in the document may indicate that this
was not in reality a joint grant but one made by Eadgifu in her own right (perhaps as a
widow, bequeathing land to the church for her own soul and that of her (dead) husband,
perhaps as a deferred bequest). Gibbs (p. 380) suggests an identification between the
donor of Weeley and the *Eideva* who was the post-Conquest holder of a manor at Lisson
Green in Middlesex, claimed by St Paul's on the basis of a disputed bequest by her
husband (see above, p. 103). But Eadgifu is a common name, the two estates are widely
separated and have no common history, and there is no obvious parallel between the two
cases to recommend the identification. An alternative avenue to explore is a possible
connection between Eadgifu and Fræwine, the beneficiary of a charter of Edward the
Confessor granting an unidentified estate at *Sciredesforde*, a copy of which was available
on the lost roll used by James and Selden (see **30**). A man of the same name was the
holder TRE of the manor at Tendring, adjacent to Weeley.

THE LONDON *CNIHTENGILD*

32

King Edward declares that his men in the gild of the English cnihtas *are to have their sake and soke, within burh and without.* [A.D. 1042 × 1044]

Q. Glasgow, University Library, Hunter U. 2. 6, 149r: copy, s. xiv/xv
   Rubric: Carta sancti Edwardi
R. London, Corporation of London Records Office, Letter Book C, 134v: copy, s. xv
S. London, Corporation of London Records Office, *Liber Dunthorne*, 79r: copy, s. xv
Ed.: a. Coote 1881, p. 481, from R and S, with translation p. 480–1
    b. Sharpe, *Letter-Book C*, p. 218, from R
    c. Ballard, *Borough Charters*, pp. 126–7, from a modern transcript of Q, with translation, p. 527
    d. Harmer, *Writs*, pp. 234–5 (no. 51), from Q, with translation, p. 235
Translated: Brooke and Keir, *London*, pp. 96–7; Douglas and Greenaway, *EHD II*, no. 273 (p. 1015)
Listed: Sawyer 1103
Edited from Q

Eadþard cyncg gret Ælfþard biscop 7 Þulfgar minne port gerefa 7 ealle þa burhþare on Lundene freonlice,[a] 7 ic cyþe eop þ ic þille þ mine men on Ænglisce cnihte gilde beon heore sace 7 heore socne purðe, binnan burh 7 butan, ofer heora land 7 ofer heora men, 7 ic þille þ heo beon spa godre lage purðe spa heo pæron on Eadgares dæge cynges 7 on mines fæder 7 spa on Cnudes, 7 ic þille eac hit mid gode geeacnian 7 ic nelle geþafian þæt heom ænig man misbeode ac beon heo ealle gesunde, 7 God eop ealle gehealde.

   [a] *For* freondlice

King Edward sends friendly greetings to Bishop Ælfweard and Wulfgar my town-reeve and all the citizens of London. And I inform you that my will is that all my men in the gild of English *cnihtas* shall be entitled to their sake and their soke, within borough and without, over their lands and over their men. And my will is that they shall be entitled to as good laws as they were in the time of King Edgar and in my father's time and similarly in Cnut's. And I will moreover augment its benefits. And I am not willing to tolerate that anyone shall do wrong to them, but may they all be prosperous. And God keep you all.

The best text of **32** is found in the cartulary of the priory of Holy Trinity, Aldgate (MS Q). For a full description, see J. Young and P.H. Aitken, *A Catalogue of the Manuscripts in the Library of the Hunterian Museum in the Unversity of Glasgow* (Glasgow, 1908), no. 215 (pp. 158–60); and for a calendar of the contents, see Hodgett, *Holy Trinity Cartulary*. The cartulary was compiled in 1425, at a time when the priory was being forced to sell off much of its endowment. The manuscript at some stage came into the possession of John Anstis (see above, pp. 73–4), who lent it to Thomas Tanner in 1713; it later passed to the Hunterian museum (see discussion of the history of the manuscript in Hodgett, *Holy Trinity Cartulary*, pp. xi–xiii; Sharpe, *Letter-Book C*, pp. xvi–xvii). The text of **32** is incorporated into a narrative account of the foundation of the *Cnihtengild* (Hodgett, *Holy Trinity Cartulary*, no. 871). The scribe may have been transcribing the original writ, or an early copy, for he has made a very good attempt at imitating the shape of some of the distinctive Anglo-Saxon letters: the runes **æ** and **þ**, with the abbreviation **þ** (*þæt*); and Insular **b, d, f, g, h, l, r**. The script of the transcript should be compared to the original writs of the Confessor represented by S 1071, 1084, 1088 (first three lines), 1105, 1140, 1156: and see also John Guillim's facsimile of **28** (Plate 2).

MSS R and S are copies of the writ in fifteenth-century letter-books preserved in the archive of the Corporation of London, probably compiled separately from the Holy Trinity cartulary but again associated with other documents concerning the *Cnihtengild*. It seems likely that MS R is the exemplar of MS S. In both texts there is frequent misreading of **ri** for Insular **r**, which indicates that the scribe or scribes may have been copying directly from the original document. These manuscripts have no superior readings and therefore no variants are given here. Ballard used a nineteenth-century transcript of the Holy Trinity cartulary in the Guildhall Library (GL 122).

Holy Trinity Priory was founded by Queen Matilda in 1108, as the successor to a church dedicated to the Holy Cross and St Mary Magdalen, which had been built by a certain Sired and which had an association with Waltham Holy Cross (founded 1062; see Hodgett, *Holy Trinity Cartulary*, p. 224; and discussion of the Waltham connection in Haslam 1988). There is a possibility that Sired was the canon of St Paul's mentioned in Domesday Book as the holder of land in Stepney (GDB 127r, 130r; *DB Middx*, 3:2, 15:1); he may or may not be Sired the priest, who entered the community of Christ Church in Canterbury, apparently in the eleventh century (Douglas and Greenaway, *EHD II*, p. 1023). According to the narrative in the cartulary, the *Cnihtengild* was dissolved in 1125 and its lands and privileges were made over to Holy Trinity; the date might be slightly astray, for the charter of Henry I confirming this grant has been dated to 1121–2 (Hodgett, *Holy Trinity Cartulary*, nos. 871, 998; Douglas and Greenaway, *EHD II*, nos 276–7). The rights of jurisdiction inherited from the *Cnihtengild* remained immensely important to the priory and were cited in litigation as late as the thirteenth century (see Hodgett, *Holy Trinity Cartulary*, nos 109, 960, 962, 968, and *ibid.*, pp. xvii–xviii; Brooke and Keir, *London*, pp. 35–6); this must have encouraged the priory to preserve the older documentation.

The small corpus of documentation relating to the London *Cnihtengild* comprises **32**, plus writs of William II and Henry I confirming its land and privileges, with a narrative of its foundation and dissolution, and charters associated with the latter (for texts and discussion, see Douglas and Greenaway, *EHD II*, nos 273–8; Coote 1881; Hodgett, *Holy Trinity Cartulary*, nos 871–5, 998). According to the narrative, the gild was founded in the reign of Edgar (957–75) by thirteen knights who obtained from the king an area of derelict land in the eastern part of London. The gild's territory and jurisdiction, as defined by Edgar, is said to have embraced the extramural area outside Aldgate known as the Portsoken, which stretched down to the Thames; and it also included property within the walls, and rights over the Surrey bank of the river facing Portsoken, as far south as the gild-members could throw their lances (see Brooke and Keir, *London*, p. 98; and for a useful map of the Portsoken area, see Haslam 1988, p. 37). This last provision has been dismissed as an 'absurd rigmarole' (Brooke and Keir, *London*, p. 98), but a similar procedure involving the throwing of a taper-axe was used to define the boundaries of liberties at Sandwich and Fordwich in Kent (S 959; Brooks and Kelly, *Christ Church*, no. 120; Brooks, *Church of Canterbury*, p. 386 n. 111). The burgesses who dissolved the gild in 1125 are said to have been descendants of the original founders; among their number was Ralph, son of Algod, a canon of St Paul's and the first prebendary of Rugmere (Brooke and Keir, *London*, p. 343). They laid Edward's charter (presumably **32**) on the altar of Holy Trinity and sent a representative to King Henry for his confirmation.

There is continuing debate about the character and function of the *Cnihtengild* (see Stenton, *Preparatory to ASE*, pp. 32–5; Harmer, *Writs*, pp. 231–4; Brooke and Keir, *London*, pp. 96–8; Haslam 1988). **32** and the Holy Trinity narrative would seem to indicate that the London gild was founded in Edgar's reign (although it could also be the case that the narrative tradition was extrapolated from the reference to Edgar in the writ, and that the actual foundation was earlier). The Old English word *cniht* typically means 'servant' or 'retainer', but that is unlikely to be the sense here, for the members of the gild mentioned in the twelfth-century documentation include leading citizens and merchants (Stenton, *Preparatory to ASE*, p. 32). There were similar organisations at Winchester and Canterbury after the Conquest, and the latter is mentioned in a ninth-century document that could be an original, but is perhaps more likely to be a later copy (S 1199; Brooks and Kelly, *Christ Church*, no. 87; and see also Biddle, *Winchester* pp. 236, 335–6). It has been suggested that the original London *cnihtas* were the responsible servants of magnates owning property in London, appointed to exploit the markets for their lords' benefit, who later became independent traders (Stenton, *Preparatory to ASE*, p. 33). An alternative possibility, in the light of recent emphasis on the sophistication and scope of the late Anglo-Saxon state, would be to see the London *cnihtas* as in origin representatives of the royal administration—thegns and reeves responsible for levying the city taxes and tolls, regulating the markets and mint, and supervising the judicial process. It has been suggested that the administration of towns in the late Anglo-Saxon period may have been partly carried out by a city patriciate (see the discussion of the evidence for royal agents in Campbell 1987, especially pp. 209–11). There may be an example in the family of Deorman of London, who would appear to have acted as moneyers over generations, with individual family members also turning up as a canon of St Paul's, an alderman and a justiciar (P. Nightingale, 'Some London Moneyers and Reflections on the Organisation of English Mints in the Eleventh and Twelfth Centuries', *Numismatic Chronicle* cxlii (1982), pp. 34–50; *eadem, Mercantile Community*, chapter 2; Campbell 1987, p. 210). Deorman's son was one of the *cnihtas* who dissolved the gild in 1125.

It has been argued that the original function of the gild was a military one, to defend the City against attack from the east. This role would have diminished after the building of the Tower, which might provide a context for the abolition of the gild under the Normans (Brook and Keir, *London*, p. 98). One commentator has seen the ultimate origin of the *Cnihtengild* in Alfred's refurbishment of the City after 886; he suggests that the gild was formed in the mid tenth century as the successor to an earlier organisation of citizens with the duty of defending the City from the east (Haslam 1988). But it is unlikely that the gild had a purely military character. Its activities in some respects may have mirrored those of the Anglo-Saxon gilds at Abbotsbury, Bedwyn, Cambridge and Exeter, whose statutes have survived (see Whitelock, *EHD*, nos 136–9). These were fellowships of mutual support and loyalty, with a particular emphasis on social gatherings, and on the funeral-arrangements of the gild-brothers and the provision of funeral masses. In connection with this latter point, the gilds tended to be closely associated with minsters (see discussion in Rosser 1988). It has been argued that the London gild had an early association with the church of St Mary Magdalen that was the predecessor of Holy Trinity; that this church may have been founded in Alfred's time, with a *parochia* corresponding to the ward of Aldgate; and, further, that the Aldgate minster was itself dependent on a postulated early mother-church at Waltham in Essex (Haslam 1988). Against this is the detail in the Holy Trinity narrative to the effect that St Mary Magdalen was founded by Sired, and the fact that the proliferation of churches with lay founders in the city would seem to be a feature of the late tenth and eleventh centuries (see pp. 34–5).

A detail that needs some kind of explanation is the emphasis on the London gild being an association of *English* 'knights', presumably to distinguish it from groups with a different identity. It has been suggested that King Edward was concerned to promote the privileges of an English organisation in order to counterbalance the power of the Danish housecarls established in London by Cnut (Nightingale 1987, p. 577; see above, pp. 40–2). The housecarls had military functions, but were also involved in enforcing taxation (Campbell 1987, pp. 201–4). Alternatively, the word *Ænglisce* may have been interpolated into the document at some stage, perhaps to reinforce the English character of this city institution in the face of the introduction of new Norman officials (see Brooke and Keir, *London*, p. 29, for the continuing importance of the English element in the Anglo-Norman city).

The authenticity of English writs is always difficult to evaluate, especially in the case of a document such as **32** for which there are no precise parallels. The exemplar of the copy in MS Q would seem to have been written in eleventh-century minuscule (see above), and there is no detail of the document that is overtly suspicious (see Harmer, *Writs*, p. 234). The first addressee is Bishop Ælfweard, so the date must lie between Edward's accession in 1042 and the bishop's death in July 1044 (so, very early in the reign). Also mentioned in the address is Wulfgar the port-reeve, who is referred to in a post-Conquest document (Hodgett, *Holy Trinity Cartulary*, no. 1072) and who is probably identical with Ulf, called port-reeve in S 1119 and shire-reeve in S 1121 (Brooke and Keir, *London*, pp. 193–4, 371). In terms of its structure and wording, **32** is very close to Edward's writ for St Paul's (**28**). There is a general consensus that royal writs by this date were usually drawn up by royal scribes, so the similarity between the two London writs could be cause for suspicion—it may be that the St Paul's writ was forged on the basis of **32** (see the commentary to **28**). Harmer comments that the linguistic forms of **32** are mainly compatible with the mid eleventh century, although the termination *-a* has been replaced by *-e* in words like *cnihte*, *godre*, *heore*, which is a later change.

APPENDIX I

Letter of Wealdhere, bishop of London,
to Archbishop Berhtwald. [A.D. 704 × 705]

A. BL Cotton Aug. ii. 18: original, s. viii[in], vellum, 145 × 363 mm
    Endorsements: (1) *in a contemporary hand:* A UALDH[ARIO] domino [*gap*] Berctua[ld]; (2) *in a hand of s. xii:* Epistola inutilis
Ed.: a. Smith, *Bede*, pp. 783–4, from A
    b. Haddan and Stubbs, iii. 274–5, from A
    c. *BMFacs.*, i. 5 (facsimile of A)
    d. Birch 115, from A
    e. *ChLA*, iii, no. 185 (facsimile of A)
    f. Chaplais 1978, pp. 22–3, with facsimile of A, plates, 1, 2
    g. Chaplais, *Essays*, XIV, pp. 22–3, with facsimile of A, plates, 1, 2
Translated: Whitelock, *EHD*, no. 164 (pp. 792–3)
Listed: Sawyer 1428b; Hart, *ECE*, no. 6

Domino reuerentissimo et catholicorum patrum[a] praeconiis beatificando Berctualdo totius Brettanię gubernacula regenti Ualdharius tuę almitatis suplex[b] salutem.

Quęrere etenim tuę sanctitatis consilium prospere rebus succedentibus tuisque sapientissimis iussionibus famulari animus deuotus mihi semper inerat. Quanto magis in aduersis et in difficilibus rerum euentibus tuę prouidę considerationis industriam consulari uoluntaria necessitas meam insciolam paruitatem perurget[c]. Inde ergo nunc instante necessitatum causa quid agi debeat tuę beniuolentię ingenium flagitando inquirere opere pretium reor. Latere quidem tuam notitiam potuisse non arbitror quanta et qualia inter regem. Uest Sęxanorum. nostrique pagi[d] regnatores discordiarum iurgia interim pululabant[e]. Et quod adhuc infelicius est ecclesiastici etiam in hanc ipsam dissensionem qui sub ipsis regiminis gubernacula sortiuntur uolentes nolent⟨esque⟩[f] de utraque parte inplicantur. Sepe tamen in utrorumque partium conuentibus pacem uerbis firmabant foedusque ingerunt[g] ut exules eliminarentur a nobis et ipsi nobis inferre non molirentur tantum malum quantum minabant dictis. Quę omnia opere adhuc non inplebantur[h]. Ante paucos autem dies hoc placitum communi consensione condixerunt ut in idus kalendarum Octobrium[i] in loco qui dicitur Bregunt ford omnes aduenissent reges ambarum partium episcopi et abbates iudicesque reliquos. Et ibi adunato concilio omnium dissimultatum causę determinarentur[j] et in quo unusquisque conuictus sit offendisse alio recta emendatione satisfaciat. Huic autem[k] concilio illis rogantibus nostrique iuuentibus[l] propriisque causis nostrae ecclesię cogentibus mé praesentem inesse condecet maximę utrisque promittentibus illam pactionis condicionem sé obseruaturos quam ego et eorum praesul pacifice et unianimiter paciscebamur. Inde per omnipotentem rerum conditorem tuę sanctitatis priuelegium*m* obsecro ut mihi innotescere digneris quid de hac ré agere debeam quia nullo modo possum inter illos reconciliare et quasi obses pacis fieri nisi maximum communionis consortium inter nos misceatur. quod nec uolo nec ausus sum agere nisi tuę licentię uoluntas adnuerit quia memor sum quomodo in praeteriti anni sinodo statutum est illis non communicandum si non tuum iudicium in ordinatione episcoporum implere festinarent quod adhuc neglectui habentes non perficiebant Ideo ergo licet illis inuitantibus nostrique suplicantibus*n* tui oris imperio obedire memet ipsum amplius paro. Tuque obtime pater uetere prudenti consilio ut uel consentiam uoci deprecantium si ita placuerit uel subter fugiam et mé ipsum a conloquio huis*o* concilii subtraham sit ita iustum iudicaueris*p*. tantum ut omni modo in eodem sensu tecum*q* semper maneam. Hac enim pro causa ad conuentum Coenredi regis episcoporum\que/*r* eius et ducum reliquorum*s* quem nuper de reconciliatione Aelfdrydę in\ter/*t* se habuerunt licet aduocatus non ueni. Quia ignarus fui quid de hac re tuę religionis praerogatiua decreuere*u* uoluisset ut postquam hoc dedicerim liberius consentissem si non aliorum inuentione me prius miscuissem. Quid plura elego quę elegeris rennuo*v* que rennueris*v* et id ipsum in omnibus tecum sapiam.

 Hoc tibi per litteras intimare curaui ne inter plures deuulgatum innotescat—
—Orantem pro nobis almitatem uestram diuina trinitas iugiter tuere dignetur.

a patruum *corrected to* patrum A   *b* A *spelling for* supplex   *c* perurbget *corrected to* perurget A   *d* pagie *corrected to* pagi A   *e* A *spelling for* pullulabant   *f* Supplied *(MS damaged)*   *g* For inierunt   *h* non iinplebantur *corrected to* non inplebantur A   *i* There is some error here; perhaps read idus Octobrium *(15 Oct.) or* pridie kalendarum Octobrium *(30 Sept.)*   *j* determirarentur *corrected to* determinarentur   *k* Abbreviation for autem written above line   *l* A *spelling for* iubentibus   *m* A *spelling for* priuilegium   *n* A *spelling for* supplicantibus   *o* For huius   *p* Remainder of line left blank   *q* Word followed by erasure *(space for approximately six letters)*   *r* 'que' added below line   *s* Word followed by eius *(cancelled)*   *t* in *corrected to* inter   *u* For decernere   *v* A *spelling for* renuo/renueris

This letter was preserved in the archive of Christ Church, Canterbury. It has been exhaustively analysed by Pierre Chaplais, who has established that it is an original and that it can be classified as the earliest surviving letter close from western Europe (see Chaplais 1978). The sheet has a horizontal format and is very lightly ruled. It was written by a single scribe, in a cursive Insular minuscule: script features include flamboyant **gi**, **ri** and **ti** ligatures (e.g. *magis*, l. 2; *industriam*, l. 3; *beatificando*, l. 1); wedged or hooked ascenders, curving to the left; occasionally open **a** (e.g. *patruum*, l. 1); **d** usually straight-backed, but occasionally uncial (e.g. *debeam*, l. 12); tall-E ligatures; e-caudata; subscript **i** (*beatificando*, l. 1); final **m** with last minim extended (e.g. *patruum*, l. 1); **p** with cleft between downstroke and bowl; occasionally open initial **q** (e.g. que, l. 7); low **s**. The relatively small number of abbreviations include the Insular compendia for *autem*, *per*, *est*;

a semi-colon for final *-us*; suspended nasals. The script seems perfectly acceptable for the implied date. There seems no good reason to follow Bruckner's suggestion that the document is a copy of the late eighth century at the earliest (*ChLA*, iii. no. 185); see Chaplais 1978, pp. 6–7. The text is written in nineteen lines, with the final line inset; all the margins are very narrow.

The proof of originality is to be found in the folding and endorsement of the sheet. There are two vertical and two horizontal folds. Using the position of the first and original endorsement Chaplais has reconstructed the pattern of folding (Chaplais 1978, pp. 7–17). The folded package was fastened by a separate wrapping tie, the position of which is revealed by the gap between *domino* and *Berctualdo* in the endorsement.

In the penultimate sentence of the text the bishop states that he is sending the message in writing for reasons of confidentiality (the alternative would have been to send an envoy with an oral message). It seems very likely that Wealdhere wrote the letter himself, rather than dictating it to a scribe (see Chaplais 1978, p. 17). The Latin is very confident and assured, with relatively few errors (compare the mistakes in the slightly earlier original charter of King Hlothhere in the Christ Church archive: S 8, A.D. 679). The writer has followed the conventional rules for letter-writing, and exhibits confidence in the construction of rhythmic prose (for a detailed analysis, see Chaplais 1978, pp. 18–21). It should be noticed that the priest and scholar Nothhelm, active at St Paul's in c. 731 and probably before, may have received his initial training in London in the time of Wealdhere or Wealdhere's successor Ingwald (for Nothhelm, see p. 17).

For analysis of the content of the letter, see above, p. 14.

APPENDIX 2

The Will of Bishop Theodred

T. Cambrige, UL. Ff. 2. 33, 47v–48r: copy, s. xiii[2]
U. BL Add. 14847, 17v–18r: copy of T, s. xiv
Ed.: a. Kemble 959, from T
    b. Thorpe, *Diplomatarium*, pp. 512–15, from T, with translation
    c. Birch 1008, from U and Kemble, Thorpe
    d. Whitelock, *Wills*, no. 1 (pp. 2–5), from T, with translation
    e. *Councils & Synods*, no. 21 (pp. 76–81), from T, with translation
Listed: Sawyer 1526; Hart, *ECEE*, no. 49; Gelling, *ECTV*, no. 329
Edited from T

[I]n nomine Domini nostri Iesu Christi. Ic þeodred Lundenware biscop will biquethen mine quiden mines erfes þe ic begeten habbe 7 get bigete, Godes þankes and his halegen, for mine soule 7 for min louerde þat ic under bigeat and for min eldrene and for all þe mannes soule þe ic foreþingiae and ic almesne underfongen habbe and me sie richlike for to bidden.

þat is þan erst þat he an his louerd his heregete, þat is þanne tua hund marcas*a* arede goldes and tua cuppes siluerene and four hors so ic best habbe and to suerde so ic best habbe, 7 foure schelda and foure spere and þat lond þat ic habbe at Dukeswrthe and þat lond þat ic habbe at Illyngtone and þat lond þat ic habbe at Earnningtone. And ic an Eadgiue fifti marcas*a* redes goldes.

And into sce Paules kirke mine to beste messehaclen þe hic habbe mid alle þe þinge þe þereto birið mid calice and on cuppe and mine beste masseboc and alle min reliquias þe ic best habbe into Paules kirke. And ic an þat lond aet Tit into seynte Paules kirke þen hewen to bedlonde mid al þat þe þeron stant buten þo men þe þer aren; fre men alle for mine soule. And ic an þat lond at Suthereye mid alle þe fiscoðe þe þerto bireð þen hewen into sce Paules kirke; and frie men þo men for þe bisscopes soule. And þeodred bisscop an þat lond at Tillingham into sce Paules kirke þo hewen to hare; and fre men þo men for mine soule. And ic an þat lond at Dunemowe ouer mine day into sce Paules kirke þen hewen.

And ic an þat lond at Mendham Osgote mine sustres sune ouer mine day, buten ic wille þat se minstre and*b* hide londes at Myndham to þere kirke. And ic an þat lond at Scotforð and Mydicaham into Myndham kirke þo Godes hewen. And ic an Osgot þat lond at Silham 7 at Isestede 7 at Chikeringe 7 at Aysfeld and at Wrtinham and all þe smale londe þat þereto bereð. And ic an þat lond at Horham and at Elyngtone into Hoxne into sce Aethelbrichtes kirke mid Godes hewen. And ic an þat lond at Luthinglond Offe mine sustres sune and his broþer; and fre men þo men halue and at Mindham also for þe bisscopes soule.

And ic an Osgote mine mey, Eadulfes sune, þat lond at Bertune and at Rucham and at Pakenham. And ic an þat lond at Newetune and at Horninggeshethe and at Ikewrthe and at Wepstede into sce Eadmundes kirke þen Godes hewen to are for þeodred bisscopes soule. And ic an þat lond at Waldringfeld Osgote mine sustres sune, and min hage þat ic binnin Gypeswich bouhte. And ic Wlstan þat lond at Wrtham so it stant.

And ic an into eueri bisscopes stole fif pund to delen for mine soule. And ic an þen archebischope fif markes[a] goldes. And ic an þat men dele at mine biscopriche binnen Lundene and buten Lundene .x. pund for mine soule. And ic an at Hoxne at mine biscopriche þat men dele .x. pund for mine soule. And ic wille þat men nieme þat erfe at Hoxne stand þat ic þerto bigeten habbe and dele it man on to, half into þe minstre, 7 dele for min soule. And lete men stonden so mikel so ic þeron fond; and fre man þo men all for mine soule. And ic wille þat men lete stonden at Lundenebyri so mikel so ic þeron fond, 7 nime þat ic þerto begat and dele on to, half into þe min- stre 7 half for mine soule; and fre men alle þo men; 7 do men þat ilke at Wunnemandune 7 on Sceon. And lete men stonden at Fullenham so it nu stant buten hwe mine manne fre wille. And on Denesige let stonden so mikel so ic þeron fond and dele it man on to half into þe minstre 7 half for mine soule.

And ic an into Glastingbiri .v. pund for mine soule. And ic an þeodred min wite massehakele þe ic on Pauie bouhte and 'al' þat þerto bireð 7 simbelcalice 7 þere messeboc þe Gosebrichte me biquaþ. And ic an Odgar þere gewele masse- hakele þe ic on Pauie bouhte 7 þat þerto bired. And ic an Gundwine þer oþer gewele massehakele þat is ungerenad 7 þat þe þerto bireð, and ic spratacke[c] þe rede messehakele 7 al þat þe þerto bired.

And wo so mine cuyde ofte, God him ofte heuene riches, buten he it er his ende it bete.

---

[a] *Possibly a scribal substitution for* mancusas   [b] *Some text may be missing here* (cf. Councils & Synods, *p. 78*)   [c] *Possibly for* ic spræc Ake (cf. Councils & Synods, *p. 81*)

In the name of our Lord Jesus Christ. I, Theodred, bishop of the people of London, wish to announce my will concerning my property, what I have acquired and may yet acquire, by the grace of God and his saints, for my soul and for that of my lord under whom I acquired it and for my ancestors' souls and for the souls of all the men for whom I intercede and from whom I have received alms and for whom it is fitting that I pray.

First he grants his lord his heriot, namely 200 marks of red gold and two silver cups and four horses, the best that I have, and two swords the best that I have, and four shields and four spears: and the estate which I have at Duxford [Cambs.] and the estate which I have at Illington [? Norfolk] and the estate which I have at Arrington [Cambs.]. And I grant to Eadgifu fifty marks of red gold.

At to St Paul's church [I grant] the two best chasubles that I have, with all the things which belong to them, together with a chalice and one cup. And my best mass-book and the best relics I have, to St Paul's church. And I grant to St Paul's church the estate at St Osyth [Essex], as an estate to provide sustenance for the community, with all that is on it, except the men who are there; they are all to be freed for my soul's sake. And I grant the estate at Southery [Norfolk], with all the fishing which belongs to it, to the community at St Paul's church, and the men are to be freed for the bishop's soul. And Bishop Theodred grants the estate at Tillingham [Essex] to St Paul's church to be the property of the community, and the men are to be freed for my soul. And I grant the estate at Dunmow [Essex] after my death to St Paul's church for the community.

And I grant the estate at Mendham [Suffolk] to my sister's son Osgot after my death, except that I desire that the minster [...] one hide of land at Mendham to the church. And I grant the estates at Shotford and Mettingham [both Suffolk] to Mendham church to God's community. And I grant to Osgot the estates at Syleham and at Instead and at Chirchkering and at Ashfield [all Suffolk] and at *Wrtinham* and all the small estates which are attached to these. And I grant the estates at Horham and at Athelington [both Suffolk] to Hoxne to St Æthelberht's church to God's community. And I grant the estate at Lothingland [Suffolk] to Offa my sister's son and his brother; and half the men are to be freed and also at Mendham, for the bishop's soul. And I grant to my kinsman Osgot, Eadulf's son, the estates at Barton and at Rougham and at Pakenham [all Suffolk]. And I grant the estates at Nowton and at Horningsheath and at Ickworth and at Whepstead [all Suffolk] to St Eadmund's church [i.e. Bury St Edmunds] as the property of God's community, for Bishop Theodred's soul. And I grant to Osgot my sister's son the estate at Waldringfield [Suffolk] and my messuage in Ipswich, which I bought. And I grant to Wulfstan the estate at Wortham [Suffolk] just as it stands.

And I grant to every bishop's see five pounds to be distributed for my soul. And I grant to the archbishop five marks of gold. And I grant that ten pounds be distributed for my soul at my *bishopriche*,[a] in London and outside London. And I grant that ten pounds be distributed for my soul at Hoxne at my *bishopriche*.[a] And it is my will that the stock which is at Hoxne, which I have acquired there, be taken and divided into two parts, half for the minster and half to be distributed for my soul. And as much as I found on that estate is to be left, and all the men are to be freed for my soul. And it is my wish that at London there be left as much as I found on the estate, and that which I added to it be taken and divided into two, half for the minster and half for my soul; and all the men are to be freed. And the same is to be done at Wimbledon and at Sheen [both Surrey]. And at Fulham everything is to be left as it now stands, unless one wishes to free any of my men. And at Dengie let there be left as much as I found on the estate, and let it [the rest] be divided into two, half for the minster and half for my soul.

And I grant to Glastonbury five pounds for my soul. And I grant to Theodred my white chasuble which I bought in Pavia and all that belongs to it, and a chalice for festivals and the massbook which Gosebriht bequeathed to me. And I grant to Odgar the yellow chasuble which I bought in Pavia and what belongs to it. And I grant to Gundwine the other yellow chasuble which is unornamented and what belongs to it. and I [?? promised to Acke] the red chasuble and all that belongs to it.

And whosoever detracts from my testament, may God deprive him of the kingdom of heaven, unless he make amends for it before his death.[b]

---

[a] *For the translation of this word, see p. 92*   [b] *Translation based on that in* Councils and Synods, *pp. 76–81*

This Middle English version of Theodred's will was preserved in the archive of Bury St Edmunds, and a comprehensive edition will appear in the volume now in preparation by K. Lowe and S. Foot. The content which relates to the London bishopric and St Paul's is discussed above, pp. 29–30, 92–4. For further discussion in the short term, see Whitelock, *Wills*, pp. 99–103; *Councils & Synods*, pp. 75–6.

APPENDIX 3

Two Post-Conquest vernacular documents from St Paul's

A

Agreement between Brihtric and his wife, and the canons [of St Paul's]. [s. xi²]

C. GL 25504 (*Liber L*), 29v–30r: copy s. xii[1]
Ed.: *HMC. 9th Report*, Appendix, p. 62b

þis his sy forepearde þe Brichtric 7 his gebedde habbað pið þa canonicas, þ his
þ heo sculan habban heora beira dæi anes canonikes gerihte on mete 7 on eale, 7
heo habbað geunnen hyra land þam canonike scær 7 saccleas, 7 æfter heora bera
deige beon þa canonikes eruename of ealra heora æhte, 7 þis beoð þa
gepitnisse, þ is Ægelpine Brihtmeres sune 7 Leofstan 7 Hearding 7 Bruning.

This is the agreement which Brihtric and his wife have with the canons, that is
that for both their lifetimes they shall have the right of one canon in food and in
ale, and they have given their land to the canons, exempt and not free from soke,
and after both their lifetimes the canons shall inherit all their property. And these
are the witnesses, that is, Æthelwine the son of Brihtmær and Leofstan and
Hearding and Bruning.

This Old English agreement was copied among a collection of post-Conquest documents
in the earliest of the extant cartularies from St Paul's (see above, pp. 61–2). It would
appear to have been drawn up around 1100 (as Gibbs, p. xxxix). The first witness,
Æthelwine, son of Brihtmær, may the son of Brihtmær of Gracechurch (see S 1234, probably A.D. 1052 × 1066; Brooks and Kelly, *Christ Church*, no. 183), who inherited the
proprietorship of the church of All Hallows Gracechurch and is mentioned as still alive in
a Canterbury document of *c.* 1100 (Douglas and Greenaway, *EHD II*, pp. 1022–3); a
Leofstanus appears among witnesses to a document of 1081, and his two sons were
among the burgesses who surrendered the lands of the *Cnihtengild* in *c.* 1125 (Douglas
and Greenaway, *ibid.*, no. 277; and see Davis 1925, p. 50); Hearding is perhaps the
Heardingus aurifaber who witnesses a London document of *c.* 1102; and Bruning could
be the moneyer *Brunic* who worked for Williams I and II (*ibid.*, pp. 22–3). For these, see
Ekwall, *London Personal Names*, pp. 17–18, 22–3, 46–7. A Brihtric held land at Mitcham
in Surrey from King Edward in 1066, part of which was in the hands of the cannons of
Bayeux by 1086 (GDB 31v; *DB Surrey* 5:6), but it seems unlikely that he is to be identified with the candidate for the St Paul's confraternity. Brihtric and his wife would have
promised the canons the reversion of their property in return for confraternity rights,

which evidently included a share in the distribution of bread and ale from the communal estates. For the bakehouse and brewery, see above.

B

Agreement between Æthelweard and the dean and brethren
of St Paul's, concerning half a hide at Sandon, Hertfordshire. [s. xi^{ex}]

C. GL 25504 (*Liber L*), 44v: copy, s. xii[1]
    Rubric: De Sanduna
Ed.: *HMC 9th Report*, Appendix, p. 65b

þis^a is sy forepearde þe Ægelpard hafð^b gemacad pið þonne decanus 7 pið ealle þa gebroðre of sce Paules mynstre, þ is of ane healfe hyde landes æt Sandune, þ he sceal æfrice geare gyuen .viii. horen^c for ealle þinc, 7 hi sculan baþa habban he 7 hys pif þa hpile þa hy lyfieð 7 æfter hyre begre dæge habba scs Paulus eall þ hy þær æfter belæfeð þa him mid rihte to gebyrige oppan þan ilcan lande, 7 þ he habba þ land spa spa hit nu gelogod is, 7 þis synd þa gepitnysse, þ is se decanus 7 þa fuþer arcediacones, 7 þysre geprite syndon tpa, an haben þa gebroðre 7 þ oðer Ægelpard, 7 hær pið þæs Colspegen 7 Ægelmær 7 Sexi.

^{a} His C ^{b} hafd C ^{c} For ora, *a measure of weight of silver, equivalent to 20d under William I*

This is the agreement that Æthelweard has made with the dean and with all the brethren of St Paul's minster, that is, concerning half a hide at Sandon, that he shall every year give eight ores for everything, and he and his wife shall both have it while they live and after the lifetimes of both of them St Paul shall have everything that they bequeathed to him there, with right of surety upon the same land, and that he shall have the land just as it is now arranged. And these are the witnesses: that is, the dean and the four archdeacons. And there are two copies of this writ, one held by the brethren and the other by Æthelweard. And also present were Colswegen and Æthelmær and Sexi.

This is a second Old English agreement copied into the earliest of the St Paul's cartularies, among a collection of post-Conquest documents (see pp. 61–2). It probably belongs to the last decade or so of the eleventh century. The formal witnesses are the dean and the four archdeacons; there is good reason to think that the cathedral hierarchy was not established at St Paul's until after the Conquest (see Brooke 1956, and above, pp. 45, 55). For the relationship between the archdeacons and the chapter, see Gibbs, pp. xxix–xxx. Also present were three laymen, the first two of whom, Colswegen and Æthelmær, are mentioned in the Latin charter dated 1103 which precedes the Old English document in the cartulary (*HMC 9th Report*, 65a). These two documents, with a third charter which follows them, concern successive agreements about the half-hide at Sandon, where the canons held a Domesday manor, reckoned at ten hides, of which five were demesne in 1086 (GDB 136r; *DB Herts.* 13:5). The earliest of the texts is the Old English charter, which would appear to be a simple lease of St Paul's property to Æthelweard and his wife for their lifetimes, in return for an annual payment. The document of 1103 records a confirmation of the lease, apparently after Æthelweard's death. His wife Leofgifu (*Lyveva*), daughter of Colswegen, canon of St Paul's, is to continue to hold the land and pay the rent, with the estate reverting to the church on her death. Colswegen and his brother Æthelmær promise that this condition will be observed. The third document records an agreement between the canons and Galio, concerning the half hide at Sandon 'quam tenuit Alwardus Licheberd in Sandona'. For Colswegen and Leofgifu, see also Ekwall, *London Personal Names*, pp. 50, 79; Davis 1925, pp. 47–8.

INDEXES

In these indexes ð and þ have been replaced by **th**. In addition, **w** is substituted for þ of the MSS, and **uu** is alphabetized as **w**. Editorial comments appear in square brackets. Charters are referred to by their numbers, in bold type; other references are to the pages of the introduction or the commentaries.

1. INDEX OF PERSONAL NAMES

The forms of personal names occuring in the texts are followed as far as possible, but normalized forms are given when a name occurs in more than one variant, or when the individual is discussed in the commentaries. All variants are given, except for Æ, Ae and E in both initial and medial positions. This is an index of names and titles, rather than of individuals. References to laymen with the same name and rank are normally grouped together. Ecclesiastics are, as far as possible, distinguished.

Acca, *minister*, **16**
Æbana, **1**; 136
Æg- *see* Ecg-
Æla, minister, **16**
Ælfflæd, wife of Ealdorman Brihtnoth, 38, 94–5, 100, 200–1
Ælfgar, ealdorman of Essex, 94, 168, 176
Ælfgyth, nun of Wilton, 168
Ælfheah, archbishop of Canterbury, 36–7, 39–40, 120–1
—bishop of Winchester, 117, 182
Ælfhere (Ælfere), *dux*, **12**; 162–3
—ealdorman, **22**; 190
Ælfhun (Ælfun), bishop of London, **22, 23**; 37, 39, 120–1, 180, 186, 190
Ælfred (Alfred), king of the West Saxons, 9, 23–9, 90
—*dux*, **16, 23** [*probably for* Ælfhere]
Ælfric, archbishop of York, **27**; 204
—abbot [of Malmesbury], **12**; 163
—abbot, **22, 23**; 190
—*deacon*, **23**; 190
Ælfsige (Ælsi), abbot of *Cowwaforde* [? Copford, Essex], **22**; 190 [*possibly for* Ælfwig]

—king's thegn, **22**; 190
—*satrapa regis*, **23**; 190
Ælfstan, bishop of London, **12, 21**; 32–5, 38, 95–7, 119–20, 162–3, 185, 200
—bishop of Rochester, 119–20
—abbot, **12**; 162–3
—*dux*, **16**
Ælfthryth, 222
Ælfweard (Ælfward), bishop of London, **32**; 40, 42, 81, 121, 209, 216–19
Ælfwig (Ælfwius, Ælwi), bishop of London, **26, 27**; 39–40, 121, 202–5
—abbot [? of Westminster], **23**; 190
Ælfwine, bishop of London, 103
—bishop of Lichfield, **11**; 160
—bishop of Winchester or Elmham, **27**; 101, 204–5
Ælfwynn, daugher of Ealdorman Æthelred and Æthelflæd, 156
Æscwine, king of the West Saxons, 136
—**1**
Æthelbald (Ædilbaldus, Æthilbaldus, Edilbaldus), king of the Mercians, **7, 8**; 15–16, 144, 148–52

233

2. INDEX OF PLACE-NAMES

3. LATIN GLOSSARY

Acheron (n.) [**19**]: Hell

alienigenus (n.) [**9**]: stranger, non-kinsman

altithronus (adj.) [**10**]: high-throned [epithet of Deity]

anathema (n.) [**1, 16**]: curse of excommunication

antistes (n.) [**21**]: bishop

archipræsul (n.) [**12, 20b**]: archbishop

archispeculator (n.) [**19b, 20b, 20c**]: archbishop

argenteus/um (n.) [**9**]: silver coin, especially a shilling

basileus (n., from Greek βασιλεύς) [**17, 23, 31**]: king

basilica (n.) [**12**]: church

canna (n.) [**6A**]: ? term for weight or measure of silver

cartula (n.) [**8, 10, 16, 21**]: charter

cassatus (n.) [**6, 10, 15, 17, 18**]: measure of land, a hide

cleronomus (n.) [**17**]: heir

cyrographum [**6**]: written record, charter

eleemosyna (n.) [**7**]: alms, charity

gehenna (n.) [**21**]: Hell

genealogia (n.) [**30**]: family, kin-group

herebus (n., spelling of *erebus*) [**23**]: Hell

hydra (n.) [**19**]: snake, serpent, demon

ierarchia (n.) [**11**]: hierarchy

karacter (n.) [**10**]: letter

liber (n.) [**10**]: book *hence* landbook, charter

manca (n., spelling for *mancusa*) [**16**]: mancus [a gold coin, or its equivalent in gold or silver, with a value of 30 silver pence] *manens* (n.) [**2, 3, 9**]: measure of land, a hide

mansa (n.) [**12, 14, 19***a*, **23, 29**]: a measure of land, a hide

mansio (n.) [**16**]: a measure of land, a hide

marenatha (n.) [**16**]: anathema

metropolitanus (n.) [**12**]: metropolitan, archbishop

monialis (n.) [**14**]: nun

notamen (n.) [**5**]: name

omnipatrans (n.) [**17**]: the all-accomplisher [epithet of the Deity]

optimas (n.) [**11**]: nobleman

peripsema (n., from Greek περίψημα) [**18**]: off-scouring, rubbish [a word which owes its currency among draftsmen of charters to Aldhelm]

præsul (n.) [**1**]: bishop

princeps (n.) [**16, 21**]: nobleman, ealdorman

privilegium (n.) [**12**]: charter granting privileges

quisquiliae (n. pl.) [**18**]: waste, rubbish [a word which owes its currency among draftsmen of charters to Aldhelm]

sanctimonialis (n.) [**17**]: nun

satrapa (n., from Greek σατράπης) [**23**]: military official, governor: *hence* thegn, ealdorman

scedula (n.) [**10**]: charter, record

scismata (n. pl., a spelling for *schismata*) [**21**]: quarrels

senator (n.) [**10**]: senior man, nobleman

subregulus (n.) [**11**]: sub-king, subordinate ruler

subthronizatus (p.p.) [**17**]: enthroned

syngraphum (n.) [**6**]: written record, charter

tauma (n., from Greek letter *tau*) [**20***b*]: cross-shaped mark

tenebrarius (adj.) [**19***a*]: pertaining to darkness

thelonarius (n.) [**8**]: toll-collector

trabeatus (adj.) [**20***b*]: wearing the robe of office

vectigal (n.) [**8, 16**]: tax, tribute

victriagius (adj.) [**20***b*]: victory-bearing

virgula (n., diminutive of *virga*, 'staff, episcopal staff') [**20***b*]: ? cross, cross-shaped mark

4. DIPLOMATIC INDEX

1. *Verbal Invocations and Proems*

(a) *Invocations*

In Christi nomine, **1**

In nomine Dei patris et summi saluatoris, **8**

In nomine Dei summi, **2**

In nomine Dei summi ipsoque inperpetuum Domino nostro Iesu Christo regnante ac disponente…, **16**

In nomine Domini Dei saluatoris nostri Iesu Christi, **7, 26**

In nomine Domini et saluatoris nostri Iesu Christi, **23**

In nomine Domini nostri Iesu Christi, **3**

In nomine Domini nostri Iesu Christi saluatoris, **4, 12, 29**

In nomine Domini nostri Iesu Christi saluatoris mundi, **6**

Regnante inperpetuum Domino nostro Iesu Christo, **9**

Regnante inperpetuum et mundi monarchiam gubernante altithroni patris sobole, **10**

(b) *Proems*

Ea que legaliter salubriterque determinantur, **29**

Ea quæ secundum decreta canonum, **6**

Ea que secundum legem salubriter diffiniuntur, **12**

Licet sermo sacerdotum et decreta, **4**

Quia unicuique homini in hac mortali uita, **8**

2. *Dispositive Words*

(a) *Present tense*

concedo, **1, 8, 15, 26**

do, **2, 18***a*, **19***a*

dono, **7**

tribuo, **14**

(b) *Past tense*

concessimus, **23**   donare decrevi, **7**
confirmaui, **26**   largitus sum, **17**
contuli, **21**   proferre largirique decreueram, **3**

3. *Royal Styles*

	(A) *Dispositive Section*	B) *Subscription*
Æthelberht, **1**	rex	
Æthelred, **2**	rex Merciorum	
Offa, **4**	rex Eastsaxonum	
Coenred, **5***a*	rex Merciorum	
Offa, **5***b*	rex Merciorum	
Swæfred, **6**	rex Eastsaxonum	
Æthelbald, **7**	rex Merciorum	rex
Æthelbald, **8**	rex Merciorum	rex
Sigeric, **9**		rex orientalium Saxonum
Edward, **10**		rex
Æthelstan, **11**		rex
Æthelstan, **12**	rex Anglorum	
Eadred, **14**	rex Anglorum cæterarum gentium in circuitu persistentium gubernator et rector	
Eadwig, **15**		rex Anglorum
Edgar, **16**	rex	rex
Edgar, **17**	Anglorum basileus	
Æthelred, **20**		totius Angliæ rex
Æthelred, **21**	rex	
Æthelred, **23**	Anglorum basileus	
Cnut, **26**	Anglorum rex	
Edward, **29**	rex Anglorum